AND THEN THE WORLD BLEW UP

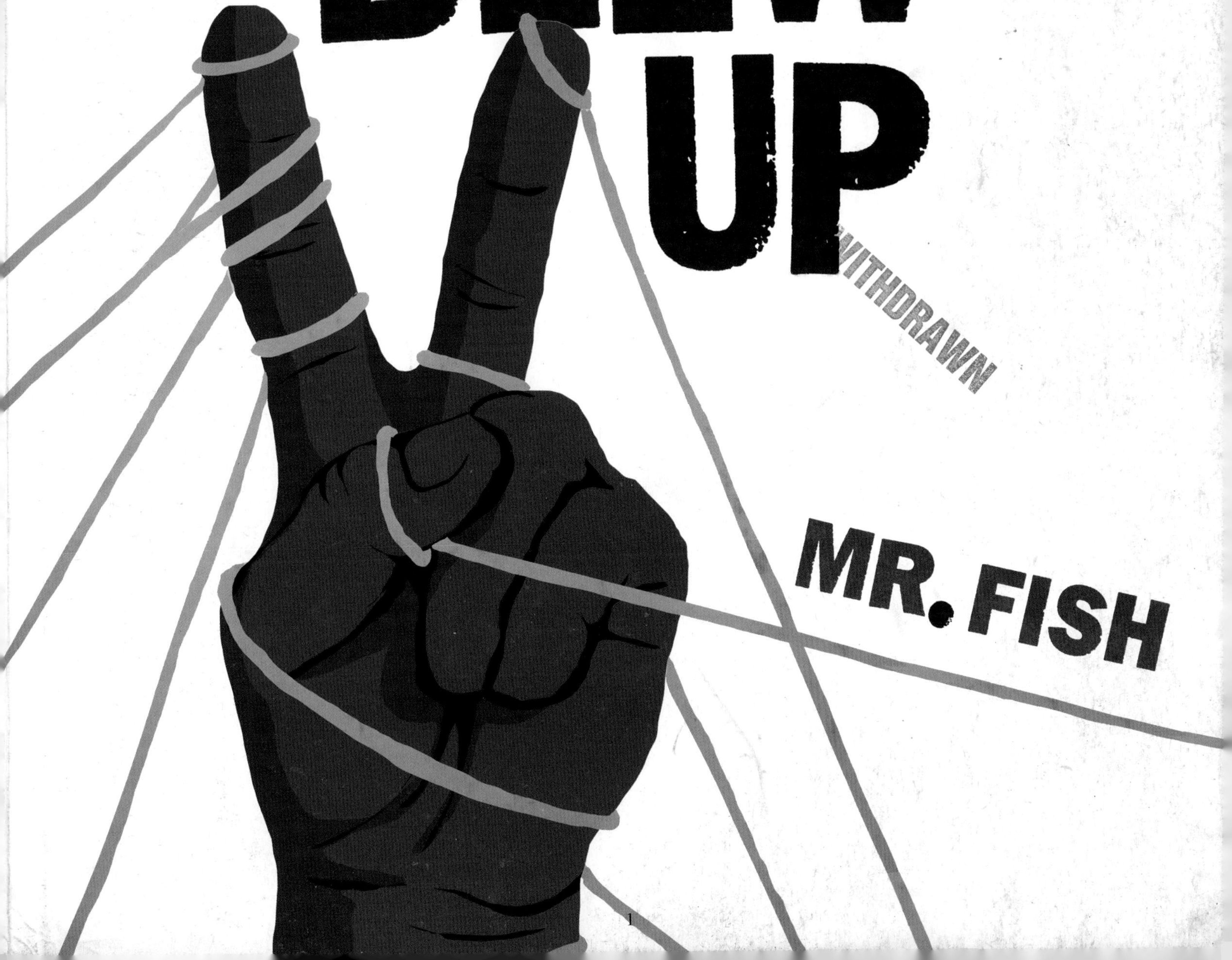

MR. FISH

Editor: Gary Groth
Designer: Dwayne Booth
Production: Preston White
Proofreader: Conrad Groth
Associate Publisher: Eric Reynolds
Publisher: Gary Groth

And Then the World Blew Up contains artwork and essays previously unpublished anywhere outside of Mr. Fish's ever-blackening soul. Material previously published first appeared in Truthdig, *Harper's Magazine*, *The Nation* and the *LA Weekly*. (For a complete list of publications that have printed the author's work, please refer to his FBI file.)

Cover image: *Go Back to Sleep, America — Nothing to See Here*, for Truthdig, 2016

Fantagraphics Books Inc.
7563 Lake City Way NE
Seattle, WA 98115

www.fantagraphics.com
facebook.com/fantagraphics
@fantagraphics

ISBN: 978-1-68396-042-3
Library of Congress Control Number: 2017938224

First printing: November 2017
Printed in Korea

For Dinah and Djuna,
who, everyday, give me everything
all at once

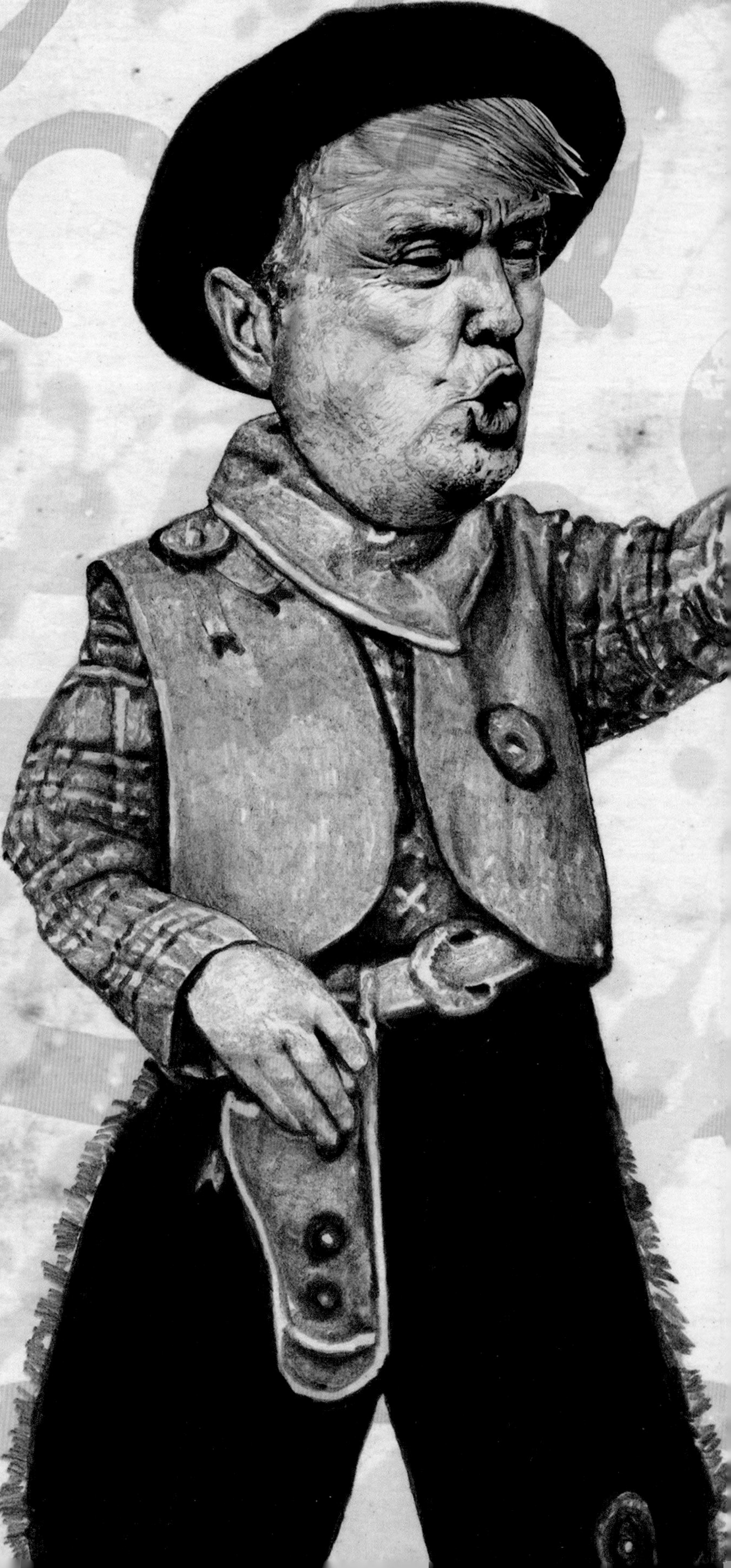

CONTENTS

Enjoy!

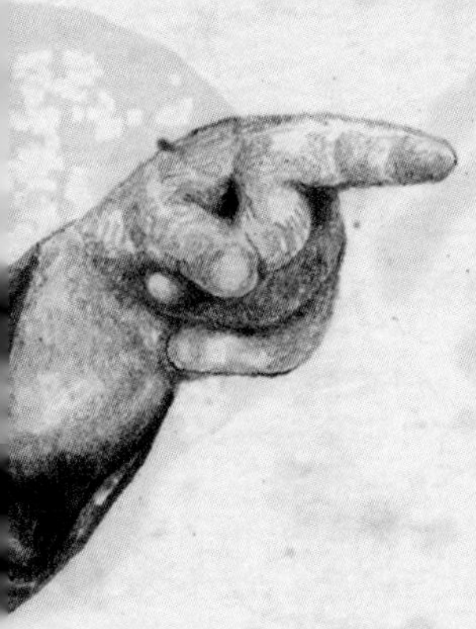

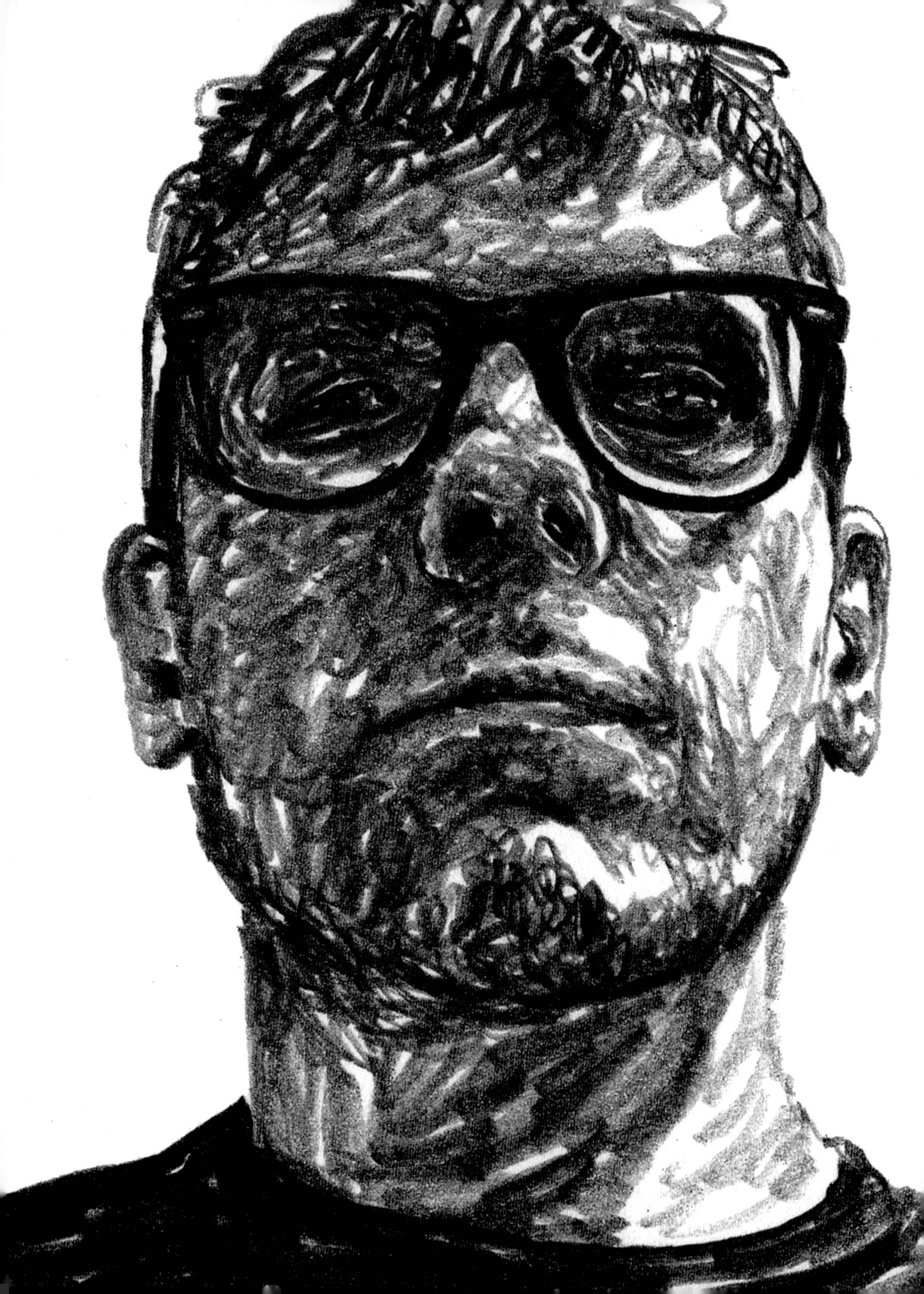

AUTHOR'S NOTE

I'VE WRITTEN ELSEWHERE how I'd accidentally fallen into the profession of editorial cartooning, having drawn my first cartoons not for publication but rather as visual shorthand to be reinterpreted later on as text for lengthier pieces of writing. This book represents the complete role reversal in recent years of that process, which is now led by the writing of prose that is later rigorously mined for cartoons and satirical drawings. Therefore, each chapter included in this book is a demonstration of how an aggregation of words can be deconstructed and rearticulated and broken down into bite-size pictorial pieces, their diction and syntax stripped to the skin and their subtext exposed for all of us to revere, ogle or condemn in accordance with how well we tolerate nudity.

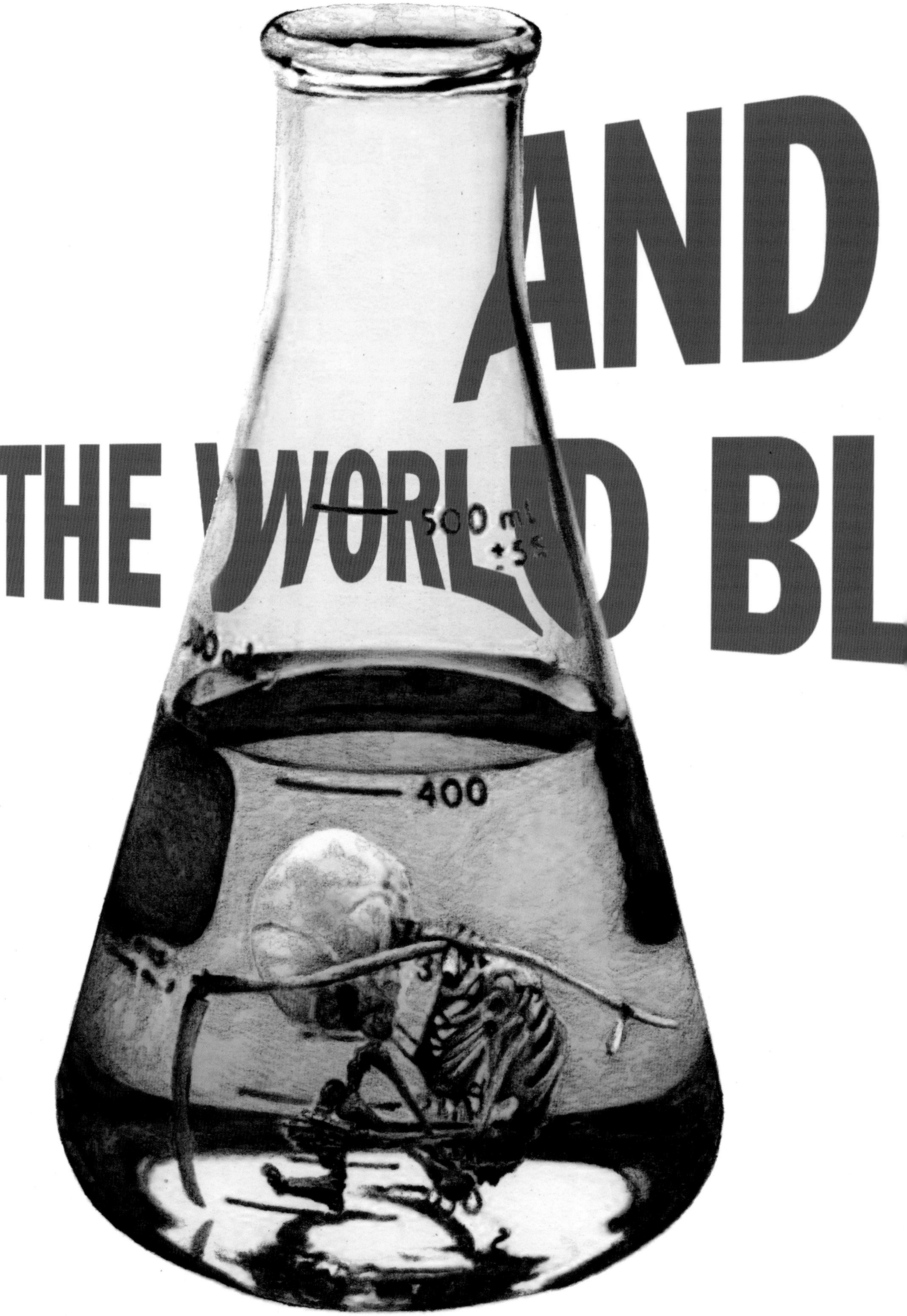
AND
THE WORLD BL
500 ml
400

THEN
EW UP
1

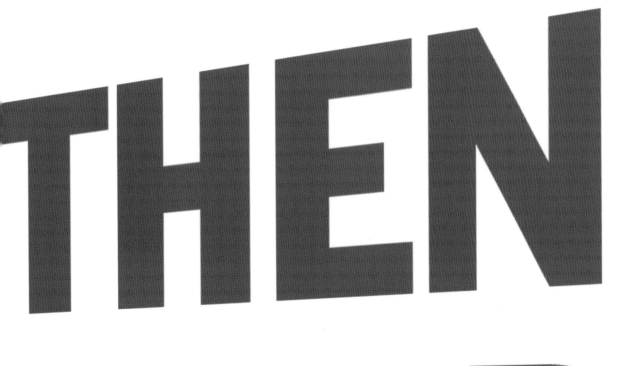

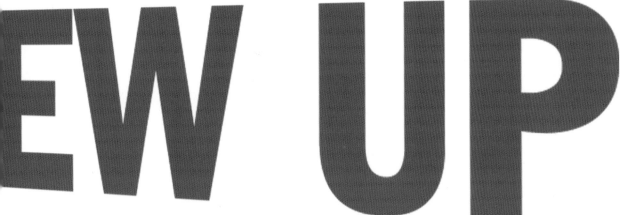

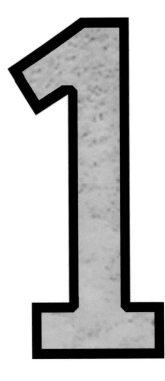

And Then the World Blew Up

ONE OF THE more absurd beliefs commonly held by democratic societies is that consensus equates to wisdom, or at least to a vague approximation of the truth. It doesn't. In fact, the only thing that consensus equates is compromise, and the only thing that placates the distaste of compromise and makes its conciliatoriness at all acceptable is camaraderie. Remember, there is nothing that sustains stupidity like a family or a crowd or a nation, the desire to be camouflaged inside a cookie cutter multiplicity in the name of self-preservation always preferable to the stark vulnerability offered by the flamboyantly independent mind.

In other words, barring exploration of the most obvious fact that people prefer the company of other people over solitude because without other people we lack a reflective surface upon which we rely for confirmation of our own identity and that without such an echo we have no presence in the world, we are a negotiated concession to the demands of cowardice, for cowardice makes us inconspicuous and inconspicuousness is the greatest survival strategy there is. But what happens when we, ourselves, become our own predators, having tamed the rapacious climate and all manner of jungle beast long ago? Banishment from the tribe makes us vulnerable to the tribe, and as long as there is a perceived safety in numbers and sufficient paranoia in the culture to warrant conformity as a strategy that keeps us safe through invisibility, there will never be any reason whatsoever to choose the brutal truth over the dozing satisfaction that comes from acquiescence to conventionality; that is, from maximizing our size by becoming part of the whole rather than minimizing the impact of our footprint upon the soft ground of credulity by remaining puny and alone.

On the morning of the 2017 Presidential Inauguration, while driving with two friends in the direction of the D.C. Metro through a January drizzle as tinny and panicked as joyous baby spiders, I passed an unremarkable Maryland house on an unremarkable street in an unremarkable neighborhood with an unremarkable front yard that the winter months turned into rusty stubble and bald earth. What caught my eye and made me momentarily think that something remarkable might be going on at the center of this wholly unremarkable scene was an oscillating sprinkler set out in the middle of the lawn wearily pissing its redundancy in the rain. Having spent the previous two years watching a pair of similarly monotonous candidates grind away incessantly for the purpose of

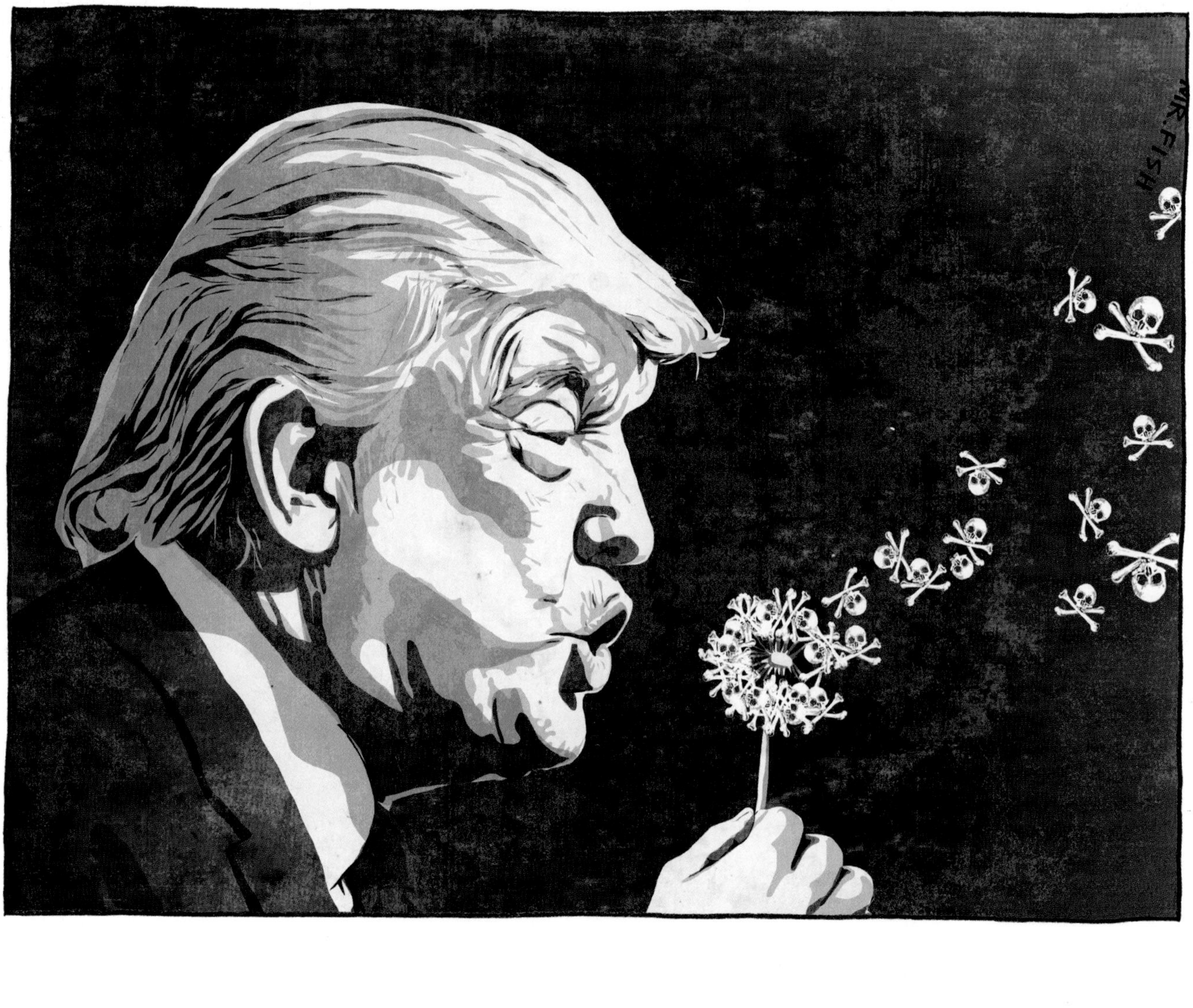
MR. FISH

contributing more and more vitriol and suspicion to a culture drowning in rage and paranoia, this small demonstration of futility masquerading as purposeful functionality gave me every reason to think that we as a nation were finally and irrevocably doomed, the mutilating pointlessness of our electoral politics finally pervasive and bewitching enough to have cursed even inanimate objects. Like magnetic fibers trained to attract what they once repelled through vigorous and prolonged stroking, the endless repetition of nonsense had miraculously breeched the cellular barrier of the biomass and become subatomic inside matter, itself.

It's amazing what relentless stroking can accomplish.

The title of this chapter comes from the closing sentence of a short story called "The Flight of the Igatu," written by my best friend, Tom, while we were in high school together and still best friends, decades before George W. Bush's War on Terror turned us into mocking and incredulous strangers in an instant, him being for the war and me being against his right to have an opinion contrary to my own. The argument started in a restaurant, and I think I probably offended him when I made fun of his girlfriend for telling me that America was heroic because it liberated a camp in Eastern Europe that her grandparents were in during the Second World War, the idea being that the proposed liberation of Iraq by Halliburton, Agility Logistics and the Kuwait Petroleum Corporation was going to be the same thing. I told her that calling America a hero for liberating a prison 60 years ago was like calling a pedophile a nice guy upon hearing that back in the 1940s he bought an ice cream cone for a little boy instead of raping him. Much to my regret, I have not seen Tom's face since Baghdad was bravely snatched from Saddam Hussein's blood-soaked pincers by cherry-cheeked American soldiers and turned into Nashville and everybody was saved and democracy spread throughout the Middle East like *Moorsoldatenlied* through Dachau. GOP bless us. GOP bless us, every one.

I admit that it wasn't very nice to ridicule my best friend's girlfriend in public and then to use the startling image of a child being fucked up the ass as the *pièce de résistance* capping my heartfelt plea for more peace, love and understanding to exist between people—I'm not sure the Sermon on the Mount or Martin Luther King's "I Have a Dream" speech would have been improved by the parable of the abducted 5-year-old and the pantless and bonered masochist—but I've never cared much about being nice or being liked or understood by anybody other than myself. Cyril Connelly once said that it was "better to write for yourself and have no public, than to write for the public and have no self." I'd suggest that the wisdom of that quote might even be elevated by swapping out the word *write* for the word *live*—fuck consensus, fuck popularity! In fact, I've always been suspicious of faddish universality as a valuable and common currency and never wanted to willingly surrender my sense of self to the bogus economy of

the domesticated herd. To think or dress or act like everybody else was what you did when you didn't recognize the spooky thrill of thinking and dressing and acting like yourself. More than that, consensus driven popularity in art, politics and religion always signaled mediocrity to me, or, even worse than mediocrity, it represented a homogenized substitute for what had the potential to be an eminently more usable and revealing and constructive form of expression. Look what popularity did to jazz, communism and Christianity, for example. Mention those things to a contemporary American audience, and consensus opinion will have you talking about Kenny G, neo-Sovietism and a brutally pious totalitarian mythology that celebrates an apocalyptic rapture and the joyous annihilation of all but the most sexually repressed and cheerfully intolerant among us. Fuck that! Permitted to retain their uncommodified and non-mass-marketed origins, each of those anti-establishmentarianism concoctions might still be urging us in the direction of self-exploration, celebrated pluralism and intrinsic human equality.

Months after Trump's election, as it will no doubt be true years hence, I feel no different about the unalterable collapse of civil society and, in fact, am starting to wonder if I haven't always assumed we were doomed by bullshit's inevitable triumph over virtue and that the only reason why I haven't been living in full acknowledgement of that fact is because I, like everybody else, prefer to be assuaged of misery by hope than crippled by hopelessness. Then again, maybe I've allowed myself to become blind to the pervasiveness of bullshit as both a friend and foe to how I interact with the world. Perhaps I, like

GIVE ME YOUR TIRED, YOUR POOR, YOUR HUDDLED MASSES YEARNING TO BREATHE FREE . . . OR I'LL FIND AND KILL THEM MYSELF

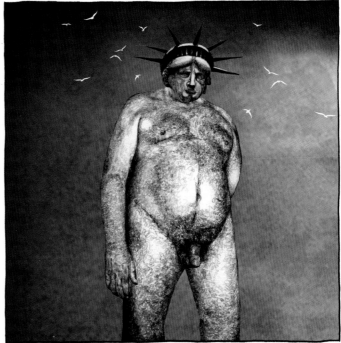

MR. FISH

everybody else, have been way too forgiving of the bullshit that buoys my ego and way too intolerant of the bullshit that exists in opposition to my complacency. After all, who among us has not come upon the kindling of a rainbow or the hushed serenity of a morning snow or the disarming enormity of a star-filled sky and not turned the egocentricity of their elation into proof of genuine affection from the universe? Conversely, who has not been brutalized by bad luck and retaliated against the world by snarling and launching a megaton stink eye into the exposed groin of Creation, as if rage was an effective deterrent to misfortune? And, finally, who of us has not suffered collateral injury or tangential jubilation from being caught in the crossfire of others similarly engaged with the notion that their moods are contingent upon their compatibility with an innate morality that is as much a part of the permanence of nature as gravity, sunlight and electromagnetism?

Bull·shit (bo̊ol'shĭt') *n.* 1. the dung of optimism, pessimism and indifference, used to fertilize the lethal delusion that human thought is the equivalent of objective reality. 2. A colorless, odorless and combustible cognitive gas found in the meaning of life.

Here is a photograph that I took during the 2017 Women's March in Washington D.C. With all access to the Internet being jammed by Homeland Security and no way to connect with the friends I'd arrived with, I decided to document my experience of being wedged in among the shrugged shoulders of half a million protestors, all of us drowning in an ocean of pink hats, placards and more positive energy and rage-soaked glee than anybody knew what to do with.

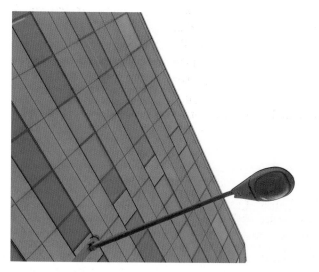

The perspective offered by the photograph, while improvised in a fit of claustrophobic panic, was inexorably linked to a memory that was all at once soothing and much more relevant to the moment that I was in than even the moment that I was in.

Here's what happened.

I was 14, ready to start high school, and it was just after dinner on the last day of summer vacation in the Alabama portion of Southern New Jersey, where the only black people I ever saw were sunburned Italians, and the only culture to which I had access was a miniature golf course that had a

white whale at its 18th hole with the word *DICK* carved into its face by an unintentionally literate hoodlum. This was in 1979, just a year before the gruesome murder of John Lennon and the even more gruesome election of Ronald Reagan into the White House, neither tragedy I've ever completely recovered from, and my mood was rapidly filling with a dread like wet cement as I looked to the horizon as it filled with storm clouds.

With the first day of classes sitting like a thug on the other side of sundown, thumping its great club of institutionalized disapproval of all that I ever hoped to become against its very dull palm, I was determined to yank my bike from the loud gewgaws crammed inside the garage for one last ride through the woods to the lake. There I planned on stripping down to my underwear and, for one last time before homework and curfew turned me into something so much less spectacular, to catapult myself from my bike and charge through the mosquitoes and the weeds and plunge myself into the root beer brown water and press down into the cool slime of the lake bed, one of the larger rocks rolled over onto my belly, and lay there in my diving mask and snorkel watching night come from three feet underwater. The snorkel I used, stowed in a rotten log at the water's edge and always requiring a quick enema to purge spiders and ants from its gut, had been made using three separate snorkels, one roll of black electrical tape and a small piece of dirty Styrofoam that acted as the cartilage that kept the nostril of the whole contraption set firmly against the breeze above the water. Sucking on the sky as if it were an impossibly huge bong containing all the magnificent lies that made a 14-year-old boy feel as if he were no more accountable to the treachery of things than a piece of cherry smoke, I would lounge beneath the water near enough to napping to savor complete relaxation without sleeping through it, a living angel hovering weightless inside an atmosphere of water and peering down upon heaven, pitying the ethereal souls there for not knowing the bliss of living inside meat so moved by both the buoyancy and confinement of flesh.

The thunderstorm came maybe ten minutes after I'd set the rock onto my stomach and pinned myself, nude this time, to the muck clinging like green mucus to the floor of the lake. Tucked safely enough below the horizon of the water for the lightning to require hours of digging with a bucket to find me, I experienced what every great composer must've been searching for in the composition of his symphonies yet was never able to capture, largely because of the crappy visuals that polite society demanded he use when communicating his music—namely, the image of one man waving a stick around above the heads of a large group of other men, and eventually some women, all of them dressed as an immense waitstaff. Occasionally there was permitted the added visual of actors behaving flamboyantly inside the magnification of jewel-encrusted opera glasses; however, small improvement, particularly when the actors seldom even sang, much less spoke, in the language or century of their audience.

My symphony, on the other hand, was automatically relevant and began with a sky swelling dramatically into a fantastic bruise, heavy with the telepathy of a God weary of his

I contributed to the perpetuation of a ruling class that pretends to need my vote to do whatever the fuck it wants

MR. FISH

own sweet understanding of everything and wishing that he could know less and explode into sand like a mountain aching to be touched by the bare feet of his own estranged children. This effect was followed by dainty water rings piccoloing in a flurry of O's as lightly as tiny bells and leading ultimately to the sort of crescendo that one might imagine the conception of the universe must've looked like: static full of flashes of fire, physics in the throes of intercourse, nudity capable of no further lewdness, a nakedness stripped to the atomic level. It was a violence that poked such excitement into my soul that once it ended there was the sensation that I'd been emptied, that my spirit had been pulled out of me, leaving me to gather, like collecting coins from a dark theater's floor, memories of what my prior spirituality must've been, its value invisible to me. Twenty minutes after the storm, I emerged from the water feeling incomplete, like a loose confederacy of dishonest recollections, or at least a ghost that had been stitched together so weakly that my very will to be seemed in danger of fragmenting inside the vibration of my own footfalls as I pushed my bike through the steamy air back to the garage, the chemistry of my insides stirred hard into a swirling cloud of undrinkable water. It was as if that by removing my voice from all conversation about the world I was finally able to recognize, with great humility, that the world was not enhanced by my excessively verbal participation in it, but rather I was enhanced by the world whose inarticulate physics were precisely what gave me license to participate in the machinery of my very existence.

In my silence at 14 upon leaving the lake, which would echo in the future silence that would come upon me at the realization on election night that Donald Trump would be our next president, I felt not unlike the word *fuck* and that, in the face of reality's illiteracy, I was suddenly permitted the grace of getting to exist merely as typeface against pulp, my obscenity made completely irrelevant by the indifference of the corporeal world toward the King's English. In an instant, I felt as if I could mean so much more by meaning so much less than the bogus definition previously attached to me by the capricious folly of language. Like an emancipated slave allowed to suddenly become invisible inside a free society, I could finally experience the thrill of watching life proceed without the disruptive influence of my presence. By no longer adding my own voice to the ceaseless blathering that constituted the cacophonous schizophrenia that was the public consciousness, I could finally feel as if I were communing with the wordless truth that lay beyond human comprehension like edifying bones concealed beneath flesh. "Silence is the universal refuge," Thoreau said, "the sequel to all dull discourses and all foolish acts," which is why I've always believed that poetry is uniquely qualified to reveal how shamelessly inadequate our brains are, when compared with our hearts, at recognizing how best to bridge the gap between who we are as people and what we pretend to be as citizens: Because poetry isn't about assembling the right words to illuminate specific aesthetic and emotional insights about the world but rather to put together word combinations that actually remove the focus from the limitations of the text, allowing the unsayable to be said. After all, isn't it the function of poetry to leave one speechless and profoundly well informed at the same time? In fact, it's arguable that the moment one seizes upon a concept of the world to explain and comprehend the world, one has already sacrificed the only true method available to him or her for integrating and then collaborating with the world, namely the humility and the wisdom to listen while the world explained itself; *no*, while the world *demonstrated* itself.

I've written one poem in my life, which was published, celebrated by a dedicated readership whose numbers didn't quite rival those of the average laughing hyena litter and then forgotten, leaving me to forever hang up the quill, cape and conceit for bardic superstardom. I was 25 at the time and the composition was called "Rastreppo the Acrobatic Clown Gave Himself a Blowjob," and this is how it went:

Neato

The poem is listed on my curriculum vitae and now I teach at two Ivy League universities and, being a college drop out, am not qualified to be my own TA.

Neato, indeed.

When 19th-century French philosopher, philologist and historian, Ernest Renan, said, "Our opinions become fixed at the point where we stop thinking," without meaning to he was elucidating on our likely self-annihilation by auto-catatonic asphyxiation, on our mass suicide by consensual pacification in the name of unanimity. How? By telling autocrats how much easier it is to manipulate society from the top down by ceasing contemplation than it is to perpetuate curiosity and critical thinking from the bottom up. After all, in both free and tyrannical societies there are agreeable rewards for acquiescence to authority and adverse penalties for dissent. There are also innumerable distractions in both free and tyrannical societies that are deliberately designed to prevent full analysis and rigorous scrutiny of substantive issues. Dispatch jackbooted goons with live ammunition to the village square, and there will be no congregation of disgruntled citizens amassing as an angry mob to demand peace, love and understanding from an oppressive government. Give everybody a machine that provides people with the option to virtually congregate in a virtual village square as a virtual mob and demand peace, love and understanding from an oppressive government and, for both options, the diffusion of meaningful political engagement in the real world is exactly the same.

Anyway, I was always jealous of that closing sentence of Tom's and swore to him that I'd steal it one day and pretend that it was my own. And though it might appear as if that time has finally arrived, I'd suggest that it hasn't, for what made the closing line so brilliant in 1984 was that it was simultaneously hilarious — because it didn't allow for the complexity of the narrative, which was expertly constructed, wonderfully compelling and fraught with heroes and villains and grand schemes targeting love, revenge and power, to resolve — and it was also the most succinct portrayal of the disconnect between perceived reality and authentic reality that I'd ever seen at 17. It isn't anymore. In fact, I feel no more obligated to credit "The Flight of the Igatu" for showing me how the human race could spontaneously combust for inexplicable yet completely plausible reasons than I do to credit *Star Trek* for cell phones or Aldous Huxley for the NSA or The Book of Revelations for doomsday. In other words:

And just as America was ready to be great again...

The democracy has timed out
The elected leadership is taking way too fucking long to respond.
The system of checks and balances could be irrevocably corrupted. Try not to trust that the government has your best interest at heart.
If you are unable to give a shit about what happens to the human species, check your connection to all living things that surround you.
If your ability to experience love and empathy and concern for your fellow human being is being blocked by a religious or political ideology, you're an asshole.
Try Again
MR. FISH

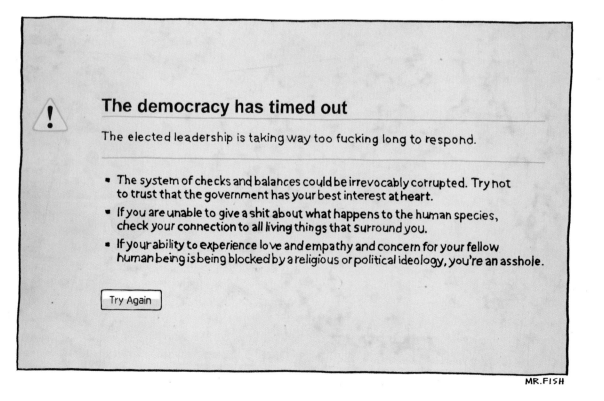

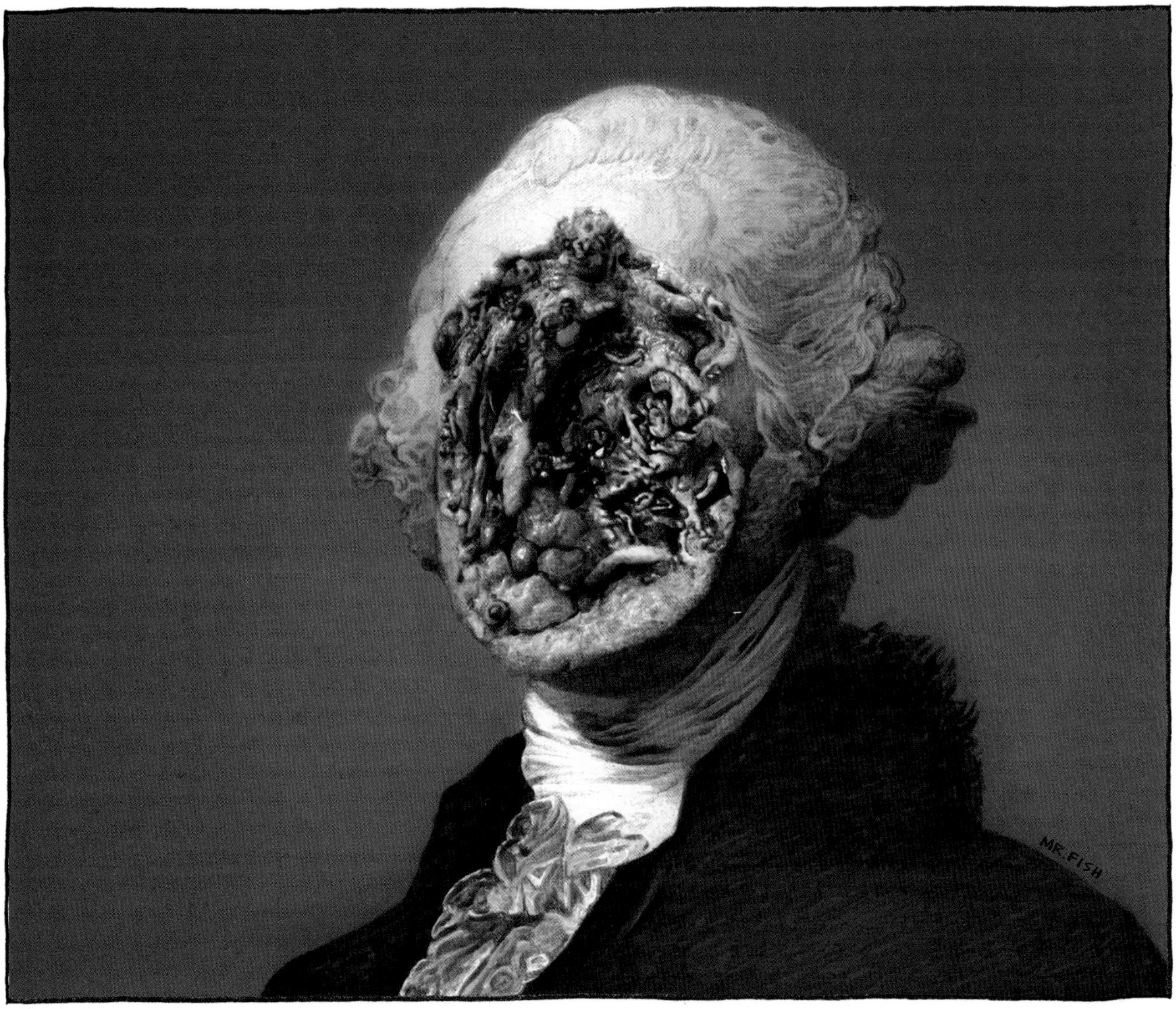
MR.FISH

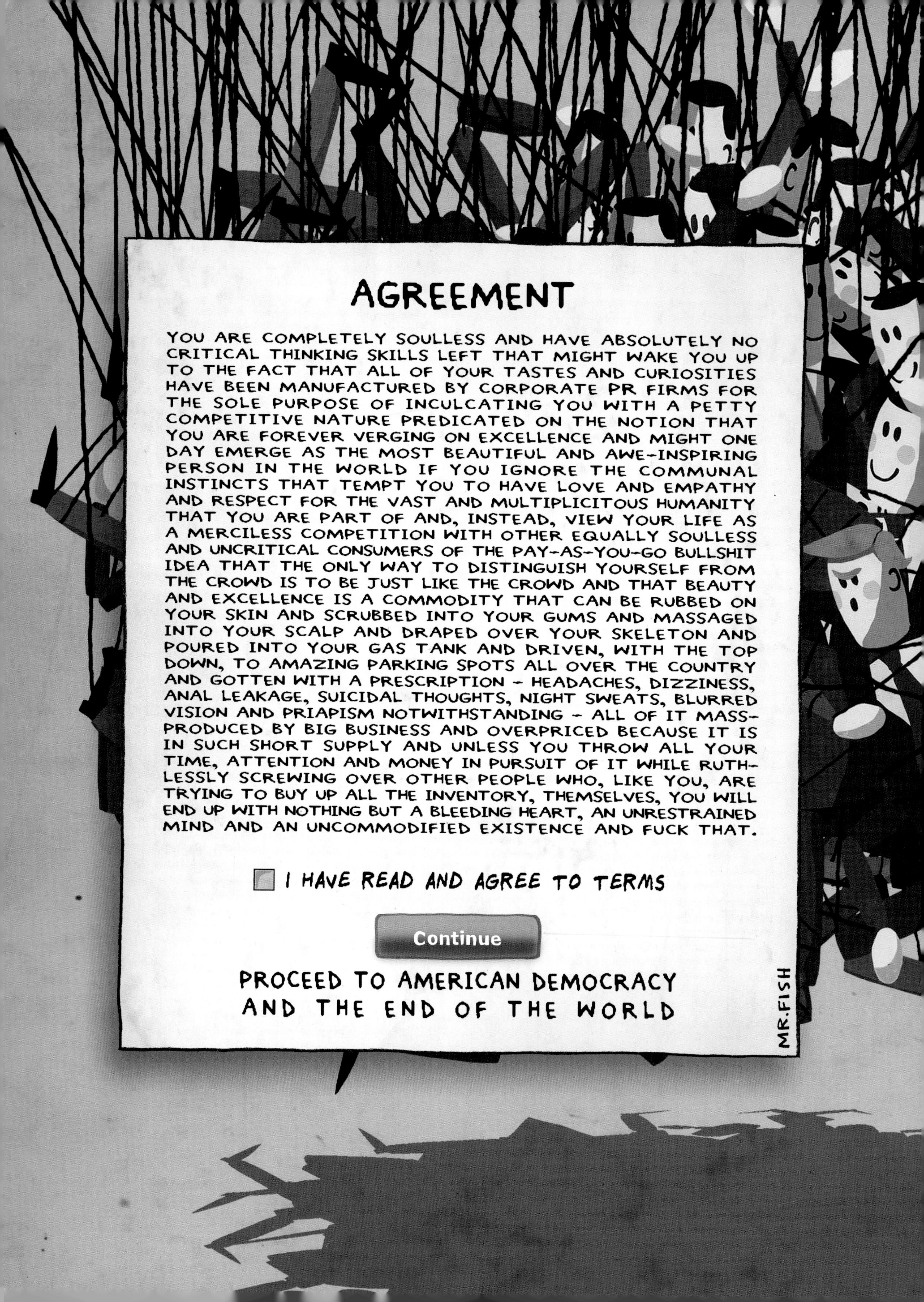
AGREEMENT
YOU ARE COMPLETELY SOULLESS AND HAVE ABSOLUTELY NO CRITICAL THINKING SKILLS LEFT THAT MIGHT WAKE YOU UP TO THE FACT THAT ALL OF YOUR TASTES AND CURIOSITIES HAVE BEEN MANUFACTURED BY CORPORATE PR FIRMS FOR THE SOLE PURPOSE OF INCULCATING YOU WITH A PETTY COMPETITIVE NATURE PREDICATED ON THE NOTION THAT YOU ARE FOREVER VERGING ON EXCELLENCE AND MIGHT ONE DAY EMERGE AS THE MOST BEAUTIFUL AND AWE-INSPIRING PERSON IN THE WORLD IF YOU IGNORE THE COMMUNAL INSTINCTS THAT TEMPT YOU TO HAVE LOVE AND EMPATHY AND RESPECT FOR THE VAST AND MULTIPLICITOUS HUMANITY THAT YOU ARE PART OF AND, INSTEAD, VIEW YOUR LIFE AS A MERCILESS COMPETITION WITH OTHER EQUALLY SOULLESS AND UNCRITICAL CONSUMERS OF THE PAY-AS-YOU-GO BULLSHIT IDEA THAT THE ONLY WAY TO DISTINGUISH YOURSELF FROM THE CROWD IS TO BE JUST LIKE THE CROWD AND THAT BEAUTY AND EXCELLENCE IS A COMMODITY THAT CAN BE RUBBED ON YOUR SKIN AND SCRUBBED INTO YOUR GUMS AND MASSAGED INTO YOUR SCALP AND DRAPED OVER YOUR SKELETON AND POURED INTO YOUR GAS TANK AND DRIVEN, WITH THE TOP DOWN, TO AMAZING PARKING SPOTS ALL OVER THE COUNTRY AND GOTTEN WITH A PRESCRIPTION - HEADACHES, DIZZINESS, ANAL LEAKAGE, SUICIDAL THOUGHTS, NIGHT SWEATS, BLURRED VISION AND PRIAPISM NOTWITHSTANDING - ALL OF IT MASS-PRODUCED BY BIG BUSINESS AND OVERPRICED BECAUSE IT IS IN SUCH SHORT SUPPLY AND UNLESS YOU THROW ALL YOUR TIME, ATTENTION AND MONEY IN PURSUIT OF IT WHILE RUTHLESSLY SCREWING OVER OTHER PEOPLE WHO, LIKE YOU, ARE TRYING TO BUY UP ALL THE INVENTORY, THEMSELVES, YOU WILL END UP WITH NOTHING BUT A BLEEDING HEART, AN UNRESTRAINED MIND AND AN UNCOMMODIFIED EXISTENCE AND FUCK THAT.
I HAVE READ AND AGREE TO TERMS
Continue
PROCEED TO AMERICAN DEMOCRACY AND THE END OF THE WORLD
MR.FISH

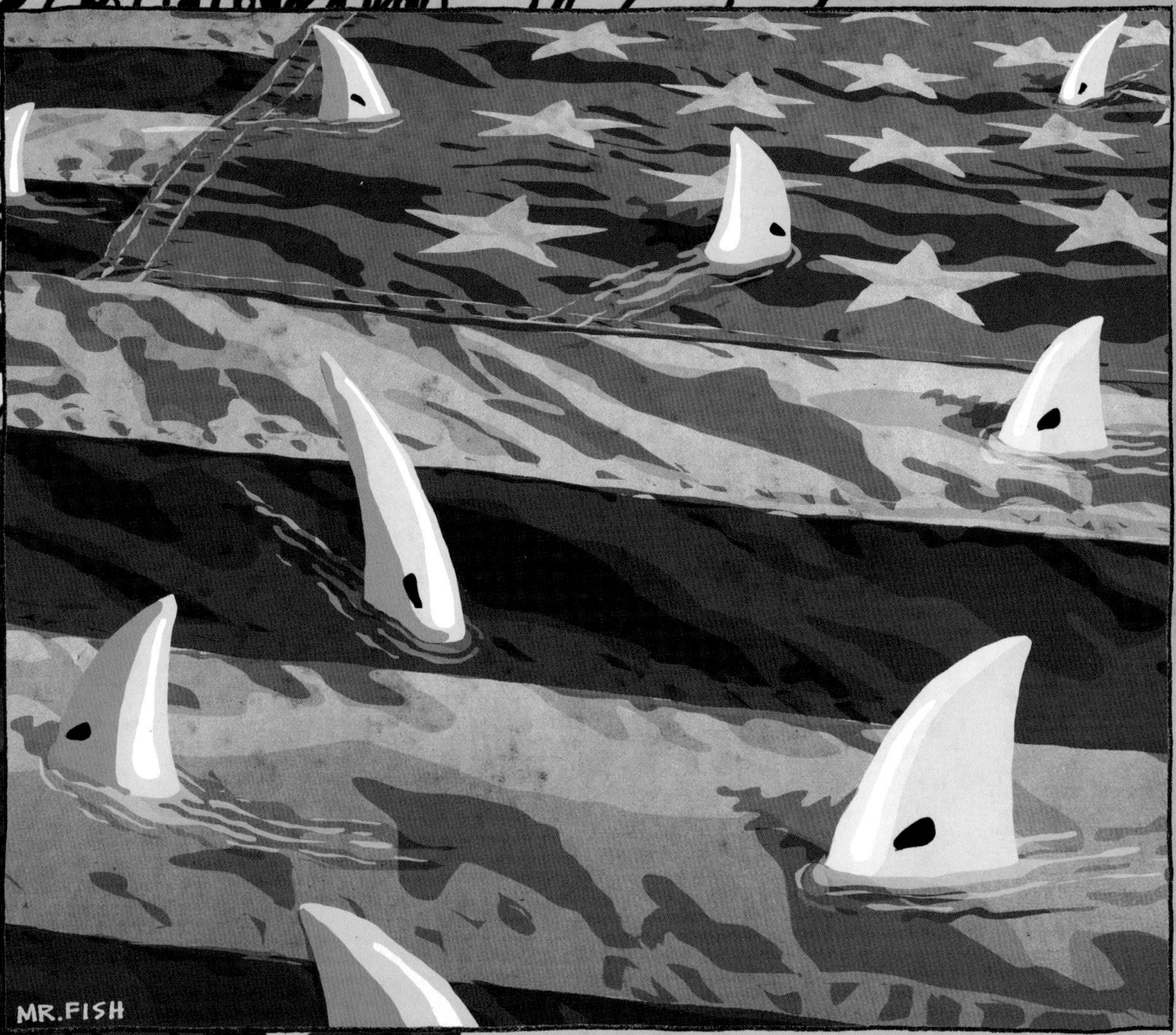
MR.FISH

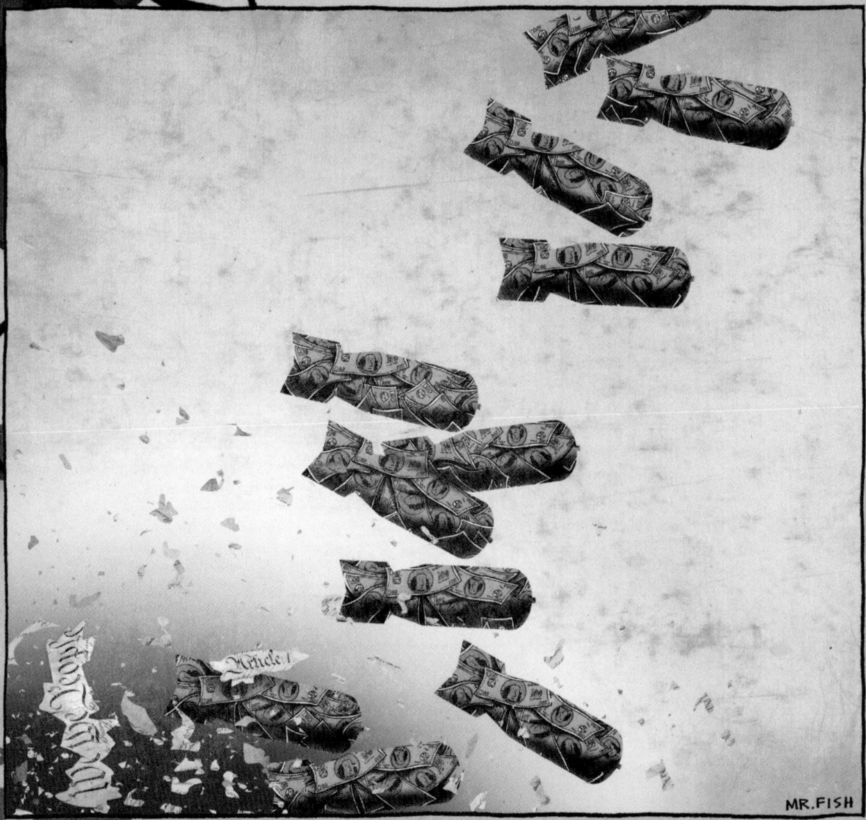
Article 1
MR.FISH

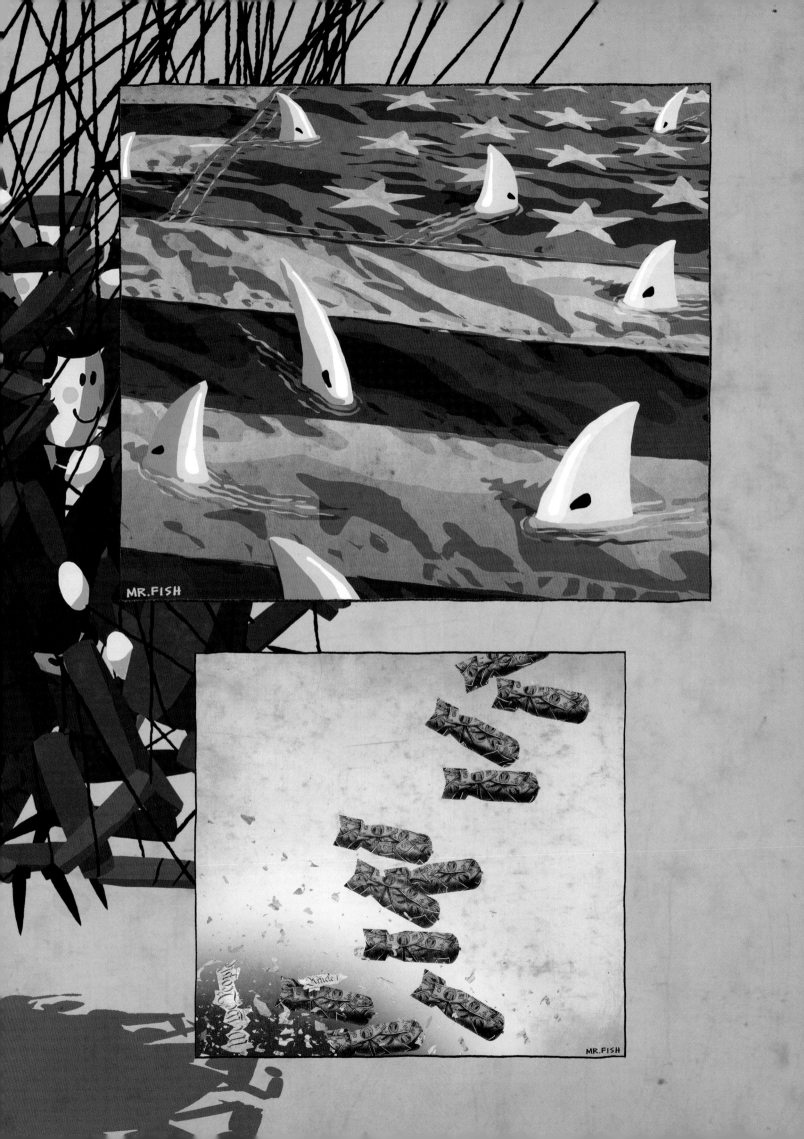

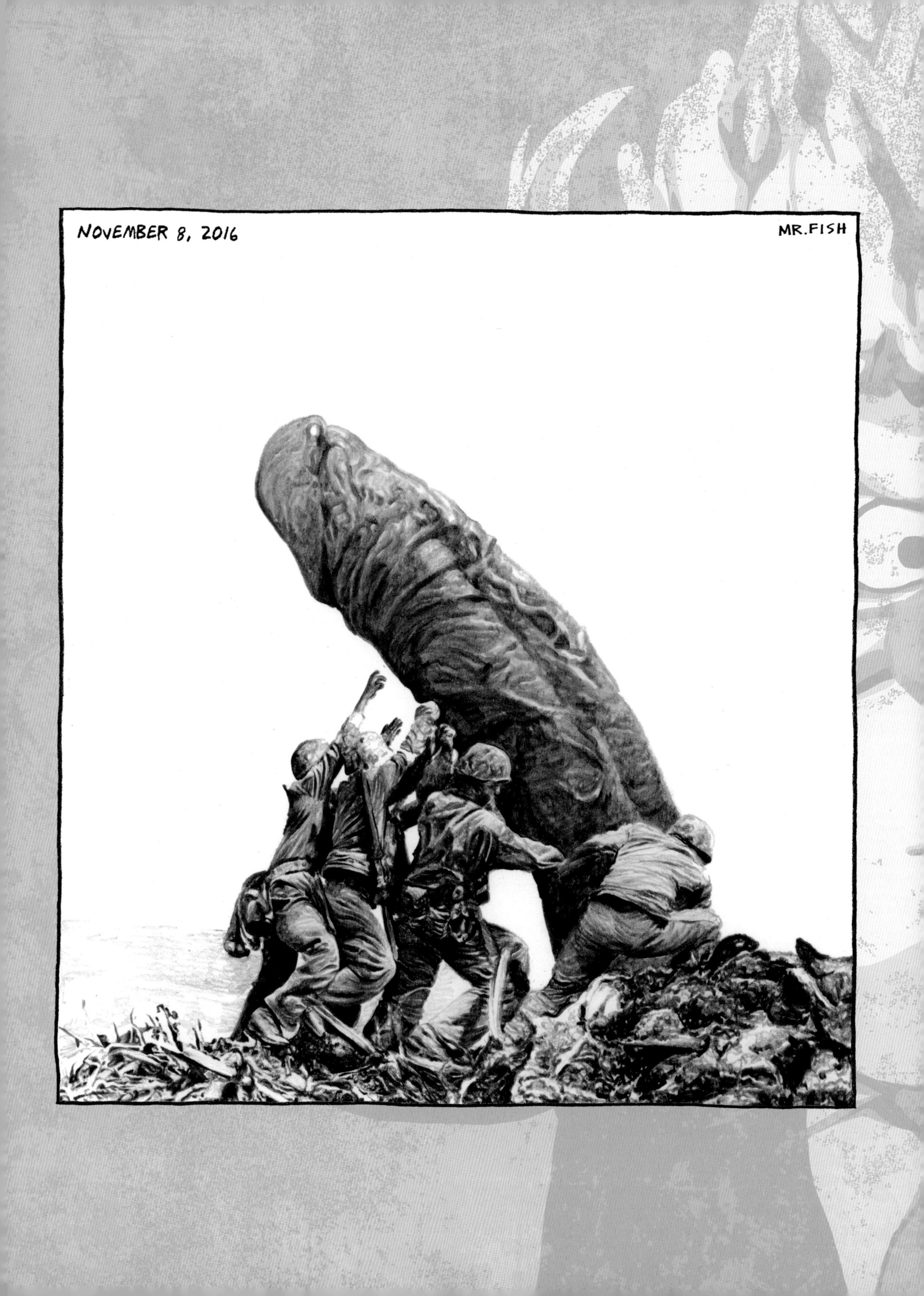
NOVEMBER 8, 2016
MR.FISH

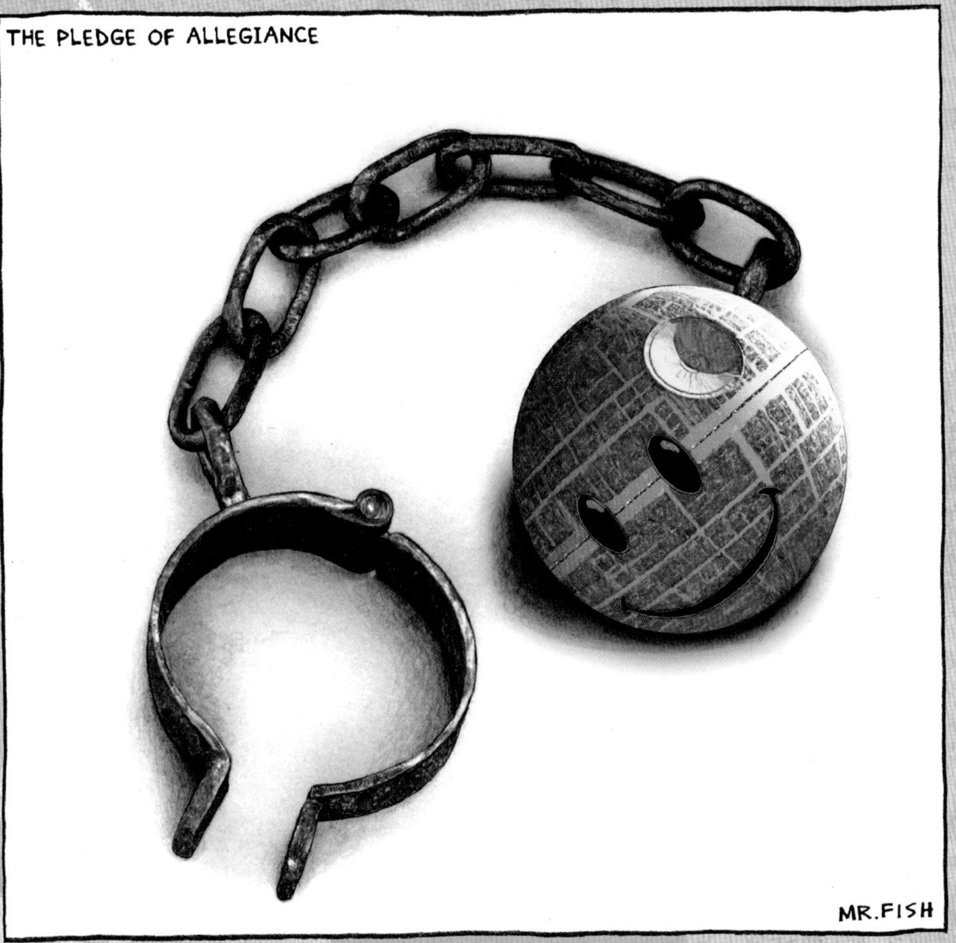
THE PLEDGE OF ALLEGIANCE
MR.FISH

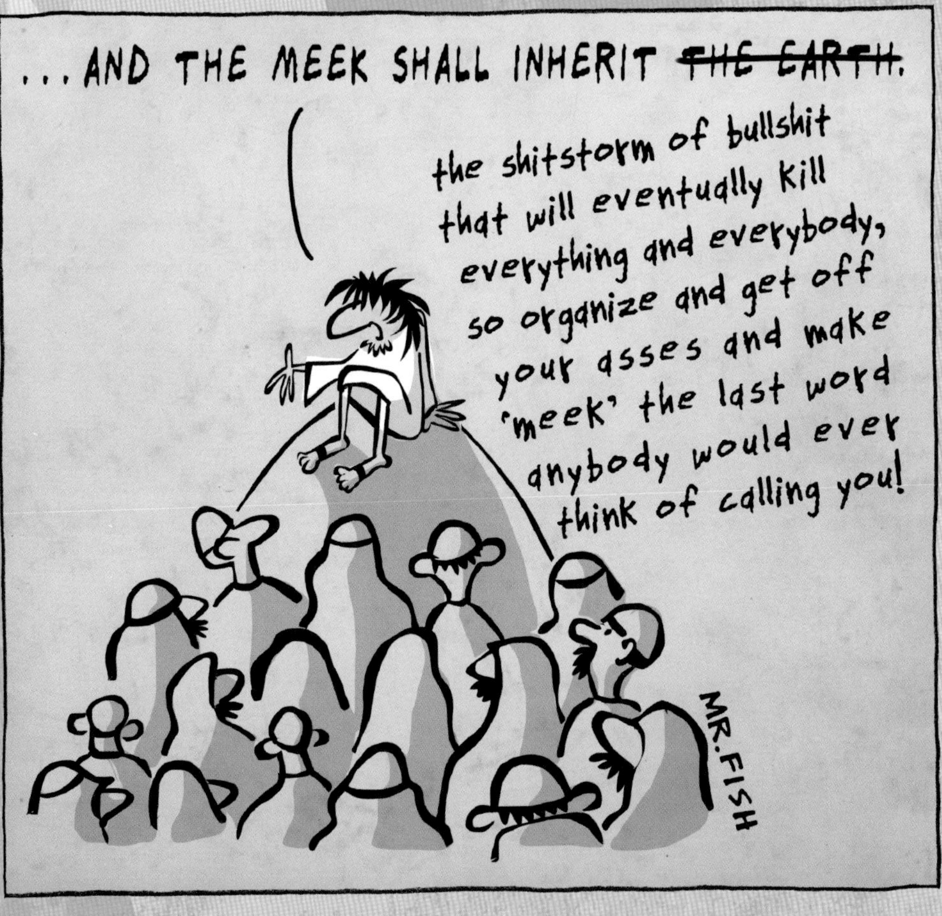
...AND THE MEEK SHALL INHERIT ~~THE EARTH~~.
the shitstorm of bullshit that will eventually kill everything and everybody, so organize and get off your asses and make 'meek' the last word anybody would ever think of calling you!
MR.FISH

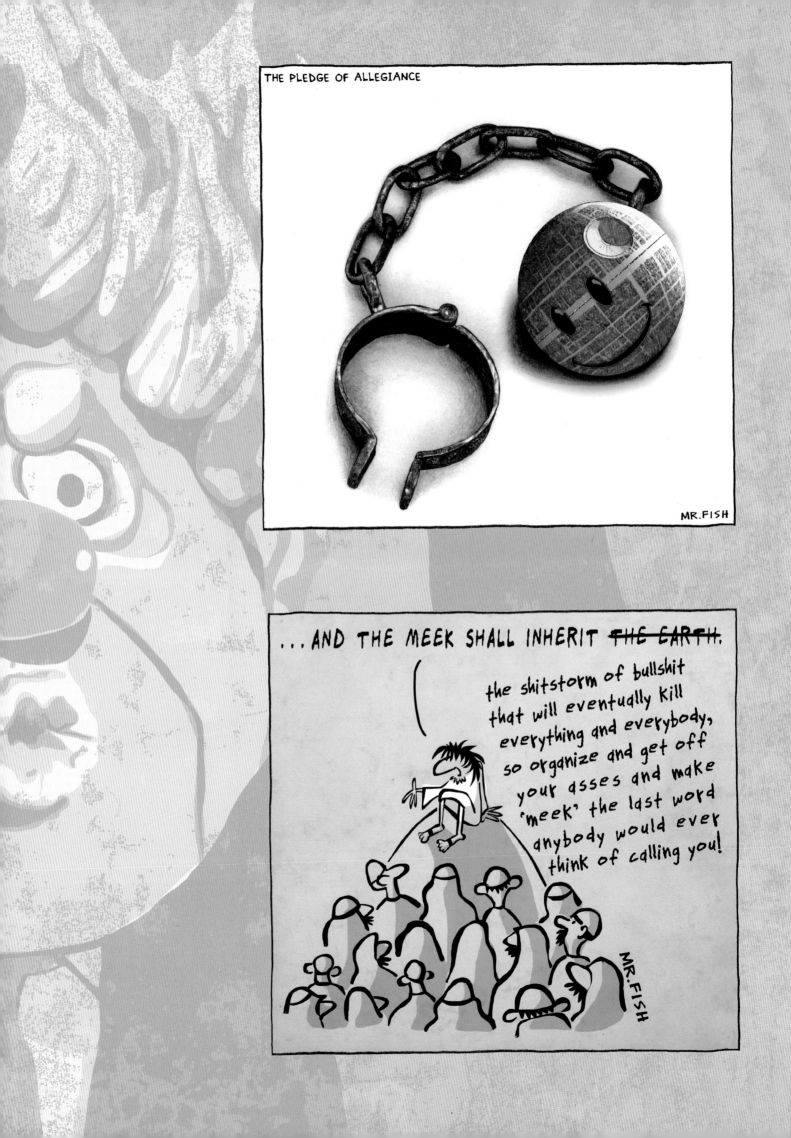

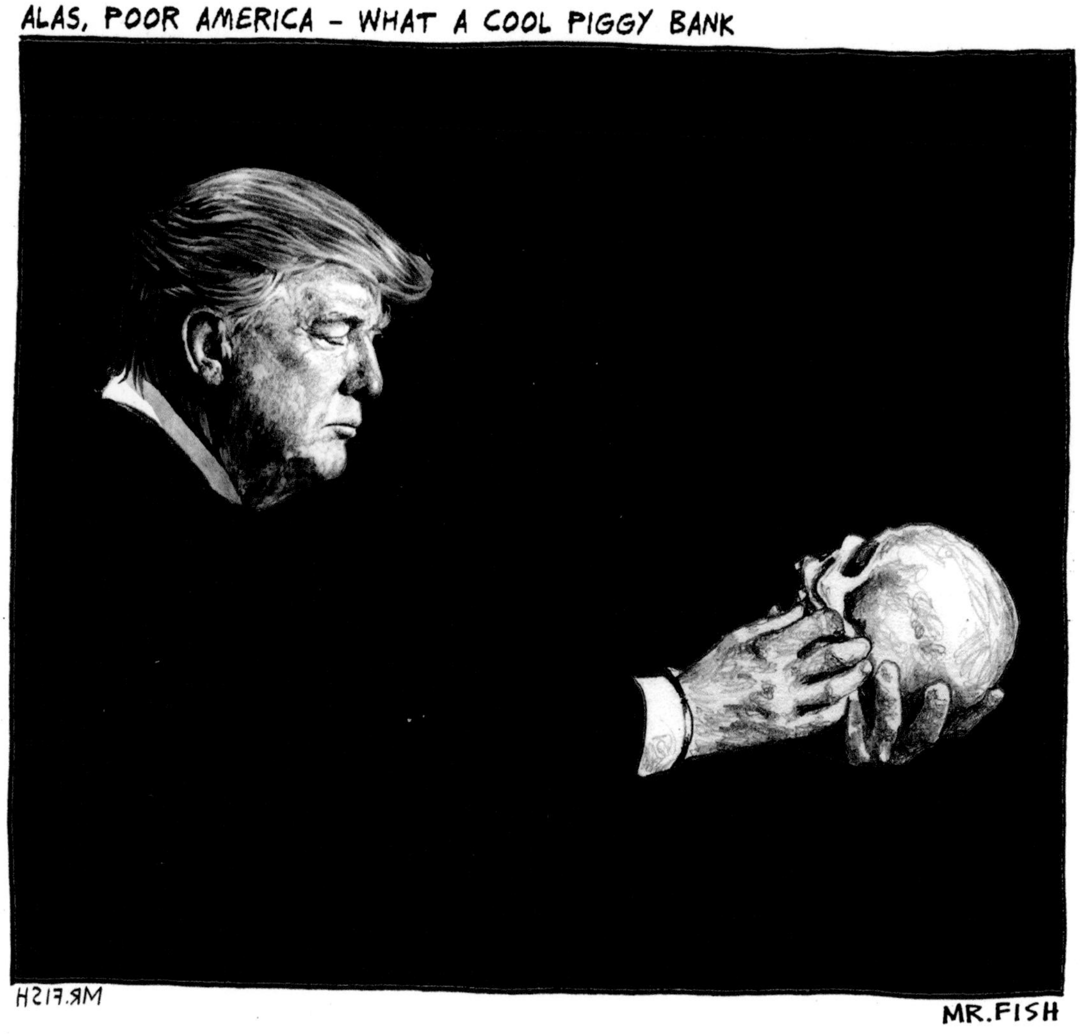
ALAS, POOR AMERICA - WHAT A COOL PIGGY BANK
MR.FISH
MR.FISH

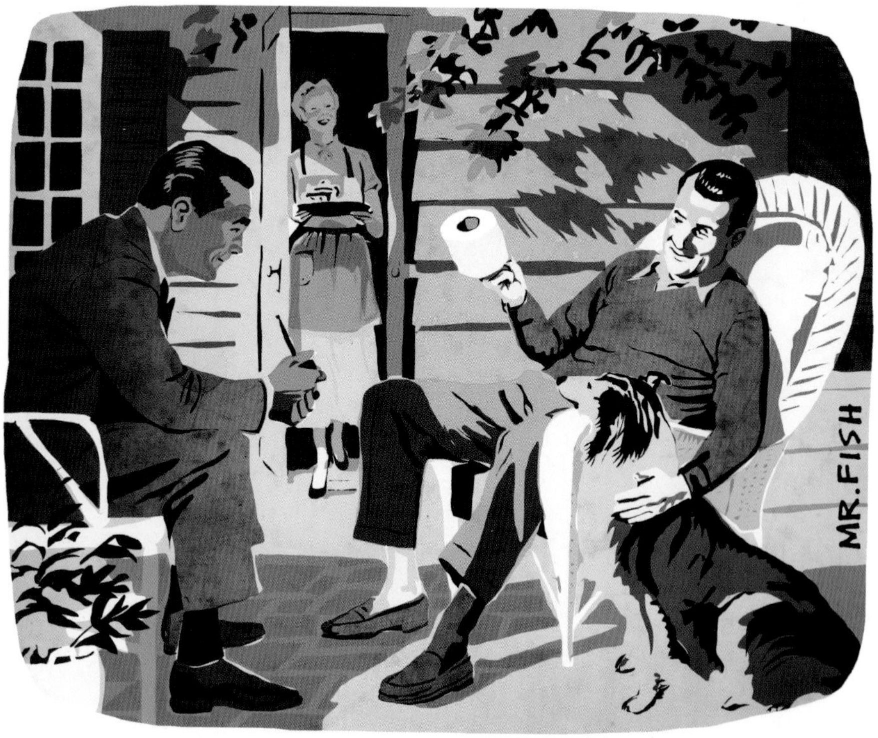
MR.FISH

"The worst thing about losing Rosalita to Trump's massive deportation roundups is that she didn't leave the operating instructions for this, which makes me a little less optimistic about how great America is about to become."

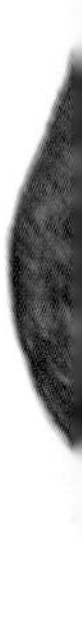

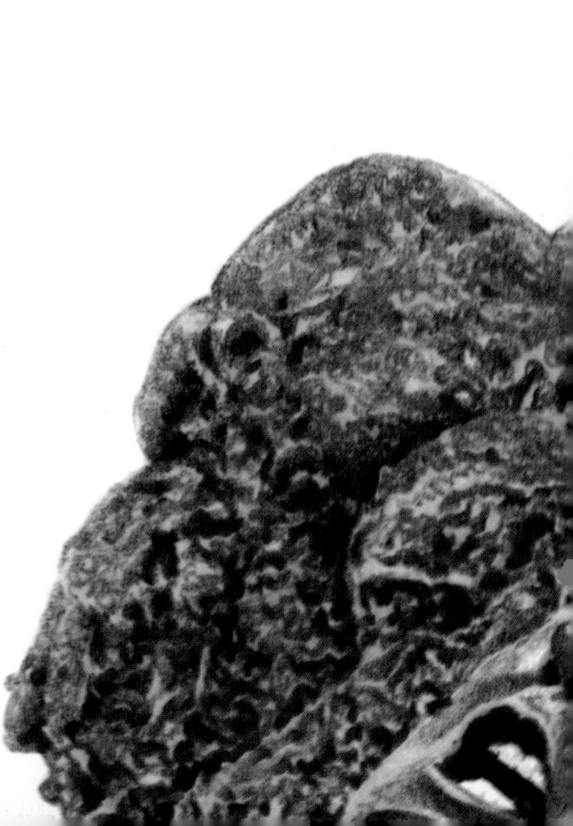

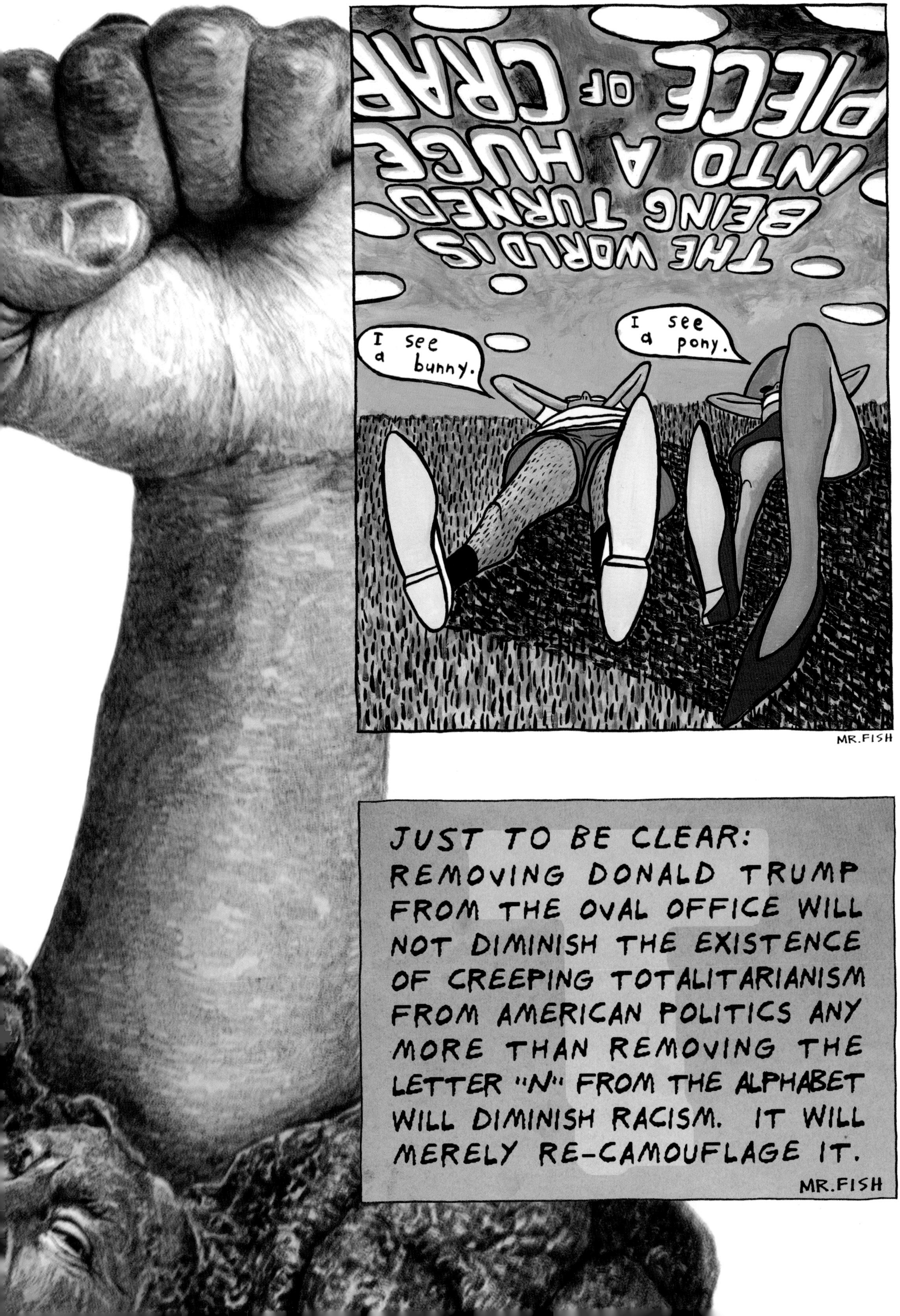
THE WORLD IS BEING TURNED INTO A HUGE PIECE OF CRAP
I see a bunny.
I see a pony.
MR.FISH
JUST TO BE CLEAR: REMOVING DONALD TRUMP FROM THE OVAL OFFICE WILL NOT DIMINISH THE EXISTENCE OF CREEPING TOTALITARIANISM FROM AMERICAN POLITICS ANY MORE THAN REMOVING THE LETTER "N" FROM THE ALPHABET WILL DIMINISH RACISM. IT WILL MERELY RE-CAMOUFLAGE IT.
MR.FISH

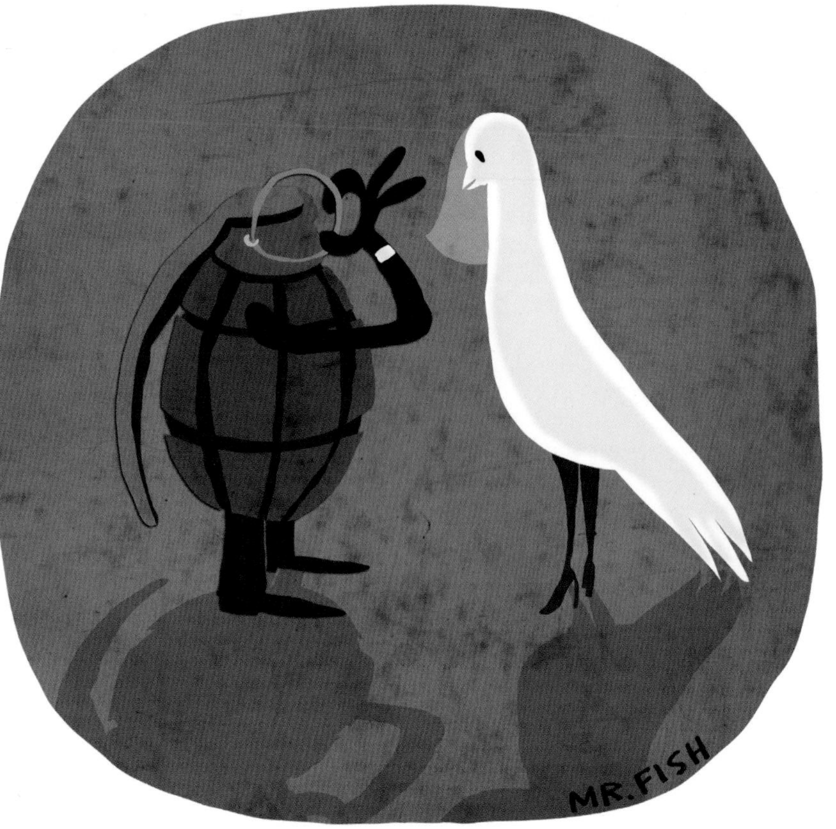
MR.FISH

"With this ring . . ."

JESUS COMING BACK, BUT ONLY FOR A MINUTE, AND THEN LEAVING AGAIN

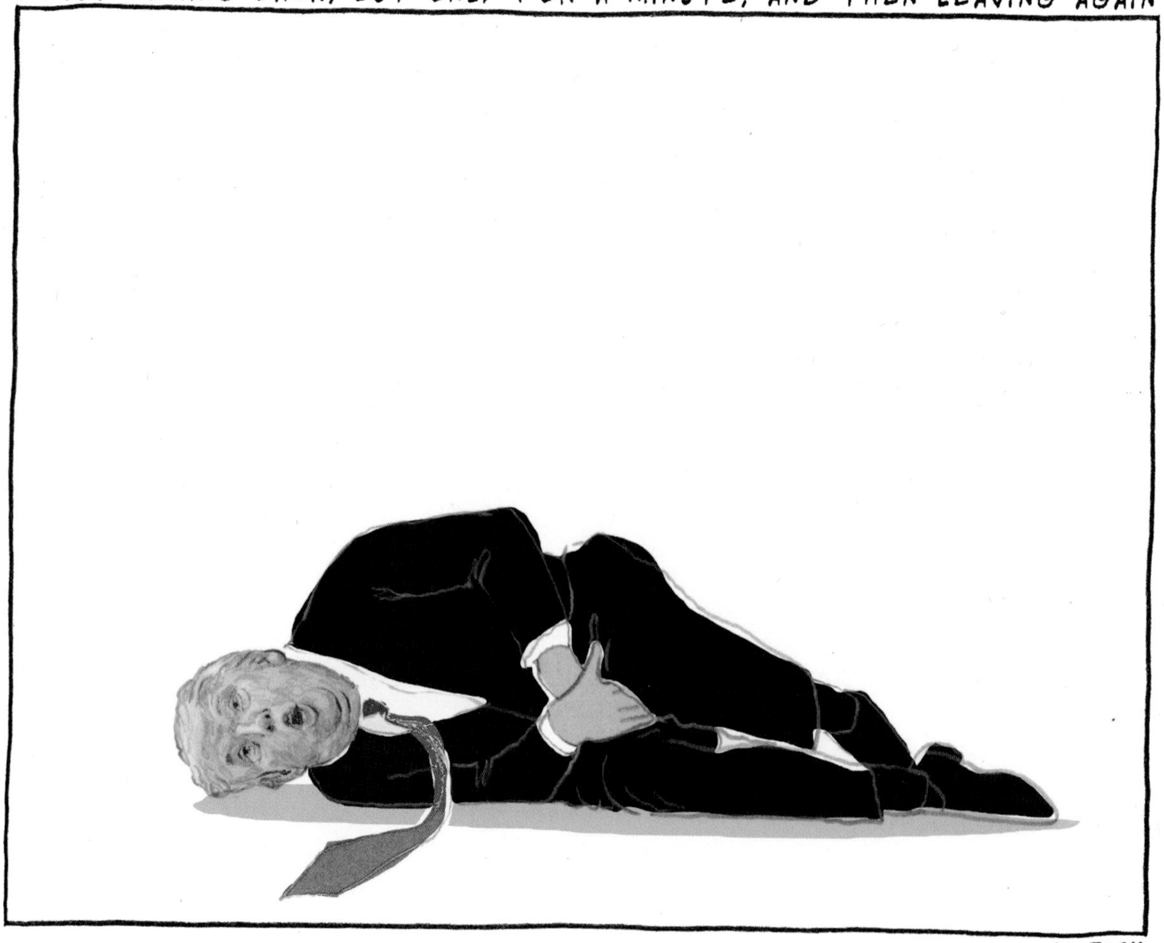

MR.FISH

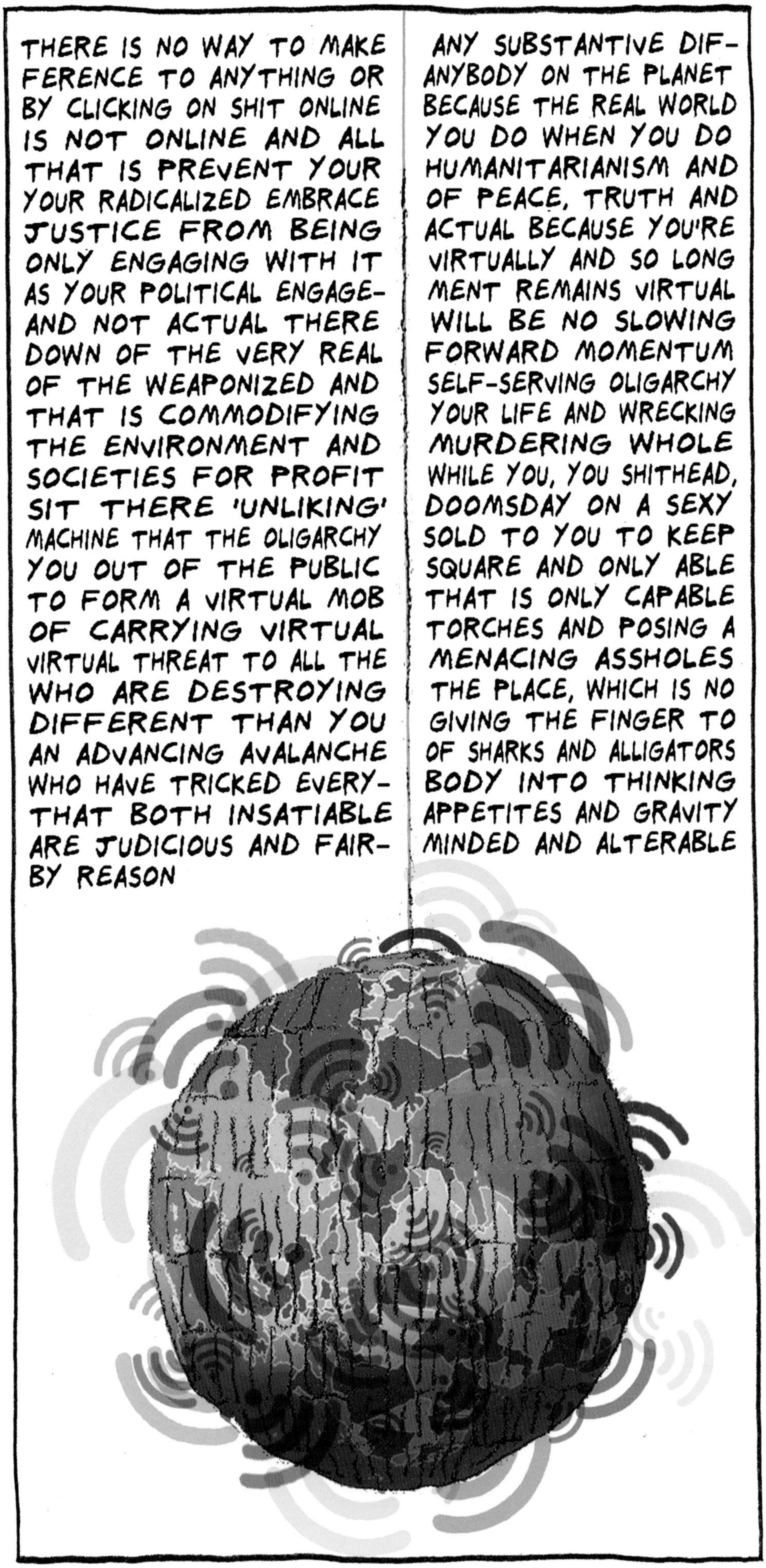
THERE IS NO WAY TO MAKE ANY SUBSTANTIVE DIF-
FERENCE TO ANYTHING OR ANYBODY ON THE PLANET
BY CLICKING ON SHIT ONLINE BECAUSE THE REAL WORLD
IS NOT ONLINE AND ALL YOU DO WHEN YOU DO
THAT IS PREVENT YOUR HUMANITARIANISM AND
YOUR RADICALIZED EMBRACE OF PEACE, TRUTH AND
JUSTICE FROM BEING ACTUAL BECAUSE YOU'RE
ONLY ENGAGING WITH IT VIRTUALLY AND SO LONG
AS YOUR POLITICAL ENGAGE- MENT REMAINS VIRTUAL
AND NOT ACTUAL THERE WILL BE NO SLOWING
DOWN OF THE VERY REAL FORWARD MOMENTUM
OF THE WEAPONIZED AND SELF-SERVING OLIGARCHY
THAT IS COMMODIFYING YOUR LIFE AND WRECKING
THE ENVIRONMENT AND MURDERING WHOLE
SOCIETIES FOR PROFIT WHILE YOU, YOU SHITHEAD,
SIT THERE 'UNLIKING' DOOMSDAY ON A SEXY
MACHINE THAT THE OLIGARCHY SOLD TO YOU TO KEEP
YOU OUT OF THE PUBLIC SQUARE AND ONLY ABLE
TO FORM A VIRTUAL MOB THAT IS ONLY CAPABLE
OF CARRYING VIRTUAL TORCHES AND POSING A
VIRTUAL THREAT TO ALL THE MENACING ASSHOLES
WHO ARE DESTROYING THE PLACE, WHICH IS NO
DIFFERENT THAN YOU GIVING THE FINGER TO
AN ADVANCING AVALANCHE OF SHARKS AND ALLIGATORS
WHO HAVE TRICKED EVERY- BODY INTO THINKING
THAT BOTH INSATIABLE APPETITES AND GRAVITY
ARE JUDICIOUS AND FAIR- MINDED AND ALTERABLE
BY REASON

MR. FISH

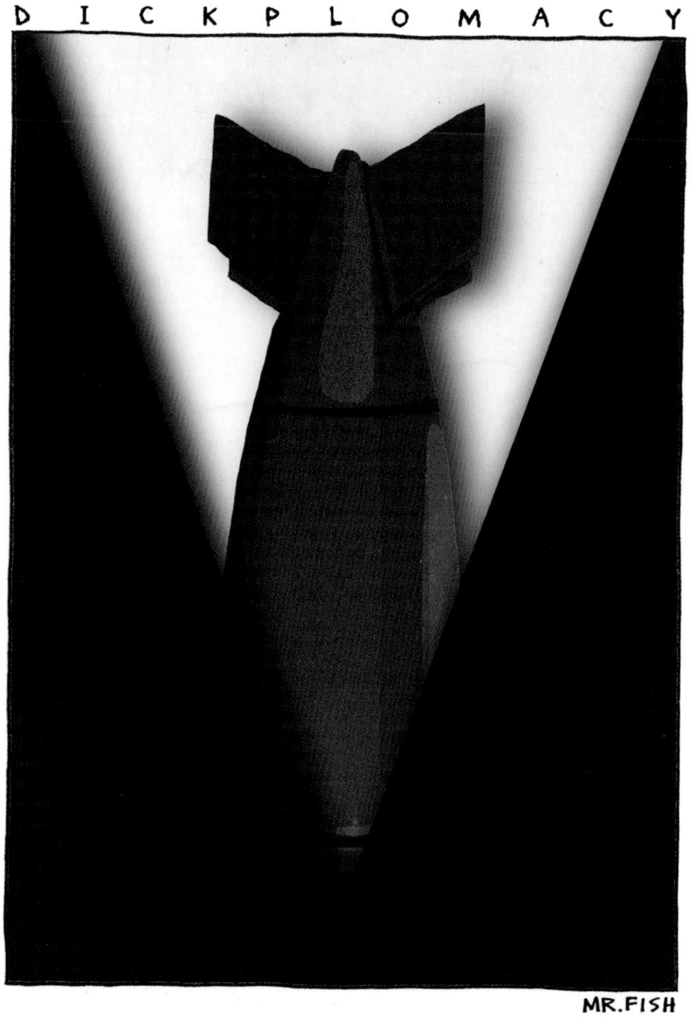
DICKPLOMACY
MR.FISH

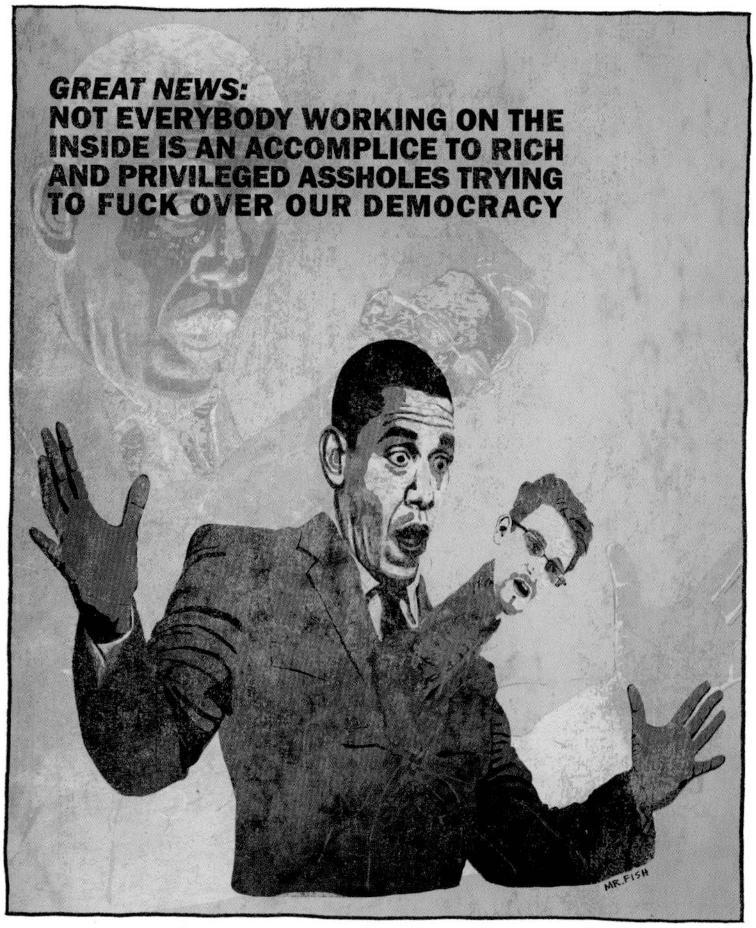
GREAT NEWS:
NOT EVERYBODY WORKING ON THE INSIDE IS AN ACCOMPLICE TO RICH AND PRIVILEGED ASSHOLES TRYING TO FUCK OVER OUR DEMOCRACY
MR.FISH

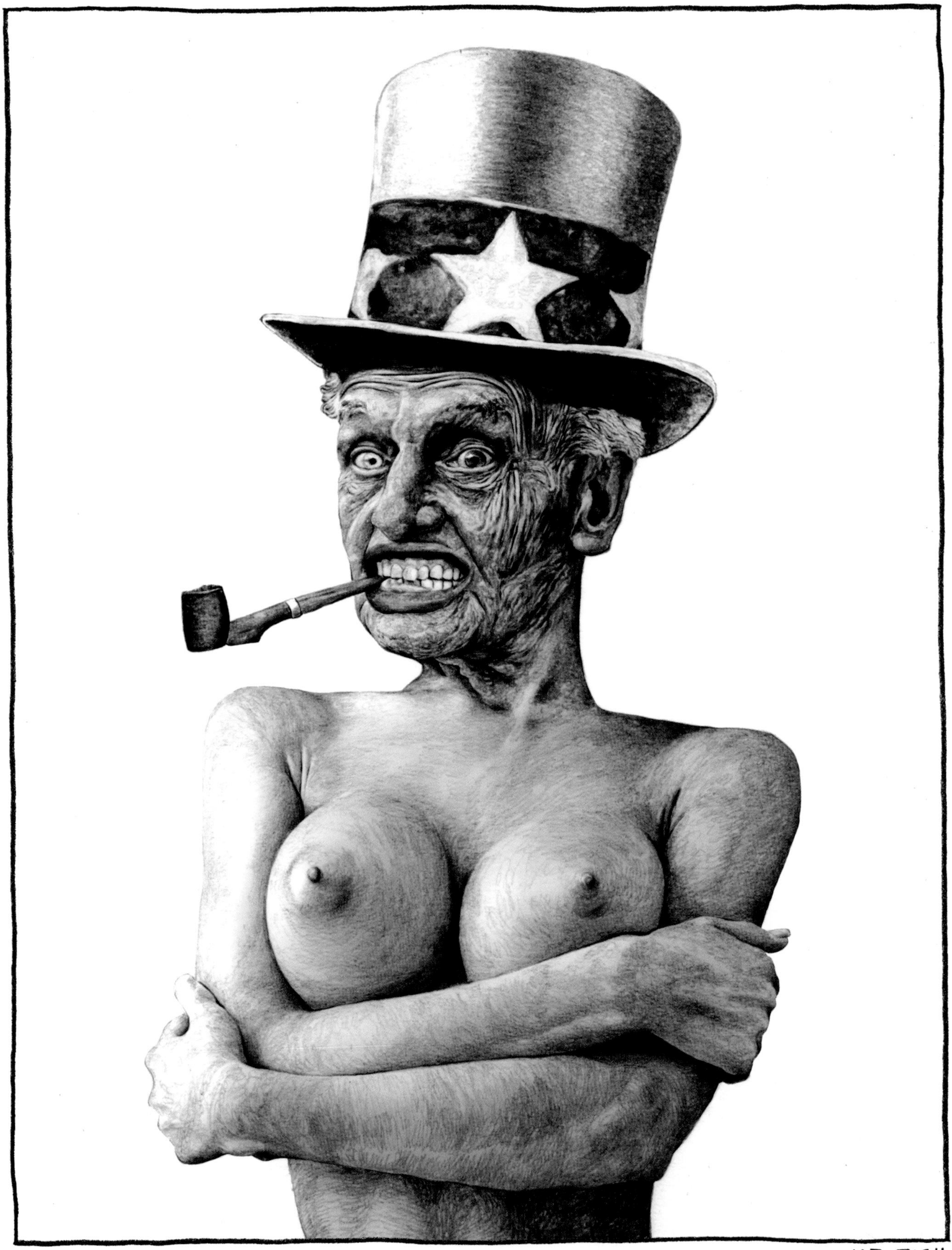
MR. FISH

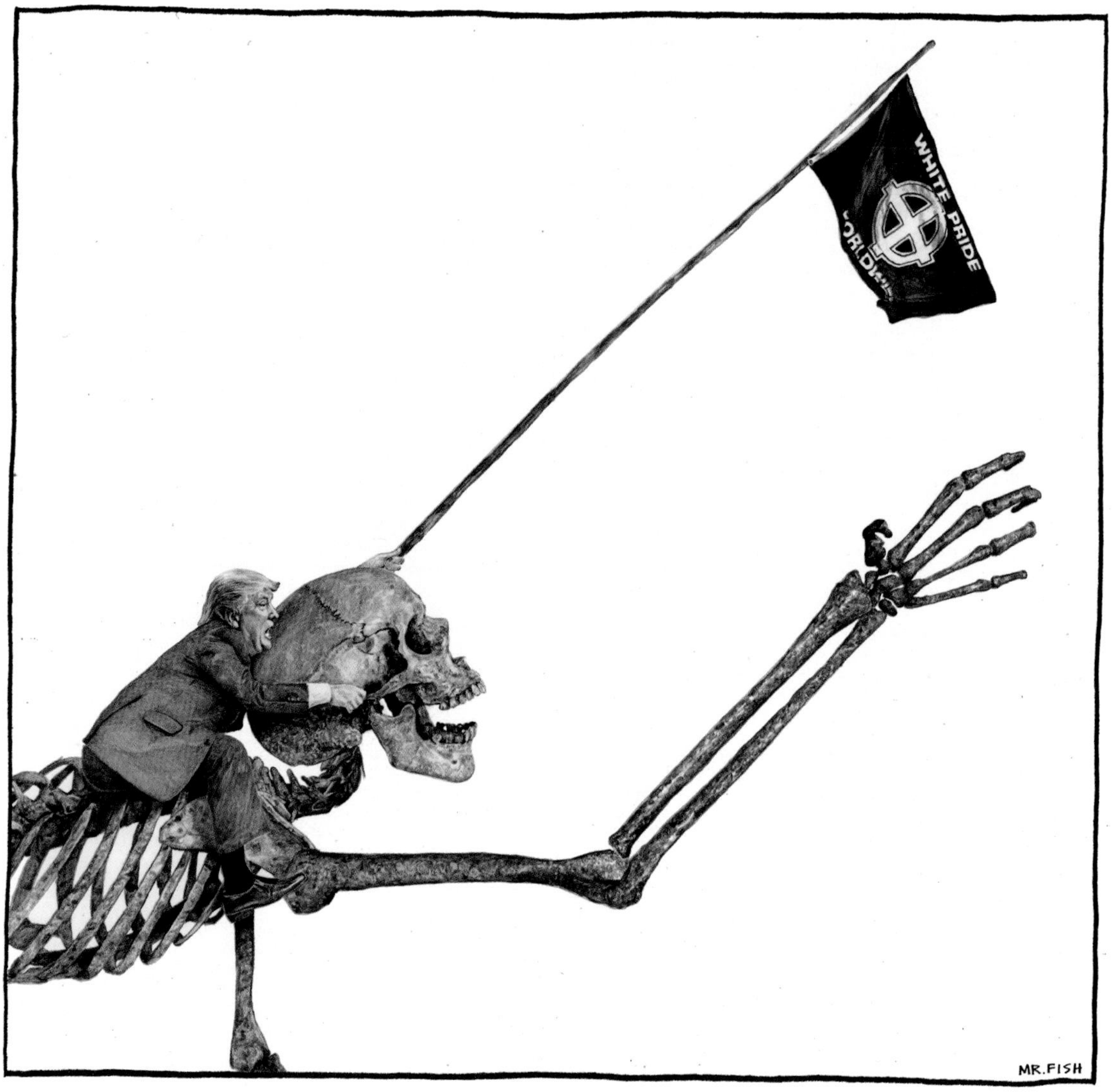
WHITE PRIDE
MR.FISH

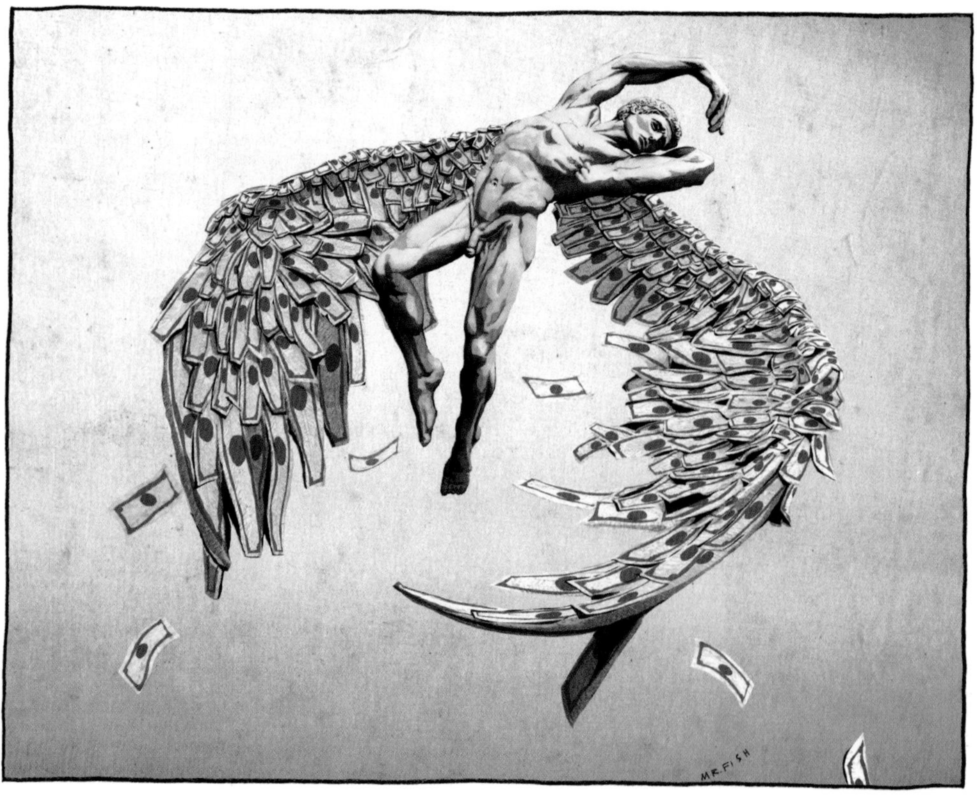
MR.FISH

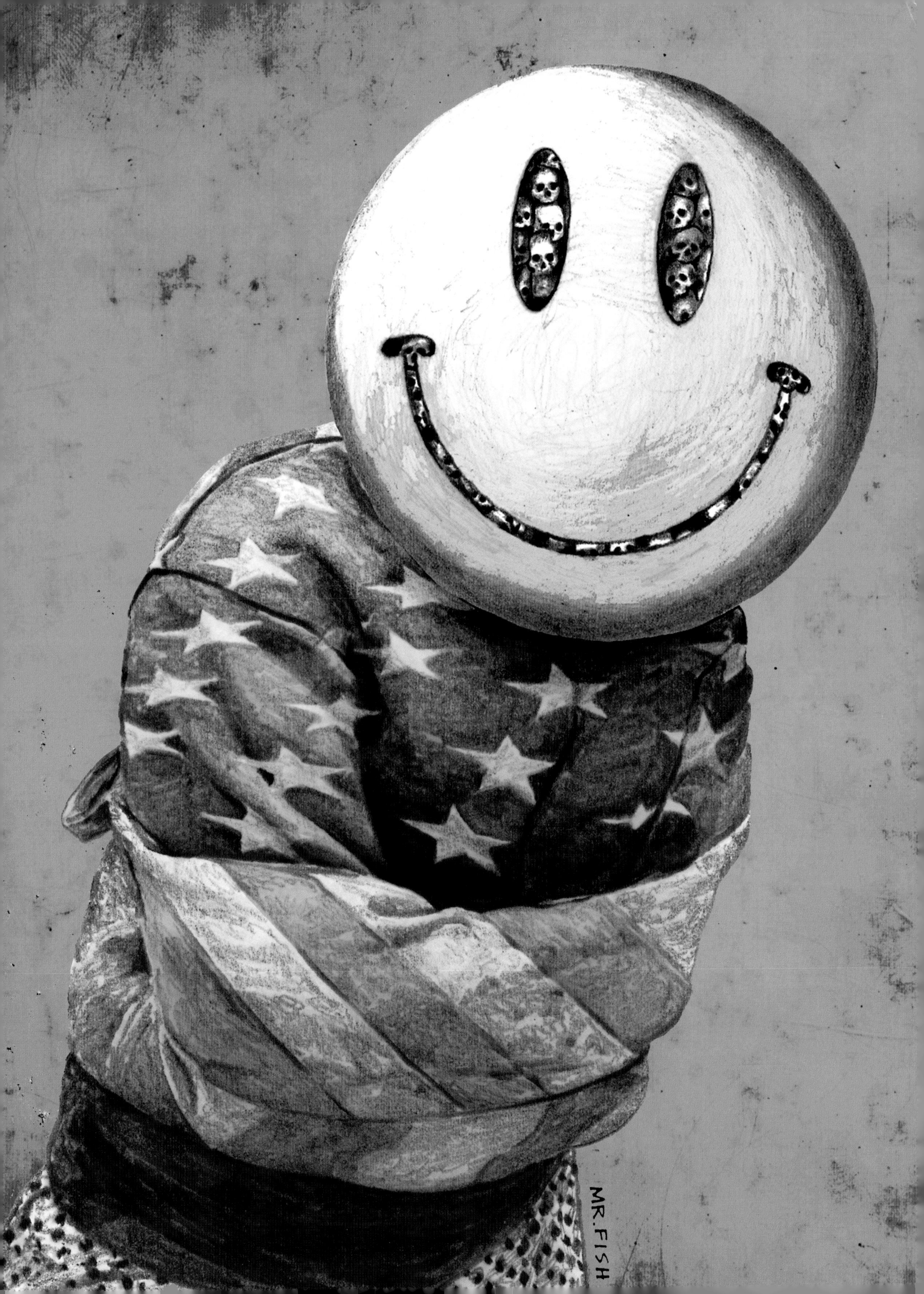
MR.FISH

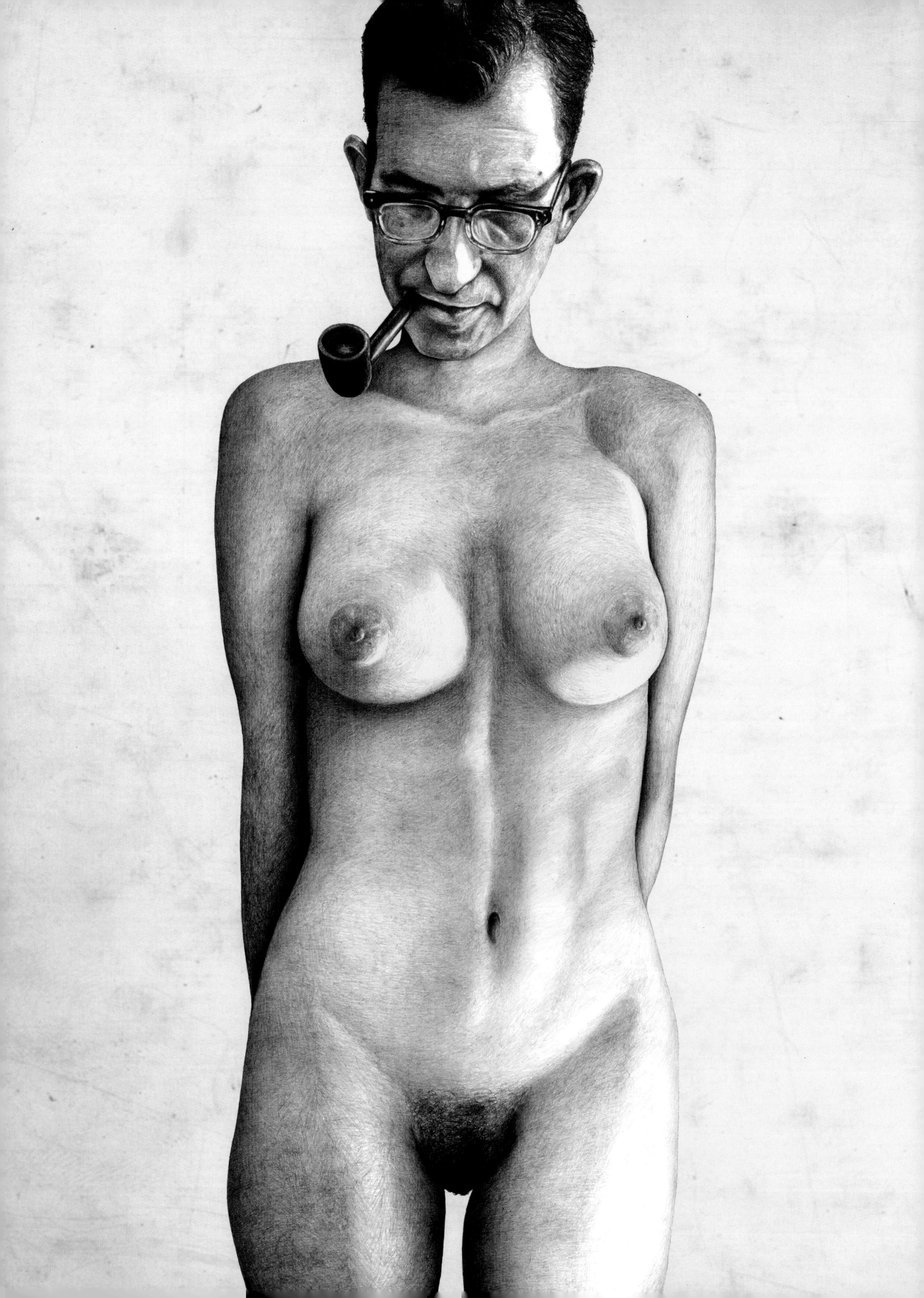

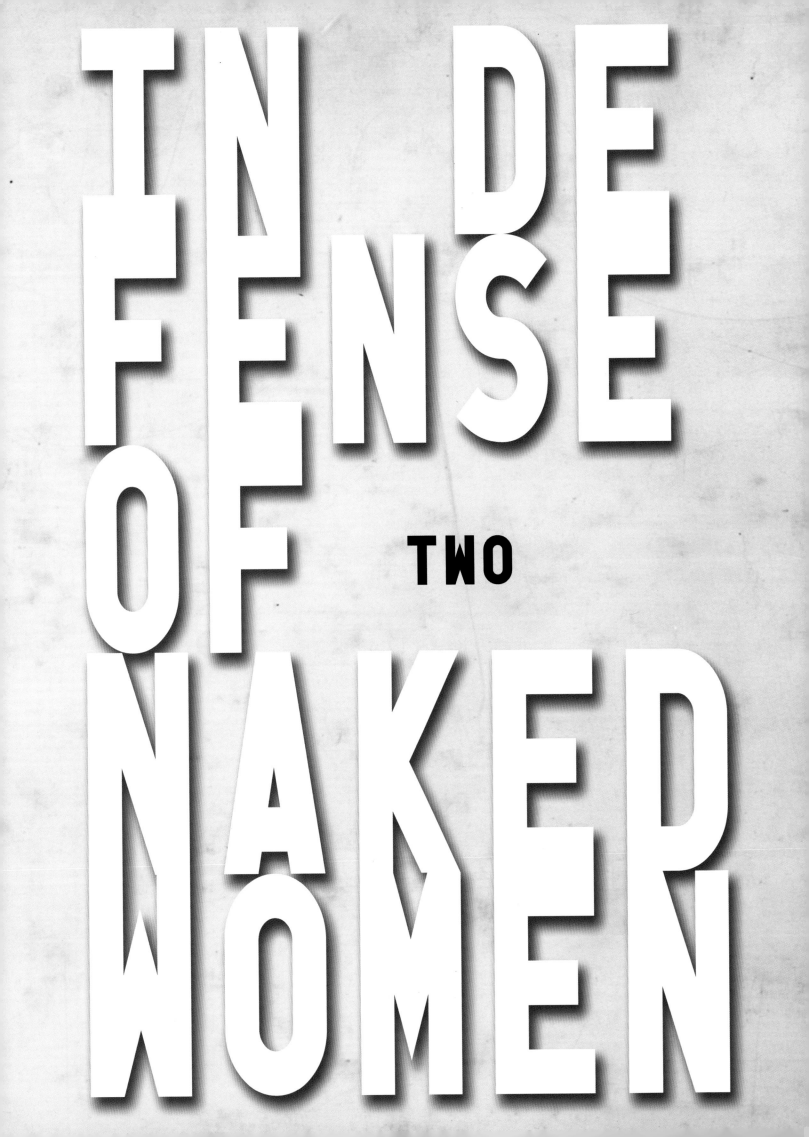

IN DE
FENSE
OF
TWO
NAKED
WOMEN

In Defense of Naked Women

I USED TO be 11. Occasionally, I am 11 again. I'm OK with that. I have a theory that by the time people reach 13 they've experienced every age they will ever experience in their lifetimes; 14 does not exist. Nobody, for example, has ever been kinder or more conniving than when they were 6, nor has anybody ever had an orgasm that was more mature than one had at 13. All that any of us have after we turn 14 are the prejudices and affections that were formed during the previous 13 years, and that, after slightly more than a decade's worth of rehearsal with our families, friends and neighbors, will then find either confirmation or argument with the outside world.

Of course, sometimes, after suffering a certain amount of pain over some of the more incessant arguing with the outside world, we might look for and find other people lucky enough to have formed personalities more nobly equipped to communicate peaceably with the parts of the outside world that exist contrary to our makeup, and we learn to either pantomime their comfort or to seek lifelong distraction inside their joy. And they don't even have to be real, these pacifying people, nor do they have to be people, necessarily; sometimes they're simply movies or sermons or books or television shows or political platforms or advertising campaigns. If we're lucky, we might be able to convince ourselves, lying on our deathbeds, that Jesus Christ can't wait to shake hands with us because we're such close friends with Spock, Oprah Winfrey, Giorgio Armani and every bald eagle in North America.

The 13th-century Sufi poet Jalaluddin Rumi said that a person was just as aware of what his or her life was about as a pencil was of what it was writing. Of course, if Rumi were alive today he'd be Afghani, having come from the Balkh region of Persia, and he'd no doubt spend an inordinate amount of time in airport security having both his accent and his sneakers checked for explosives. "We said remove your head, A-rab, and place it into the plastic tub for X-ray!"

(Pause to allow for sound of veteran clapping his hooks together.)

Freezing my nuts off at 3 a.m. on the rooftop of a parking garage at a movie theater on Sunset Boulevard in Hollywood, CA, in the spring of 2005, I found myself thinking about the Susan Sontag quote that said 10 percent of any population is cruel, no matter what, and that 10 percent is merciful, no matter what, and that the remaining 80 percent could be moved in either direction. Down below dressed in rubber and plastic and burlap and armed to the teeth with battery-operated weaponry and corrective lenses strode hundreds of space aliens, robots, senators, queens, lords, storm troopers and an elite infantry of disparate knights, call them Jedis of chess and masturbation, into the lobby for the 3:30 showing of *Star Wars III: Revenge of the Sith* (or *Shit*, if you decided to defer to the greater wisdom of the spell-checker on your laptop) and I rushed to join them, eager to mock them while secretly hoping that the movie might blow the mind of the 13-year-old that I knew piloted my orgasms and yippied and yahooed at fireworks and excessive violence and defecating zoo animals and the non-taxing demand of reacting to something completely meaningless. My costume? Somebody way too cool to give a Sith, of course.

Watching the movie, I was reminded of something that a 20th-century Spanish poet said about the United States of America. He said that it was the most primitive society on Earth with the greatest technology.

On. Off.

During the springtime of my first pass at 11, in 1977, I saw both the original *Star Wars* movie and had my first look at

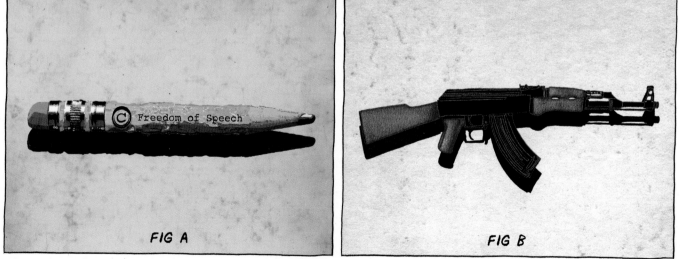

WHICH OF THESE WEAPONS WOULD YOU CHOOSE FOR YOURSELF AND WHICH WOULD YOU CHOOSE FOR YOUR ENEMY IN A CONFLICT WHERE YOU WANTED TO WIN?
© Freedom of Speech
FIG A
FIG B
MR.FISH

WAR   PEACE

MR.FISH

hardcore pornography. The movie, everybody knows—many too well; the pornography nobody but my best friend JJ knows, having come from his mother's nightstand and presented to me one day after school in the form of playing cards, the deck having been pinned beneath the intimidating guard dog of a dildo big enough to roll out cookie dough for the veiniest hamantaschen imaginable. The cards featured terrifying close-ups of wide-open vaginas, each of which looked more like an emergency room Polaroid of a fireworks accident than anything that I imagined one day wanting to put my mouth on. Still, there was something about these overexposed snapshots of drooling, red-faced little gargoyles, these bearded and gaping wounds that pulled a nurturing sympathy from the Florence Nightingale deep inside my groin who, taping her pen against a clipboard and narrowing her beatific gaze, suggested excessive caulking as a fix, that hypnotized me. Part of me knew that this queen of hearts and this nine of diamonds and this ace of spades wasn't really just a picture of some strange girl's *natural eius debent* – Latin for *stinky surprise* – but rather represented a vast and impending scenario that I needed to prepare for. So, thrilling to both and embarrassed by neither, I spent my prepubescent years attempting to move inert objects with my mind while simultaneously recalling the contents of those playing cards as if cramming for a test that rote memorization alone would carry me through.

So, what did one have to do with the other? What did trying to master telekinesis ultimately have to do with my greater understanding of each glistening fold and each ripening contour of the female *whatchamacallit?*

Maybe it was this: Contrary to the popular idea of feminism, I decided that experiencing a woman as a sexual object wasn't inherently a bad thing. I, for one, love being objectified during sex, particularly when the object that I'm being thought of seems able to exist without the incessant commentary of my personality to define or justify it, like a sunset beautiful without the explanation of science, or a poem moving without a syllabus, or a smile infectious without the psychological profile to categorize it. Or, more specifically, a 20-inch wiener dog playful enough not to require any interference from the sap holding the leash. What was bad, I decided, about thinking of people exclusively as a sexual object was that you missed being able to experience them as anything else, thereby making them completely invisible when dressed and breathing normally—a point of view, mind you, that I had when I was 5 years old and surrounded by girls just as likely as I was to pick their nose and swear and piss in the woods. Feminism suffers, I think, when *it attempts to deny a woman access to the complete freedom that comes with all that lies between despicability and respectability.*

A cunt and a vagina, it turns out, are exactly the same thing. (Pause, repeat.)

Star Wars thus became for me a similar victim of pigeonholiness—that is, neither a work of great hero mythology that informed some deeper understanding of the human soul nor a huge, steaming piece of pop culture so idiotic that exposure to its stench had the unfortunate effect of retarding the otherwise perfectly indifferent perception that we lived in a completely Wookie-less universe (if you call that *living*). Specifically, while the entire Star Wars saga might be little more than an exercise in crappy storytelling, perhaps even an unwitting champion of lazy politics predicated on the notion that there existed absolute good and absolute evil in the world and that people might legitimately be objectified as either black or white chess pieces and that the gigantic mechanism of the cosmos was a fair and noble construct that rewarded the pure and punished the wicked, it was still nothing but a fairytale concocted by a high-functioning imbecile, a genius of howling mediocrity named George Lucas whose story was no more or less outrageous than the Bible or the Constitution or the Quran. What my thoughts about feminism taught me about Lucas was that I shouldn't objectify his idiocy, nor should I objectify the idiocy of what the Bible or the Constitution or the Quran demanded of the portion of the world begging exemption from surrendering to a global world order unfamiliar to them.

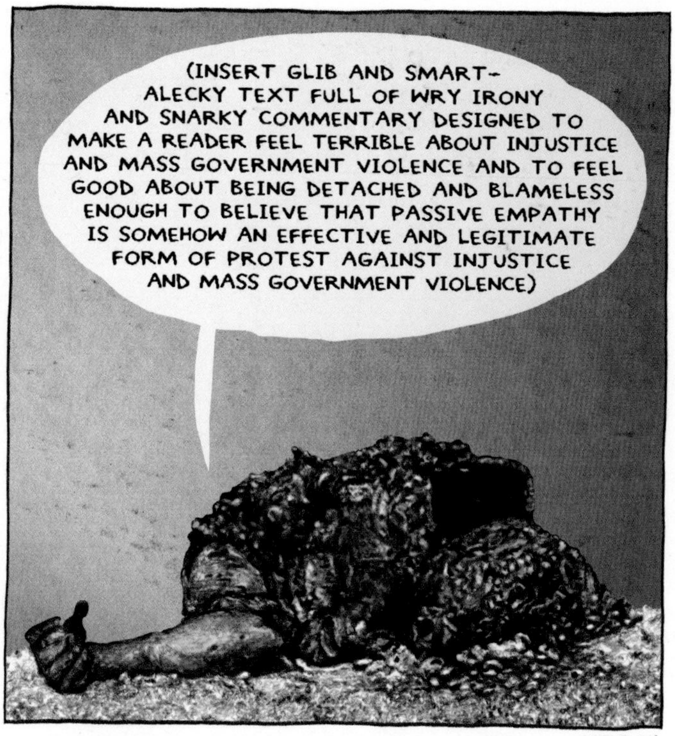
(INSERT GLIB AND SMART-ALECKY TEXT FULL OF WRY IRONY AND SNARKY COMMENTARY DESIGNED TO MAKE A READER FEEL TERRIBLE ABOUT INJUSTICE AND MASS GOVERNMENT VIOLENCE AND TO FEEL GOOD ABOUT BEING DETACHED AND BLAMELESS ENOUGH TO BELIEVE THAT PASSIVE EMPATHY IS SOMEHOW AN EFFECTIVE AND LEGITIMATE FORM OF PROTEST AGAINST INJUSTICE AND MASS GOVERNMENT VIOLENCE)
MR.FISH

I figured that as long as George Lucas kept his morally simplistic perversions behind closed theater doors, then he wasn't hurting anybody. Same with George Washington. And, dare I say, ISIS, Osama bin Laden and Adolf Hitler. As long as the door that we're talking about is kept unlocked and has a WELCOME matt on both sides and all the EXIT signs inside are clearly marked. Or, at the very least, if not all that, then at least a sign at the door warning of the health hazards of entering: *Exposure to philosophy enclosed has been known to waste an inordinate amount of time and to cause rampant self-aggrandizement, corruption of all human decency and, ultimately, death.*

In the spring of 2004, I downloaded a video file onto my computer and watched U.S. contractor Nicholas Berg getting his head sawed off by a bunch of Middle Eastern men in ski

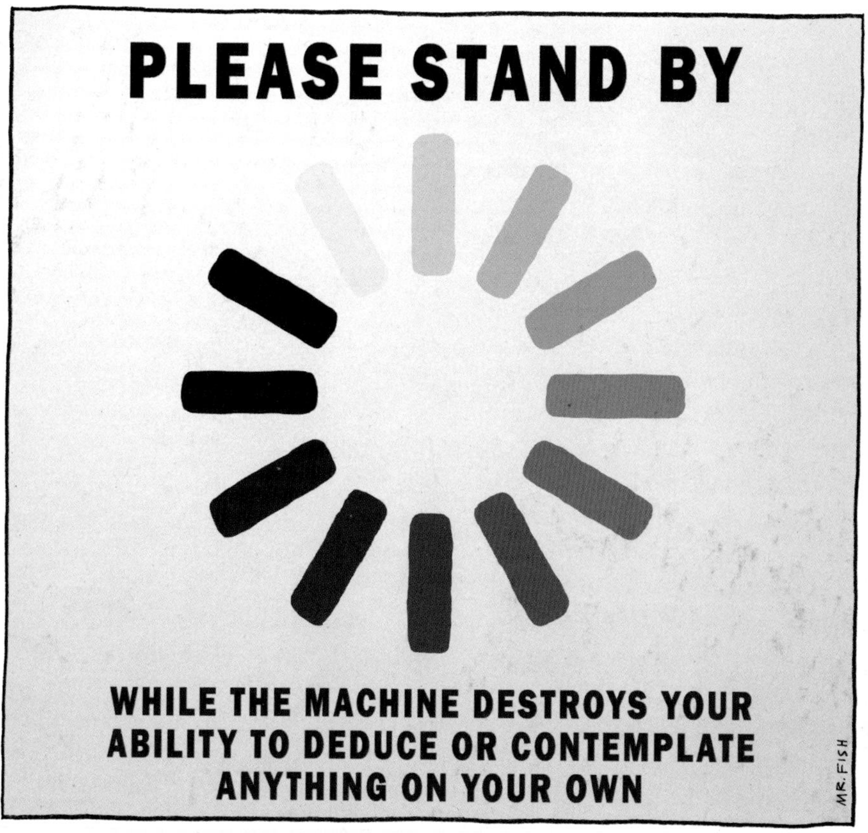
PLEASE STAND BY
WHILE THE MACHINE DESTROYS YOUR ABILITY TO DEDUCE OR CONTEMPLATE ANYTHING ON YOUR OWN
MR. FISH

masks. After all, I figured, if you're interested in what death might look like, having heard about it your whole life, what kind of pictures can you expect to get of all the informative beheading and de-limbing and vaporizing of all the civilians that the United States does from 15,000 feet up, where the only indication that you might get of having committed all that killing is perhaps a tiny green light flashing on a computer screen, the same technology used to indicate when the French fries are ready to be removed from the fryer at McDonald's? I then spent the next 20 minutes following the Berg beheading calling friends to tell them not to do what I'd done, that my whole physiology had changed as a result of what I'd seen and that I would forever be at least one degree colder at my core. I explained how the execution wasn't interesting to look at on any level whatsoever, making me worry that Hollywood might not be doing its job. Tragedy, it turns out, plays a lot better when it's massive and when a lot of people die all at once and from some distance, as in Titanic or Godzilla or even, truth be told, the daytime toppling of the two tallest buildings in the world by two crashed airplanes, horrible sadness and bone-crushing dread aside. Sure, if Berg had been torn apart by a disintegrating skyscraper shot from a news camera in New Jersey, or if he'd been seized by a Tyrannosaurus Rex and then eaten, his murder might've been easier for me to process, but only because my eyes would've mostly been on the dinosaur and not on the agony of the dinosaur's lunch, baby-faced and wearing an orange jumpsuit and barefoot.

The 11-year-old that I once was was the one who wanted to see the beheading, and not because when I was 11 I was particularly enamored with the brutality of torture, Polaroids of

fireworks accidents aside, but rather because most 11-year-olds want to see things that they've never seen before, whether it's a baseball game or a moon rock or the birth of a litter of slimy purple puppies or a self-induced cyanide poisoning at a sentencing in a courtroom or a Facebook murder or a subway suicide or a shark attack; newness, tragic or comic, is the reason why we wake up in the morning.

Think and Do:

A friend of mine once told me that the best indicator of a video store's quality, back when there were video stores, was whether or not it carried gay porno, back when gay porno was exotic. "A place brave enough to stock *Shaving Ryan's Privates* and *Blood Sausage*," he explained, "is not concerned with promoting a version of the world where only one kind of joy is tolerated or where a difference of opinion is considered either too embarrassing to contemplate or too contrary to go divinely unpunished." He loved how for a lot of super-benevolent, love-thy-neighbor Christian-types the only purpose of fucking was for the procreation of more and more Christians who would promise to be intolerant of any orgasm that didn't contribute to the breeding of more and more intolerance of any orgasm that didn't contribute to the breeding of more and more intolerance of any orgasm that didn't contribute... well, you get the idea. Anyway, he saw procreation-exclusive screwing as being roughly equivalent to telling people that they were only allowed to die of old age. "And that's why we're completely fucked as a species," he said, "because most people in the world don't realize that trying has very little to do with it."

AMERICA WINNING AT CHESS

MR. FISH

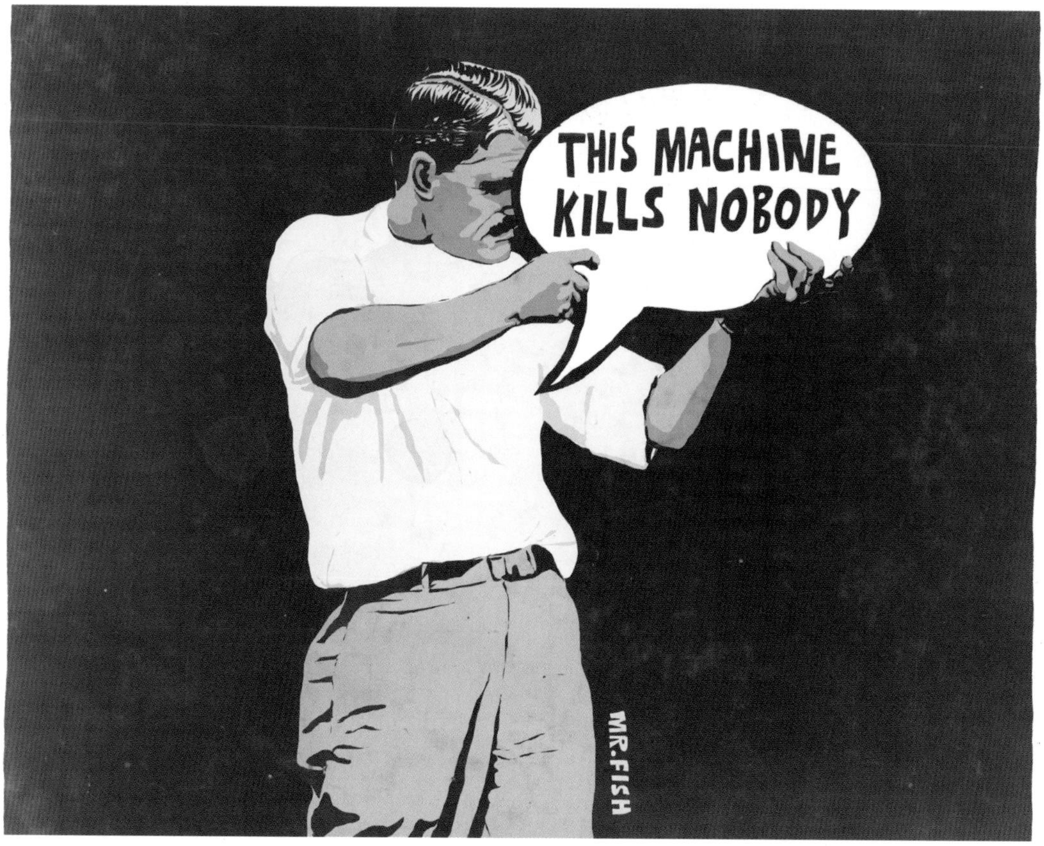
THIS MACHINE KILLS NOBODY
MR. FISH

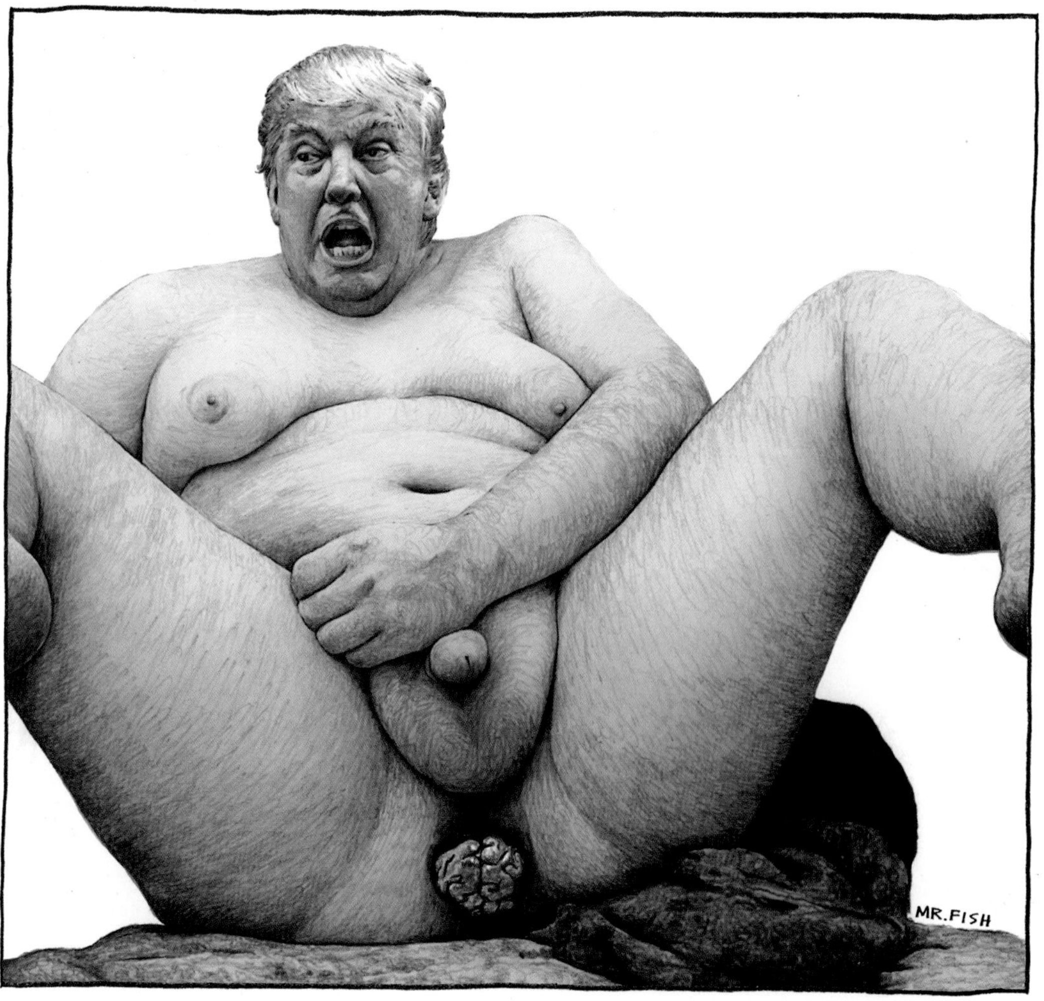
MR. FISH

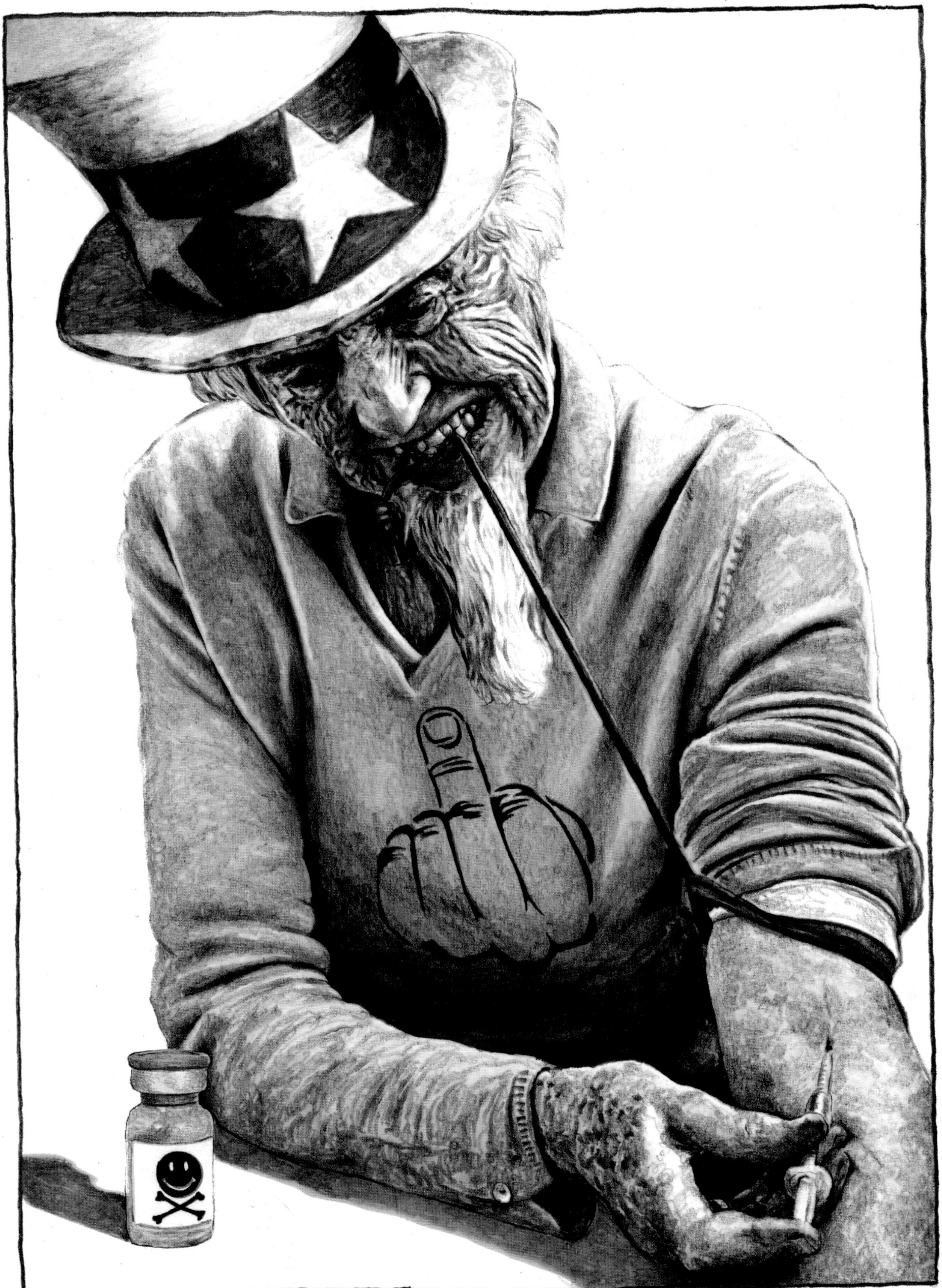
MR. FISH

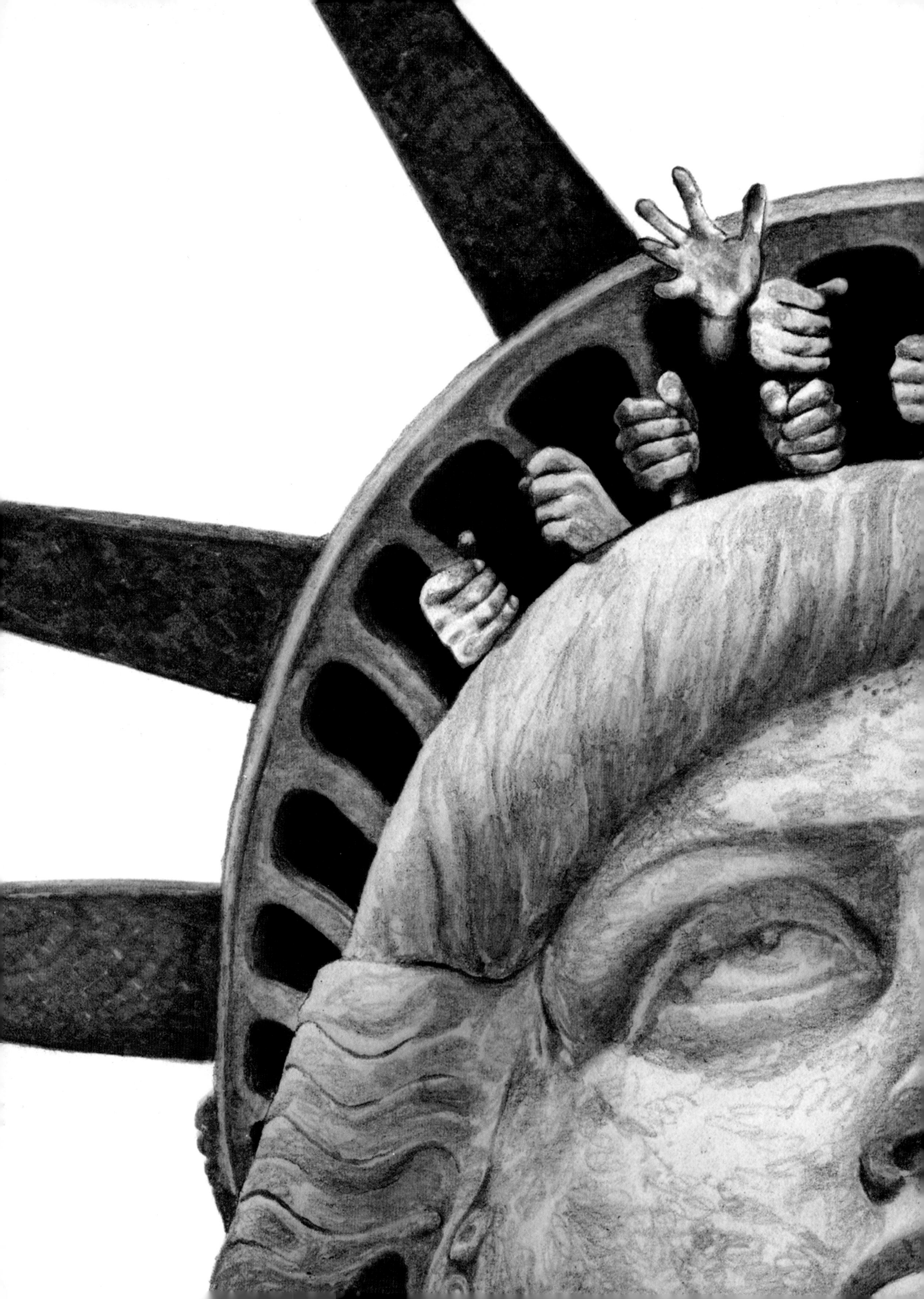

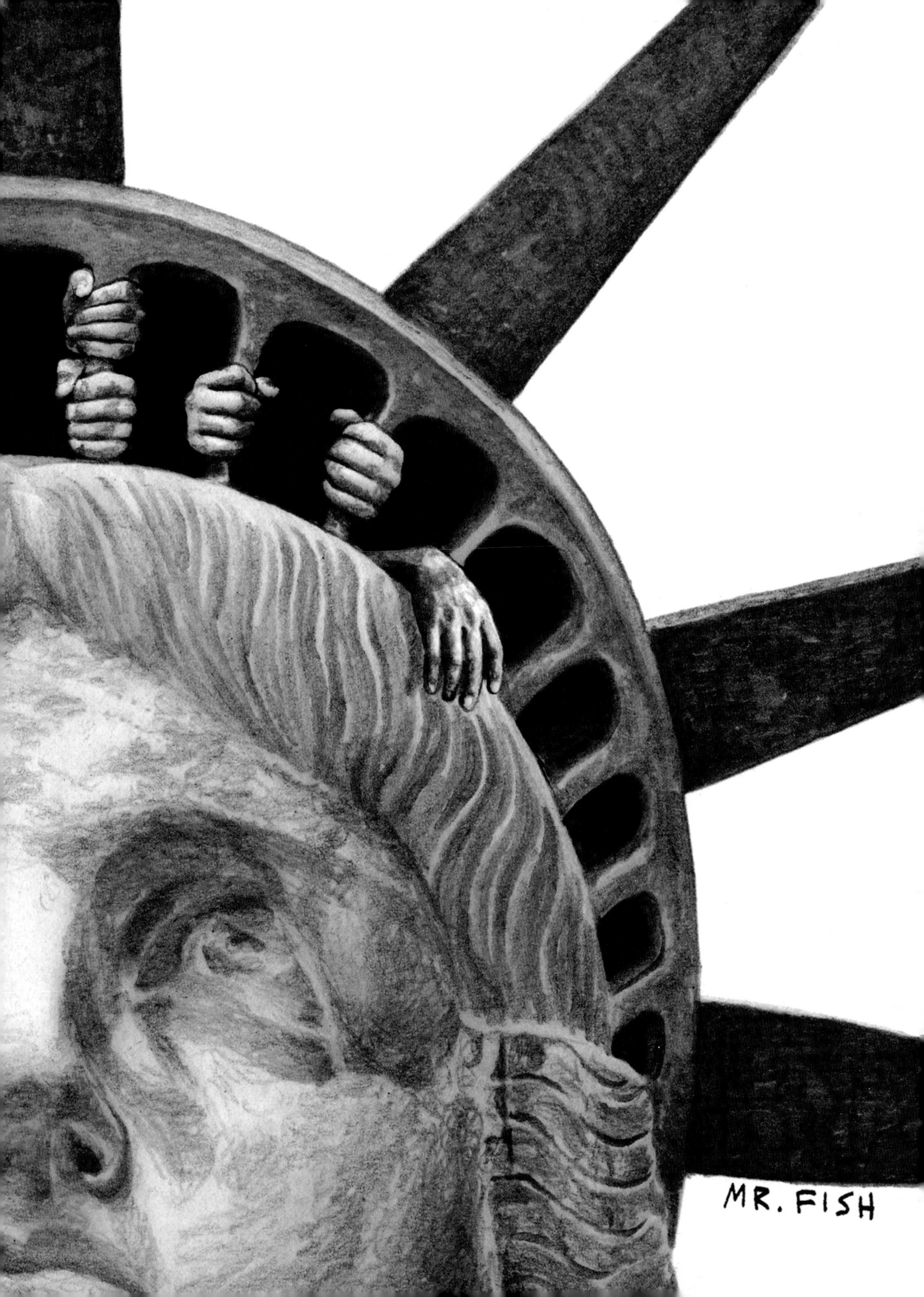
MR. FISH

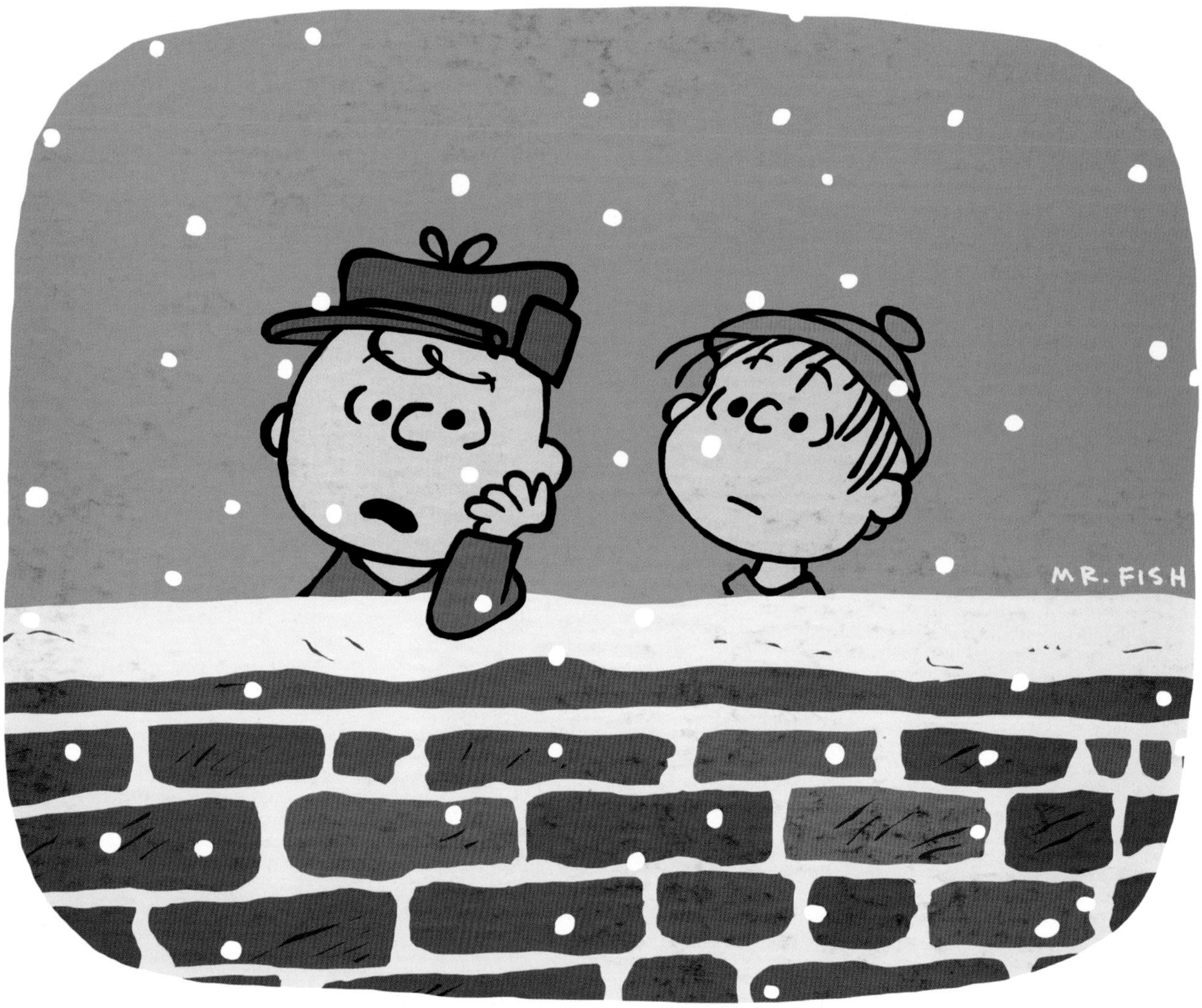
MR. FISH

"I know it's Christmas, Linus, and that you think the only way to celebrate the holiday is to ignore all the crass commercialization that makes December 25th nothing but a finish line contrived by multinational corporations looking to maximize their profits by turning us all into mindless consumers of capitalistic frivolity, but isn't Christianity just another form of bullshit anti-intellectualism designed to brainwash us into thinking we're somehow incomplete without surrendering our life to it? I mean, how is handing over our personal integrity to the bogus claims of advertising agencies any more fucked up than relinquishing our common sense to a 2000-year-old religion based on superstition, shame, misogyny, tribalism, zero science and a mental patient's concept of good and evil? I don't know – somehow I don't think you being a little Jesus freak will be enough to sustain me this year. What I'm saying, I guess, is that it's time for me to grow up and walk away from our friendship, leave you alone to waste your life throwing rocks at the moon while I start hanging out with deeper thinkers who don't look like they just shit their pants whenever I mention Fauvism, the Enlightenment, phenomenology or Jack Kerouac."

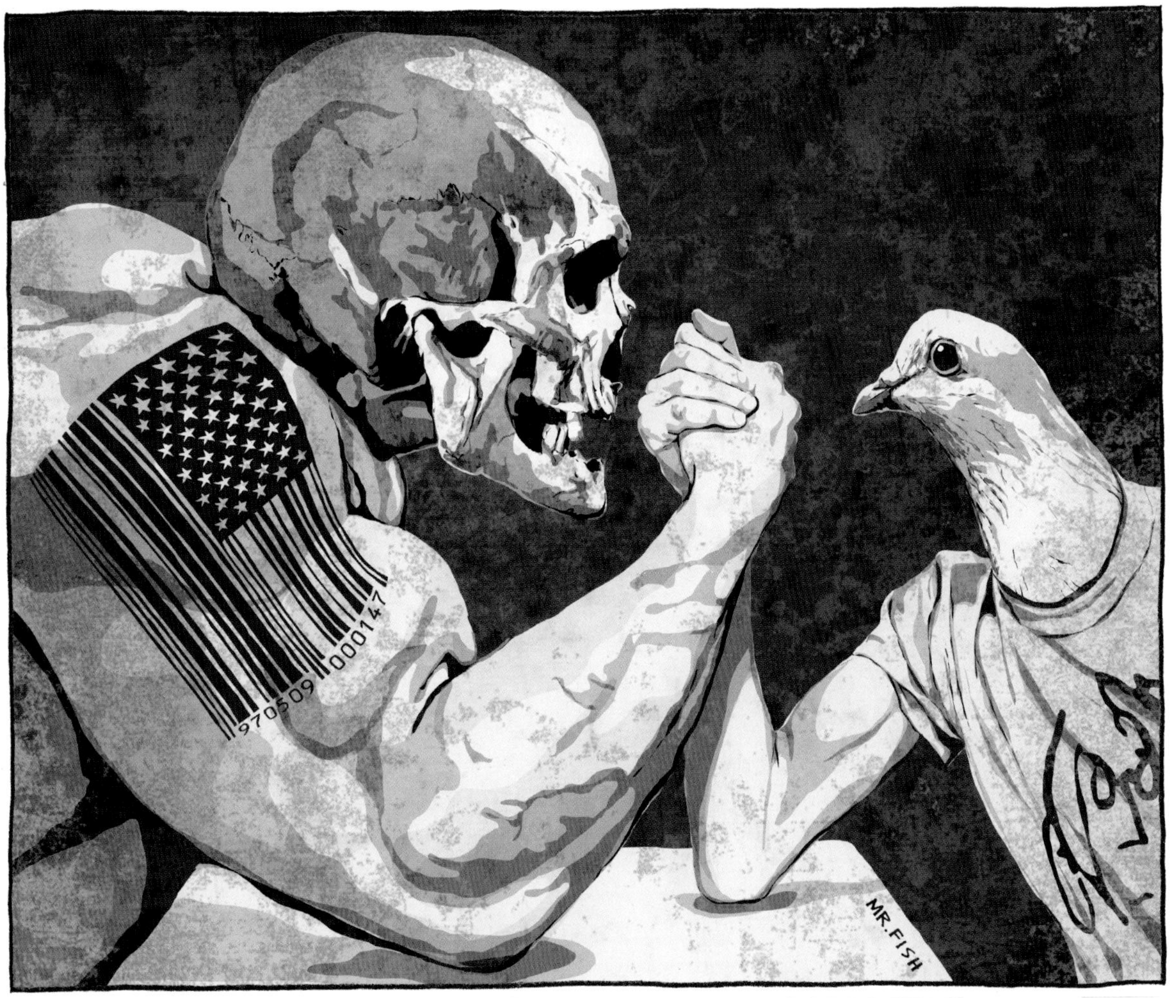
970509 000147
MR.FISH

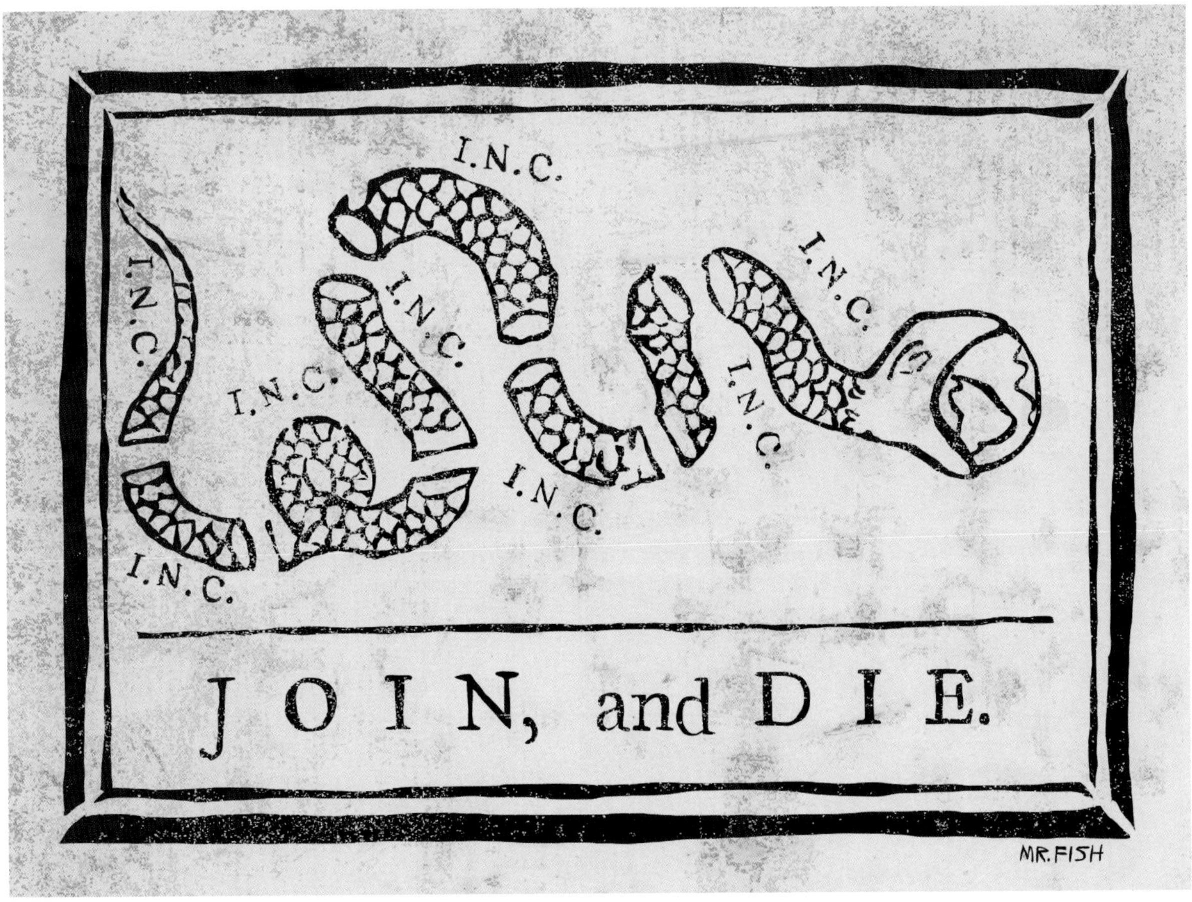
I.N.C.
I.N.C.
I.N.C.
I.N.C.
I.N.C.
I.N.C.
I.N.C.
I.N.C.
JOIN, and DIE.
MR.FISH

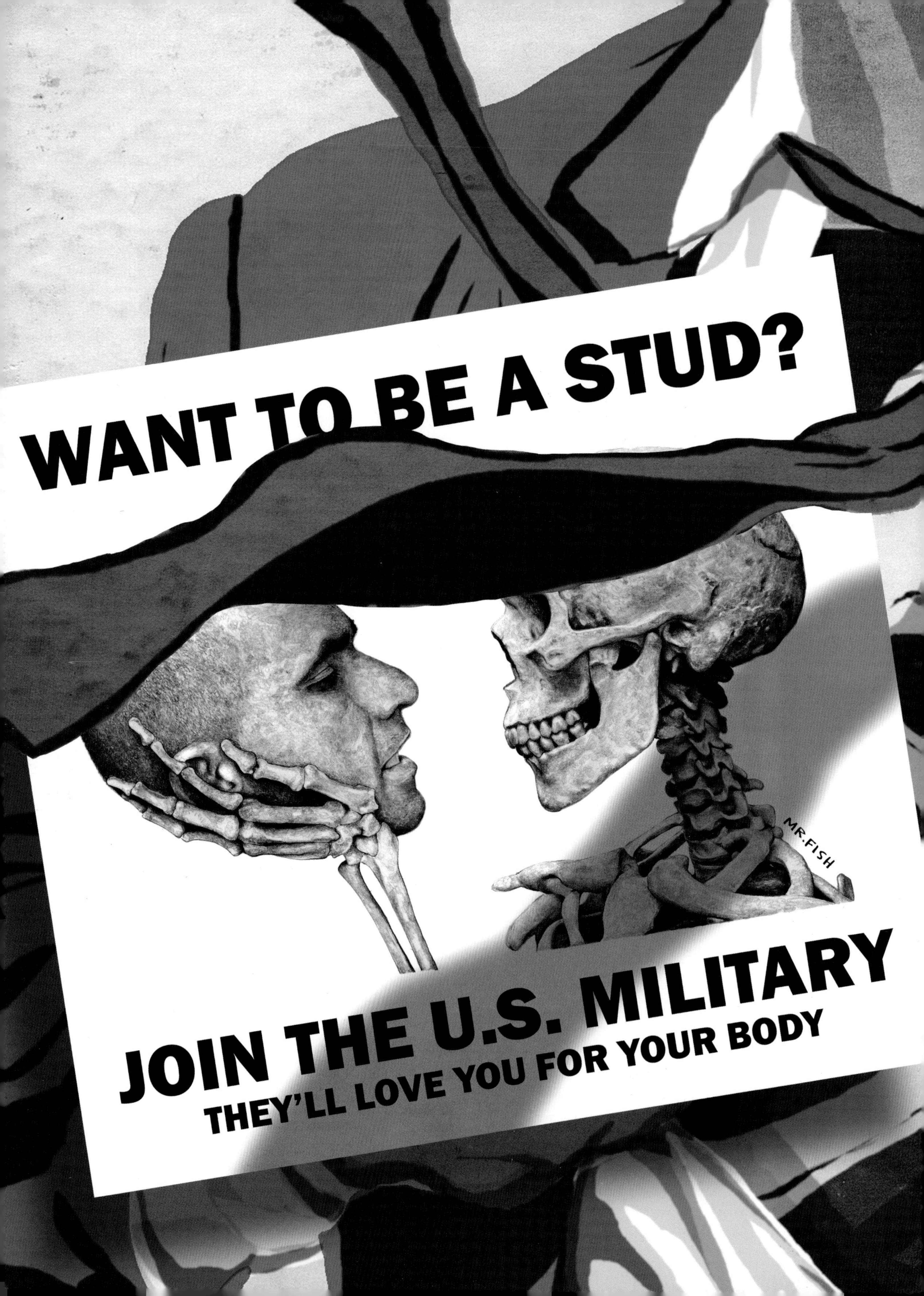
WANT TO BE A STUD?
MR.FISH
JOIN THE U.S. MILITARY
THEY'LL LOVE YOU FOR YOUR BODY

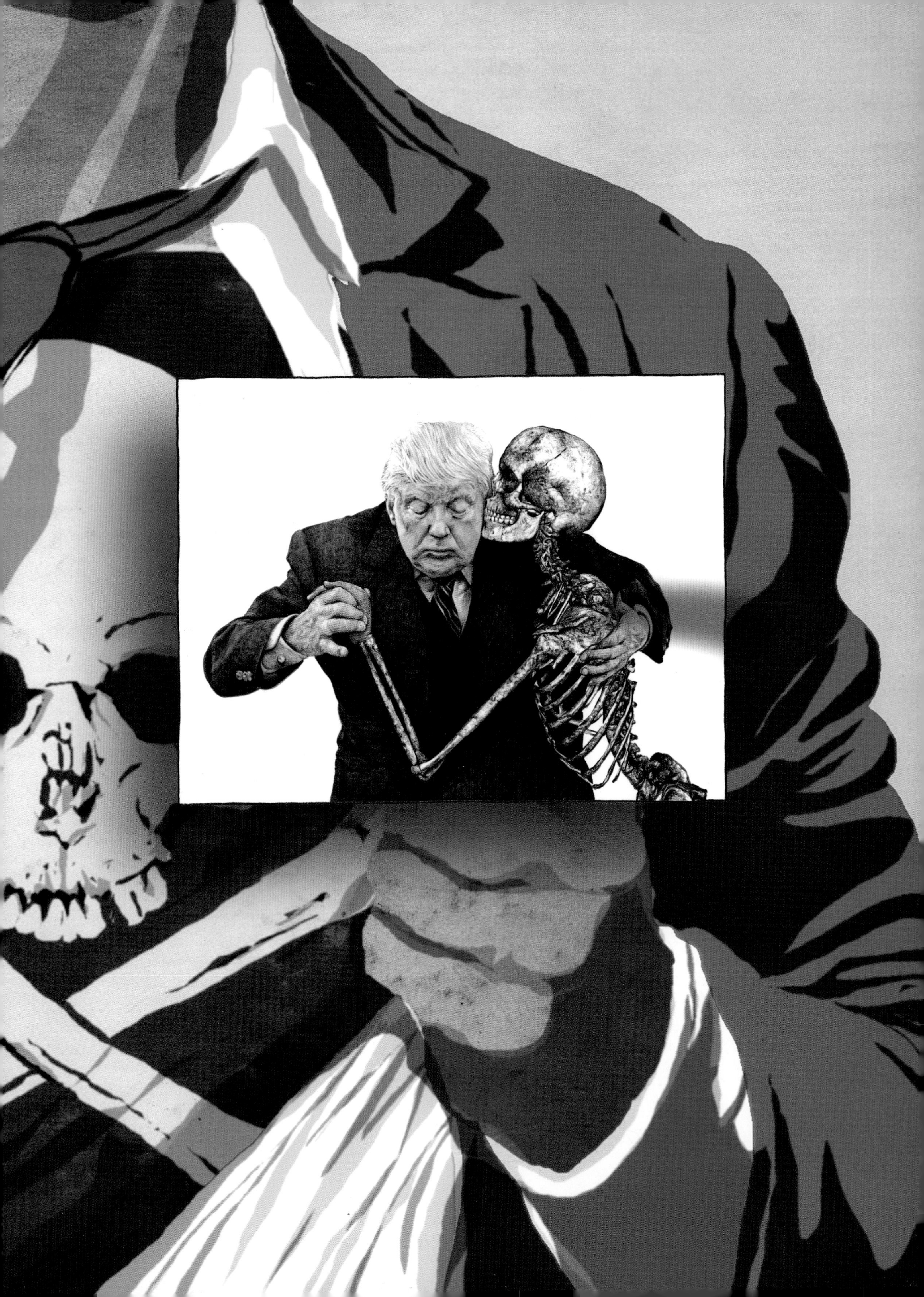

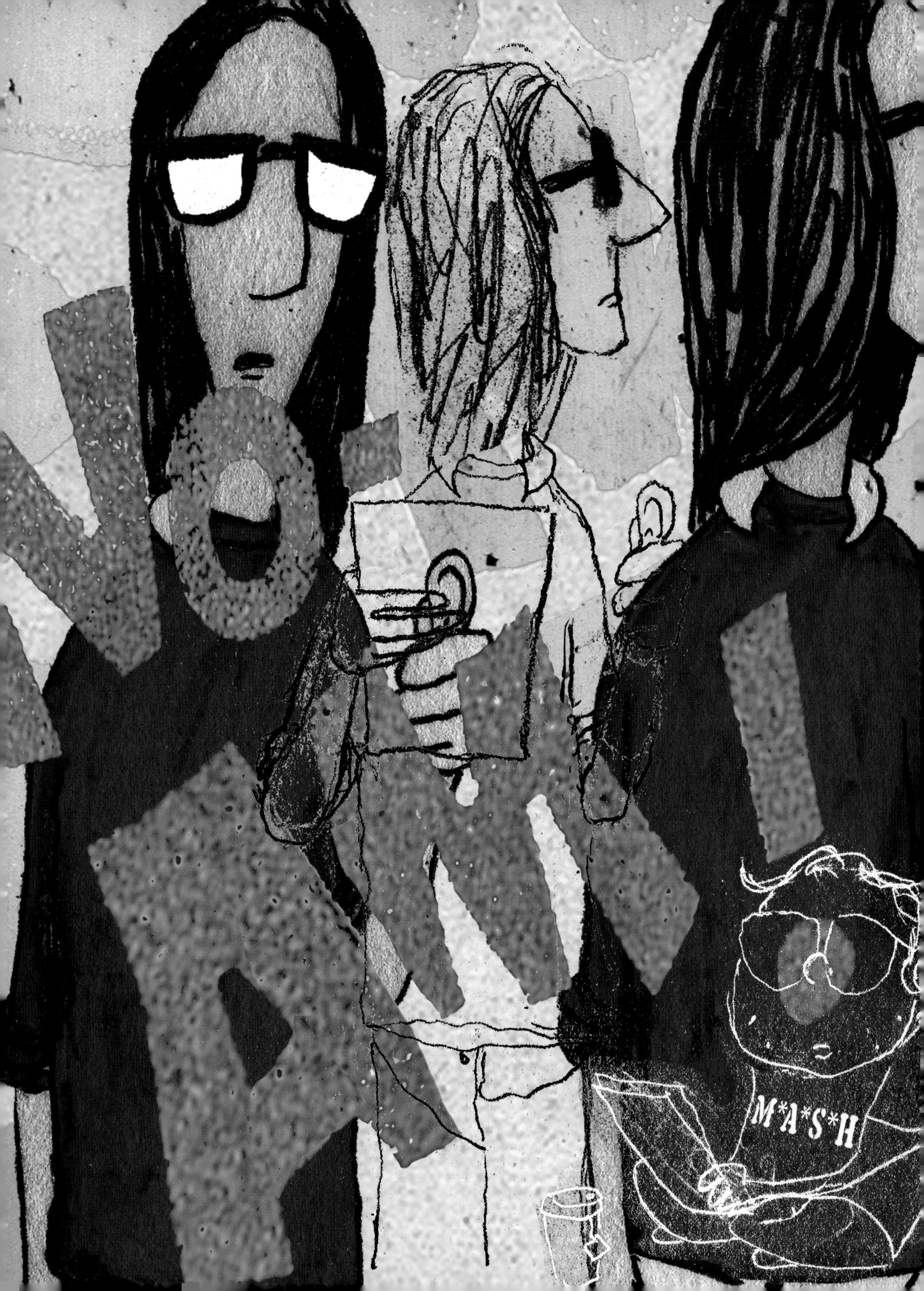
M*A*S*H

LEND ME YOUR EAR 3

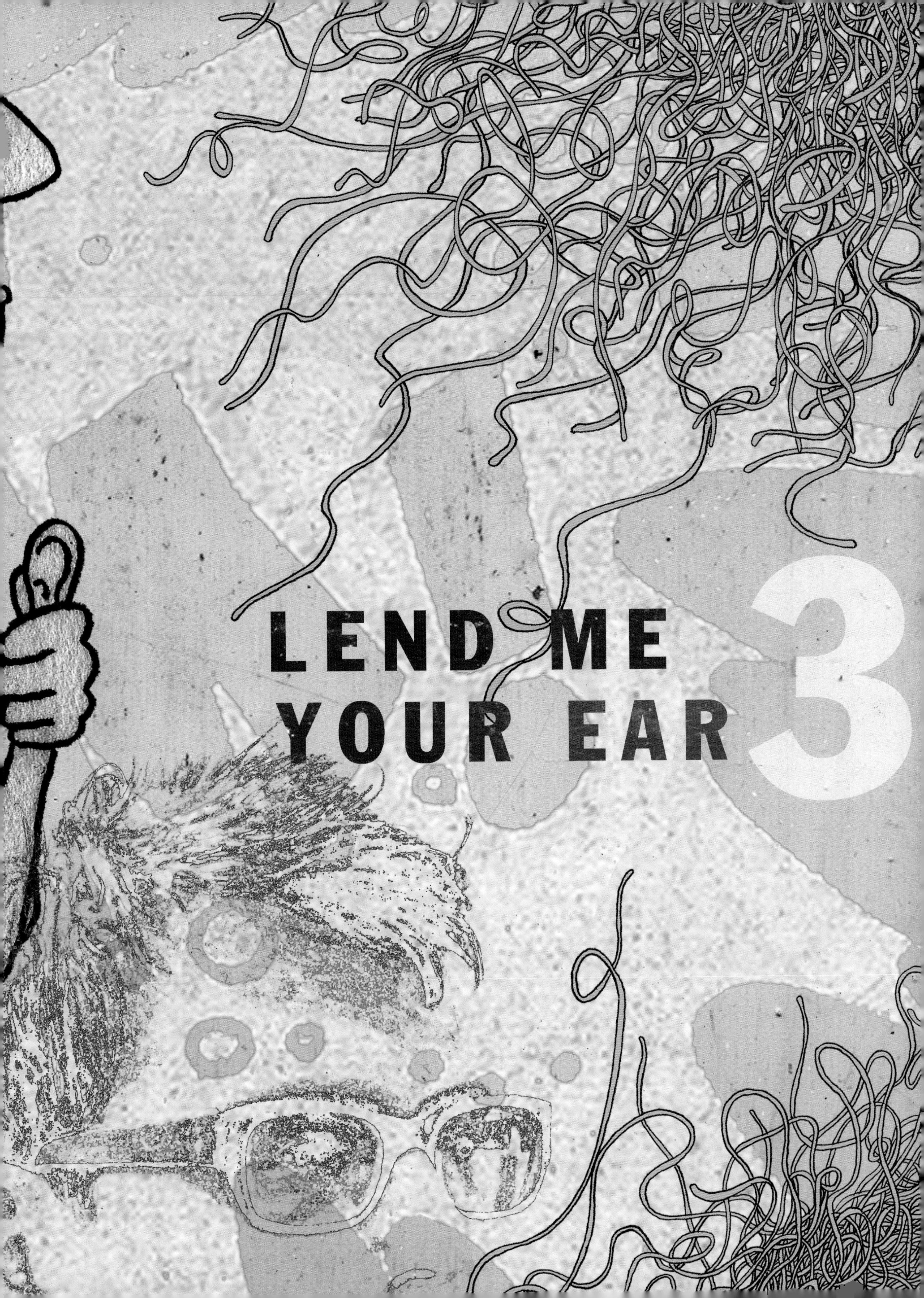

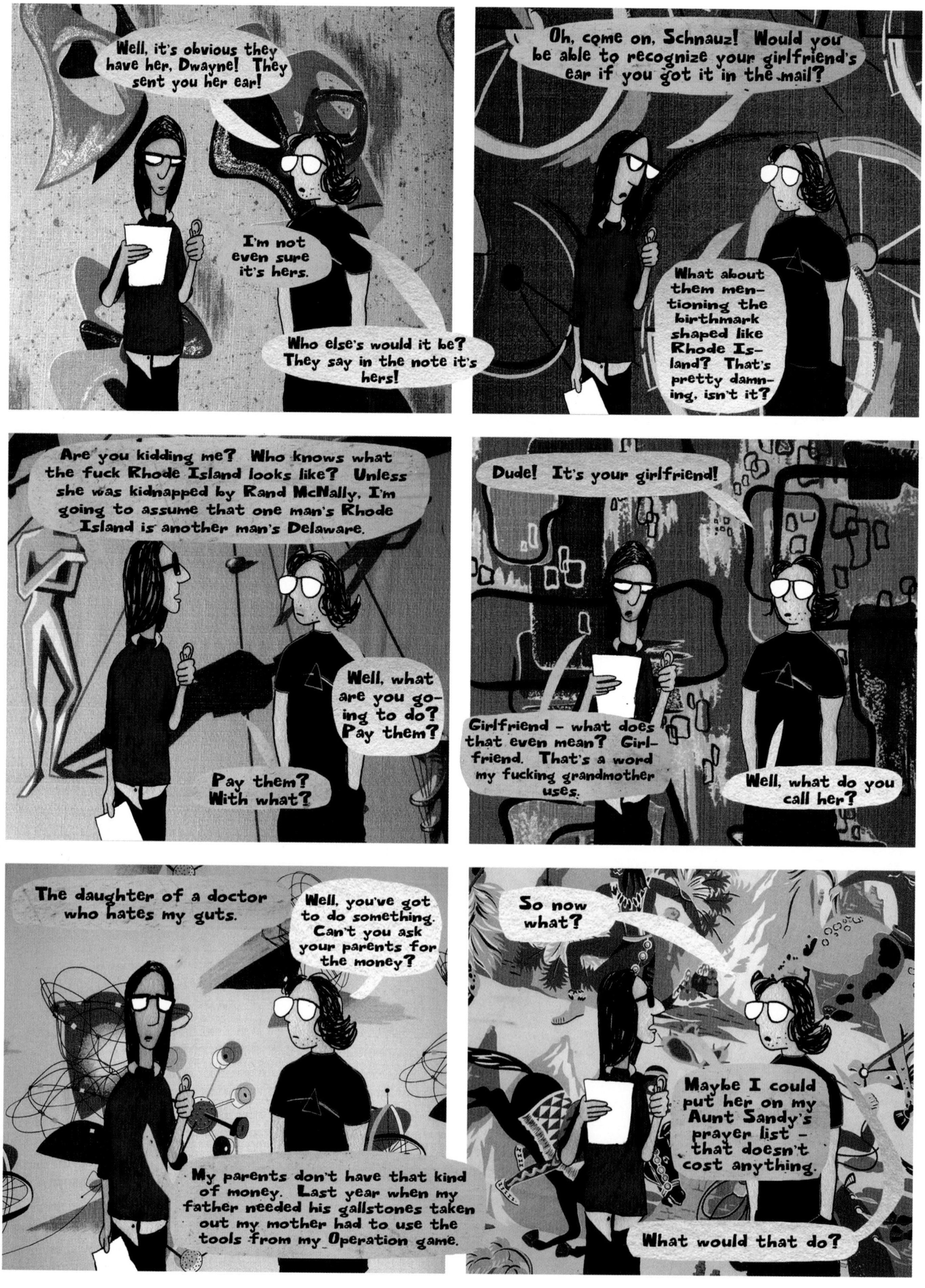
Well, it's obvious they have her, Dwayne! They sent you her ear!
I'm not even sure it's hers.
Who else's would it be? They say in the note it's hers!
Oh, come on, Schnauz! Would you be able to recognize your girlfriend's ear if you got it in the mail?
What about them mentioning the birthmark shaped like Rhode Island? That's pretty damning, isn't it?
Are you kidding me? Who knows what the fuck Rhode Island looks like? Unless she was kidnapped by Rand McNally, I'm going to assume that one man's Rhode Island is another man's Delaware.
Well, what are you going to do? Pay them?
Pay them? With what?
Dude! It's your girlfriend!
Girlfriend - what does that even mean? Girlfriend. That's a word my fucking grandmother uses.
Well, what do you call her?
The daughter of a doctor who hates my guts.
Well, you've got to do something. Can't you ask your parents for the money?
My parents don't have that kind of money. Last year when my father needed his gallstones taken out my mother had to use the tools from my Operation game.
So now what?
Maybe I could put her on my Aunt Sandy's prayer list - that doesn't cost anything.
What would that do?

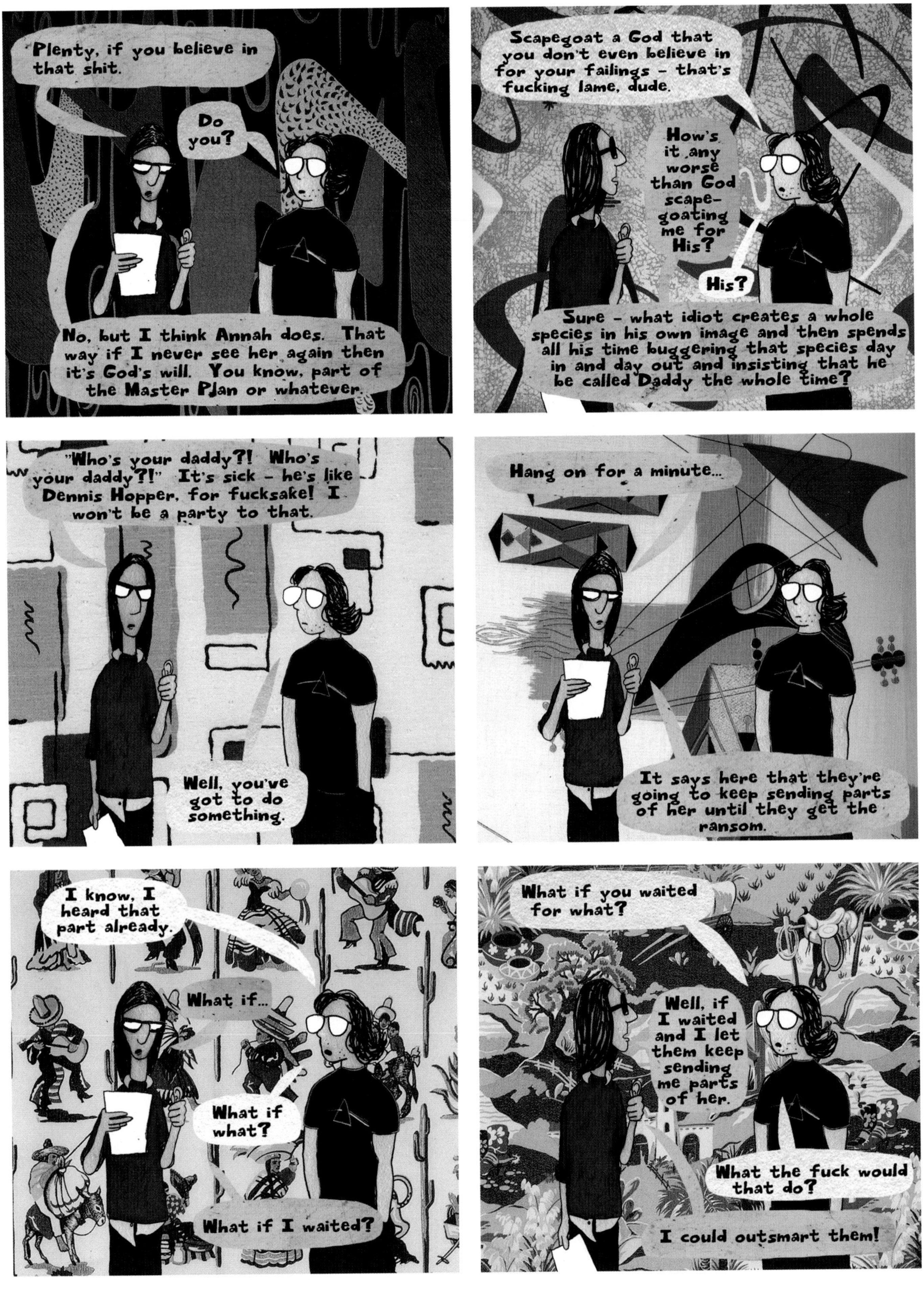

Plenty, if you believe in that shit.
Do you?
No, but I think Annah does. That way if I never see her again then it's God's will. You know, part of the Master Plan or whatever.
Scapegoat a God that you don't even believe in for your failings - that's fucking lame, dude.
How's it any worse than God scape-goating me for His?
His?
Sure - what idiot creates a whole species in his own image and then spends all his time buggering that species day in and day out and insisting that he be called Daddy the whole time?
"Who's your daddy?! Who's your daddy?!" It's sick - he's like Dennis Hopper, for fucksake! I won't be a party to that.
Well, you've got to do something.
Hang on for a minute...
It says here that they're going to keep sending parts of her until they get the ransom.
I know, I heard that part already.
What if...
What if what?
What if I waited?
What if you waited for what?
Well, if I waited and I let them keep sending me parts of her.
What the fuck would that do?
I could outsmart them!

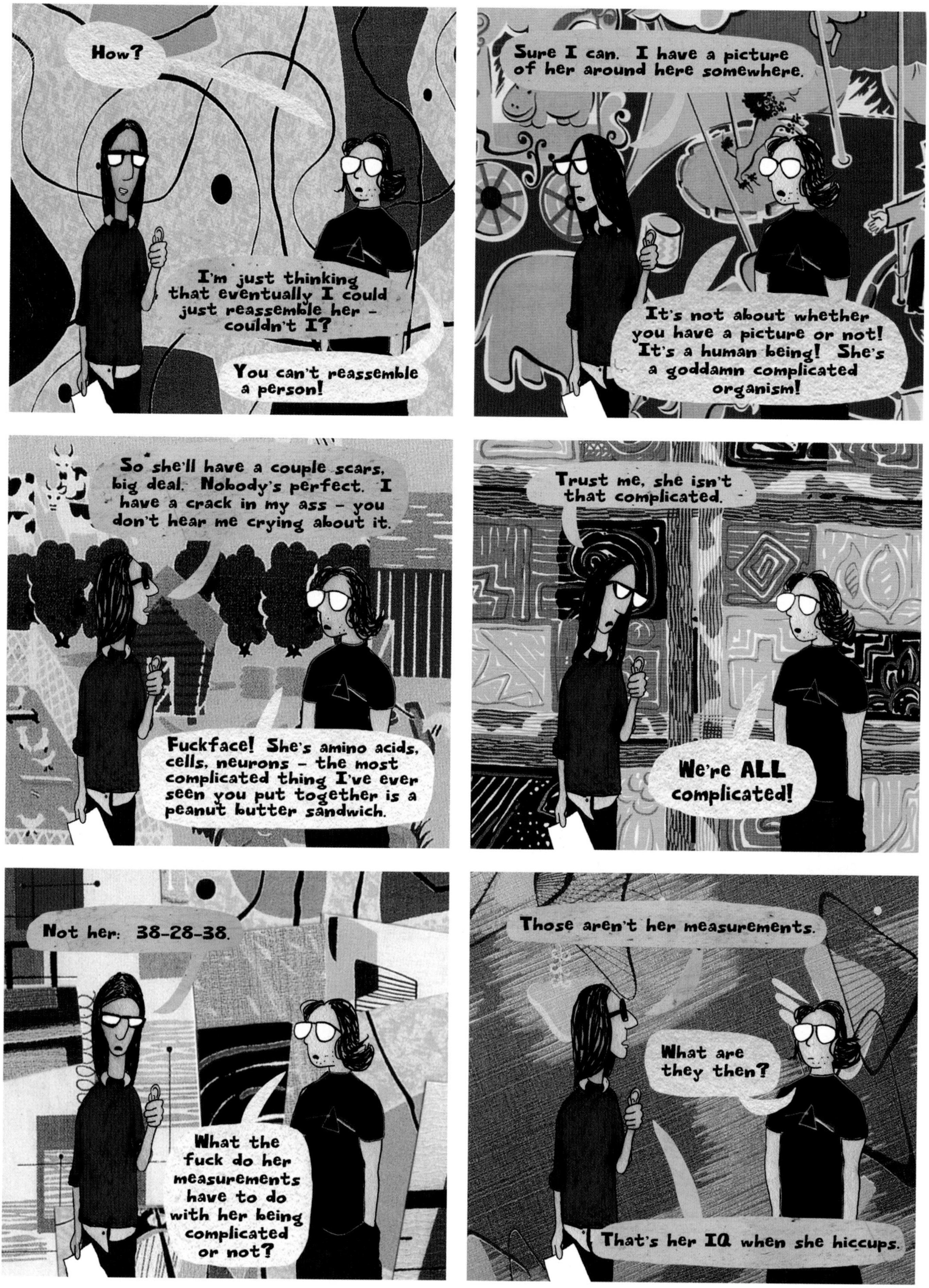
How?
I'm just thinking that eventually I could just reassemble her - couldn't I?
You can't reassemble a person!
Sure I can. I have a picture of her around here somewhere.
It's not about whether you have a picture or not! It's a human being! She's a goddamn complicated organism!
So she'll have a couple scars, big deal. Nobody's perfect. I have a crack in my ass - you don't hear me crying about it.
Fuckface! She's amino acids, cells, neurons - the most complicated thing I've ever seen you put together is a peanut butter sandwich.
Trust me, she isn't that complicated.
We're ALL complicated!
Not her: 38-28-38.
What the fuck do her measurements have to do with her being complicated or not?
Those aren't her measurements.
What are they then?
That's her IQ when she hiccups.

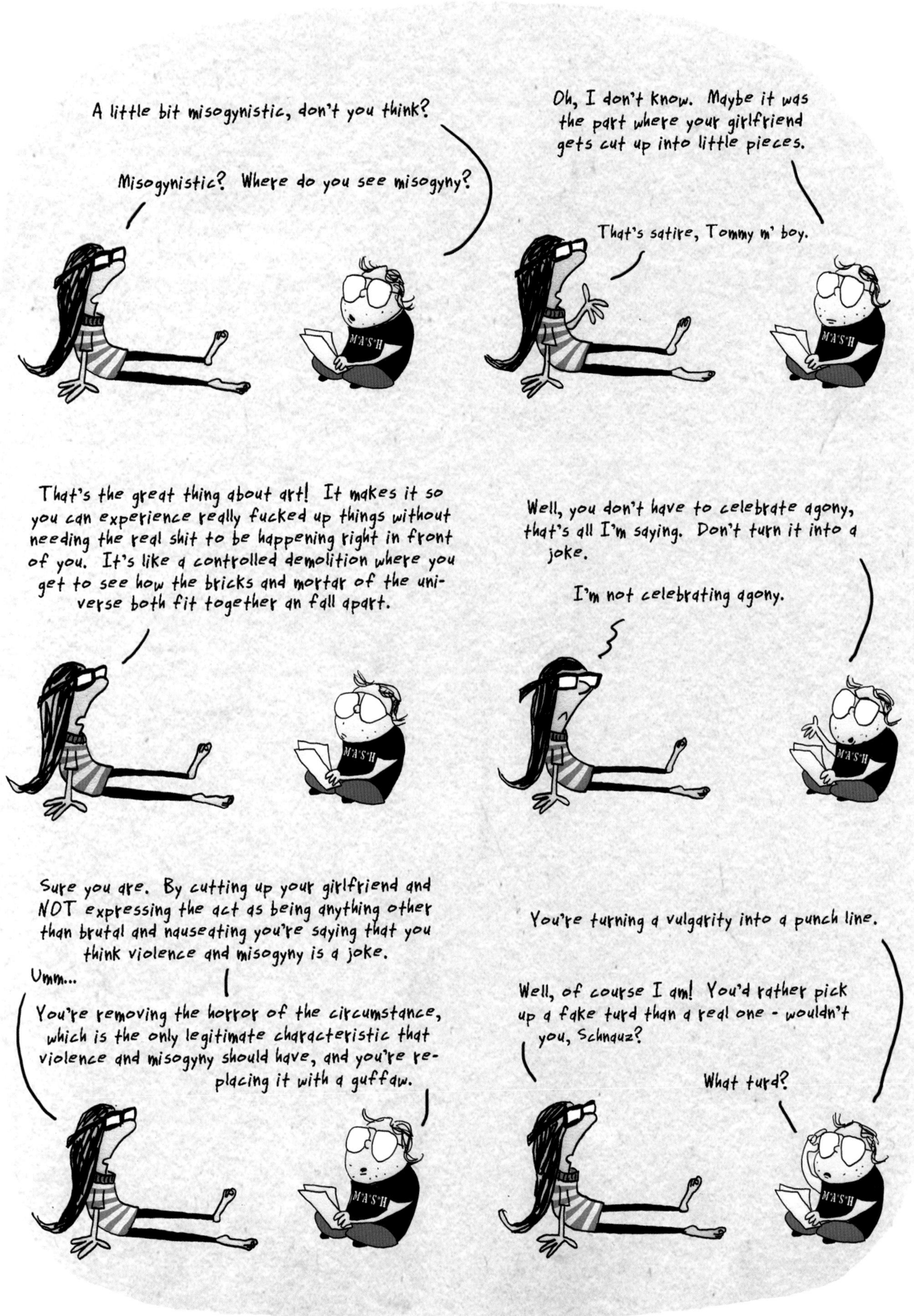
A little bit misogynistic, don't you think?
Misogynistic? Where do you see misogyny?
Oh, I don't know. Maybe it was the part where your girlfriend gets cut up into little pieces.
That's satire, Tommy m' boy.
M*A*S*H
That's the great thing about art! It makes it so you can experience really fucked up things without needing the real shit to be happening right in front of you. It's like a controlled demolition where you get to see how the bricks and mortar of the universe both fit together an fall apart.
Well, you don't have to celebrate agony, that's all I'm saying. Don't turn it into a joke.
I'm not celebrating agony.
Sure you are. By cutting up your girlfriend and NOT expressing the act as being anything other than brutal and nauseating you're saying that you think violence and misogyny is a joke.
Umm...
You're removing the horror of the circumstance, which is the only legitimate characteristic that violence and misogyny should have, and you're replacing it with a guffaw.
You're turning a vulgarity into a punch line.
Well, of course I am! You'd rather pick up a fake turd than a real one - wouldn't you, Schnauz?
What turd?

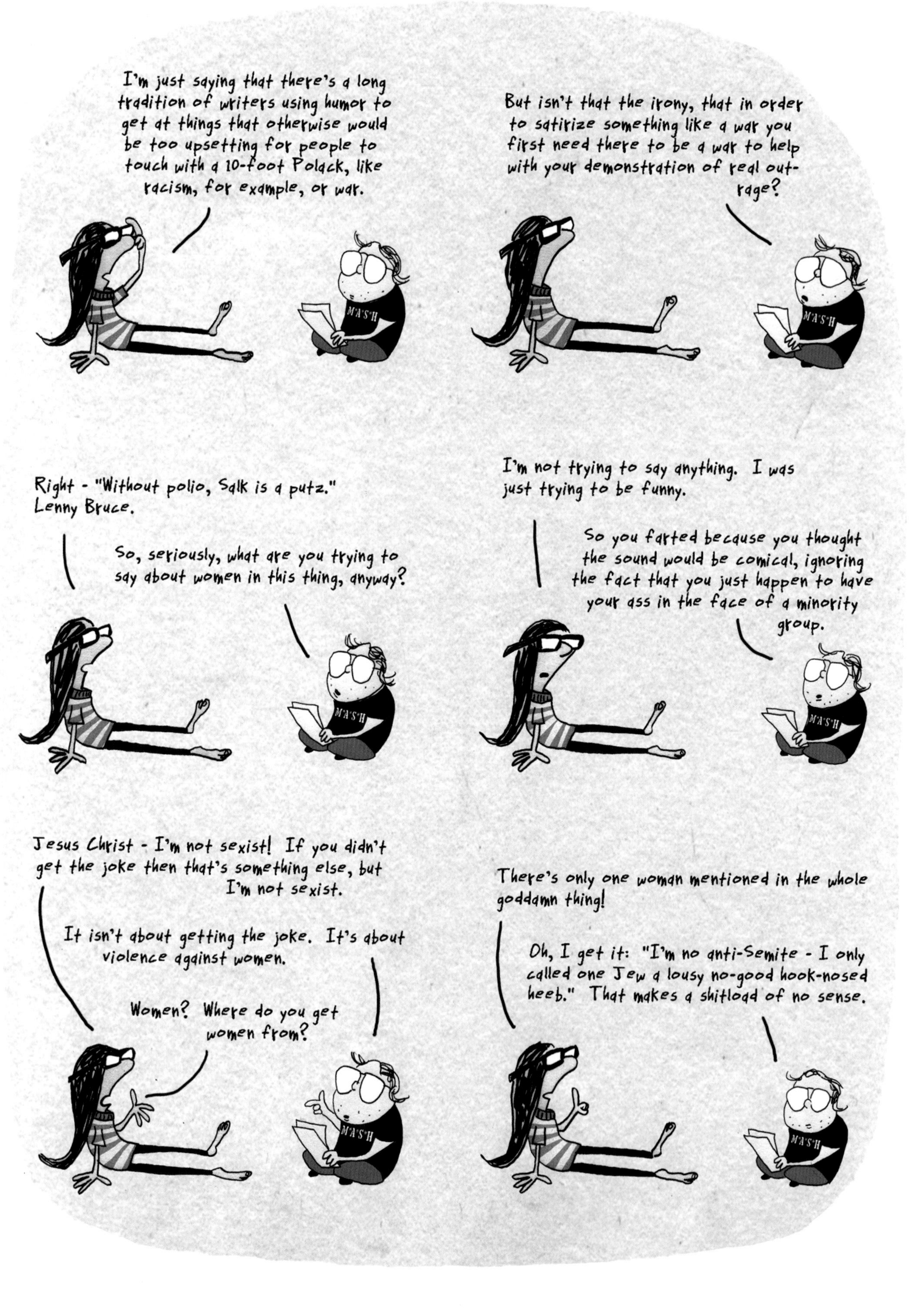

I'm just saying that there's a long tradition of writers using humor to get at things that otherwise would be too upsetting for people to touch with a 10-foot Polack, like racism, for example, or war.
But isn't that the irony, that in order to satirize something like a war you first need there to be a war to help with your demonstration of real outrage?
Right - "Without polio, Salk is a putz." Lenny Bruce.
So, seriously, what are you trying to say about women in this thing, anyway?
I'm not trying to say anything. I was just trying to be funny.
So you farted because you thought the sound would be comical, ignoring the fact that you just happen to have your ass in the face of a minority group.
Jesus Christ - I'm not sexist! If you didn't get the joke then that's something else, but I'm not sexist.
It isn't about getting the joke. It's about violence against women.
Women? Where do you get women from?
There's only one woman mentioned in the whole goddamn thing!
Oh, I get it: "I'm no anti-Semite - I only called one Jew a lousy no-good hook-nosed heeb." That makes a shitload of no sense.
M*A*S*H

First of all, just because I happen to mention a single female character in a story doesn't automatically mean that I'm commenting on all women everywhere!

Pretending that one woman has the responsibility of representing ALL women is what's sexist.

A human being isn't a brussel's sprout - love one, you love them all. Hate one, you hate 'em all. That's nonsense!

I just think that you shouldn't denigrate people for a joke, that's all. It's lazy.

Listen, douchebag, don't let your love of people become so pathological that you refuse to learn anything from human despicability.

Don't become somebody who can't see the lynchings for the trees.

I don't even know what that means...

I'm just saying that real prejudice can only qualify as real discrimination if it's intentional, if the purpose is to incite contempt for a specific group of people.

In other words, if somebody laughs at some incredibly inappropriate joke about pedophilia it doesn't automatically mean that he or she is an advocate for adults getting to fuck uncooperative 4-year-olds.

So, let me get this straight - if somebody's intention is to bring about world peace by slaughtering all the Christians...

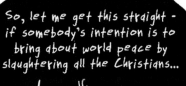

...or Armenians or Indians or Infidels, say, I shouldn't criticize his magnanimity?

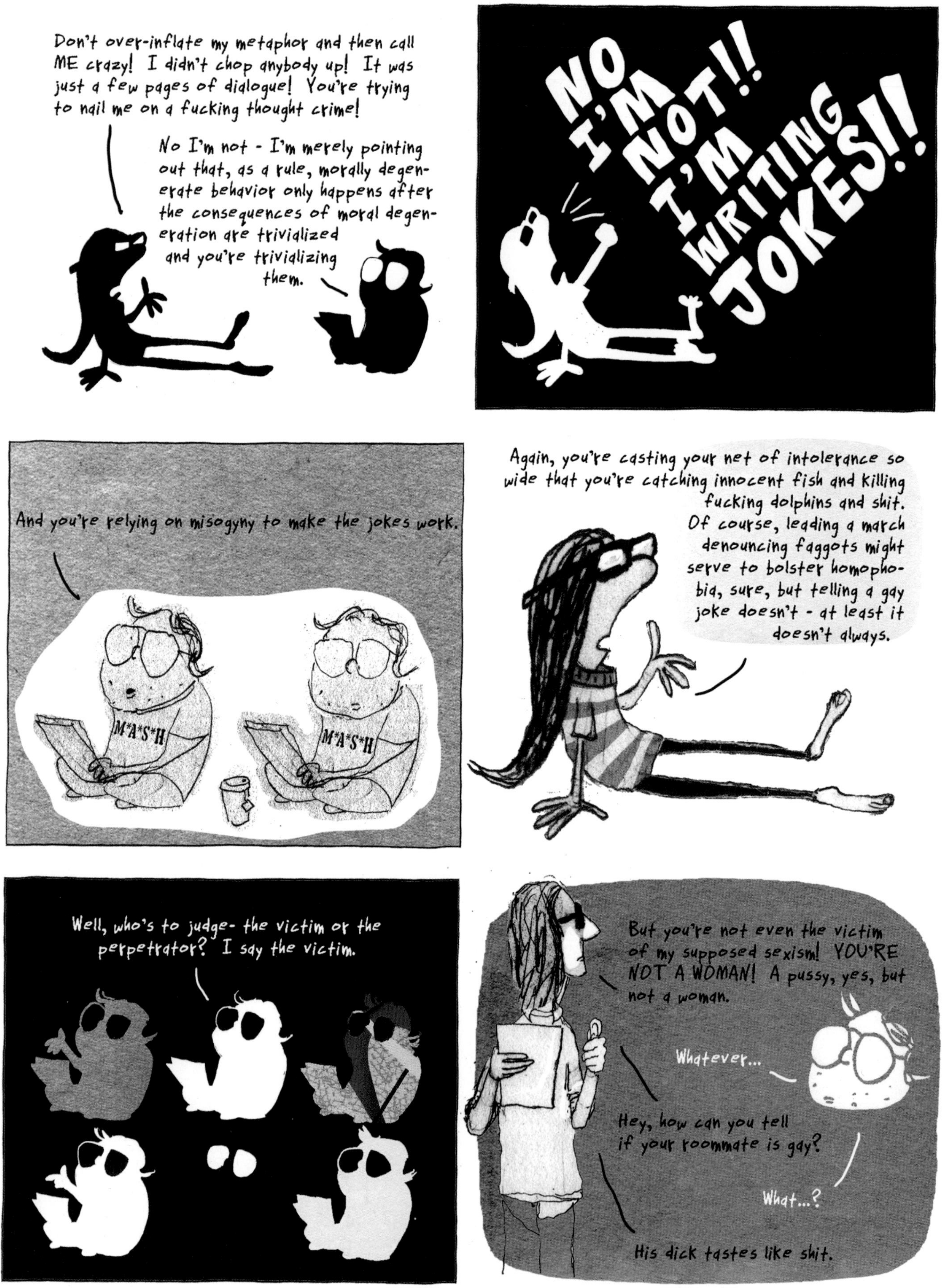

Don't over-inflate my metaphor and then call ME crazy! I didn't chop anybody up! It was just a few pages of dialogue! You're trying to nail me on a fucking thought crime!
No I'm not - I'm merely pointing out that, as a rule, morally degenerate behavior only happens after the consequences of moral degeneration are trivialized and you're trivializing them.
NO I'M NOT!! I'M WRITING JOKES!!
And you're relying on misogyny to make the jokes work.
M*A*S*H
M*A*S*H
Again, you're casting your net of intolerance so wide that you're catching innocent fish and killing fucking dolphins and shit. Of course, leading a march denouncing faggots might serve to bolster homophobia, sure, but telling a gay joke doesn't - at least it doesn't always.
Well, who's to judge- the victim or the perpetrator? I say the victim.
But you're not even the victim of my supposed sexism! YOU'RE NOT A WOMAN! A pussy, yes, but not a woman.
Whatever...
Hey, how can you tell if your roommate is gay?
What...?
His dick tastes like shit.

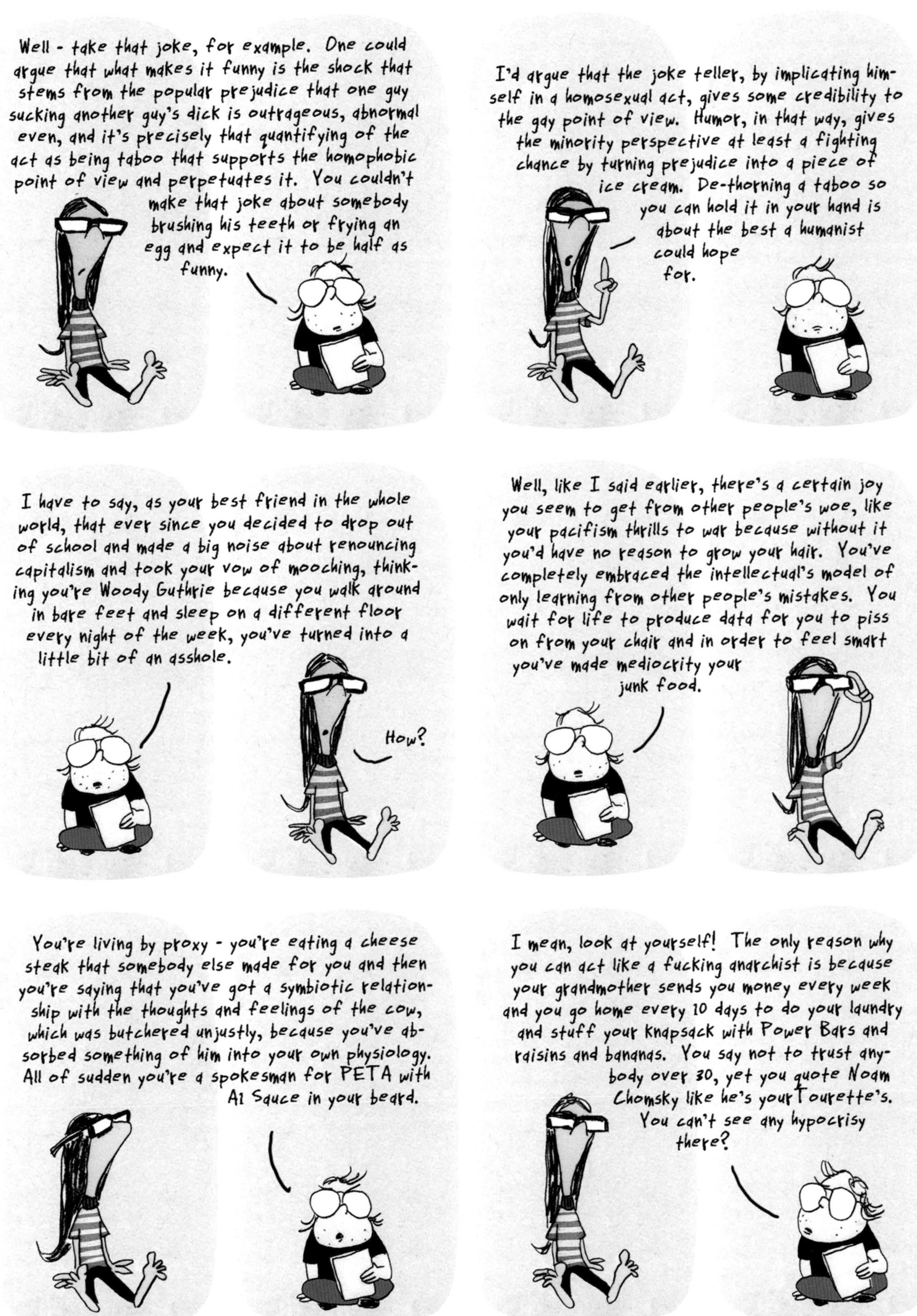
Well - take that joke, for example. One could argue that what makes it funny is the shock that stems from the popular prejudice that one guy sucking another guy's dick is outrageous, abnormal even, and it's precisely that quantifying of the act as being taboo that supports the homophobic point of view and perpetuates it. You couldn't make that joke about somebody brushing his teeth or frying an egg and expect it to be half as funny.
I'd argue that the joke teller, by implicating himself in a homosexual act, gives some credibility to the gay point of view. Humor, in that way, gives the minority perspective at least a fighting chance by turning prejudice into a piece of ice cream. De-thorning a taboo so you can hold it in your hand is about the best a humanist could hope for.
I have to say, as your best friend in the whole world, that ever since you decided to drop out of school and made a big noise about renouncing capitalism and took your vow of mooching, thinking you're Woody Guthrie because you walk around in bare feet and sleep on a different floor every night of the week, you've turned into a little bit of an asshole.
How?
Well, like I said earlier, there's a certain joy you seem to get from other people's woe, like your pacifism thrills to war because without it you'd have no reason to grow your hair. You've completely embraced the intellectual's model of only learning from other people's mistakes. You wait for life to produce data for you to piss on from your chair and in order to feel smart you've made mediocrity your junk food.
You're living by proxy - you're eating a cheese steak that somebody else made for you and then you're saying that you've got a symbiotic relationship with the thoughts and feelings of the cow, which was butchered unjustly, because you've absorbed something of him into your own physiology. All of sudden you're a spokesman for PETA with A1 Sauce in your beard.
I mean, look at yourself! The only reason why you can act like a fucking anarchist is because your grandmother sends you money every week and you go home every 10 days to do your laundry and stuff your knapsack with Power Bars and raisins and bananas. You say not to trust anybody over 30, yet you quote Noam Chomsky like he's your Tourette's. You can't see any hypocrisy there?

TOM: You like to shock people by drawing yourself naked
       in all your self-portraits for art class, big dumb
       cock hanging out, yet back at the dorm you dry yourself
       in the shower with the curtain closed. You couldn't
       even tell your mother that you dropped out or school -
       you made your brother do it.

DWAYNE: Now wait a minute - that's not true!

Tom: The point is that none of your so-called theories
       have ever been tested in any real life situations.

DWAYNE: None?

TOM: Maybe some, but none of the major ones.

DWAYNE: Like what?

TOM: Like you telling everybody that homosexuality is no
       big deal, and you're right, but you've never even
       shared an umbrella with a dude much less had his balls
       on your chin. You're for the legalization of marijuana,
       but you've never even smoked a joint, much less finished
       a whole beer.

DWAYNE: And I'm guessing that you abhor slavery because
       you grew up picking cotton for free in the scorching
       Alabama sun with nothing but the gospel and your banjo
       playing to sustain you. Or was it because slavery is
       conceptually abhorrent, just like it's conceptually
       abhorrent to kill somebody, which we should all know
       without rehearsal?

TOM: But that's what I'm saying, that so long as all you
       have informing your life philosophy is conceptual
       truisms you'll be nothing but a blowhard elitist. A
       snob.

DWAYNE: My life philosophy isn't just conceptual truisms!

TOM: I'm just saying that aren't you at all curious to get
      out of your safe zone just to test your bravery, even
      if it's just every once in awhile? I'm telling you as
      your oldest friend that you could stand to suffer
      some common humilities to see if your personal opinions
      and internal commandments can survive being submerged
      in actual human blood and not just black ink. Most
      self-proclaimed heroes shit their pants on the battle-
      field and I'm betting that you're no different, which
      is by no means a dig - it just means that you're like
      everybody else. Isn't that a huge part of your commie
      ideal?

DWAYNE: Alright - tell me what to do, comrade. I don't give
      a shit. Test my bravery.

TOM: Cut off all your hair. See if you still feel like
      a fucking hippie without the costume.

DWAYNE: That's all?

TOM: And honor the bet that you welched on from
      Thanksgiving.

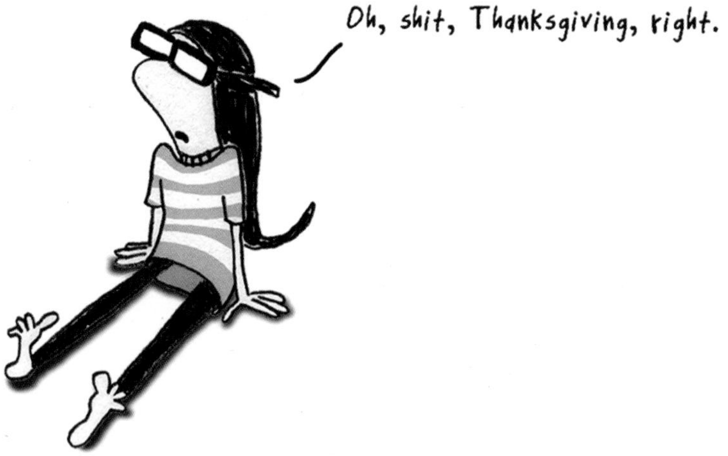
Oh, shit, Thanksgiving, right.

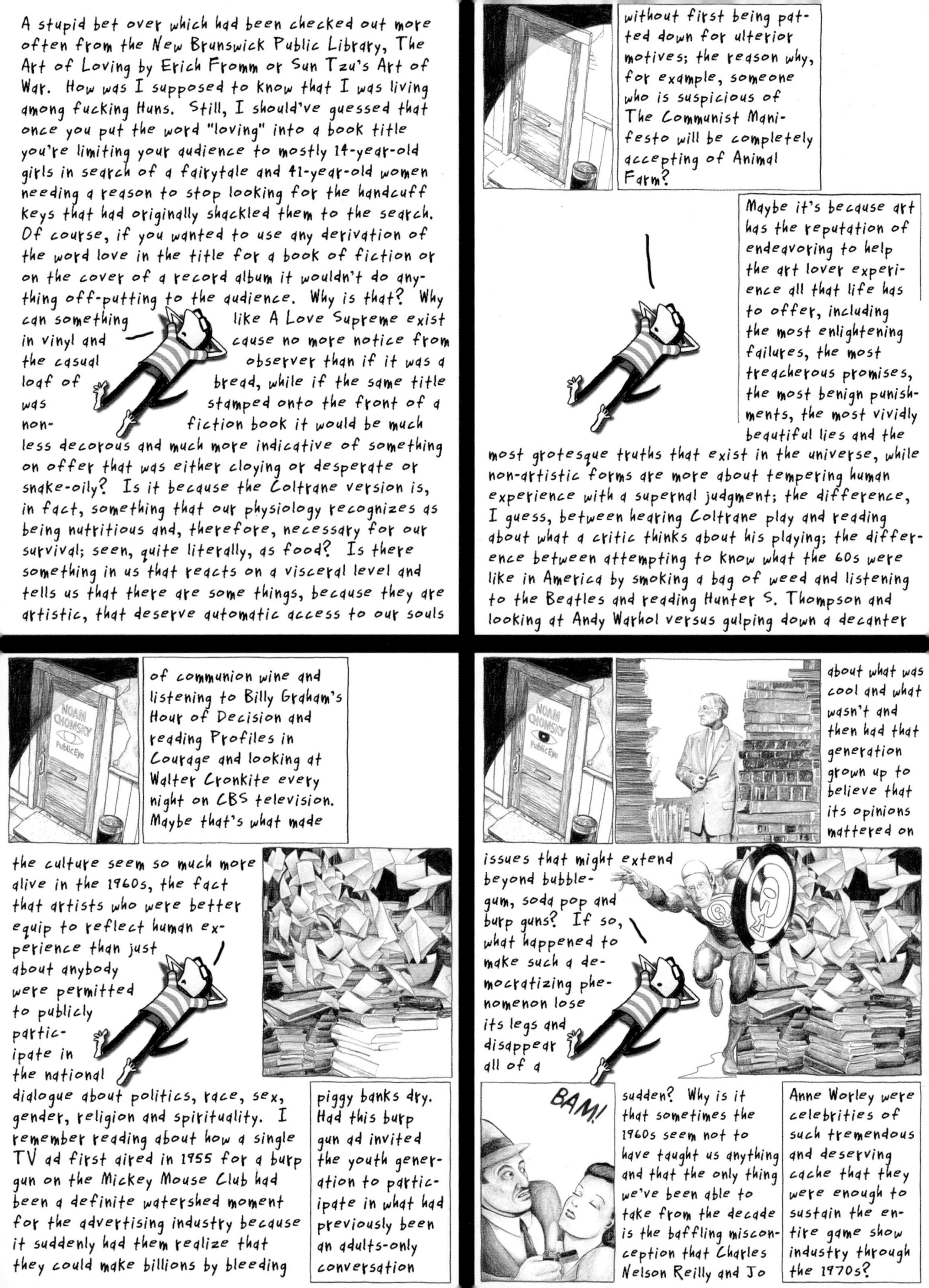
A stupid bet over which had been checked out more often from the New Brunswick Public Library, The Art of Loving by Erich Fromm or Sun Tzu's Art of War. How was I supposed to know that I was living among fucking Huns. Still, I should've guessed that once you put the word "loving" into a book title you're limiting your audience to mostly 14-year-old girls in search of a fairytale and 41-year-old women needing a reason to stop looking for the handcuff keys that had originally shackled them to the search. Of course, if you wanted to use any derivation of the word love in the title for a book of fiction or on the cover of a record album it wouldn't do anything off-putting to the audience. Why is that? Why can something like A Love Supreme exist in vinyl and cause no more notice from the casual observer than if it was a loaf of bread, while if the same title was stamped onto the front of a non-fiction book it would be much less decorous and much more indicative of something on offer that was either cloying or desperate or snake-oily? Is it because the Coltrane version is, in fact, something that our physiology recognizes as being nutritious and, therefore, necessary for our survival; seen, quite literally, as food? Is there something in us that reacts on a visceral level and tells us that there are some things, because they are artistic, that deserve automatic access to our souls
without first being patted down for ulterior motives; the reason why, for example, someone who is suspicious of The Communist Manifesto will be completely accepting of Animal Farm?
Maybe it's because art has the reputation of endeavoring to help the art lover experience all that life has to offer, including the most enlightening failures, the most treacherous promises, the most benign punishments, the most vividly beautiful lies and the most grotesque truths that exist in the universe, while non-artistic forms are more about tempering human experience with a supernal judgment; the difference, I guess, between hearing Coltrane play and reading about what a critic thinks about his playing; the difference between attempting to know what the 60s were like in America by smoking a bag of weed and listening to the Beatles and reading Hunter S. Thompson and looking at Andy Warhol versus gulping down a decanter
NOAM CHOMSKY
Public Eye
of communion wine and listening to Billy Graham's Hour of Decision and reading Profiles in Courage and looking at Walter Cronkite every night on CBS television. Maybe that's what made
the culture seem so much more alive in the 1960s, the fact that artists who were better equip to reflect human experience than just about anybody were permitted to publicly participate in the national dialogue about politics, race, sex, gender, religion and spirituality. I remember reading about how a single TV ad first aired in 1955 for a burp gun on the Mickey Mouse Club had been a definite watershed moment for the advertising industry because it suddenly had them realize that they could make billions by bleeding
piggy banks dry. Had this burp gun ad invited the youth generation to participate in what had previously been an adults-only conversation
NOAM CHOMSKY
Public Eye
about what was cool and what wasn't and then had that generation grown up to believe that its opinions mattered on
issues that might extend beyond bubblegum, soda pop and burp guns? If so, what happened to make such a democratizing phenomenon lose its legs and disappear all of a
BAM!
sudden? Why is it that sometimes the 1960s seem not to have taught us anything and that the only thing we've been able to take from the decade is the baffling misconception that Charles Nelson Reilly and Jo
Anne Worley were celebrities of such tremendous and deserving cache that they were enough to sustain the entire game show industry through the 1970s?

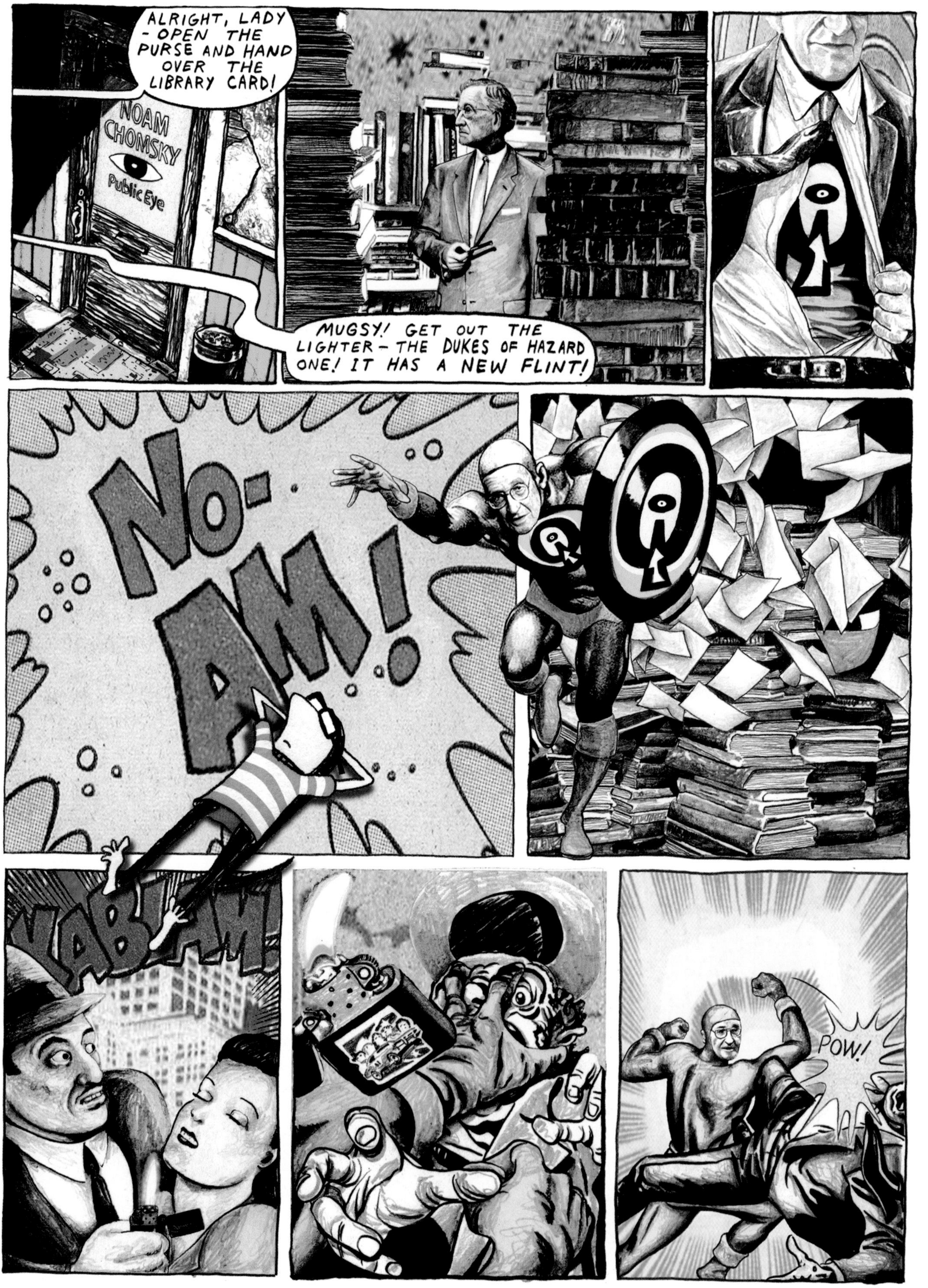
ALRIGHT, LADY - OPEN THE PURSE AND HAND OVER THE LIBRARY CARD!
NOAM CHOMSKY
Public Eye
MUGSY! GET OUT THE LIGHTER - THE DUKES OF HAZARD ONE! IT HAS A NEW FLINT!
NO-AM!
ABLAM!
POW!

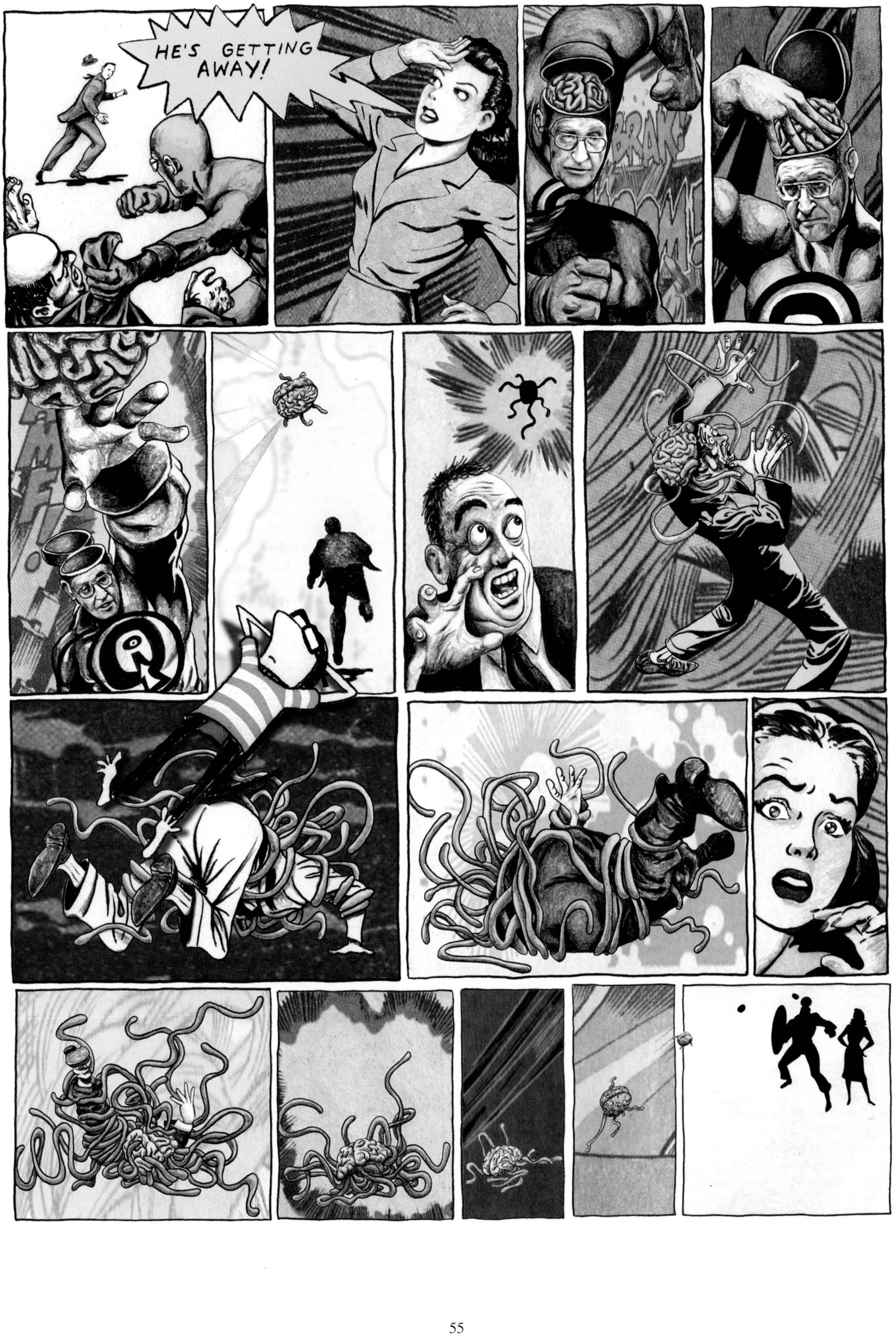
HE'S GETTING AWAY!

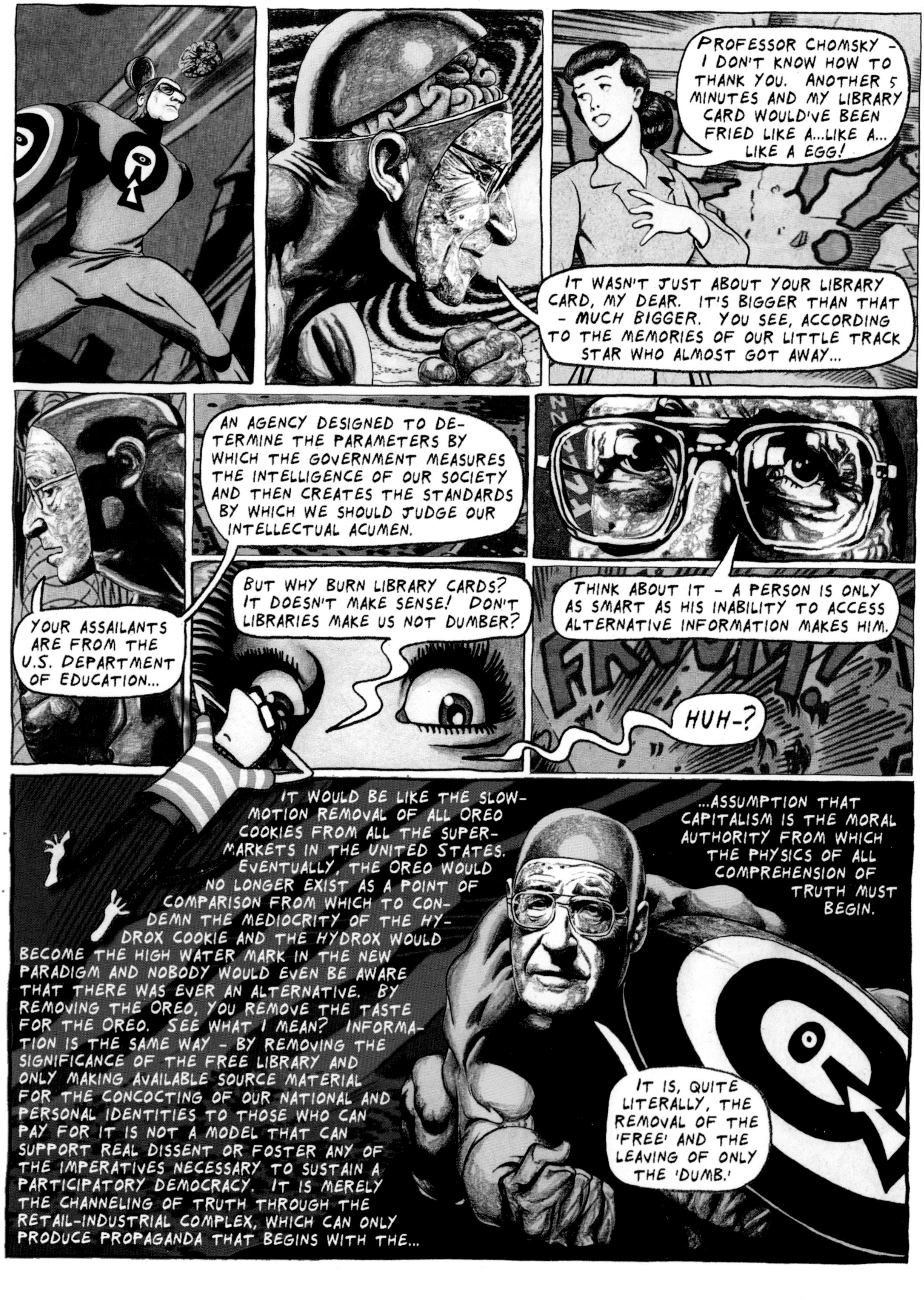
PROFESSOR CHOMSKY - I DON'T KNOW HOW TO THANK YOU. ANOTHER 5 MINUTES AND MY LIBRARY CARD WOULD'VE BEEN FRIED LIKE A...LIKE A... LIKE A EGG!
IT WASN'T JUST ABOUT YOUR LIBRARY CARD, MY DEAR. IT'S BIGGER THAN THAT - MUCH BIGGER. YOU SEE, ACCORDING TO THE MEMORIES OF OUR LITTLE TRACK STAR WHO ALMOST GOT AWAY...
YOUR ASSAILANTS ARE FROM THE U.S. DEPARTMENT OF EDUCATION...
AN AGENCY DESIGNED TO DETERMINE THE PARAMETERS BY WHICH THE GOVERNMENT MEASURES THE INTELLIGENCE OF OUR SOCIETY AND THEN CREATES THE STANDARDS BY WHICH WE SHOULD JUDGE OUR INTELLECTUAL ACUMEN.
BUT WHY BURN LIBRARY CARDS? IT DOESN'T MAKE SENSE! DON'T LIBRARIES MAKE US NOT DUMBER?
THINK ABOUT IT - A PERSON IS ONLY AS SMART AS HIS INABILITY TO ACCESS ALTERNATIVE INFORMATION MAKES HIM.
HUH-?
IT WOULD BE LIKE THE SLOW-MOTION REMOVAL OF ALL OREO COOKIES FROM ALL THE SUPERMARKETS IN THE UNITED STATES. EVENTUALLY, THE OREO WOULD NO LONGER EXIST AS A POINT OF COMPARISON FROM WHICH TO CONDEMN THE MEDIOCRITY OF THE HYDROX COOKIE AND THE HYDROX WOULD BECOME THE HIGH WATER MARK IN THE NEW PARADIGM AND NOBODY WOULD EVEN BE AWARE THAT THERE WAS EVER AN ALTERNATIVE. BY REMOVING THE OREO, YOU REMOVE THE TASTE FOR THE OREO. SEE WHAT I MEAN? INFORMATION IS THE SAME WAY - BY REMOVING THE SIGNIFICANCE OF THE FREE LIBRARY AND ONLY MAKING AVAILABLE SOURCE MATERIAL FOR THE CONCOCTING OF OUR NATIONAL AND PERSONAL IDENTITIES TO THOSE WHO CAN PAY FOR IT IS NOT A MODEL THAT CAN SUPPORT REAL DISSENT OR FOSTER ANY OF THE IMPERATIVES NECESSARY TO SUSTAIN A PARTICIPATORY DEMOCRACY. IT IS MERELY THE CHANNELING OF TRUTH THROUGH THE RETAIL-INDUSTRIAL COMPLEX, WHICH CAN ONLY PRODUCE PROPAGANDA THAT BEGINS WITH THE...
...ASSUMPTION THAT CAPITALISM IS THE MORAL AUTHORITY FROM WHICH THE PHYSICS OF ALL COMPREHENSION OF TRUTH MUST BEGIN.
IT IS, QUITE LITERALLY, THE REMOVAL OF THE 'FREE' AND THE LEAVING OF ONLY THE 'DUMB.'

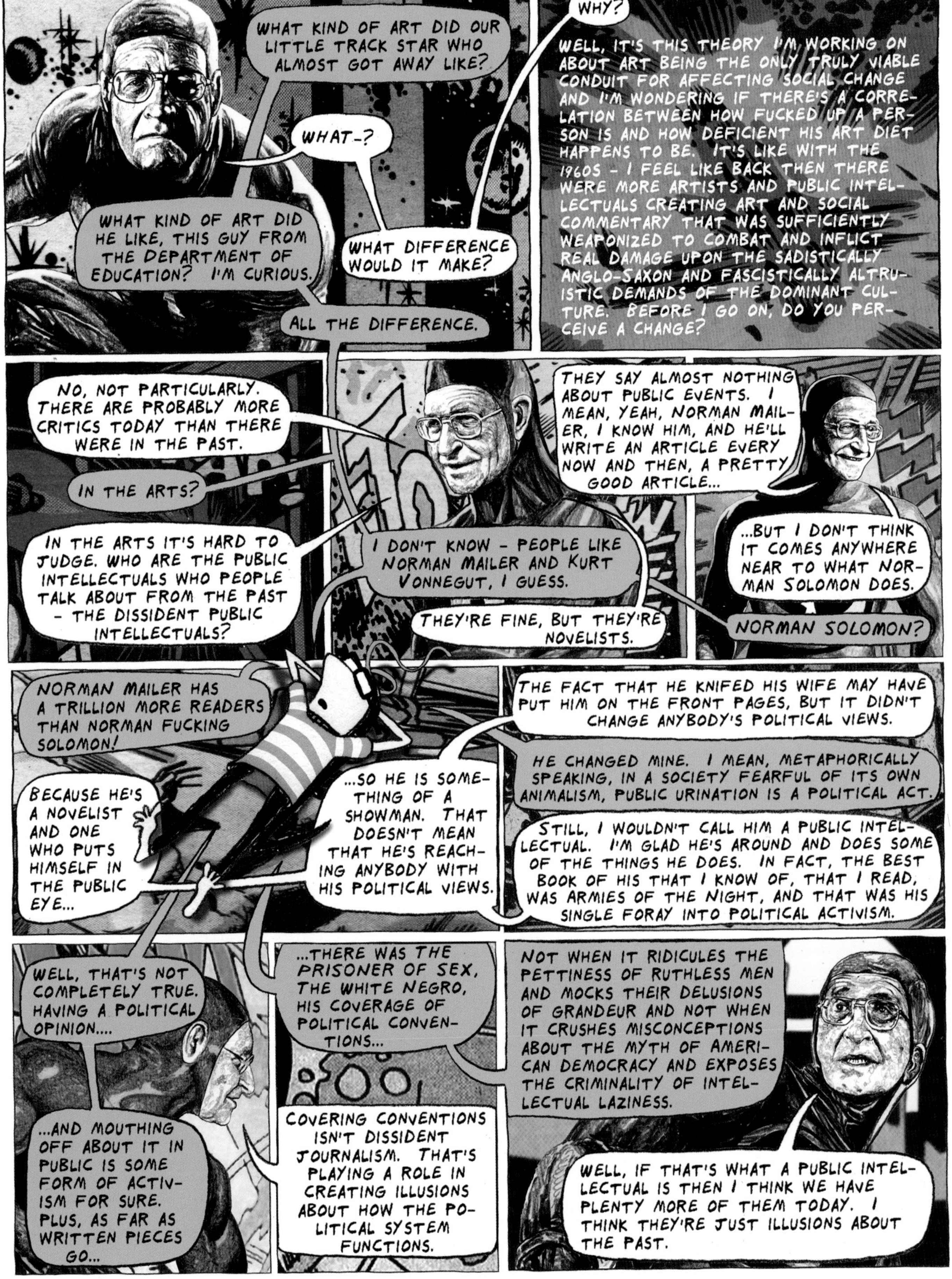
WHAT KIND OF ART DID OUR LITTLE TRACK STAR WHO ALMOST GOT AWAY LIKE?
WHAT-?
WHAT KIND OF ART DID HE LIKE, THIS GUY FROM THE DEPARTMENT OF EDUCATION? I'M CURIOUS.
WHAT DIFFERENCE WOULD IT MAKE?
ALL THE DIFFERENCE.
WHY?
WELL, IT'S THIS THEORY I'M WORKING ON ABOUT ART BEING THE ONLY TRULY VIABLE CONDUIT FOR AFFECTING SOCIAL CHANGE AND I'M WONDERING IF THERE'S A CORRELATION BETWEEN HOW FUCKED UP A PERSON IS AND HOW DEFICIENT HIS ART DIET HAPPENS TO BE. IT'S LIKE WITH THE 1960S - I FEEL LIKE BACK THEN THERE WERE MORE ARTISTS AND PUBLIC INTELLECTUALS CREATING ART AND SOCIAL COMMENTARY THAT WAS SUFFICIENTLY WEAPONIZED TO COMBAT AND INFLICT REAL DAMAGE UPON THE SADISTICALLY ANGLO-SAXON AND FASCISTICALLY ALTRUISTIC DEMANDS OF THE DOMINANT CULTURE. BEFORE I GO ON, DO YOU PERCEIVE A CHANGE?
NO, NOT PARTICULARLY. THERE ARE PROBABLY MORE CRITICS TODAY THAN THERE WERE IN THE PAST.
IN THE ARTS?
IN THE ARTS IT'S HARD TO JUDGE. WHO ARE THE PUBLIC INTELLECTUALS WHO PEOPLE TALK ABOUT FROM THE PAST - THE DISSIDENT PUBLIC INTELLECTUALS?
I DON'T KNOW - PEOPLE LIKE NORMAN MAILER AND KURT VONNEGUT, I GUESS.
THEY'RE FINE, BUT THEY'RE NOVELISTS.
THEY SAY ALMOST NOTHING ABOUT PUBLIC EVENTS. I MEAN, YEAH, NORMAN MAILER, I KNOW HIM, AND HE'LL WRITE AN ARTICLE EVERY NOW AND THEN, A PRETTY GOOD ARTICLE...
...BUT I DON'T THINK IT COMES ANYWHERE NEAR TO WHAT NORMAN SOLOMON DOES.
NORMAN SOLOMON?
NORMAN MAILER HAS A TRILLION MORE READERS THAN NORMAN FUCKING SOLOMON!
BECAUSE HE'S A NOVELIST AND ONE WHO PUTS HIMSELF IN THE PUBLIC EYE...
...SO HE IS SOMETHING OF A SHOWMAN. THAT DOESN'T MEAN THAT HE'S REACHING ANYBODY WITH HIS POLITICAL VIEWS.
THE FACT THAT HE KNIFED HIS WIFE MAY HAVE PUT HIM ON THE FRONT PAGES, BUT IT DIDN'T CHANGE ANYBODY'S POLITICAL VIEWS.
HE CHANGED MINE. I MEAN, METAPHORICALLY SPEAKING, IN A SOCIETY FEARFUL OF ITS OWN ANIMALISM, PUBLIC URINATION IS A POLITICAL ACT.
STILL, I WOULDN'T CALL HIM A PUBLIC INTELLECTUAL. I'M GLAD HE'S AROUND AND DOES SOME OF THE THINGS HE DOES. IN FACT, THE BEST BOOK OF HIS THAT I KNOW OF, THAT I READ, WAS ARMIES OF THE NIGHT, AND THAT WAS HIS SINGLE FORAY INTO POLITICAL ACTIVISM.
WELL, THAT'S NOT COMPLETELY TRUE. HAVING A POLITICAL OPINION....
...AND MOUTHING OFF ABOUT IT IN PUBLIC IS SOME FORM OF ACTIVISM FOR SURE. PLUS, AS FAR AS WRITTEN PIECES GO...
...THERE WAS THE PRISONER OF SEX, THE WHITE NEGRO, HIS COVERAGE OF POLITICAL CONVENTIONS...
COVERING CONVENTIONS ISN'T DISSIDENT JOURNALISM. THAT'S PLAYING A ROLE IN CREATING ILLUSIONS ABOUT HOW THE POLITICAL SYSTEM FUNCTIONS.
NOT WHEN IT RIDICULES THE PETTINESS OF RUTHLESS MEN AND MOCKS THEIR DELUSIONS OF GRANDEUR AND NOT WHEN IT CRUSHES MISCONCEPTIONS ABOUT THE MYTH OF AMERICAN DEMOCRACY AND EXPOSES THE CRIMINALITY OF INTELLECTUAL LAZINESS.
WELL, IF THAT'S WHAT A PUBLIC INTELLECTUAL IS THEN I THINK WE HAVE PLENTY MORE OF THEM TODAY. I THINK THEY'RE JUST ILLUSIONS ABOUT THE PAST.

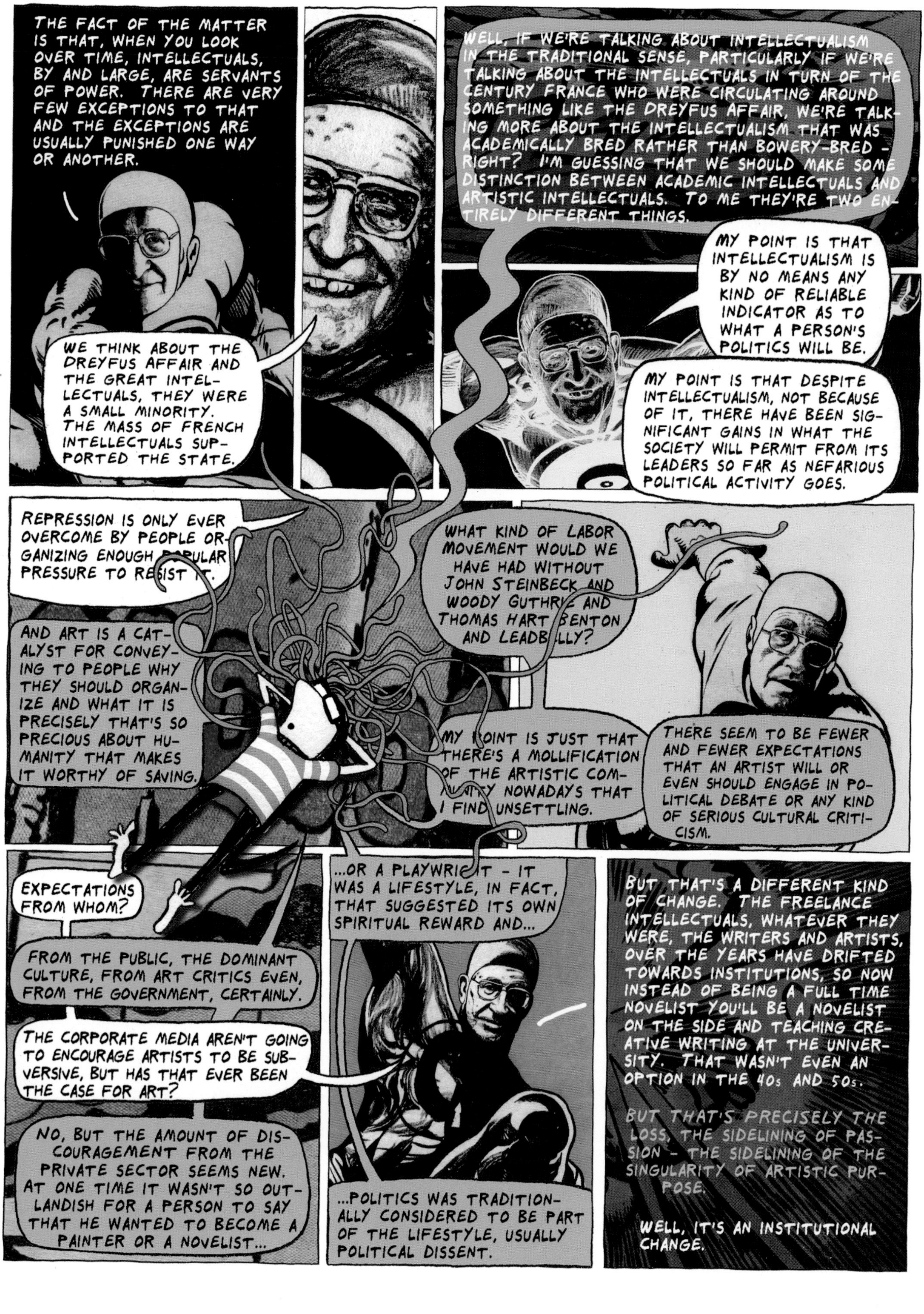
THE FACT OF THE MATTER IS THAT, WHEN YOU LOOK OVER TIME, INTELLECTUALS, BY AND LARGE, ARE SERVANTS OF POWER. THERE ARE VERY FEW EXCEPTIONS TO THAT AND THE EXCEPTIONS ARE USUALLY PUNISHED ONE WAY OR ANOTHER.
WE THINK ABOUT THE DREYFUS AFFAIR AND THE GREAT INTELLECTUALS, THEY WERE A SMALL MINORITY. THE MASS OF FRENCH INTELLECTUALS SUPPORTED THE STATE.
WELL, IF WE'RE TALKING ABOUT INTELLECTUALISM IN THE TRADITIONAL SENSE, PARTICULARLY IF WE'RE TALKING ABOUT THE INTELLECTUALS IN TURN OF THE CENTURY FRANCE WHO WERE CIRCULATING AROUND SOMETHING LIKE THE DREYFUS AFFAIR, WE'RE TALKING MORE ABOUT THE INTELLECTUALISM THAT WAS ACADEMICALLY BRED RATHER THAN BOWERY-BRED - RIGHT? I'M GUESSING THAT WE SHOULD MAKE SOME DISTINCTION BETWEEN ACADEMIC INTELLECTUALS AND ARTISTIC INTELLECTUALS. TO ME THEY'RE TWO ENTIRELY DIFFERENT THINGS.
MY POINT IS THAT INTELLECTUALISM IS BY NO MEANS ANY KIND OF RELIABLE INDICATOR AS TO WHAT A PERSON'S POLITICS WILL BE.
MY POINT IS THAT DESPITE INTELLECTUALISM, NOT BECAUSE OF IT, THERE HAVE BEEN SIGNIFICANT GAINS IN WHAT THE SOCIETY WILL PERMIT FROM ITS LEADERS SO FAR AS NEFARIOUS POLITICAL ACTIVITY GOES.
REPRESSION IS ONLY EVER OVERCOME BY PEOPLE ORGANIZING ENOUGH POPULAR PRESSURE TO RESIST IT.
AND ART IS A CATALYST FOR CONVEYING TO PEOPLE WHY THEY SHOULD ORGANIZE AND WHAT IT IS PRECISELY THAT'S SO PRECIOUS ABOUT HUMANITY THAT MAKES IT WORTHY OF SAVING.
WHAT KIND OF LABOR MOVEMENT WOULD WE HAVE HAD WITHOUT JOHN STEINBECK AND WOODY GUTHRIE AND THOMAS HART BENTON AND LEADBELLY?
MY POINT IS JUST THAT THERE'S A MOLLIFICATION OF THE ARTISTIC COMMUNITY NOWADAYS THAT I FIND UNSETTLING.
THERE SEEM TO BE FEWER AND FEWER EXPECTATIONS THAT AN ARTIST WILL OR EVEN SHOULD ENGAGE IN POLITICAL DEBATE OR ANY KIND OF SERIOUS CULTURAL CRITICISM.
EXPECTATIONS FROM WHOM?
FROM THE PUBLIC, THE DOMINANT CULTURE, FROM ART CRITICS EVEN, FROM THE GOVERNMENT, CERTAINLY.
THE CORPORATE MEDIA AREN'T GOING TO ENCOURAGE ARTISTS TO BE SUBVERSIVE, BUT HAS THAT EVER BEEN THE CASE FOR ART?
NO, BUT THE AMOUNT OF DISCOURAGEMENT FROM THE PRIVATE SECTOR SEEMS NEW. AT ONE TIME IT WASN'T SO OUTLANDISH FOR A PERSON TO SAY THAT HE WANTED TO BECOME A PAINTER OR A NOVELIST...
...OR A PLAYWRIGHT - IT WAS A LIFESTYLE, IN FACT, THAT SUGGESTED ITS OWN SPIRITUAL REWARD AND...
...POLITICS WAS TRADITIONALLY CONSIDERED TO BE PART OF THE LIFESTYLE, USUALLY POLITICAL DISSENT.
BUT THAT'S A DIFFERENT KIND OF CHANGE. THE FREELANCE INTELLECTUALS, WHATEVER THEY WERE, THE WRITERS AND ARTISTS, OVER THE YEARS HAVE DRIFTED TOWARDS INSTITUTIONS, SO NOW INSTEAD OF BEING A FULL TIME NOVELIST YOU'LL BE A NOVELIST ON THE SIDE AND TEACHING CREATIVE WRITING AT THE UNIVERSITY. THAT WASN'T EVEN AN OPTION IN THE 40s AND 50s.
BUT THAT'S PRECISELY THE LOSS, THE SIDELINING OF PASSION - THE SIDELINING OF THE SINGULARITY OF ARTISTIC PURPOSE.
WELL, IT'S AN INSTITUTIONAL CHANGE.

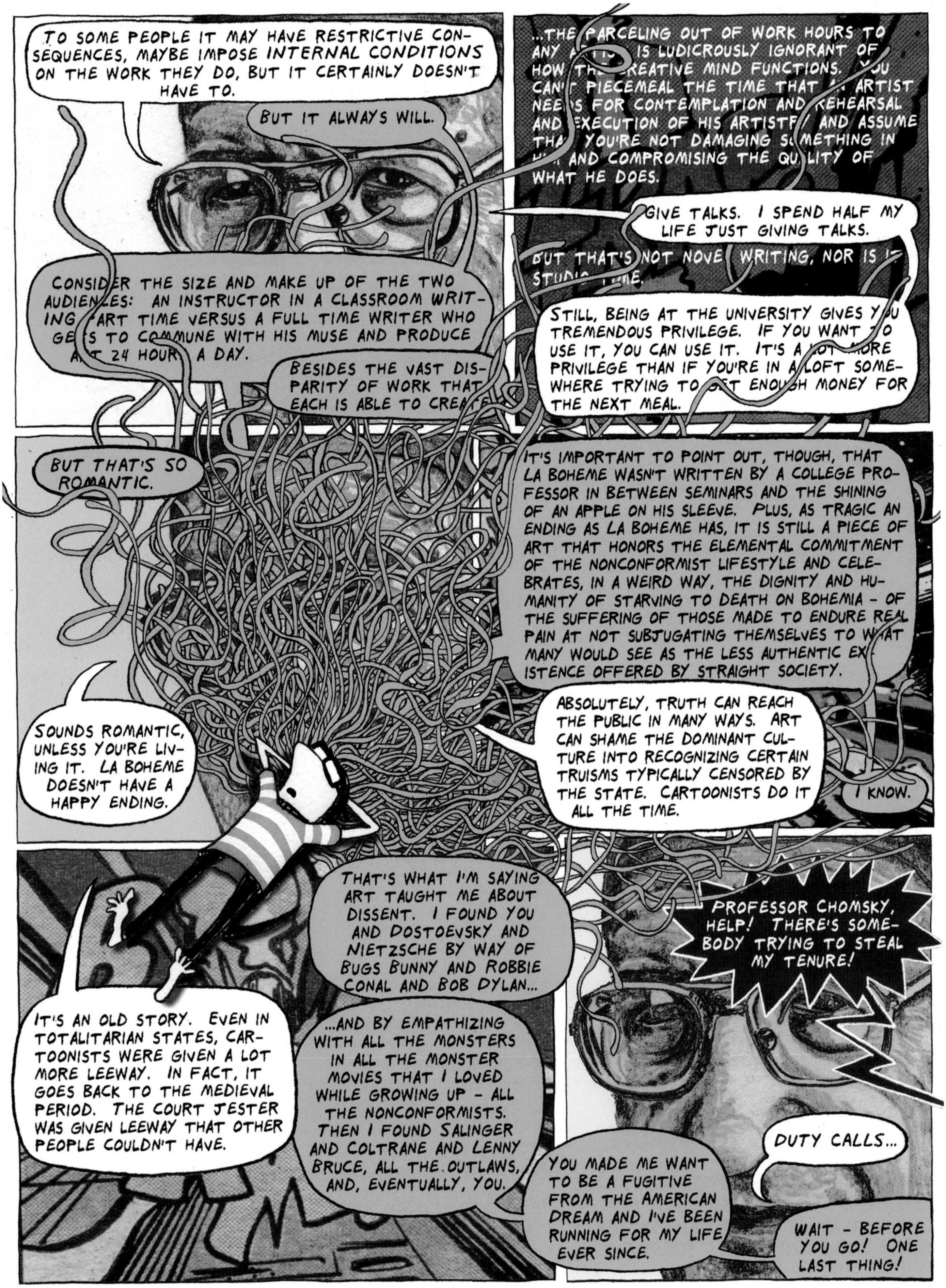
TO SOME PEOPLE IT MAY HAVE RESTRICTIVE CONSEQUENCES, MAYBE IMPOSE INTERNAL CONDITIONS ON THE WORK THEY DO, BUT IT CERTAINLY DOESN'T HAVE TO.
BUT IT ALWAYS WILL.
...THE PARCELING OUT OF WORK HOURS TO ANY ARTIST IS LUDICROUSLY IGNORANT OF HOW THE CREATIVE MIND FUNCTIONS. YOU CAN'T PIECEMEAL THE TIME THAT AN ARTIST NEEDS FOR CONTEMPLATION AND REHEARSAL AND EXECUTION OF HIS ARTISTRY AND ASSUME THAT YOU'RE NOT DAMAGING SOMETHING IN HIM AND COMPROMISING THE QUALITY OF WHAT HE DOES.
GIVE TALKS. I SPEND HALF MY LIFE JUST GIVING TALKS.
BUT THAT'S NOT NOVEL WRITING, NOR IS IT STUDIO TIME.
CONSIDER THE SIZE AND MAKE UP OF THE TWO AUDIENCES: AN INSTRUCTOR IN A CLASSROOM WRITING PART TIME VERSUS A FULL TIME WRITER WHO GETS TO COMMUNE WITH HIS MUSE AND PRODUCE ART 24 HOURS A DAY.
BESIDES THE VAST DISPARITY OF WORK THAT EACH IS ABLE TO CREATE.
STILL, BEING AT THE UNIVERSITY GIVES YOU TREMENDOUS PRIVILEGE. IF YOU WANT TO USE IT, YOU CAN USE IT. IT'S A LOT MORE PRIVILEGE THAN IF YOU'RE IN A LOFT SOMEWHERE TRYING TO GET ENOUGH MONEY FOR THE NEXT MEAL.
BUT THAT'S SO ROMANTIC.
IT'S IMPORTANT TO POINT OUT, THOUGH, THAT LA BOHEME WASN'T WRITTEN BY A COLLEGE PROFESSOR IN BETWEEN SEMINARS AND THE SHINING OF AN APPLE ON HIS SLEEVE. PLUS, AS TRAGIC AN ENDING AS LA BOHEME HAS, IT IS STILL A PIECE OF ART THAT HONORS THE ELEMENTAL COMMITMENT OF THE NONCONFORMIST LIFESTYLE AND CELEBRATES, IN A WEIRD WAY, THE DIGNITY AND HUMANITY OF STARVING TO DEATH ON BOHEMIA - OF THE SUFFERING OF THOSE MADE TO ENDURE REAL PAIN AT NOT SUBJUGATING THEMSELVES TO WHAT MANY WOULD SEE AS THE LESS AUTHENTIC EXISTENCE OFFERED BY STRAIGHT SOCIETY.
SOUNDS ROMANTIC, UNLESS YOU'RE LIVING IT. LA BOHEME DOESN'T HAVE A HAPPY ENDING.
ABSOLUTELY, TRUTH CAN REACH THE PUBLIC IN MANY WAYS. ART CAN SHAME THE DOMINANT CULTURE INTO RECOGNIZING CERTAIN TRUISMS TYPICALLY CENSORED BY THE STATE. CARTOONISTS DO IT ALL THE TIME.
I KNOW.
IT'S AN OLD STORY. EVEN IN TOTALITARIAN STATES, CARTOONISTS WERE GIVEN A LOT MORE LEEWAY. IN FACT, IT GOES BACK TO THE MEDIEVAL PERIOD. THE COURT JESTER WAS GIVEN LEEWAY THAT OTHER PEOPLE COULDN'T HAVE.
THAT'S WHAT I'M SAYING ART TAUGHT ME ABOUT DISSENT. I FOUND YOU AND DOSTOEVSKY AND NIETZSCHE BY WAY OF BUGS BUNNY AND ROBBIE CONAL AND BOB DYLAN...
...AND BY EMPATHIZING WITH ALL THE MONSTERS IN ALL THE MONSTER MOVIES THAT I LOVED WHILE GROWING UP - ALL THE NONCONFORMISTS. THEN I FOUND SALINGER AND COLTRANE AND LENNY BRUCE, ALL THE OUTLAWS, AND, EVENTUALLY, YOU.
PROFESSOR CHOMSKY, HELP! THERE'S SOMEBODY TRYING TO STEAL MY TENURE!
DUTY CALLS...
YOU MADE ME WANT TO BE A FUGITIVE FROM THE AMERICAN DREAM AND I'VE BEEN RUNNING FOR MY LIFE EVER SINCE.
WAIT - BEFORE YOU GO! ONE LAST THING!

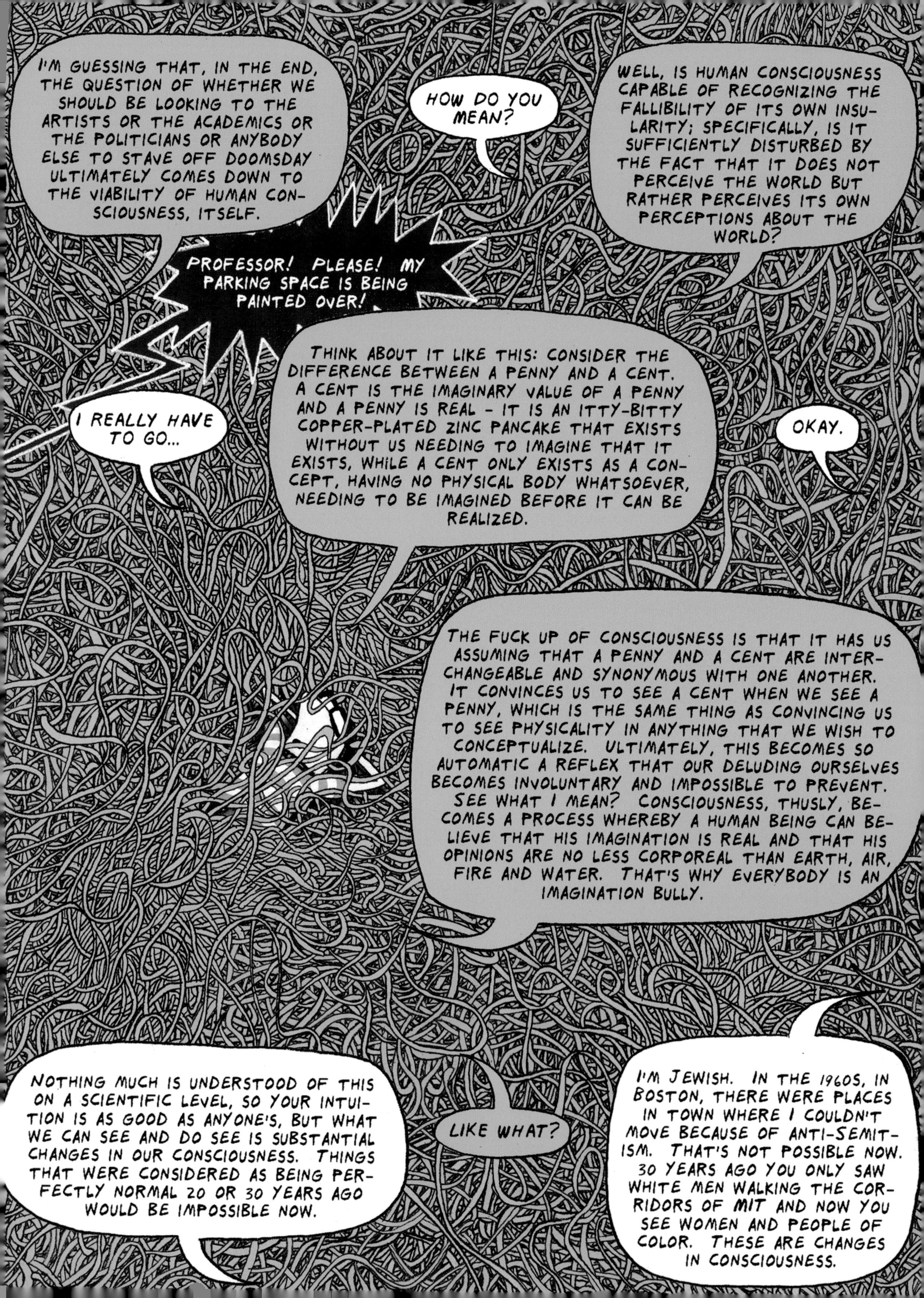
I'M GUESSING THAT, IN THE END, THE QUESTION OF WHETHER WE SHOULD BE LOOKING TO THE ARTISTS OR THE ACADEMICS OR THE POLITICIANS OR ANYBODY ELSE TO STAVE OFF DOOMSDAY ULTIMATELY COMES DOWN TO THE VIABILITY OF HUMAN CONSCIOUSNESS, ITSELF.
HOW DO YOU MEAN?
WELL, IS HUMAN CONSCIOUSNESS CAPABLE OF RECOGNIZING THE FALLIBILITY OF ITS OWN INSULARITY; SPECIFICALLY, IS IT SUFFICIENTLY DISTURBED BY THE FACT THAT IT DOES NOT PERCEIVE THE WORLD BUT RATHER PERCEIVES ITS OWN PERCEPTIONS ABOUT THE WORLD?
PROFESSOR! PLEASE! MY PARKING SPACE IS BEING PAINTED OVER!
I REALLY HAVE TO GO...
THINK ABOUT IT LIKE THIS: CONSIDER THE DIFFERENCE BETWEEN A PENNY AND A CENT. A CENT IS THE IMAGINARY VALUE OF A PENNY AND A PENNY IS REAL - IT IS AN ITTY-BITTY COPPER-PLATED ZINC PANCAKE THAT EXISTS WITHOUT US NEEDING TO IMAGINE THAT IT EXISTS, WHILE A CENT ONLY EXISTS AS A CONCEPT, HAVING NO PHYSICAL BODY WHATSOEVER, NEEDING TO BE IMAGINED BEFORE IT CAN BE REALIZED.
OKAY.
THE FUCK UP OF CONSCIOUSNESS IS THAT IT HAS US ASSUMING THAT A PENNY AND A CENT ARE INTERCHANGEABLE AND SYNONYMOUS WITH ONE ANOTHER. IT CONVINCES US TO SEE A CENT WHEN WE SEE A PENNY, WHICH IS THE SAME THING AS CONVINCING US TO SEE PHYSICALITY IN ANYTHING THAT WE WISH TO CONCEPTUALIZE. ULTIMATELY, THIS BECOMES SO AUTOMATIC A REFLEX THAT OUR DELUDING OURSELVES BECOMES INVOLUNTARY AND IMPOSSIBLE TO PREVENT. SEE WHAT I MEAN? CONSCIOUSNESS, THUSLY, BECOMES A PROCESS WHEREBY A HUMAN BEING CAN BELIEVE THAT HIS IMAGINATION IS REAL AND THAT HIS OPINIONS ARE NO LESS CORPOREAL THAN EARTH, AIR, FIRE AND WATER. THAT'S WHY EVERYBODY IS AN IMAGINATION BULLY.
NOTHING MUCH IS UNDERSTOOD OF THIS ON A SCIENTIFIC LEVEL, SO YOUR INTUITION IS AS GOOD AS ANYONE'S, BUT WHAT WE CAN SEE AND DO SEE IS SUBSTANTIAL CHANGES IN OUR CONSCIOUSNESS. THINGS THAT WERE CONSIDERED AS BEING PERFECTLY NORMAL 20 OR 30 YEARS AGO WOULD BE IMPOSSIBLE NOW.
LIKE WHAT?
I'M JEWISH. IN THE 1960S, IN BOSTON, THERE WERE PLACES IN TOWN WHERE I COULDN'T MOVE BECAUSE OF ANTI-SEMITISM. THAT'S NOT POSSIBLE NOW. 30 YEARS AGO YOU ONLY SAW WHITE MEN WALKING THE CORRIDORS OF MIT AND NOW YOU SEE WOMEN AND PEOPLE OF COLOR. THESE ARE CHANGES IN CONSCIOUSNESS.

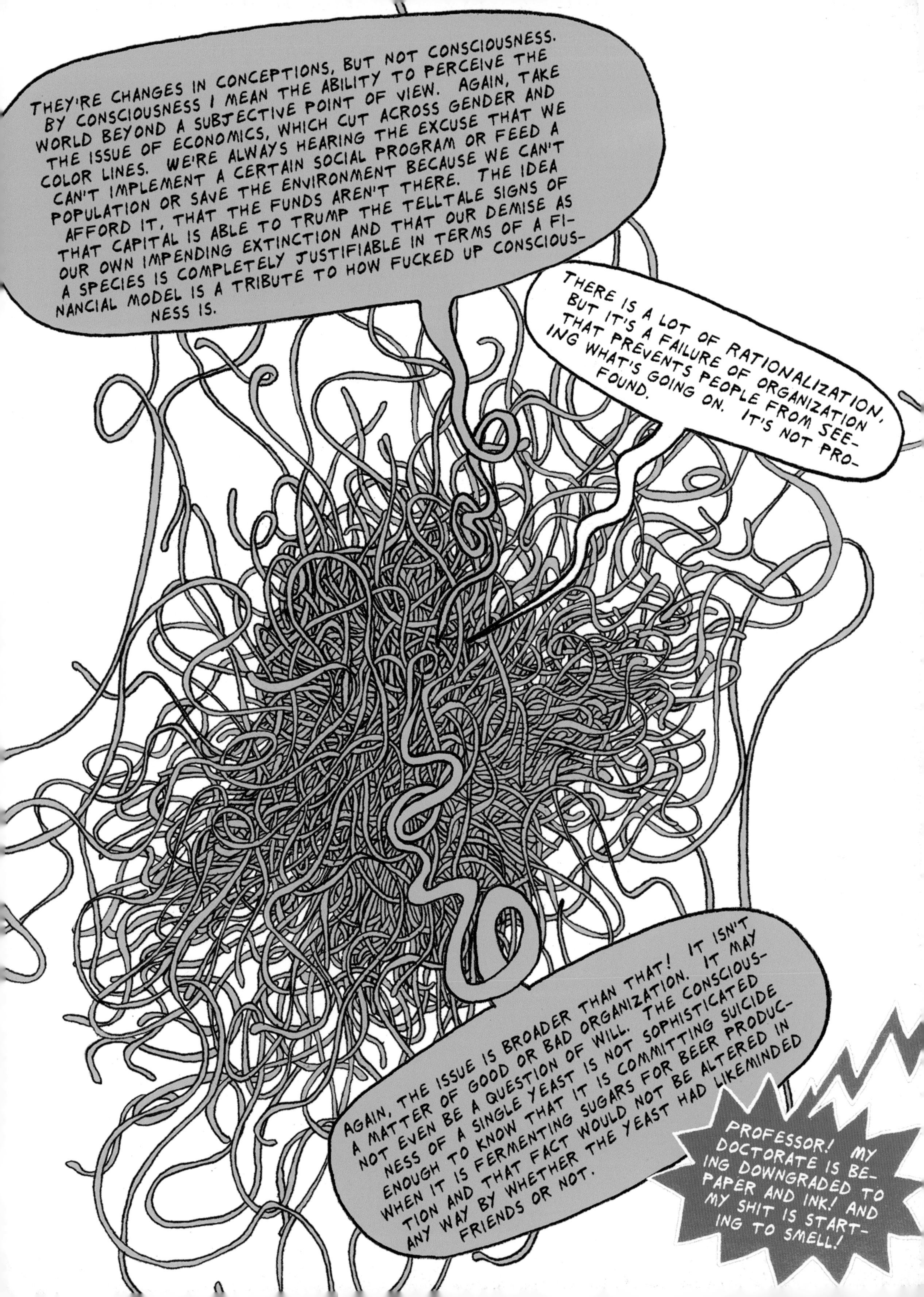
THEY'RE CHANGES IN CONCEPTIONS, BUT NOT CONSCIOUSNESS. BY CONSCIOUSNESS I MEAN THE ABILITY TO PERCEIVE THE WORLD BEYOND A SUBJECTIVE POINT OF VIEW. AGAIN, TAKE THE ISSUE OF ECONOMICS, WHICH CUT ACROSS GENDER AND COLOR LINES. WE'RE ALWAYS HEARING THE EXCUSE THAT WE CAN'T IMPLEMENT A CERTAIN SOCIAL PROGRAM OR FEED A POPULATION OR SAVE THE ENVIRONMENT BECAUSE WE CAN'T AFFORD IT, THAT THE FUNDS AREN'T THERE. THE IDEA THAT CAPITAL IS ABLE TO TRUMP THE TELLTALE SIGNS OF OUR OWN IMPENDING EXTINCTION AND THAT OUR DEMISE AS A SPECIES IS COMPLETELY JUSTIFIABLE IN TERMS OF A FINANCIAL MODEL IS A TRIBUTE TO HOW FUCKED UP CONSCIOUSNESS IS.
THERE IS A LOT OF RATIONALIZATION, BUT IT'S A FAILURE OF ORGANIZATION THAT PREVENTS PEOPLE FROM SEEING WHAT'S GOING ON. IT'S NOT PROFOUND.
AGAIN, THE ISSUE IS BROADER THAN THAT! IT ISN'T A MATTER OF GOOD OR BAD ORGANIZATION. IT MAY NOT EVEN BE A QUESTION OF WILL. THE CONSCIOUSNESS OF A SINGLE YEAST IS NOT SOPHISTICATED ENOUGH TO KNOW THAT IT IS COMMITTING SUICIDE WHEN IT IS FERMENTING SUGARS FOR BEER PRODUCTION AND THAT FACT WOULD NOT BE ALTERED IN ANY WAY BY WHETHER THE YEAST HAD LIKEMINDED FRIENDS OR NOT.
PROFESSOR! MY DOCTORATE IS BEING DOWNGRADED TO PAPER AND INK! AND MY SHIT IS STARTING TO SMELL!

I'M OFF - BUT TO ANSWER YOUR QUESTION ABOUT WHAT KIND OF ART THE GUY FROM THE DEPARTMENT OF EDU-CATION LIKED -
YEAH?
DOONESBURY, SIMON AND GARFUNKEL, GARRISON KEILLOR, HUMPHREY BOGART, WILL EISNER AND PHILLIP JOHNSON.
OH, NO...

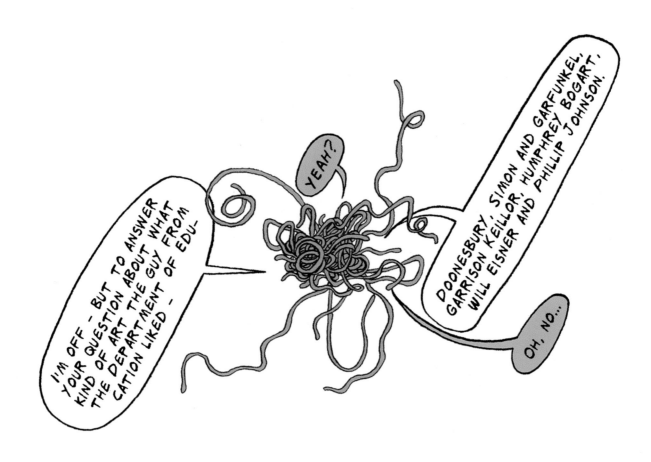

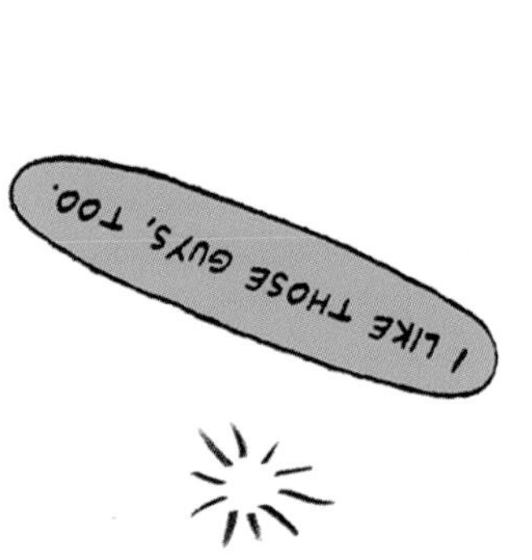
I LIKE THOSE GUYS, TOO.

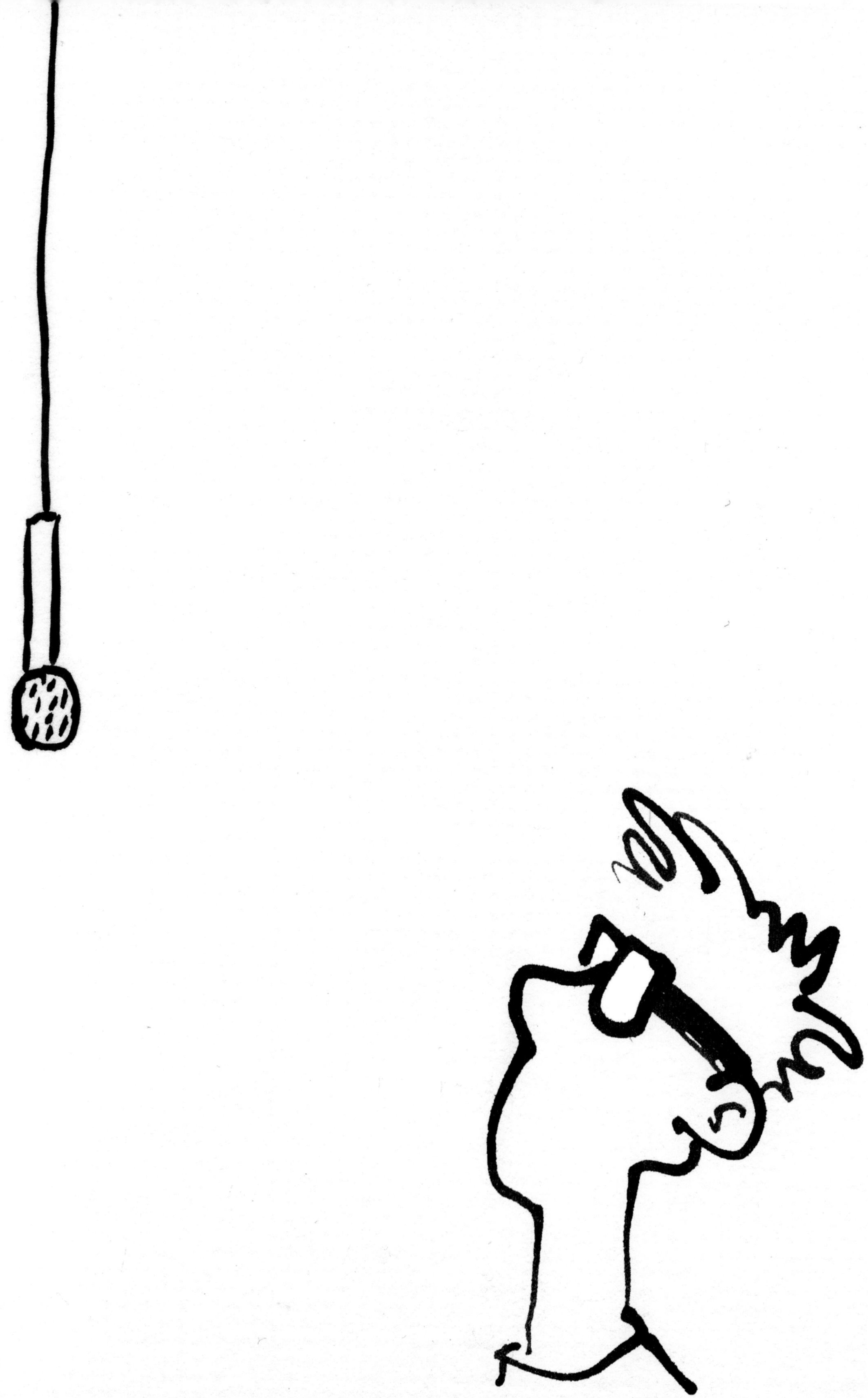

4

THE EGG AND I

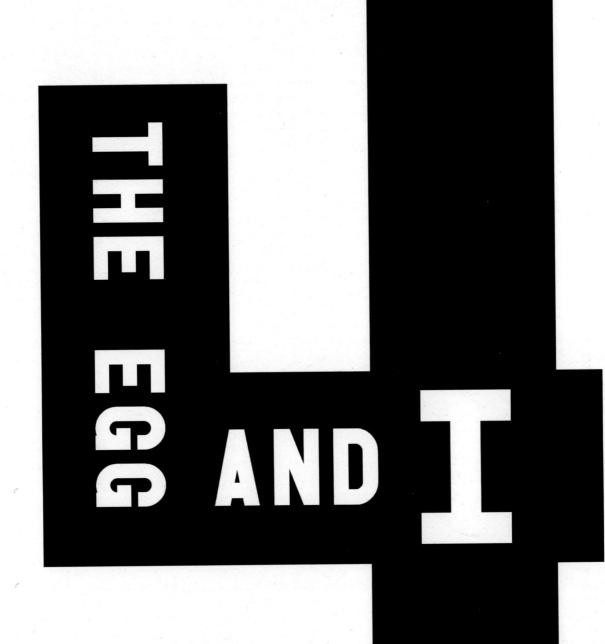

The Egg and I

AS A TEENAGER, world-renowned Oscar Wilde/Cindy Brady genius hybrid Truman Capote worked as a copy boy in the art department at *The New Yorker*. This was in the early 1940s, and one of his responsibilities, in addition to sorting cartoons for Saul Steinberg and William Steig and George Price, was to deliver the famously ill-tempered and blind humorist James Thurber to his mistress' apartment at the end of the day. Capote would wait in the living room while the couple engaged in the sort of rowdy lovemaking that he later described as the sound of hogs being butchered. He would then dress Thurber and return the satiated lecher home, oftentimes fall-down drunk, to his wife, who would undress him for bed. The helplessness of his ward made Capote feel servile and invisible, like a nanny hired to mollycoddle a spoiled rotten baby with the same exact daily routine, Monday through Friday, that began with a few drinkie-poos, followed by a walkie-poo, then an obstreperous ejaculation into a homely secretary, then a changing, then another walkie-poo and then beddy-bye.

Finally bored beyond tolerance by the scut work, Capote decided, while dressing Thurber one afternoon, to put the old man's socks on inside out. Predictably, Thurber's wife, who had dressed her husband in the morning, demanded an explanation as to why it had appeared he needed to remove his socks during the day, to which the celebrated wit is rumored to have quipped, "That fucking little queer." (Pause to allow Eustace Tilley the Walter Mitty-esque daydream of believing that he is not really just Alfred E. Neuman in silk pantaloons and a $300 hat.) Needless to say, as a result of the inverted socks, Capote was immediately relieved of his professional obligation to Thurber's vas deferens and, 70 years later, the artfulness of his extrication can still be enjoyed as thoroughly as if it were an exquisitely rendered poem designed expertly for repeated recitation.

Specifically, not only does the story testify to the power of humor to sustain a real-life parable celebrating the ingenuity of a man hoping to escape the mundane, but it is also proof that the scenic, circuitous route through life may be preferable to the more direct. Had Capote merely decided to end his association with Thurber by complaining privately to Harold Ross, the magazine's editor at the time, or by quitting, not only would the delectability of the original story have been lost forever, but so too would the example that the human experience could, at times, be lived with grace and artistry.

When I was in the eighth grade, I was arrested for throwing eggs at a pedophile's house. Let's say that her name was Deloris Keating, not true, and that I was NOT chew-my-own-foot-off jealous that my 14-year-old friend, Richie, was the one having sex with her and not me, also not true, though both details are necessary for the streamlining of the narrative. She was old, *real* old, maybe 31, and freshly divorced with three young children. Richie was her baby sitter, and every Tuesday and Thursday night he would use a hair pick to inflate his

North Jersey wopfro into a Don Henley, comb the porn star prototype mustache resting on his upper lip with a dry toothbrush, slap on enough Brut Cologne to bruise the air and walk to her house around the corner like he was Youngblood Priest in *Super Fly*. He would then watch television and drink chocolate milk with Deloris' kids, feed them macaroni and cheese on plastic Hanna-Barbera plates, get them into their pajamas and tuck them into their beds. Then, sometime around 11 o'clock, his employer would come home and take off her pants, open her blouse, turn on a porno film and rub up against her hire, stinking of Long Island Iced Teas and cigarette smoke. Minus the diseased and psychotic manipulation of a minor, plus the inexplicable preference for Betamax over VHS, it was a real Romeo and Juliet romance. That is, until Richie thought that it would be a laugh-riot to take the 17-inch zucchini she had in her bedside table, bake it at 350 degrees for an hour and return it back to its drawer as soft as a gargantuan green alien stool sample.

"What do you mean, *what did she say*?!" he barked back at me with watery eyes, momentarily forgetting that anybody with whom an adolescent boy is having sex is not so much a sex partner as an interloper encroaching on the magnificent love affair he is already having with his own genitalia. "She was pissed off—said that I was too fucking immature for her! Can you believe that shit?" he said, trying to keep the contents of his "Spider-Man" Trapper Keeper from spilling out all over the bus stop.

Five days later, on the night before Halloween, he and I, along with my big brother, Jeff, a guy named Philhower and a guy named Danny, crept out of the woods on the other side of the street in front of Deloris' house, the pockets of our jackets and hooded sweatshirts loaded with eggs, our claustrophobic blood pounding in our ears, our nervous systems overrun with something like electric spiders. I don't remember much following the order to *FIRE!* except that the one and only egg I threw

MR. FISH

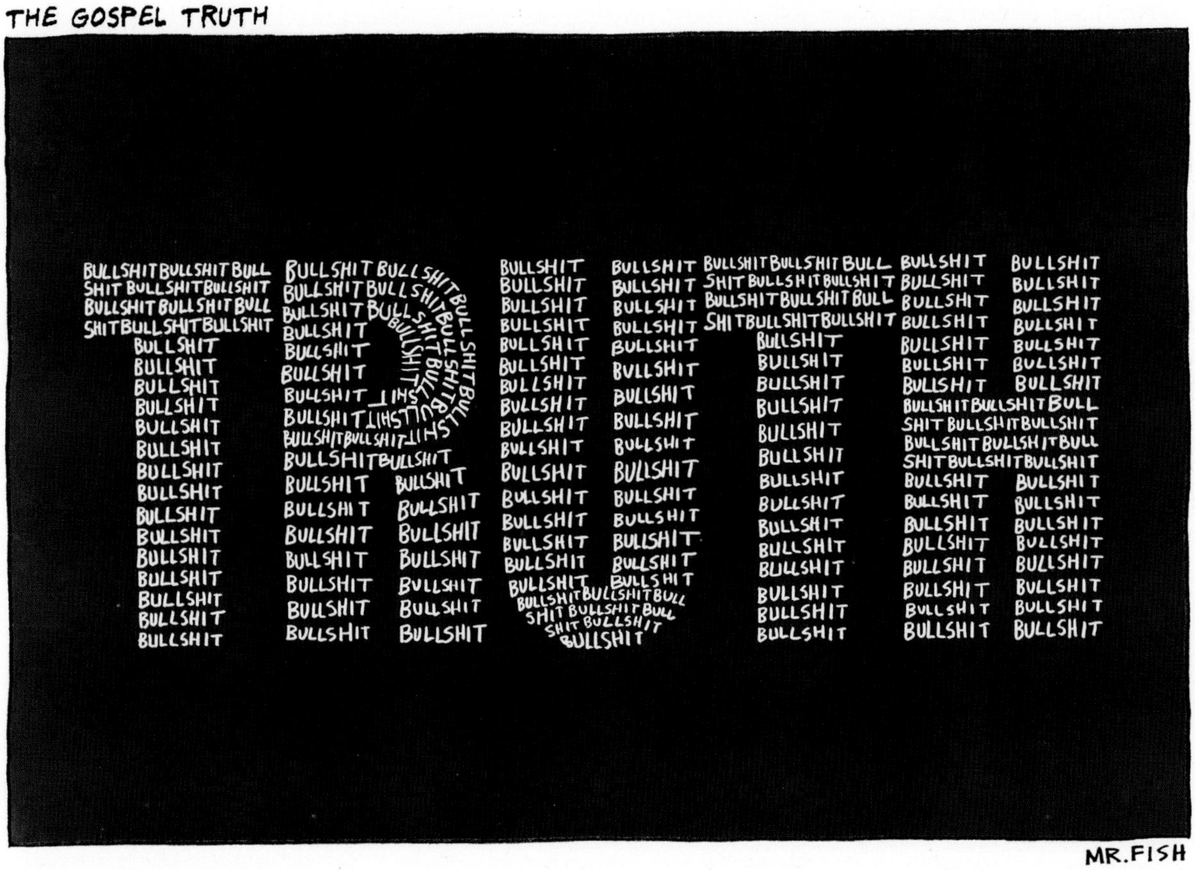
THE GOSPEL TRUTH
BULLSHIT
MR.FISH

missed its target completely and sailed over the roof. Then I remember, almost immediately, somebody yelling *RUN!* amid the mayhem of yolks exploding against shingles and shutters, at which point we ran, not for the woods, but as a sloppy disparate mob set zigzagging down the street like morons trying to outrun eyesight.

The thing about art, and I include folklore to be part of that discipline, is that it will always deepen the historical record that defines our moral and immoral certitude by insisting that the human heart, with all its contradictions and inarticulate universality, be present at the existential committee convened for the comprehension of life itself. Straight journalism, for example, or the rote memorization of theocratic balderdash or the cataloging of scientific data are certainly insufficient compilers of all that comprises the complicated identity of the whole species. Consider how unremarkable and ineffectual the 1950s and '60s would've been had the only commentary available to us been that of Walter Cronkite, Bishop Sheen and the House Un-American Activities Committee. Or try processing the great Dante-esque calamity that was the Second World War without such books as *The Naked and the Dead*, *Catch-22* and *Slaughterhouse-Five*. Additionally, no one would even know that there was ever a labor movement in this country that was vibrant and effective in teaching people how to organize and to gain both civil and workers' rights had there never been Woody Guthrie, Lead Belly, John Steinbeck, Mary Harris "Mother" Jones, Art Young, William Gropper or Thomas Hart Benton.

"I worry because I don't see any significant artwork being produced nowadays to help deepen our understanding of recent historical events beyond whatever sound bites we're given by the 24-hour news cycle," I said, standing behind a commie-red podium in front of a crowd at Revolution Books in lower Manhattan after a presentation of my cartoons. This was on the night before the night before the NYPD was covertly scheduled to dismantle the Occupy Wall Street encampment at Zuccotti Park and to wage the only sort of war that the U.S. power structure seems willing to fight anymore, both domestically and internationally. That is the sort launched against the defenseless and, preferably, the sleeping, the heroism of the cops and soldiers involved typically being determined by how squarely they're able to shoot their target in the back.

"There's no poetry in the retelling or re-examination of what we've been through over the last decade because there is no artistry in the way the memory has been rendered," I said, locking eyes with a kid in the front row who had just gotten into town from Duluth to join the fledgling OWS resistance movement as a photographer. "What source material will our children have access to when it comes to making sense of 9/11, for example? Who are they going to quote, the great Wolf

MR.FISH

Blitzer? *In My Time* by Dick Cheney? It's fucking ridiculous, and we're running out of time! Nothing will be remembered if we don't feel like retelling the story!"

"Are you going to let him burn alone, or are you going to stand up like men?" asked Officer Von Schmidt, gesturing toward a rather sullen-looking Richie while strutting back and forth in front of us in his jackboots and breeches, the brim of his policeman's cap hiding his eyes. We had been picked up by a pair of squad cars just a few blocks away from Deloris' house and returned, with egg on our shoes, to her front yard for positive identification. Nobody said a word. "You gonna act like a bunch of girls and let your buddy hang?!" Again, silence. "You call these assholes your friends?" he asked Richie, chuckling. "These aren't your friends! They don't care about you!" This from a full-grown adult who would in an hour's time respond to a 14-year-old's tearful retelling of how a mother of three children invited him to see how many of his fingers he could fit inside her at one time by saying, "Aw, come on! Don't be a baby about it! Count yourself lucky—you're a man! So how many fingers was it?"

"Yes, sir, I did it," said Philhower, looking at the ground, while another officer approached to read him his rights.

"How about you?" said Von Schmidt, moving down the line and going nose to nose with Danny, who was beginning to hyperventilate.

"Yeah," exhaled Danny, "I did it."

Von Schmidt took another step to the left. "And how about you?"

I nodded and stared at my shoes.

"You?" said Von Schmidt, stopping in front of my big brother.

"I don't know what you're talking about," said Jeff, shrugging his shoulders slightly and shaking his head in bewilderment.

"All right, get lost!" ordered Von Schmidt.

Watching Jeff casually round the corner with his hands in his pockets, not a care in the world, we all learned, perhaps too late, how the truth is sometimes way too important to be limited by the facts.

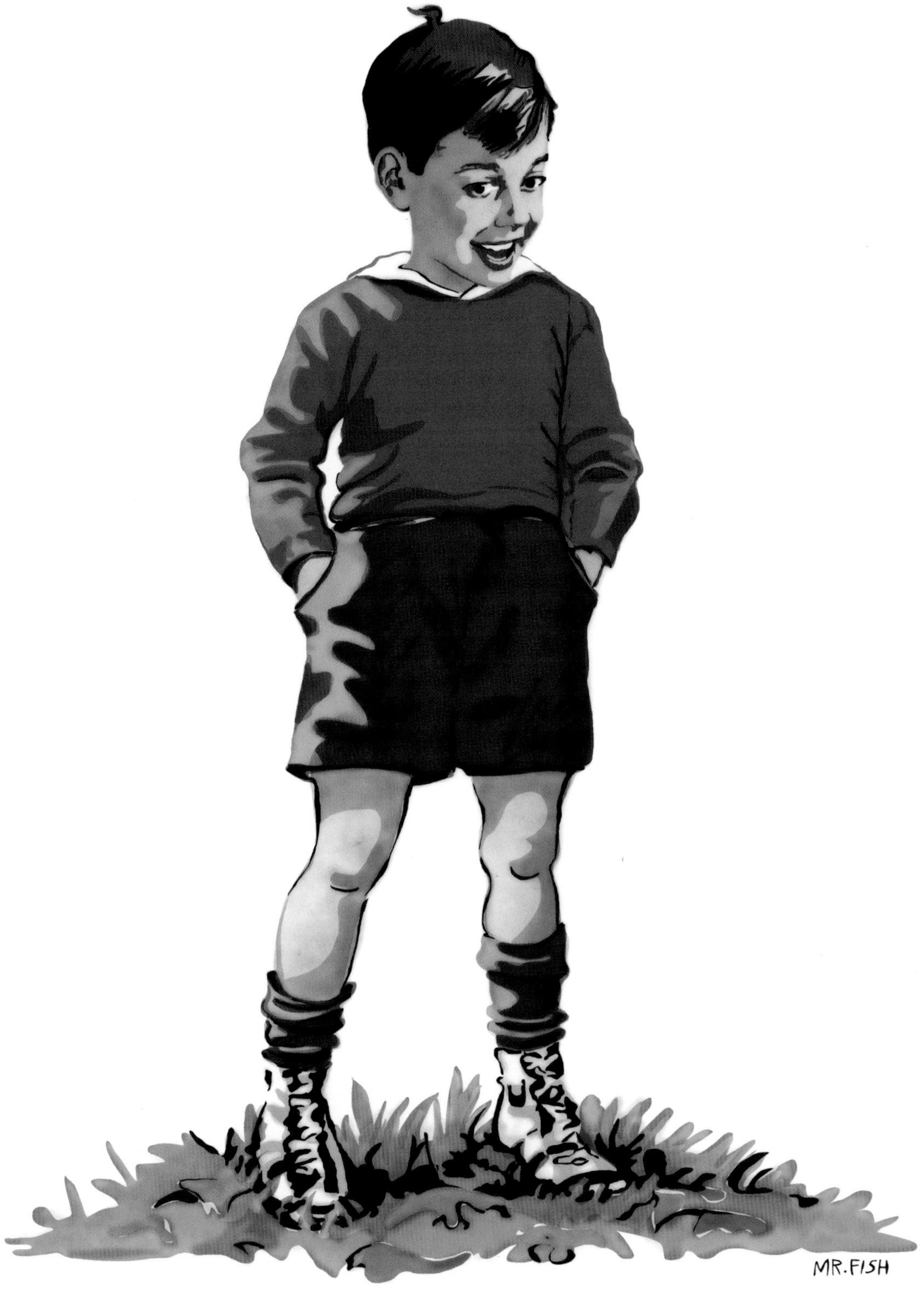
MR. FISH

Dick likes cock.

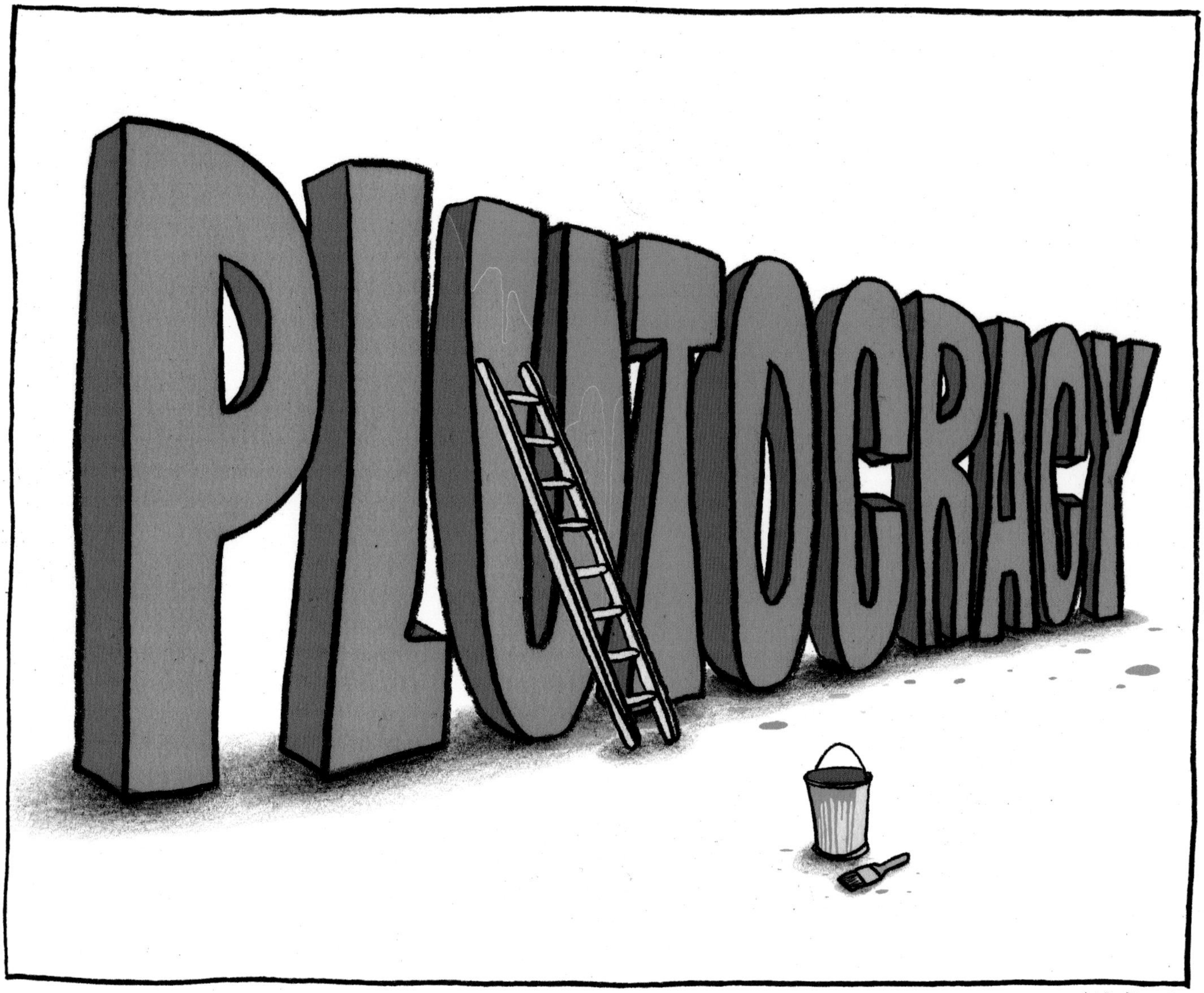
PLUTOCRACY

MR.FISH

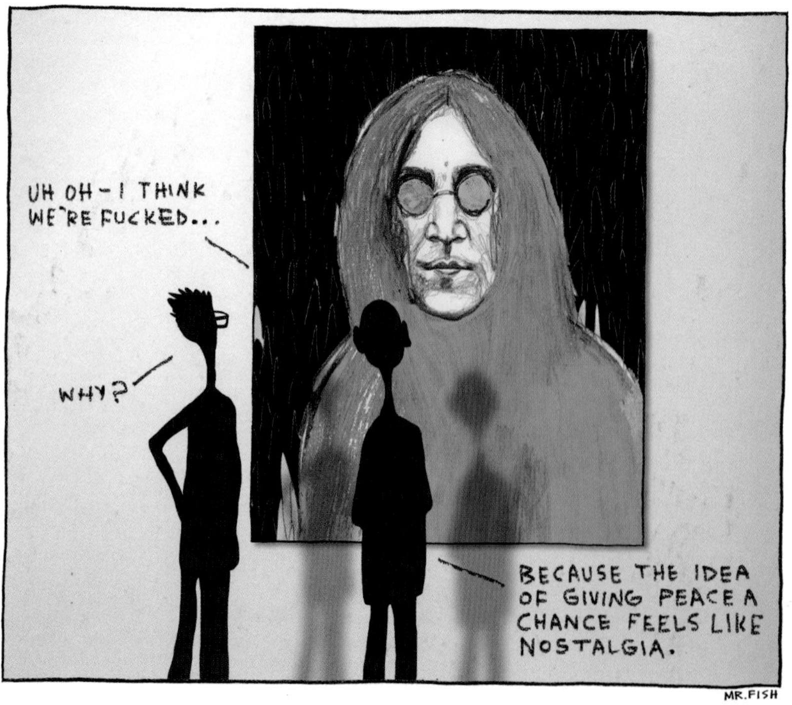
UH OH - I THINK WE'RE FUCKED...
WHY?
BECAUSE THE IDEA OF GIVING PEACE A CHANCE FEELS LIKE NOSTALGIA.
MR.FISH

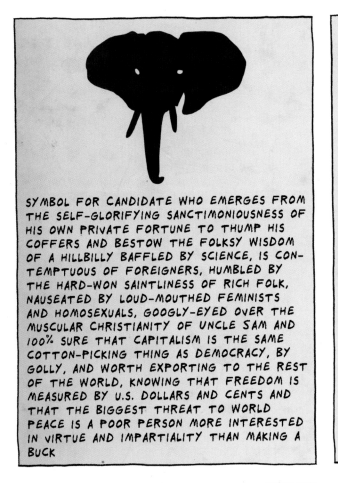

SYMBOL FOR CANDIDATE WHO EMERGES FROM THE SELF-GLORIFYING SANCTIMONIOUSNESS OF HIS OWN PRIVATE FORTUNE TO THUMP HIS COFFERS AND BESTOW THE FOLKSY WISDOM OF A HILLBILLY BAFFLED BY SCIENCE, IS CONTEMPTUOUS OF FOREIGNERS, HUMBLED BY THE HARD-WON SAINTLINESS OF RICH FOLK, NAUSEATED BY LOUD-MOUTHED FEMINISTS AND HOMOSEXUALS, GOOGLY-EYED OVER THE MUSCULAR CHRISTIANITY OF UNCLE SAM AND 100% SURE THAT CAPITALISM IS THE SAME COTTON-PICKING THING AS DEMOCRACY, BY GOLLY, AND WORTH EXPORTING TO THE REST OF THE WORLD, KNOWING THAT FREEDOM IS MEASURED BY U.S. DOLLARS AND CENTS AND THAT THE BIGGEST THREAT TO WORLD PEACE IS A POOR PERSON MORE INTERESTED IN VIRTUE AND IMPARTIALITY THAN MAKING A BUCK

SYMBOL FOR CANDIDATE WHO EMERGES FROM THE SELF-GLORIFYING SANCTIMONIOUSNESS OF HIS OWN PRIVATE FORTUNE TO THUMP HIS COFFERS AND BESTOW THE FOLKSY WISDOM OF A DEMURE AND NONTENURED COMMUNITY COLLEGE ENGLISH PROFESSOR MOVED BY THE SANCTITY OF A DOOMSDAY MACHINE FUELED ENTIRELY BY SUSTAINABLE ENERGY, GOOD INTENTIONS AND A RECYCLING PROGRAM, ALL THE WHILE GOOGLY-EYED OVER THE MUSCULAR CHRISTIANITY OF UNCLE SAM AND 100% SURE THAT CAPITALISM IS THE SAME GODDAMN THING AS DEMOCRACY, BY GOLLY, AND WORTH EXPORTING TO THE REST OF THE WORLD, KNOWING THAT FREEDOM IS MEASURED BY U.S. DOLLARS AND CENTS AND THAT THE BIGGEST THREAT TO WORLD PEACE IS A POOR PERSON MORE INTERESTED IN VIRTUE AND IMPARTIALITY THAN MAKING A BUCK

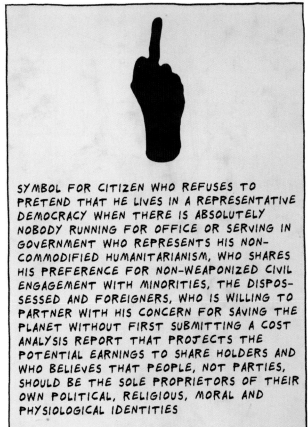

SYMBOL FOR CITIZEN WHO REFUSES TO PRETEND THAT HE LIVES IN A REPRESENTATIVE DEMOCRACY WHEN THERE IS ABSOLUTELY NOBODY RUNNING FOR OFFICE OR SERVING IN GOVERNMENT WHO REPRESENTS HIS NON-COMMODIFIED HUMANITARIANISM, WHO SHARES HIS PREFERENCE FOR NON-WEAPONIZED CIVIL ENGAGEMENT WITH MINORITIES, THE DISPOSSESSED AND FOREIGNERS, WHO IS WILLING TO PARTNER WITH HIS CONCERN FOR SAVING THE PLANET WITHOUT FIRST SUBMITTING A COST ANALYSIS REPORT THAT PROJECTS THE POTENTIAL EARNINGS TO SHARE HOLDERS AND WHO BELIEVES THAT PEOPLE, NOT PARTIES, SHOULD BE THE SOLE PROPRIETORS OF THEIR OWN POLITICAL, RELIGIOUS, MORAL AND PHYSIOLOGICAL IDENTITIES

MR. FISH

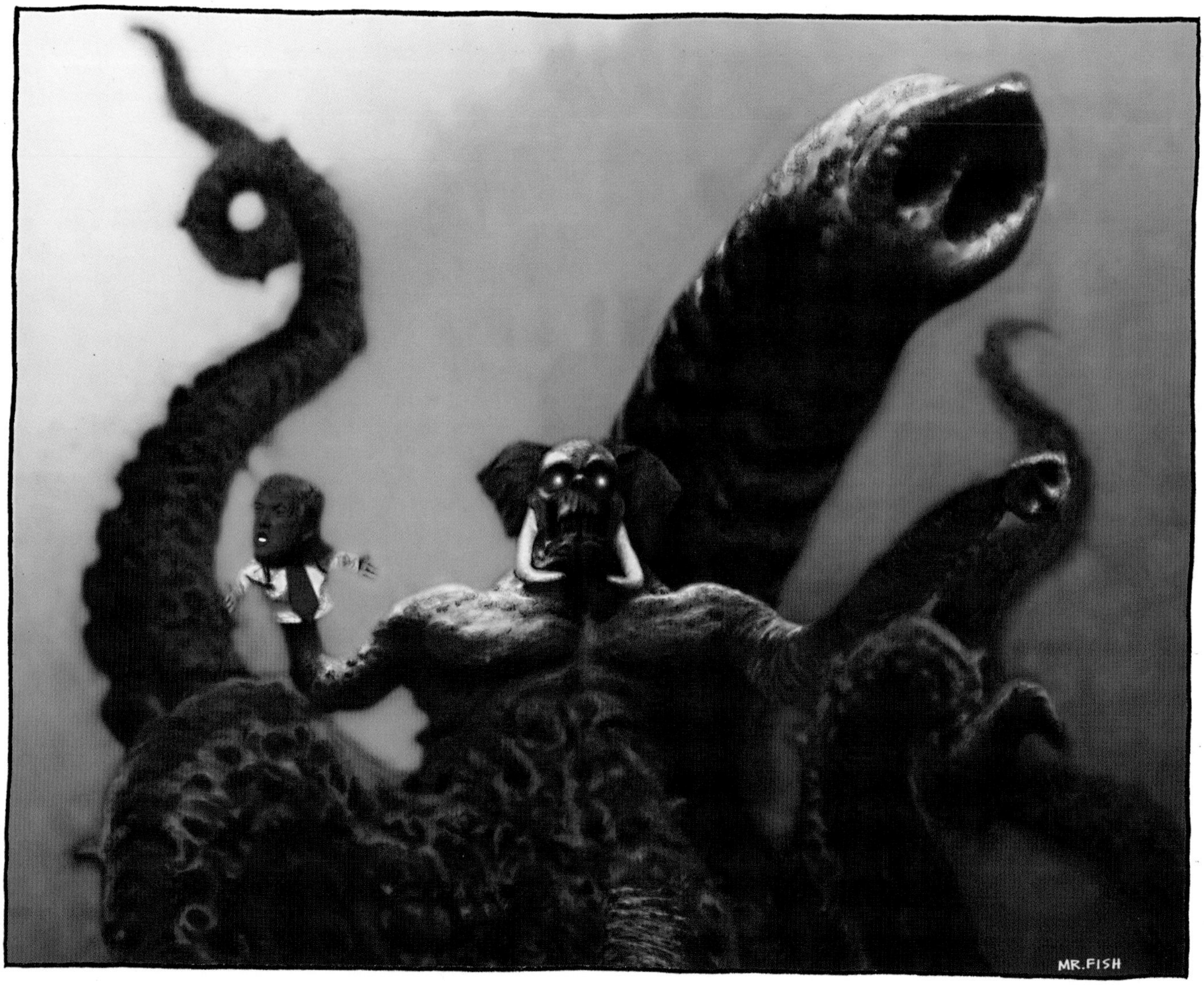
MR.FISH

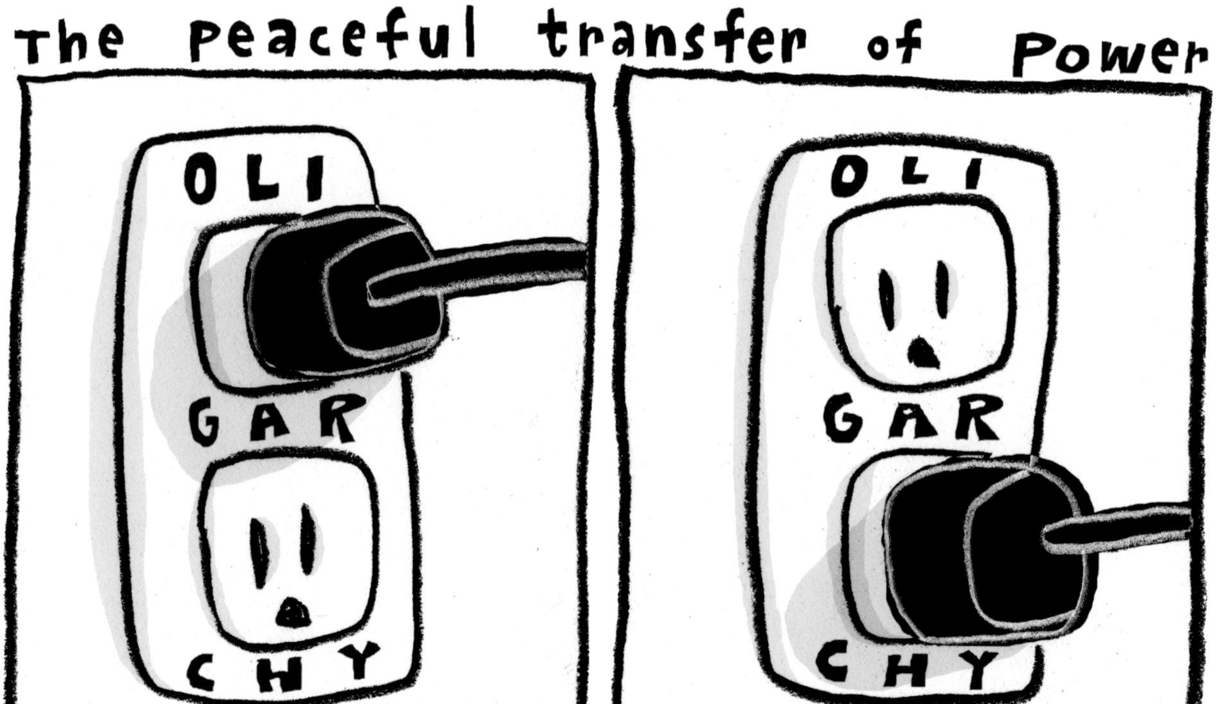
The peaceful transfer of Power
OLI
GAR
CHY
OLI
GAR
CHY
MR.FISH

ONLY A COWARD ARMS HIMSELF

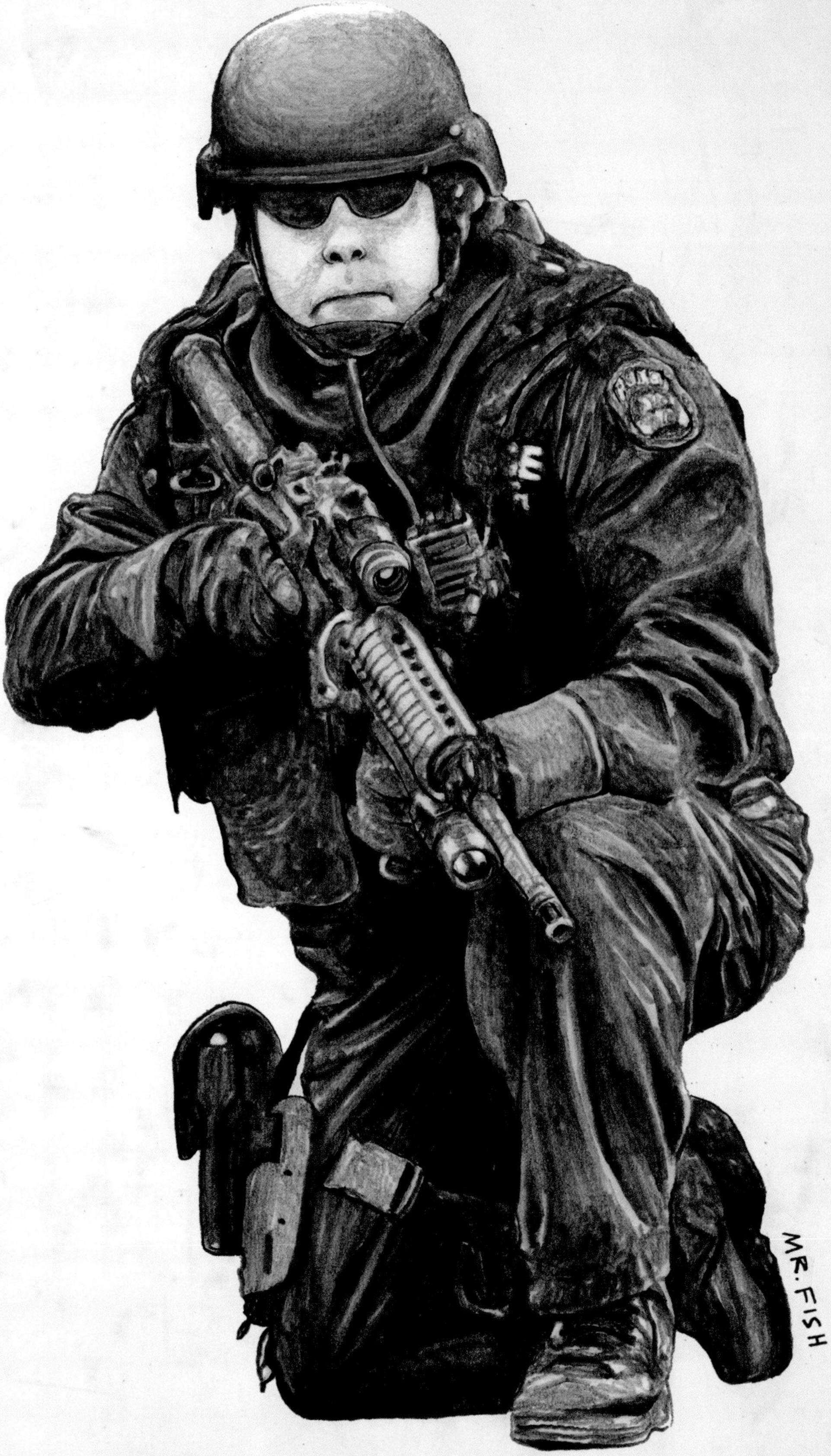
MR. FISH

AGAINST THE FIRST AMENDMENT

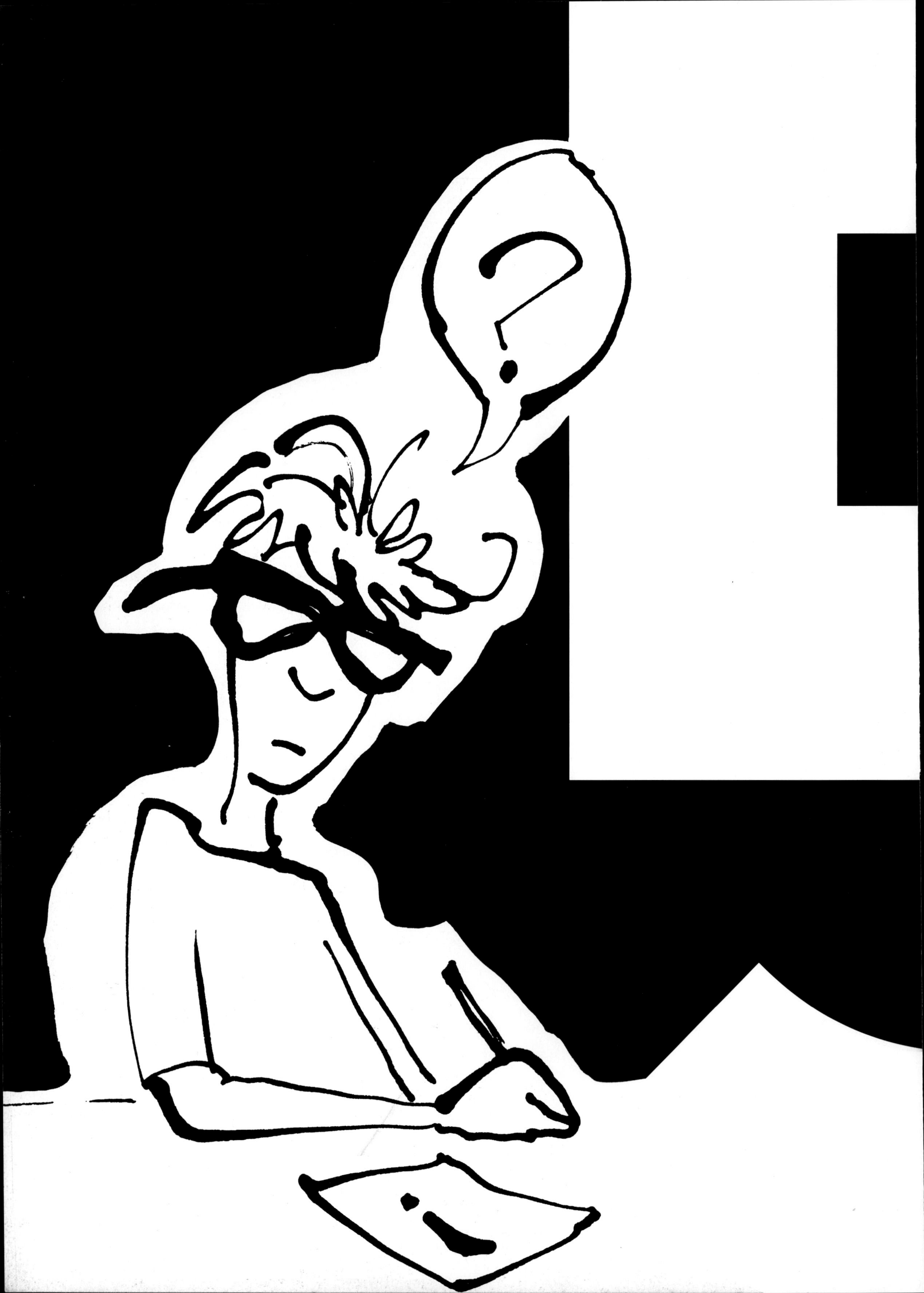

NUDE IN BLACK AND WHITE

Nude in Black and White

WHILE VISITING THE Smithsonian National Air and Space Museum in Washington, D.C., at age 11, I found out that the transparent bubble on a warplane from which a gunner fires his machine gun is called a blister. This seemed somehow appropriately unsettling, as if any aircraft misappropriated for the purpose of wreaking havoc on the soft gooey insides of human beings would, as a matter of cosmic jurisprudence, end up being covered with welts and vesications. It was like cirrhosis being visited upon an alcoholic, or syphilis upon a whore, this sudden appearance of gigantic, non-aerodynamic blisters on the lower back and belly and ass of an airplane made morally corrupt by a bug-eyed addiction to violence. Had I visited the museum only a year previously, I might've been less attuned to the engineering specifics of military aggression, preferring instead to while away the afternoon lolling around the Apollo 11 command module or gazing up at the silver underside of the Spirit of St. Louis and reveling in the pride and optimism once promised to America by famed Nazi sympathizer and eugenics enthusiast Charles Lindbergh. As it happened, however, I had recently been shown a tattered photograph of actress Susan Dey without a shirt on and my priorities had changed.

The picture, which showed every evidence that it had been burglarized with great haste from a magazine and passed around so rapaciously by the entire sixth grade that its texture had become less like paper and more like chiffon, depicted Laurie Partridge herself laying topless on an unmade bed, her mouth like a tiny bow, her pert breasts like upturned teacups, her nipples as pointy as rosebuds squeezed from a pastry bag. As base and vulgar as this description might seem to me now, there was no other way for an 11-year-old to process a naked woman as there was a newness to the female anatomy then that made objectification just another 15-letter-word that like health insurance, I'd eventually get around to caring about. That said, upon seeing the image in 1977, which I would later find out was a still from a movie called *First Love*, my politics aligned in an instant with those espoused by the character that Dey portrayed on TV. As if suddenly freed from the confines of a very dark cave, I found myself groping to gather the light that was Laurie Partridge's corny pacifism and unconvincing feminism and cheerful dedication to social justice for refuge in my soul, assuming that only a fellow hippie would ever be given access to what I knew existed beneath her fringed and floral poncho.

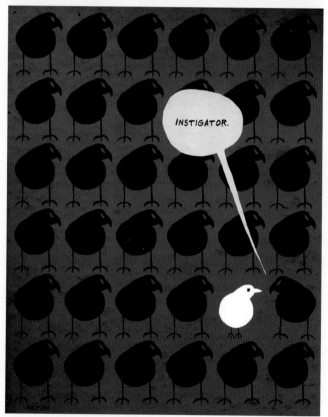

I thought about Susan Dey and blisters and being a hippie last Thursday when I found myself driving around outside the Air and Space Museum looking for a place to park. I was in D.C. for the purpose of lending my body and rancor to the Occupy Wall Street protesters gathering in Freedom Plaza for their first day of rabble-rousing. I was traveling alone—everybody else I knew had to work—and I couldn't wait to engage with likeminded strangers and experience the unique thrill that

THE EMPIRE HAS NO CLOTHES

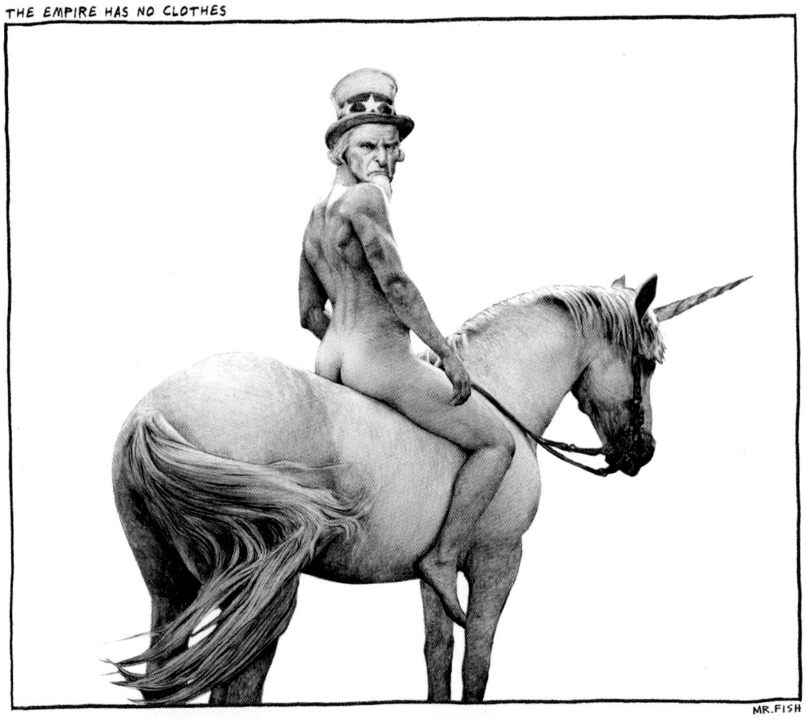
MR.FISH

comes from finding camaraderie among beatific and morally anchored interlopers. "What—?!" shouted my wife through the earpiece on my cellphone, her voice made teeny and metallic by the wafer-thin technology I held in my hand.

"I'm lost!" I shouted back above the cacophony of car and foot traffic surrounding me. "I thought I'd see other protesters carrying signs and sleeping bags and just follow them," I said, looking this way and that, "but there's nobody like that—just assholes in suits!"

"I can't hear you!" she hollered.

"Where's Freedom Plaza?!" I screamed.

"Friedman?!"

"Freedom! FREEDOM!" I said, turning heads with my inadvertent channeling of famed anti-Semite and red-faced, Jesus-loving misogynist Mel Gibson.

After being directed remotely to the protest site by my wife, who guided my trajectory expertly from a windowless room a hundred miles away, I passed through an archway at the southeast corner of Freedom Plaza that was made from a pair of papier-mâché RQ-1 Predator drones mounted on long poles, the irony of the parallelism too ham-fisted for me to appreciate. For the next two hours, I read homemade signs and chuckled at sloganeering T-shirts and spoke with revolutionaries about doomsday, foreclosure and what tomorrow should look like, listening peripherally to event organizers and enraged speakers shout into a microphone from the makeshift stage and reconfigure Marx and Debs and Guthrie into cheap rhymes and bumper sticker shorthand. "Wall Street executives are nothing but a bunch of bullies!" shrieked a bearded 30-year-old who was skinny enough to have his posture affected by the weight of his gigantic glasses. "And bullies are big! And they're mean!" he concluded, giving everybody in the audience the chance to cheer and pump their fists into the air in contempt of all the team captains in grammar school who chose them last for kickball. Cameras biopsied the scene from every angle, creating the uneasy feeling that many of the participants were not really participants at all and, instead, were spectators hoping to get a contact high from the small number of real hell-raisers trying with all their might to recast this *Fuck You* Mardi Gras against modernity, itself, into a culturally viable sit-in against rich white people, specifically.

There was a pissed-off Santa Claus in a putrid red velvet suit at the north end of the square, speaking in solidarity with the protesters yet addressing them with disdain, as if they were rabbits in his garden. "America is a fascist/corporatist state!" he spat, his big spooky old-man hands going every which way. "There hasn't been any truth in this goddamn country ever since November the twenty-second, nineteen-hundred and sixty-three!" Then he started singing "God Bless America," insisting that everybody join in.

There were Photoshopped posters of Barack Obama wearing a Hitler mustache, Benjamin Netanyahu wearing a Hitler mustache, Hillary Clinton wearing a Hitler mustache, Sarah Palin wearing a Hitler mustache, Bill O'Reilly wearing a Hitler mustache and, for those trapped in a nostalgia for simpler times, Dick Cheney and George W. Bush wearing Hitler mustaches, the little black square having become the progressives' most destructive boomeranging metaphor—a rallying cry, really, for those who prefer the big bang of moronomy over the subtle pop of irony.

There were tourists from West Palm Beach and Buffalo and St. Paul cutting through the plaza with pinched faces and raging telepathy that said, "How dare you filthy beatniks ruin our vacations by corrupting our concept of what Washington, D.C., is supposed to signify by exercising the First Amendment rights deemed sacred by every single statue and monument in town!"

There was no nuance as far as the eye could see.

"Did you ever wonder why there aren't any songs about peace on the radio?" I heard someone say over the rally's PA system as I made my way across the street, having spotted a Starbucks whose Wi-Fi signal I was hoping to cop for free through the glass. "It's because all the radios are owned by corporations!" said the voice, inciting the crowd to go apeshit with booing, many of them wearing T-shirts adorned with peace signs from Walmart and Old Navy and Urban Outfitters. Locking eyes on the wide lip of an enormous concrete planter where I noticed an empty space in between two Wall Street protesters typing on laptops, I quickened my pace, motivated by a sudden impulse to re-examine a photograph taken 67 years ago near Papua New Guinea in the South Pacific during the Second World War. "Corporations hate peace and that's why you don't hear Pete Seeger and Peter, Paul and Mary on the radio anymore!" The lone yelp of approval told me that half the audience was too young to know who Pete Seeger and Peter, Paul and Mary were and the other half seemed reluctant to throw their vocal support behind a movement that was demanding to see the safe return of "Guantanamera" and "Stewball" to commercial radio.

There's a famous black-and-white picture taken in 1944 by *Time/Life* photographer Horace Bristol of a naked PBY blister gunner during a rescue operation in Rabaul Bay. The young Navy gunner is unnamed and photographed from the back, his slim build much more gazelle-like than bull, the inhibition expressed in his body language reminiscent of the boy bathers in Thomas Eakins' 1885 masterpiece, *The Swimming Hole*. Tiny droplets of either sweat or seawater cling to the sailor's shoulders, back and in a sublime patch of sunlight gathering in a graceful swoop at the top of his ass crack. His hair is mussed and he is wearing headphones, the wartime sky seen through the giant blister that he occupies alive with the lethal bumblebees of Japanese antiaircraft fire.

Most remarkable to me about the photograph is how well it depicts the bewitching vulnerability of a human body. Here

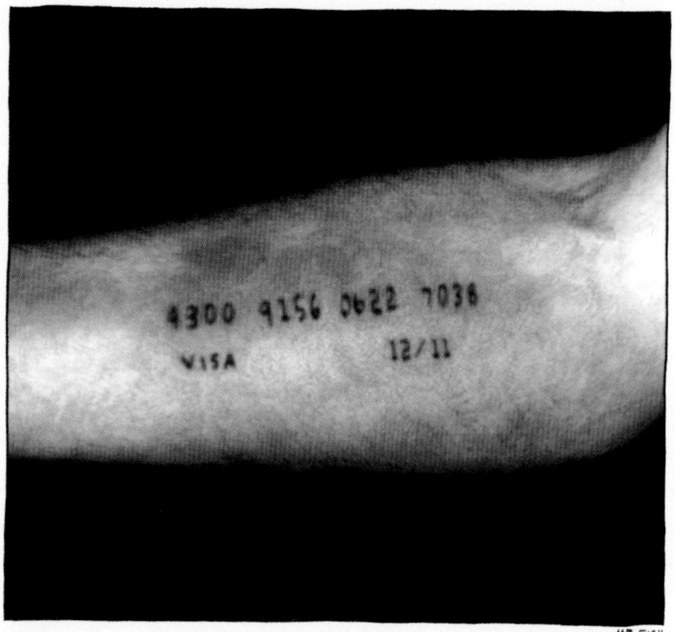
4300 9156 0622 7036
VISA 12/11
MR. FISH

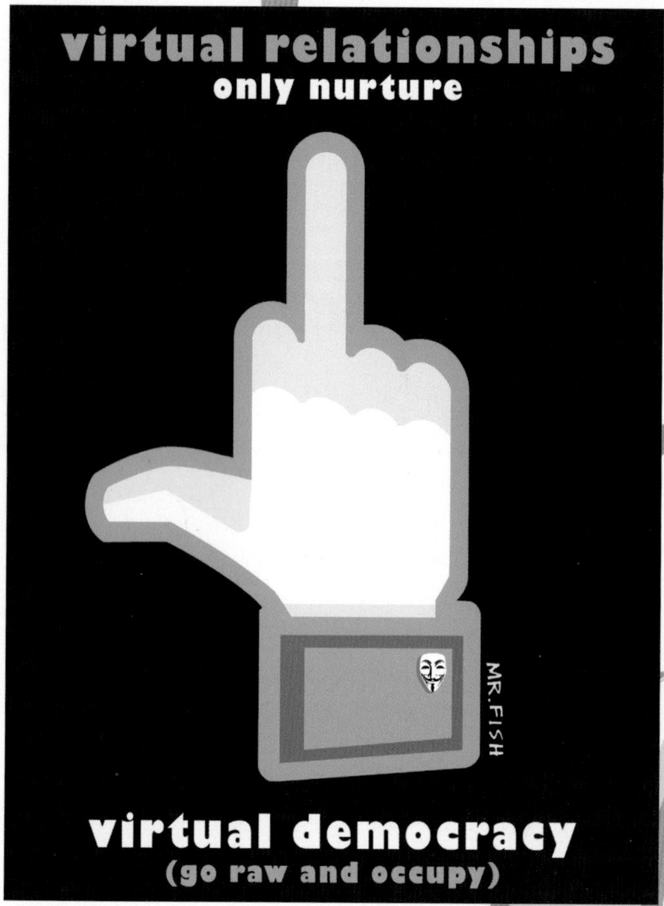
virtual relationships
only nurture
MR. FISH
virtual democracy
(go raw and occupy)

is this naked kid, no doubt thousands of miles away from his home, caged inside the ghoulish skeleton of a giant metal machine designed to both stave off and initiate the most brutal sort of mass cruelty devised by modern man, yet his political affiliations and religious convictions and cultural prejudices are rendered completely inconsequential by the tenderness of his age and the beauty of his skin and the fragility of his predicament. His existence, like the stark honesty of his physique, is elemental and harrowing and tenuous without requiring either corroboration from the intellect or rationale from some bureaucratic narrative to make sense, forcing the viewer's own human vulnerabilities to be likewise exposed and made precious and beautiful by association.

This, to me, was poetry and a much more convincing call to universal amity than Bob Gruen's photograph of John Lennon flashing the peace sign in front of the Statue of Liberty or Alberto Korda's iconic picture of Che Guevara scanning the horizon for the red dawn. For me, there has always been a huge difference between seeking inspiration on how to experience life through poetry versus searching for clear instruction on how to live life through religion or politics or economics.

"All right, losers! Either buy something or get out of here!" said a Starbucks thug waving us off the concrete planter like we were pigeons. "Go use the Internet at McDonald's!" he said, looking just as tattooed and pierced and disenfranchised as the protesters he was shooing away. I slid my computer back into my bag and returned to Freedom Plaza, remembering something Noam Chomsky said in 1967 when asked about Bob Dylan's perceived abandonment of the protest movements of the day: "If the capitalist PR machine wanted to invent someone for their purposes, they couldn't have made a better choice [than Bob Dylan]." What Dylan's detractors failed to recognize then, and maybe they still do, is how hard it is to find a rhyme for *antiestablishmentarianism* when you're trying to create art that warms the heart and feeds the soul and gives a person more than just an expert opinion upon which to rely when facing down self-righteousness.

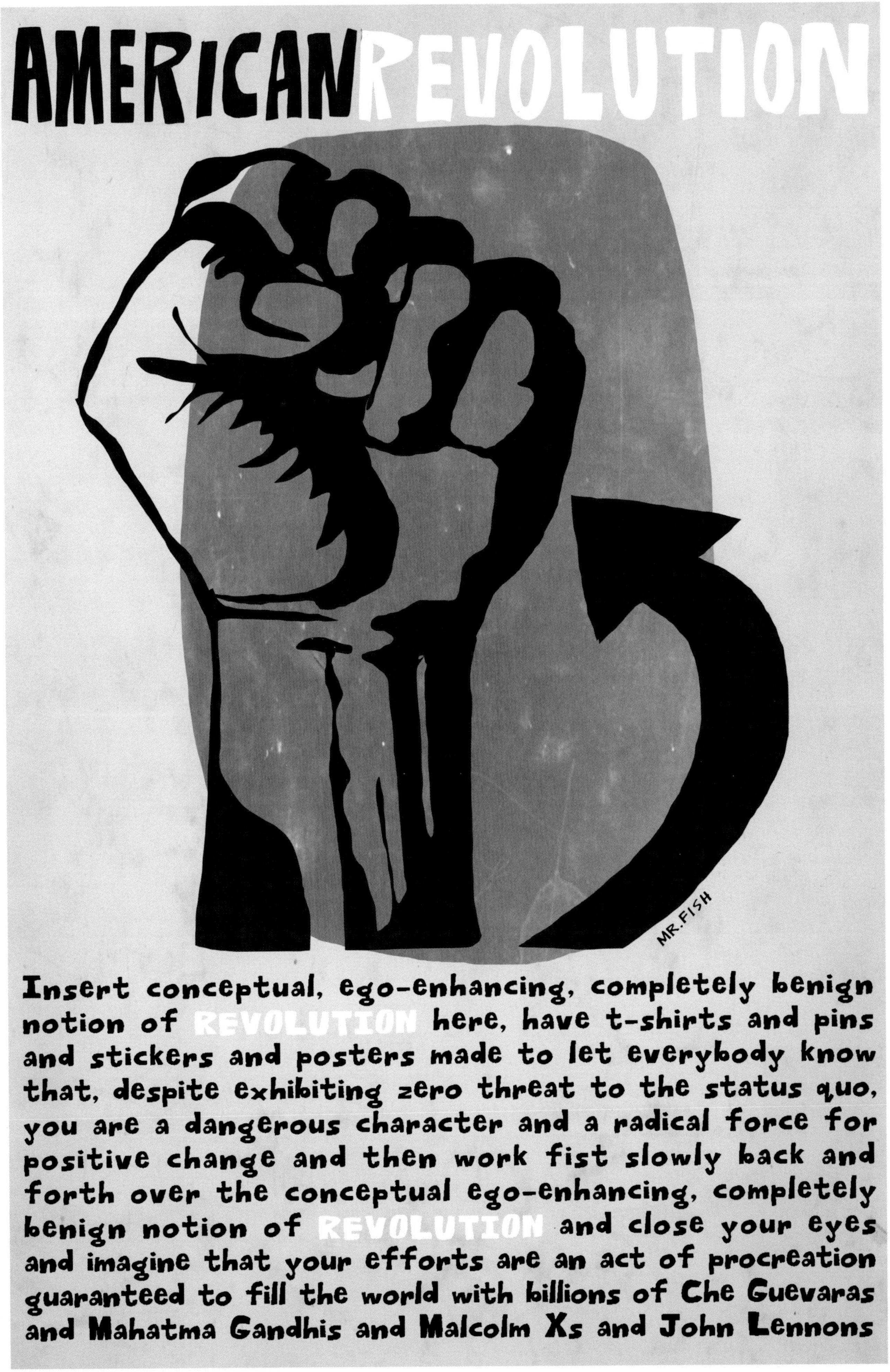
AMERICAN REVOLUTION
MR.FISH
Insert conceptual, ego-enhancing, completely benign notion of REVOLUTION here, have t-shirts and pins and stickers and posters made to let everybody know that, despite exhibiting zero threat to the status quo, you are a dangerous character and a radical force for positive change and then work fist slowly back and forth over the conceptual ego-enhancing, completely benign notion of REVOLUTION and close your eyes and imagine that your efforts are an act of procreation guaranteed to fill the world with billions of Che Guevaras and Mahatma Gandhis and Malcolm Xs and John Lennons

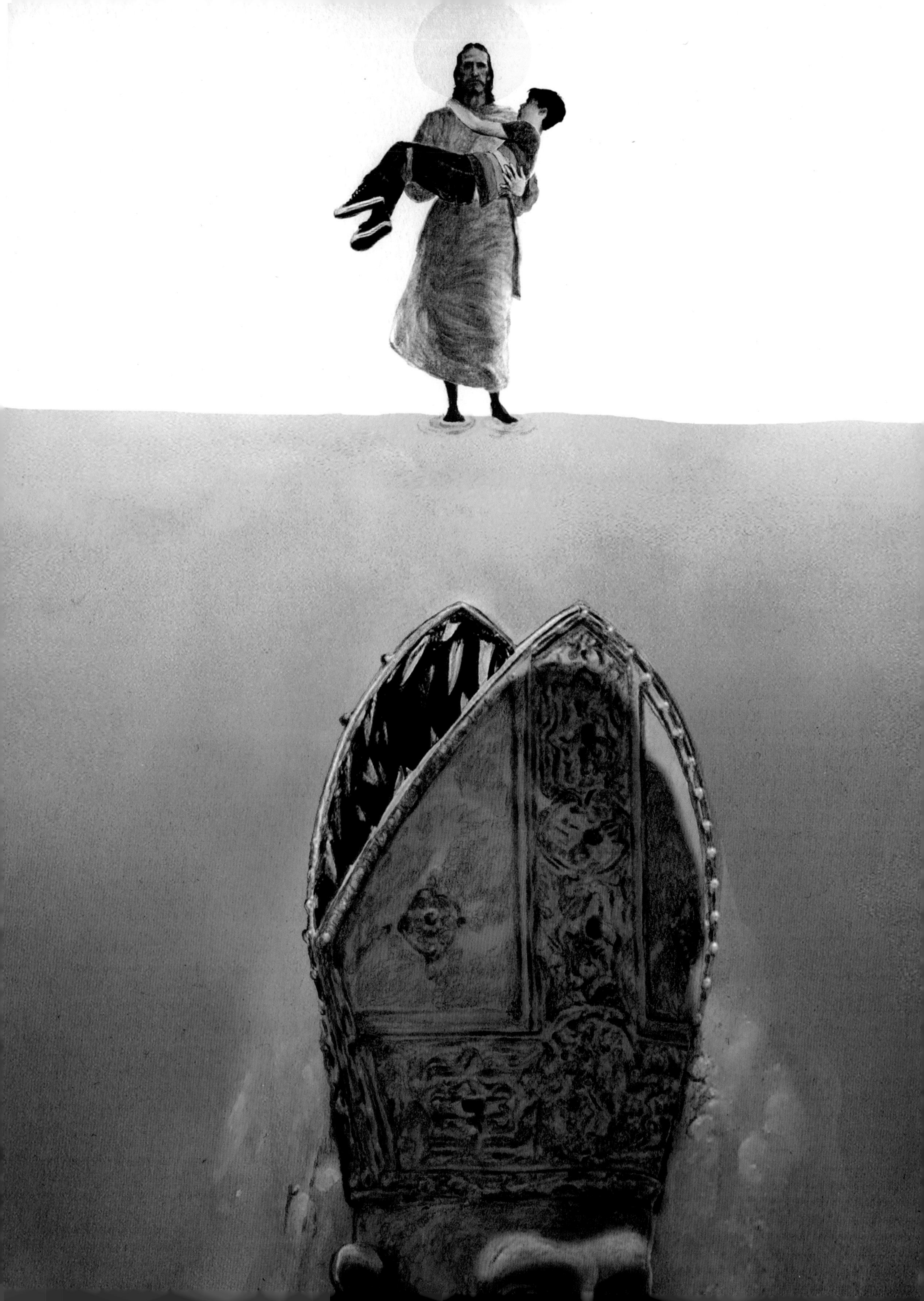

CARTOON CAPTION CONTEST

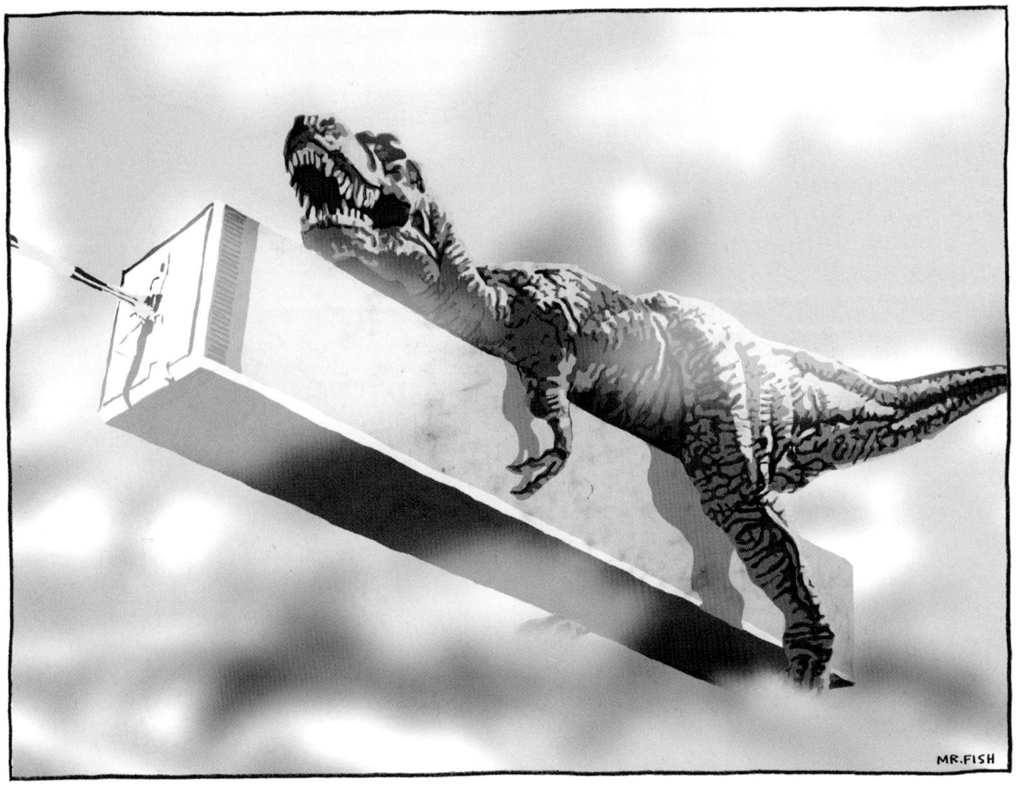
MR.FISH

"Tyrannosaurus Rex Fucking One of the Twin Towers in Heaven."
Gladys O'Harris, Maple Lake, Mn.

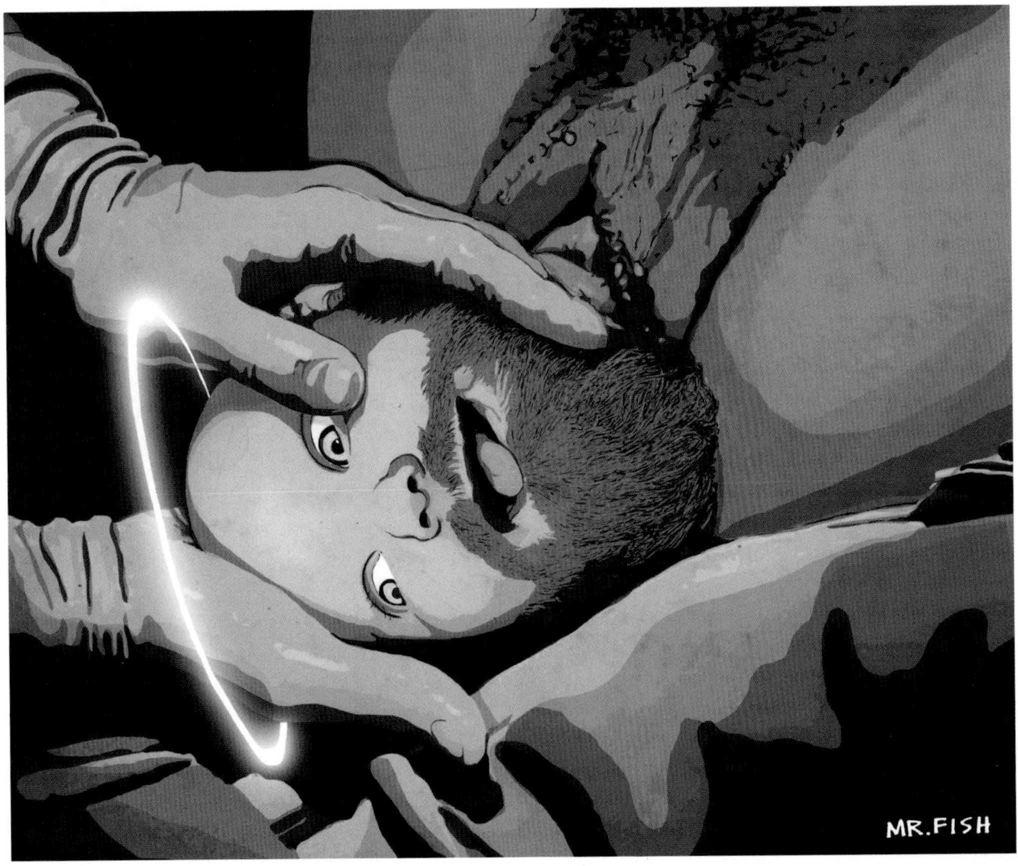
MR.FISH

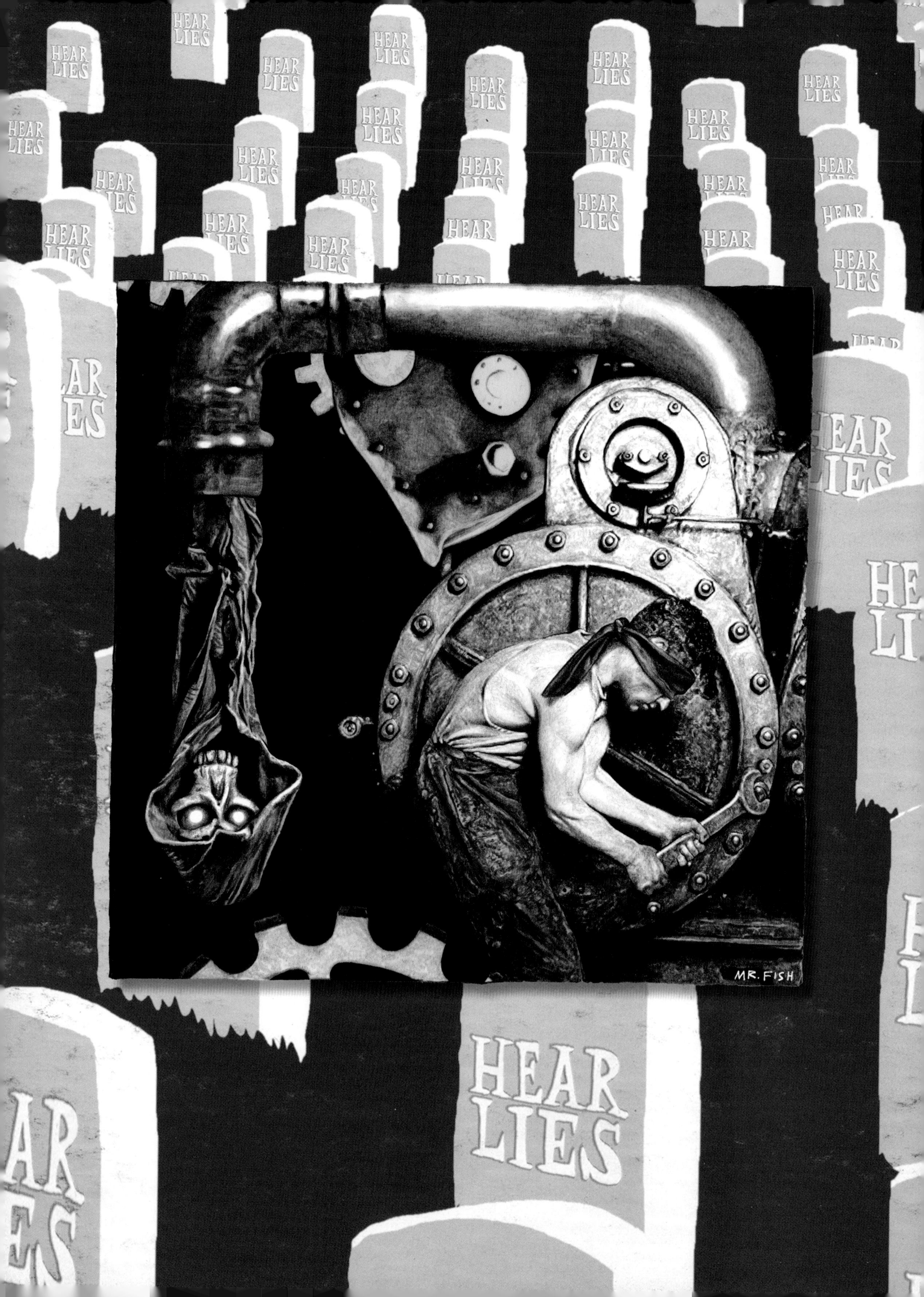
HEAR LIES
MR. FISH

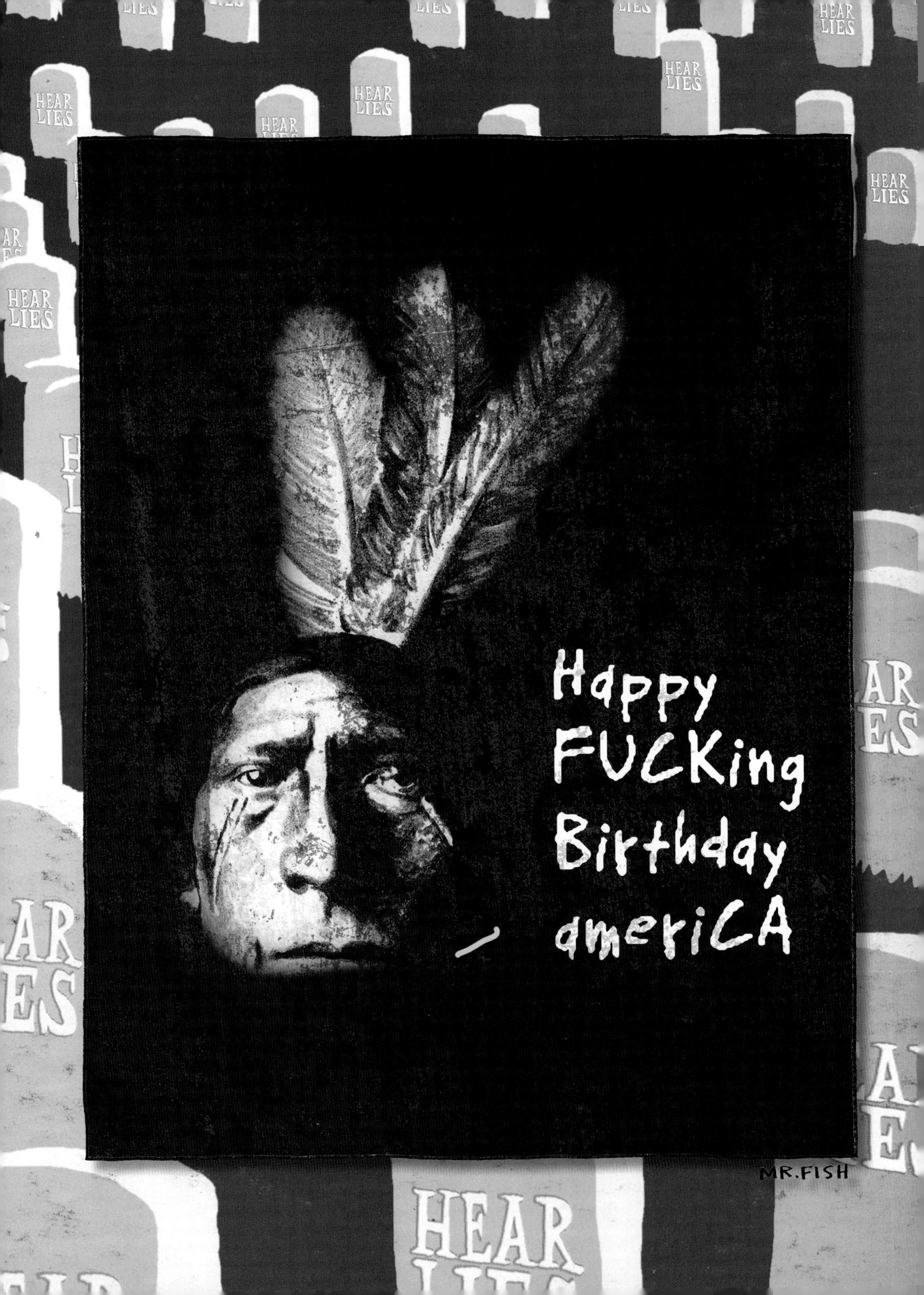
HEAR LIES
Happy FUCKing Birthday americA
MR.FISH

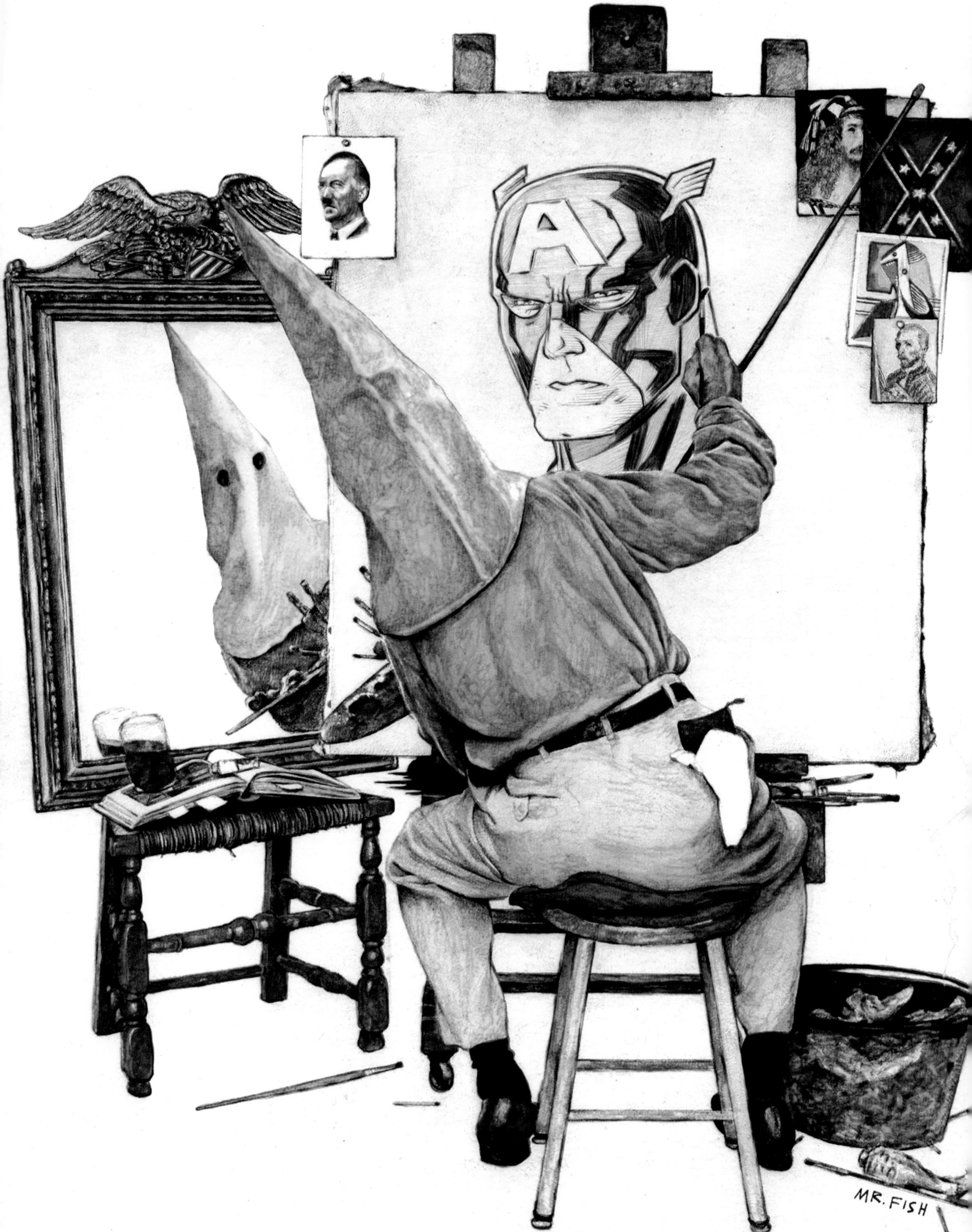
MR. FISH

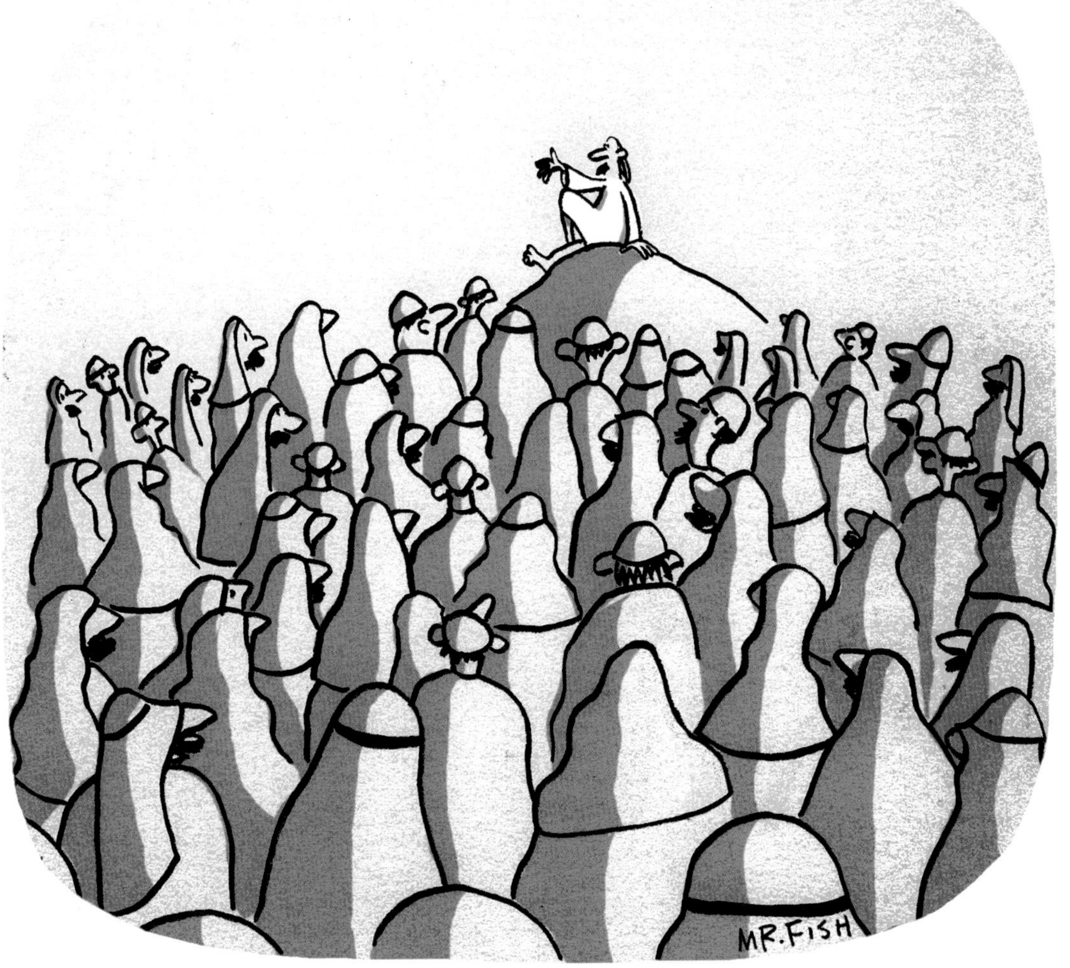
MR.FISH

". . . so go fucking be nice to each other."

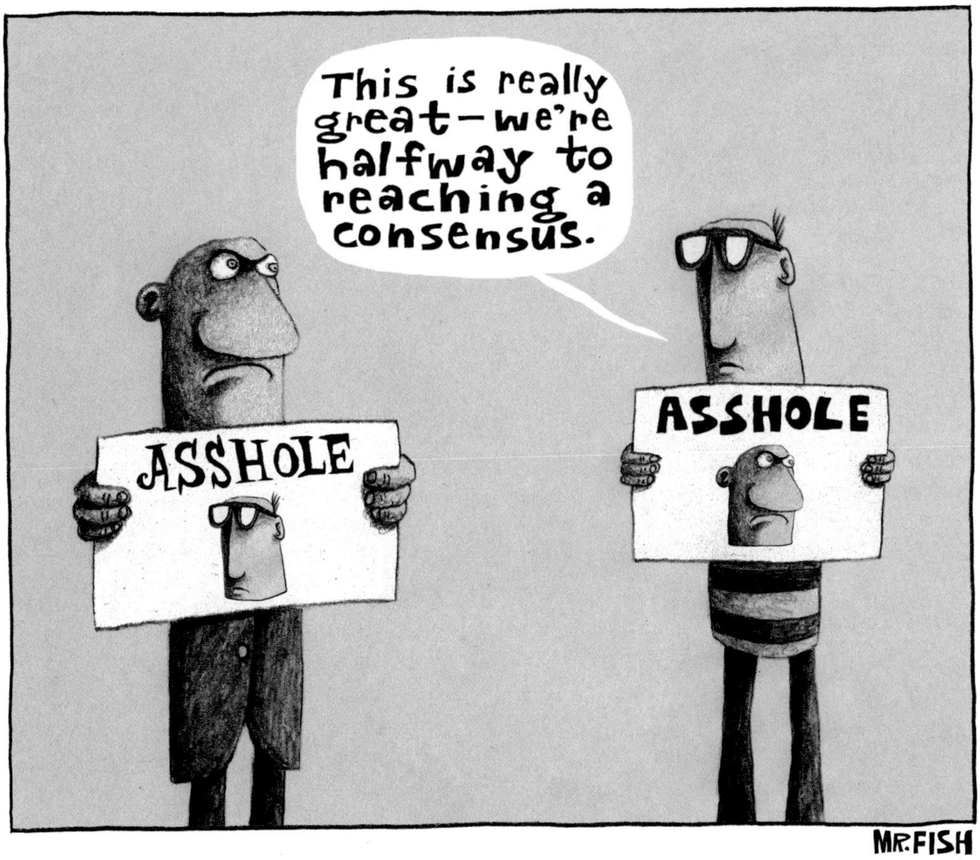
This is really great—we're halfway to reaching a consensus.
ASSHOLE
ASSHOLE
MR.FISH

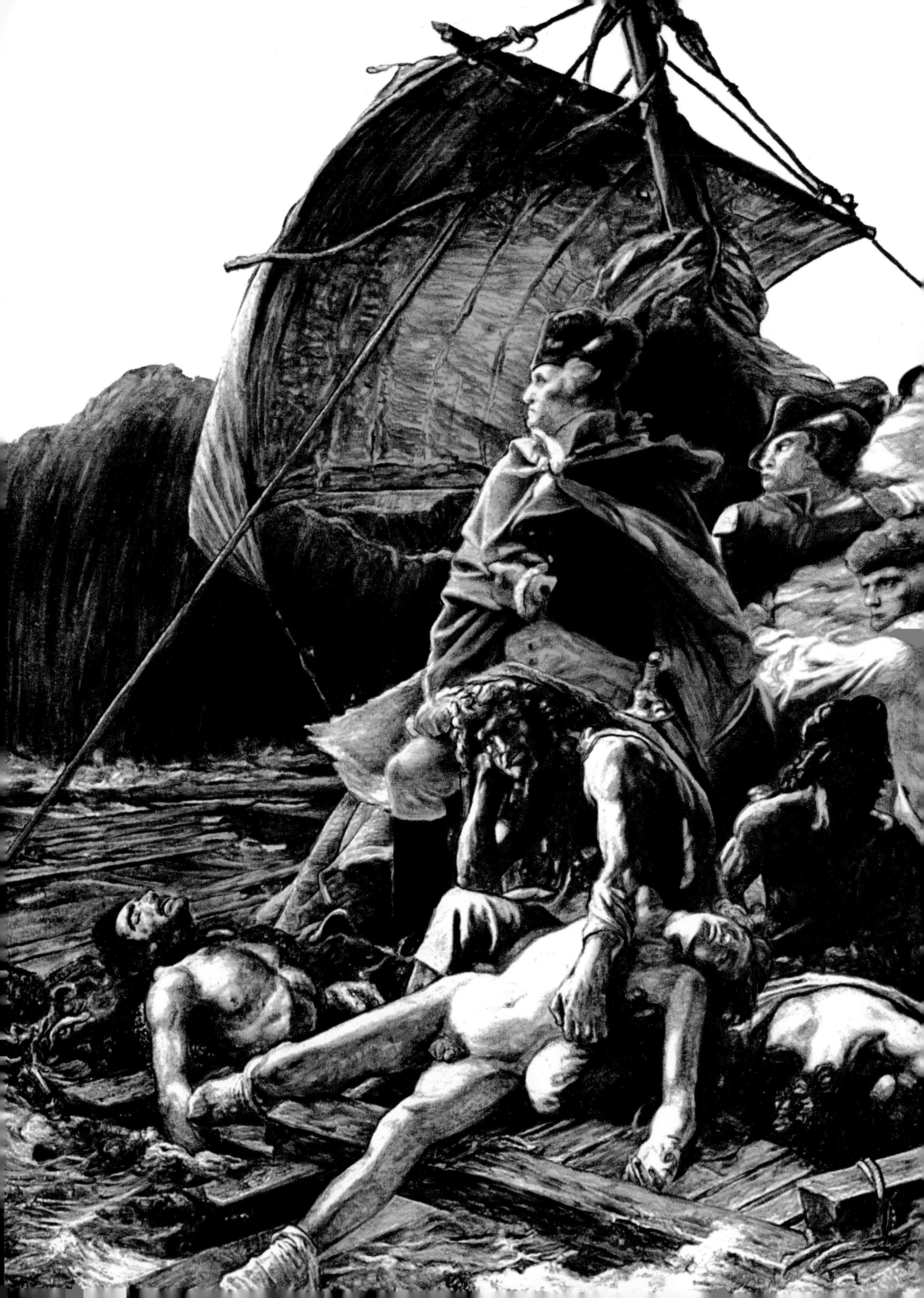

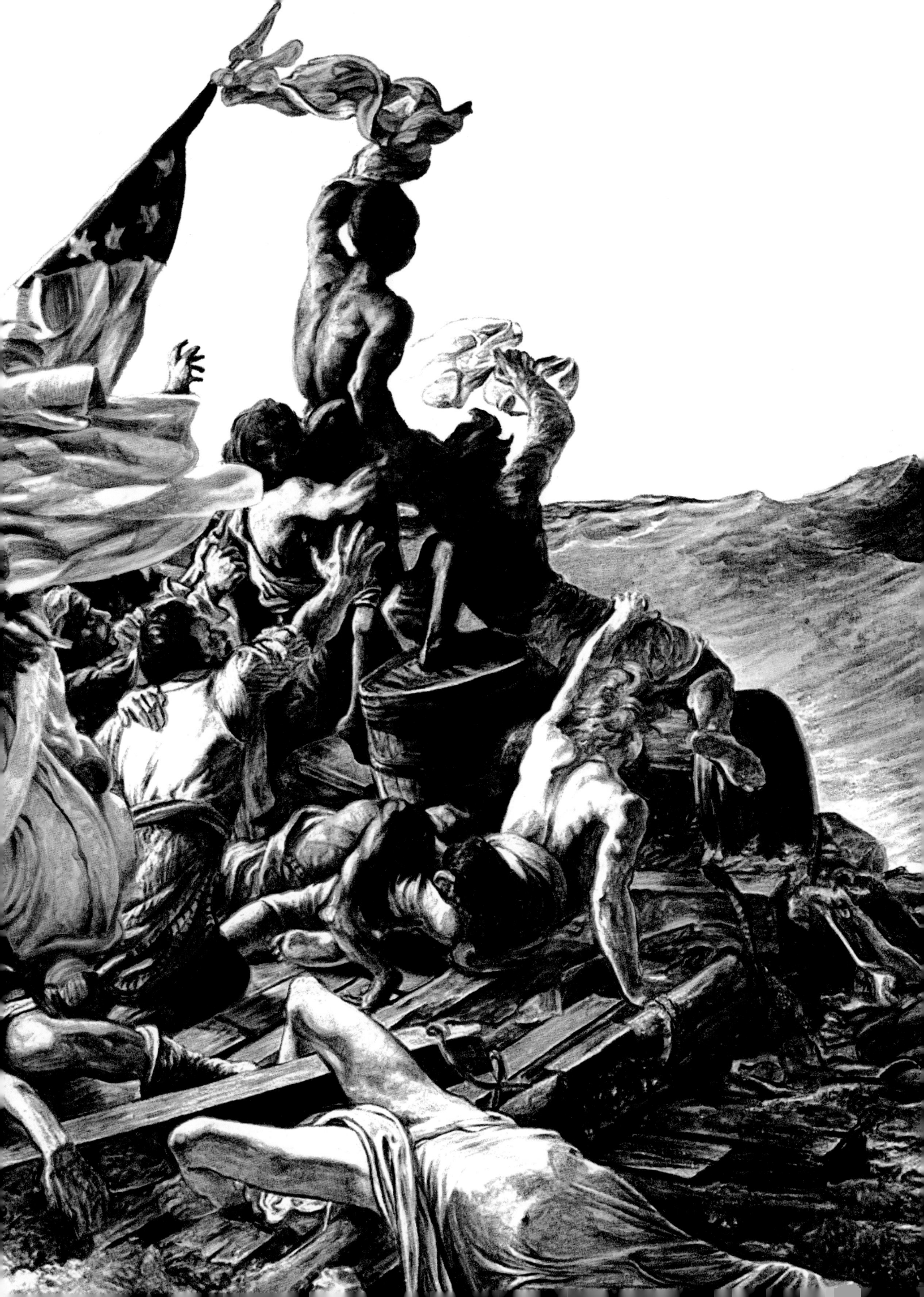

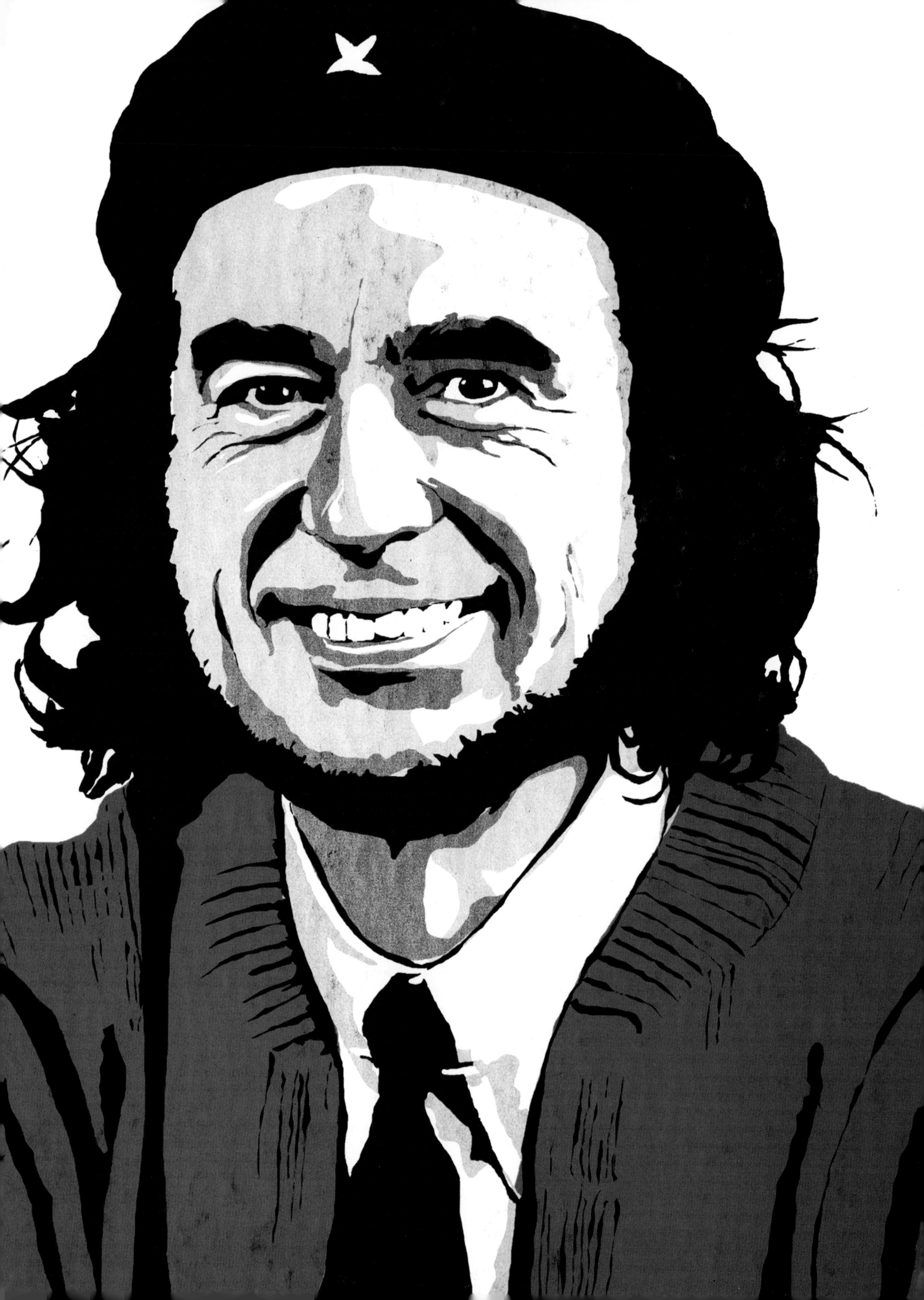

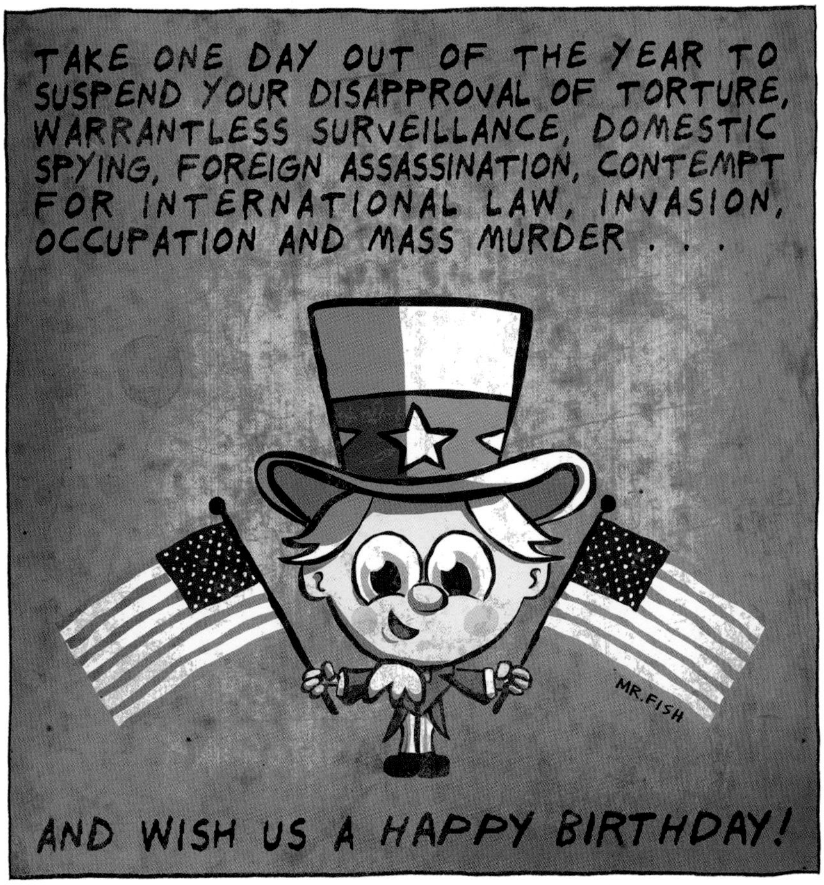
TAKE ONE DAY OUT OF THE YEAR TO SUSPEND YOUR DISAPPROVAL OF TORTURE, WARRANTLESS SURVEILLANCE, DOMESTIC SPYING, FOREIGN ASSASSINATION, CONTEMPT FOR INTERNATIONAL LAW, INVASION, OCCUPATION AND MASS MURDER . . .
MR. FISH
AND WISH US A HAPPY BIRTHDAY!

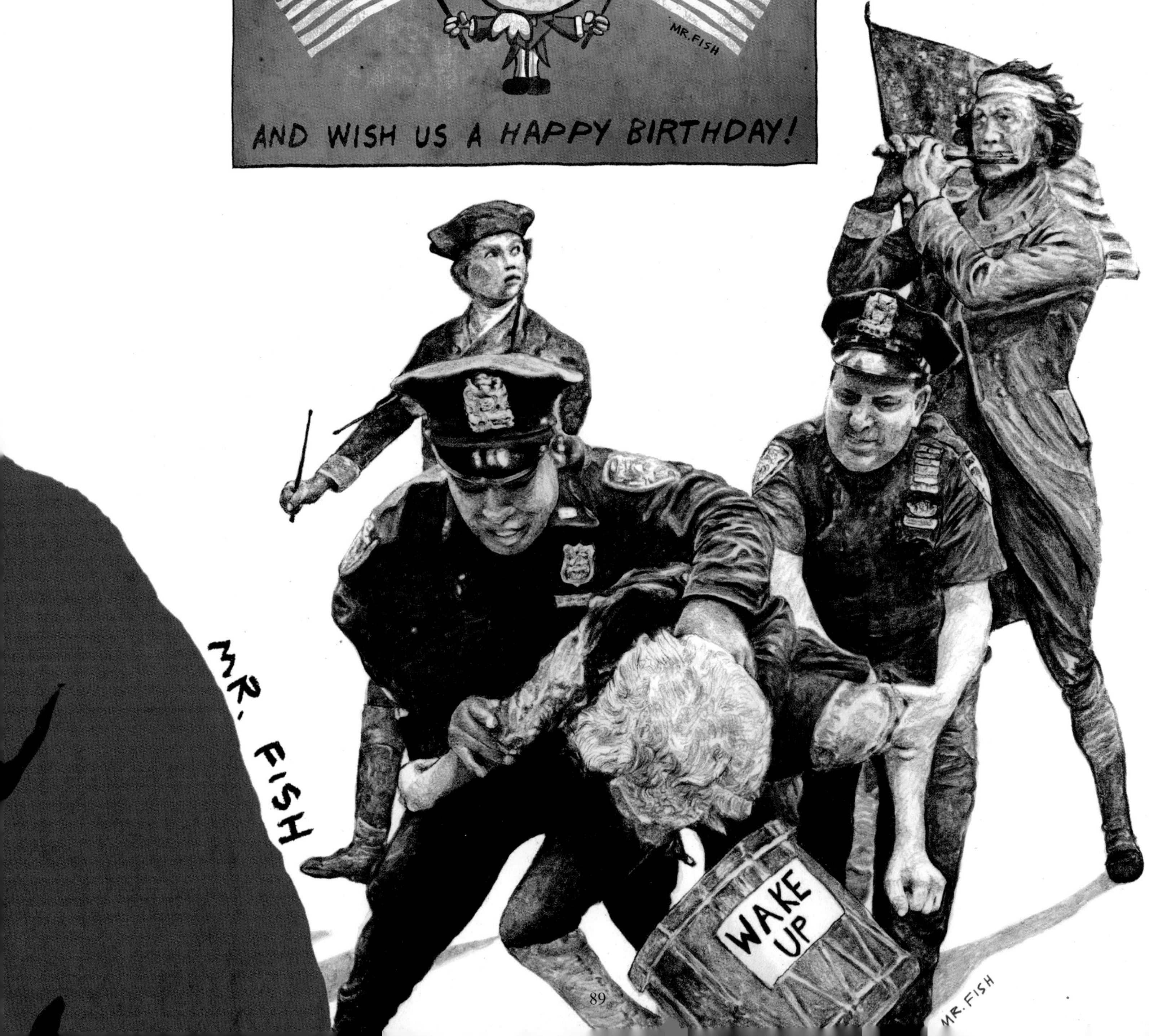
MR. FISH
WAKE UP
MR. FISH

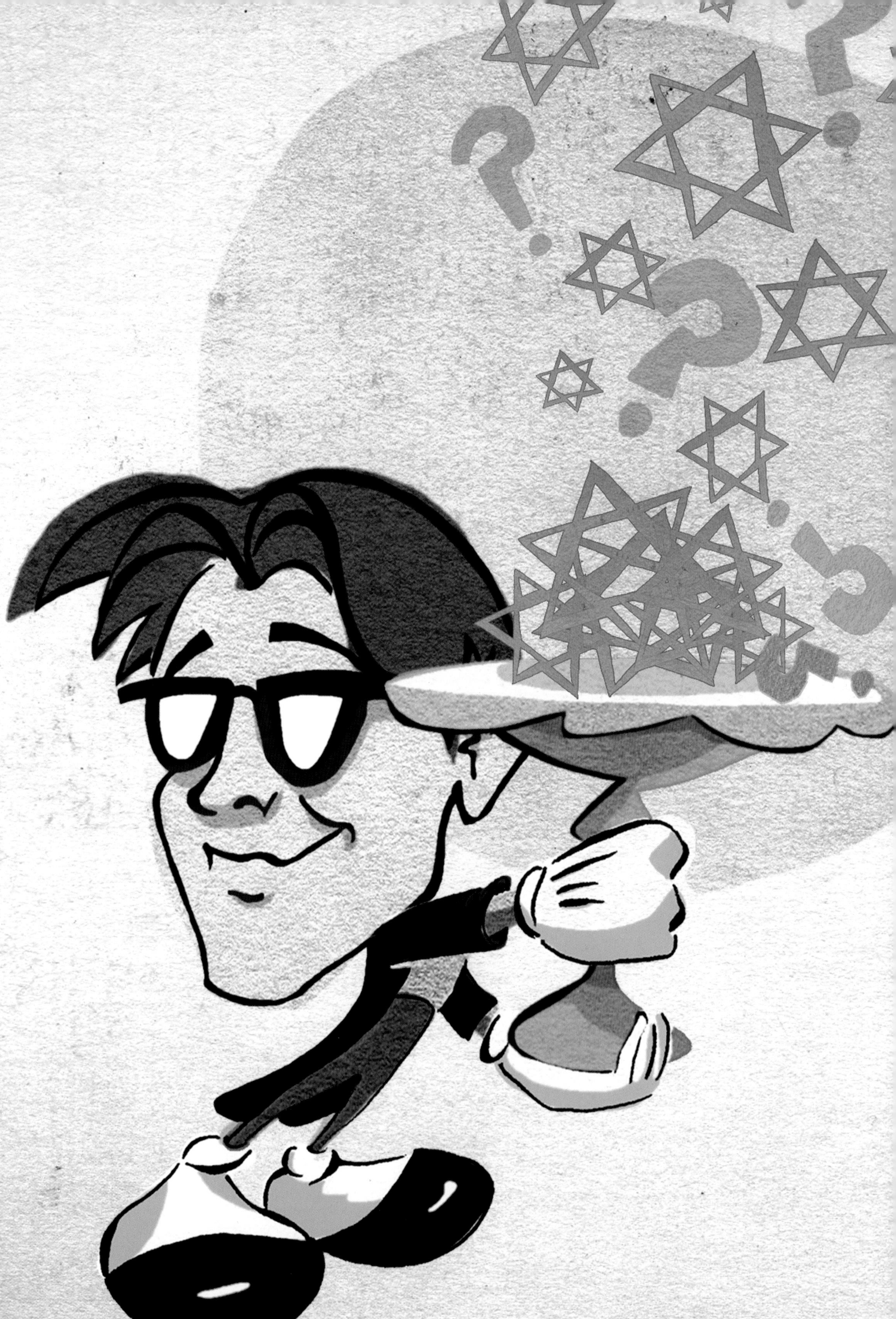

6

When Jewish upon a Star

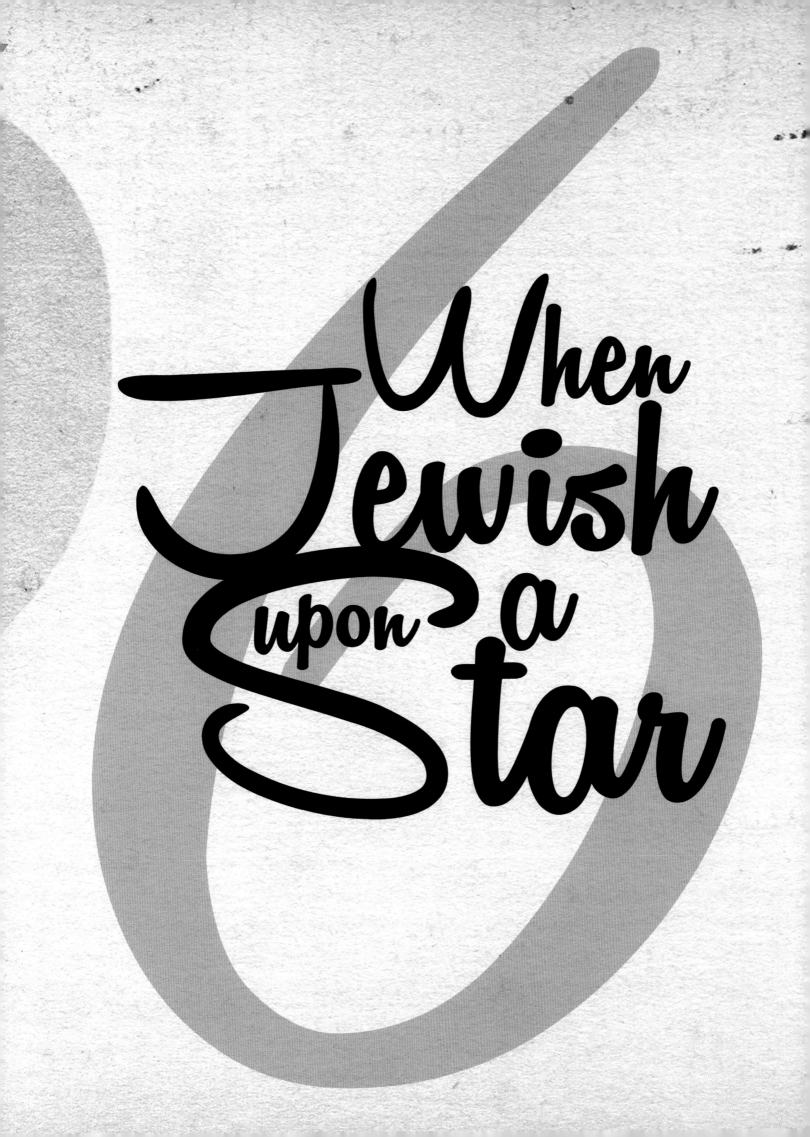

When Jewish Upon a Star

THE VOICE ON the other end of the telephone needed to make sure that I was 21. I wasn't. "I'm 22," I said, lying, figuring that 19 might as well be 22 and, anyway, this was a comedy club that I was scheduling an audition for, not the Moonlite Bunny Ranch or the FBI.

My heroes at the time were Woody Allen, Jackie Mason, Philip Roth, Neil Simon, Irving Howe, Erich Fromm, Allen Ginsberg, Arthur Miller, Abraham Maslow, S. J. Perelman, Paul Krassner, Abbie Hoffman and Groucho Marx. I'd decided, over the previous 18 months while slowly dripping out of college, that if I was ever going to succeed as a Jewish comedian and writer I needed to stop being a South Jersey Protestant virgin Fine Arts major at Rutgers University with Han Solo hair and Top-Siders and move to New York to have my inner David Cassidy exorcised from my soul, kneed in the stomach and beaten with a rusty paint bucket somewhere in Boro Park or Crown Heights.

My fascination with Judaism began when I was 12, right around the time I decided the tribe that I belonged to—the one with the John Wayne narration, the street address of *Downtown Disney: Reality in 3-Quarter Scale Facade!* and the bizarre Ameri-Christian logic, call it blatant *nepotism*, that had cast super-WASP Charlton Heston in the role of Moses—was neither honest nor intellectually curious enough to reflect the truth of existence nor the dark complexities of the human experience.

Judaism, on the other hand, as evidenced by several thousand years of recorded history and vast amounts of art and literature and kvetching, seemed to thrive on a tradition of critical self-analysis as opposed to the self-glorification of Technicolored Anglo-Saxonism. In fact, after a rather intense week over Christmas vacation in which I'd devoured *Der Antichrist* by Friedrich Nietzsche, *The Future of an Illusion* by Sigmund Freud and both *Night* and *The Trial of God* by Elie Wiesel, I suddenly realized that the atheistic evangelism that I so naturally gravitated toward was not only not wholly scientific, but actually found many of its most prominent champions and sympathizers, including Baruch Spinoza, Emma Goldman, Jacques Derrida and Karl Marx, coming from Jewish origins.

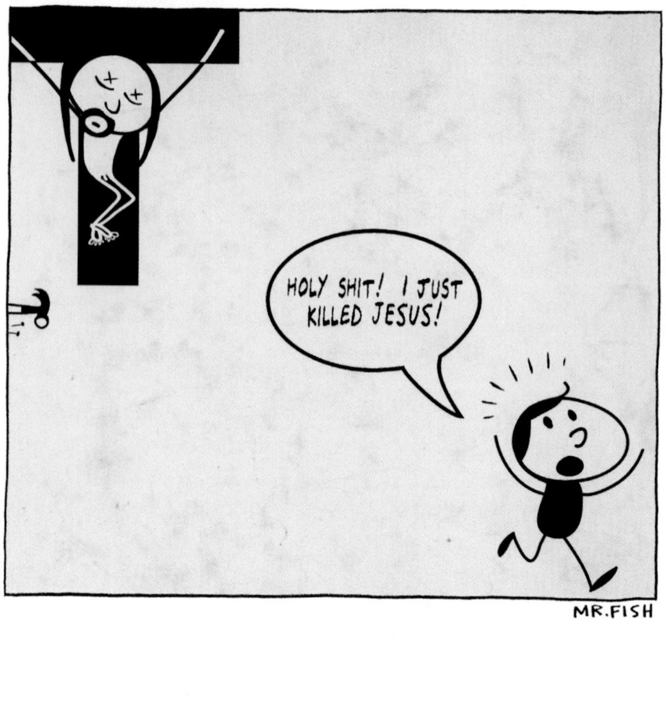
HOLY SHIT! I JUST KILLED JESUS!
MR.FISH

Even among theists who practiced the religion, rabbis included, skepticism and rigorous debate seemed to prevent the junking up of Judaism with all the superfluous voodoo and super and subhuman mascots and harrowingly hierarchical idolatry exemplified by other religions, such as Catholicism, Consumer Capitalism and Fascism.

Every day people are straying away from the church and going back to God. —Lenny Bruce

"You know, they're probably going to have to take some skin off the back of your legs for this," said my friend, Derek, one day after school while thumbing through the Yellow Pages in search of a plastic surgeon. I was at his house, as I was most afternoons, drinking a highball glass of NyQuil, which I was doing only because his parents were out and it was almost New Year's and he was driving. I had been complaining about the size of my nose all day long, saying that I wished I had a bigger one, something more Semitic and less Debbie Reynolds, and he was tired of hearing about it.

"I don't know why they can't make one bigger," I said. "They make boobs bigger, for Chrissake!" Then Derek made the comment about the extra skin. Then I changed my mind.

"Are you sure?" asked Derek. "Don't you want to be a bigger boob?"

You should have your anti-Semitic head blown off, you fucking piece of dog shit!!!! That was just one of the many suggestions made by one of the people thoughtful enough to email me in January 2009 in response to a cartoon that I'd posted online depicting Holocaust survivors holding up signs in support of the 1,000-plus Palestinians killed during what the Israelis called *Operation Cast Lead* and what the Arab world called the *Gaza Massacre*. Who better to speak in solidarity with an oppressed and quarantined and sadistically tortured population, I figured, than another famously and morbidly oppressed and quarantined and sadistically tortured population, the ethnicity of either population being grossly unimportant in the face of their common humanity?

Even my older brother, Jeff, was emailing me, although the subject of his correspondence had less to do with defending the actions of Israel and more to do with the resistance tactics of Hamas, which had been firing hundreds of Qassam rockets into Southern Israel in retaliation against the IDF's never-ending siege of Gaza—rockets that had killed, from 2000 to 2009, 22 Israelis, prompting me to wonder how devastating the retaliation might've been had Hamas been launching corn dogs instead, knowing that heart disease is responsible for killing upward of 600,000 people every year.

Jeff (via email): I guess this is what we're seeing, the final, horrible, inexcusable but typical final stages of a war. To quote Gandhi: "I object to violence because when it appears to do good, the good is only temporary; the evil it does is permanent." Hamas fights on, Israel fights on, the evil it does is permanent.

Dwayne (via email): *I'm not sure I agree with the idea that what's happening between the Israelis and the Palestinians is the end of a war. Let me bring in some other parallels to consider. Prior to the Stonewall Riots, many in the gay movement felt completely ineffectual and hopeless as a population.*

Continuously mistreated and culturally categorized as perverts and, quite literally, seen as being subhuman, gays by and large existed in varying degrees of real misery (depending on the geography) and were forced to perpetuate their own invisibility by remaining subservient to the prejudice that imprisoned them. Returning violence to the police and vice officers galvanized the movement in such a way that could've only been achieved through violence—it showed the world that there are genuine consequences for those who, both literally and figuratively, live by the sword.

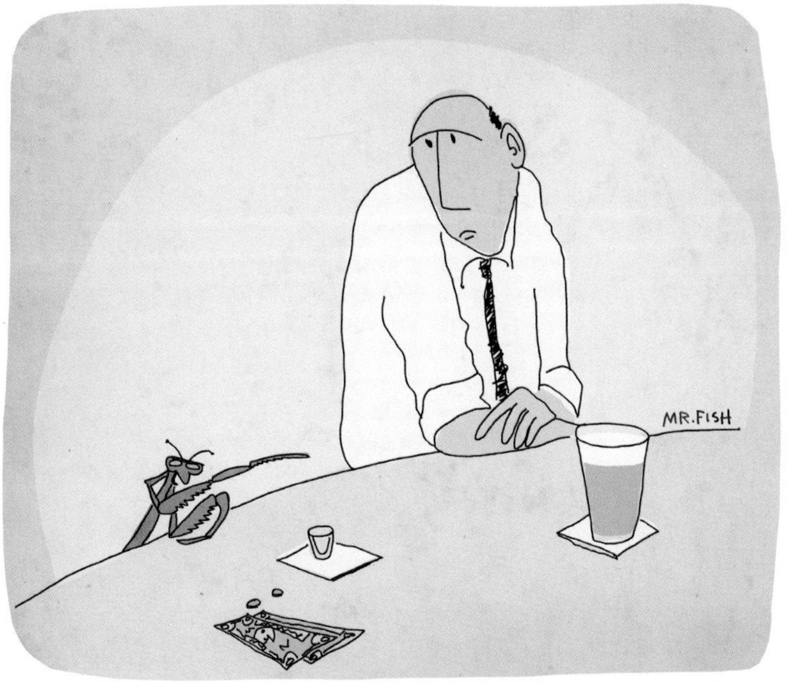
MR.FISH

"Yeah, well – you want to know what I say? I say fuck God! I've been praying night and day for thumbs, sideburns and a chick with big cans ever since I can remember and fucking look at me!"

I don't celebrate that fact as a virtue, but rather point to it as a truism of physiological physics, a cause and effect as permanent as the truism of gravity. You can will an egg to maintain its integrity with all your might while it's falling out of your hand, but you won't be able to change what happens to it once it hits the ground. Likewise, bullies don't usually possess any great talent for self-reflection and tend to learn of their own dedication to injustice by having injustice mirrored back upon them, if they ever learn. Malcolm X had much the same effect on the black movement as Stonewall had on the gays: No one should be allowed to revel in the delusion that they are so privileged that they can abuse other people and remain exempt from any blowback.

I think of Israel's "war" with Lebanon in 2006. I think of Vietnam. I think of Iraq. Ultimately, I think, it becomes an issue of personal dignity. Human beings will tend to want to fulfill the fruition promised to them by their own biologies; DNA, in addition to determining eye color and rate of tooth decay, programs us with passions for freedom and comfort and self-determination. What Gandhi and King did was a tactic for rending the whip from the hand of their oppressor, certainly, and one I find exquisitely beautiful and inspiring; however, when I see how lazy and unimaginative and tribal humanity can be I find myself unable to trust that there would be any lasting sorrow over the cruel slaughter of me and my fellow pacifists. History has shown that there would likely be a quiet celebration for the gained real estate, both physically and ideologically, left by my absence.

Really? If the cops had gone crazy and killed all the protesters and none of them fought back, every single American would know about Stonewall instead of the very small percent that do now. Further, if they had killed some cops where would the movement be?

So is it just the right amount of violence? My understanding of Stonewall is that it was not particularly an event of violence by gays inflicted on the oppressive police, but more the collection of a critical mass of people, gathered for the same reason, who got beat up by the police and fought back just enough to make it into the newspaper but not enough to demand revenge by generations of cops to come.

Not sure I agree with the mathematics. Seems that you expect not only great lessons to come from well publicized mass slaughter, but lasting ones as well, which history doesn't bear out. The Armenian holocaust didn't prevent the Jewish holocaust, nor did the Jewish holocaust teach the lesson to Israel that people should not be forced into ghetto existence and systematically terrorized and ultimately murdered with great technological proficiency.

Also, everybody knows about both World Wars—you can't get any more public than that—and both of those wars ended with a global promise of "never again." Some promise. And, yes, there is something to be said for "just the right amount of violence." I'd rather be shot in the leg than in the head.

Yes! It feels great, especially when it's justified. Self-defense violence, revenge violence, righteous violence, holy violence. Deep down inside, I still have some programming that would make me feel wonderful if I could shoot a man in a WW II German uniform. Those fuckers! I want to chop the arms off some Rwandan Hutus! I want to laser stormtroopers!

You're forgetting General Ursus from the Planet of the Apes. *And you're precisely right about that programming, which I would argue is only slightly tamed by one's moral integrity. I doubt that a human being's natural instinct for doing whatever he can to guarantee his personal survival will ever be sublimated by the abstract notion that stepping into the buzz saw of injustice is better for the species.*

Back in the summer of 1982, I asked my mother if we had any Jewish ancestors. She was making a grilled cheese sandwich using Velveeta, Land O'Lakes butter and Wonder Bread at the time, the question no less crazy than if I'd asked an Eskimo if he had a surfing gene. I was probably wearing the yarmulke that my high school art teacher, Mr. Applebaum, had given to me and holding *Gates of Mitzvah: A Guide to the Jewish Life Cycle*

by Simeon J. Maslin, which I'd gotten for Christmas.

"Not by blood," she said, "but definitely by punch line." Then she told the parable of Benjamin J. Holtzhacker and the Captive Audience.

When my mother was in the second grade back in 1951, her teacher took some time before winter break to go around the room and ask her students to take turns naming a favorite holiday tradition that they enjoyed with their families. This was in early December, and the classroom was done up gaily in silver tinsel and pipe cleaner candy canes and cardboard Santas. Little Billy loved watching a model train circle the base of his Christmas tree while blowing real smoke. Margo felt like a Yuletide queen sitting atop her father's shoulders while her family caroled with members of their church congregation through the center of town. "How are Christmas trees and black men alike?" asked my mother when it was her turn, momentarily freezing the forward momentum of the class activity.

"I beg your pardon?" said her teacher, trying to fit the non sequitur into a nonexistent slot in her head.

I AM
CHARLIE HEBDO

MURDERED BY AL-QAEDA JIHADISTS FOR DRAWING PICTURES CONSIDERED OFFENSIVE TO ISLAM

I AM
NAJI SALIM AL-ALI

MURDERED BY DOUBLE AGENTS WORKING FOR THE NATIONAL INTELLIGENCE AGENCY OF ISRAEL FOR DRAWING PICTURES CRITICAL OF ISRAEL AND ARABIC REGIMES

I AM
MANA NEYESTANI

IMPRISONED AND TORTURED BY THE IRANIAN GOVERNMENT FOR DRAWING A COCKROACH SPEAKING AZERBAIJANI

I AM
MIKE DIANA
ALI DILEM
GERHARD HADERER
ARIFUR RAHMAN

A SHORT LIST OF CONTEMPORARY ARTISTS CENSORED, JAILED, ATTACKED, THREATENED AND EXILED . . .

...AND
ALI FERZAT
KURT WESTERGAARD
MUSA KART
WANG LIMING

FOR DRAWING PICTURES AND SOMETIMES COLORING THEM IN AND SHOWING THEM TO OTHER PEOPLE

I AM
UNEMPLOYED

MR. FISH

BECAUSE, 100 YEARS AGO, THERE USED TO BE 2000 STAFF CARTOONISTS WORKING FOR U.S. MAGAZINES AND NEWSPAPERS AND NOW THERE ARE FEWER THAN 30

"How are Christmas trees and black men alike?" asked my mother for a second time, her face as bright as a freshly halved onion. Nobody said a word. "They both have colored balls!" said my mother, turning to wink at Benjamin J. Holtzhacker, who had told her the joke and was hiding his head in the back row. My grandmother was promptly telephoned, and my mother was sent home as if she'd suddenly come down with communism and was in danger of infecting the entire school population.

Then, in mid-September of 1982, the Israeli army surrounded the Sabra and Shatila Palestinian refugee camps in Beirut and made it impossible for anybody to leave. Then it gave the green light to the Christian Lebanese Phalangists to enter the camps at night and, beneath the incandescent light cast from a thousand Israeli flares, to massacre upward of 3,000 people inside. Then I decided, for the sake of saving mine and Moses' and Sid Caesar's and Lenny Bruce's and Mort Sahl's and Noam Chomsky's and Susan Sontag's and Gloria Steinem's and Naomi Klein's and Sarah Silverman's people from succumbing to the derogation of a negative stereotype, that the State of Israel and the spiritual integrity of Judaism were two completely different things.

"You don't look 21," said Derek, as I was about to get on the train bound for New York, just as the breeze blew back my hair, revealing that I'd shaved my hairline back 2 inches from my forehead. "You don't look any older—you look like somebody who lost a bet!"

"It's a comedy club," I said, reassuring him, "it'll be too dark to see how old I am."

"You'll be standing in a fucking spotlight, you jackass!" he reminded me, making me recall a quote by Mark Twain.

If God had meant for us to be naked, we'd have been born that way.

Three hours later, I took the stage, squinting hard beneath a light bright enough to suggest interrogation, and did my best to assimilate into the questionable murkiness of my own intentions to find and hold an audience captive.

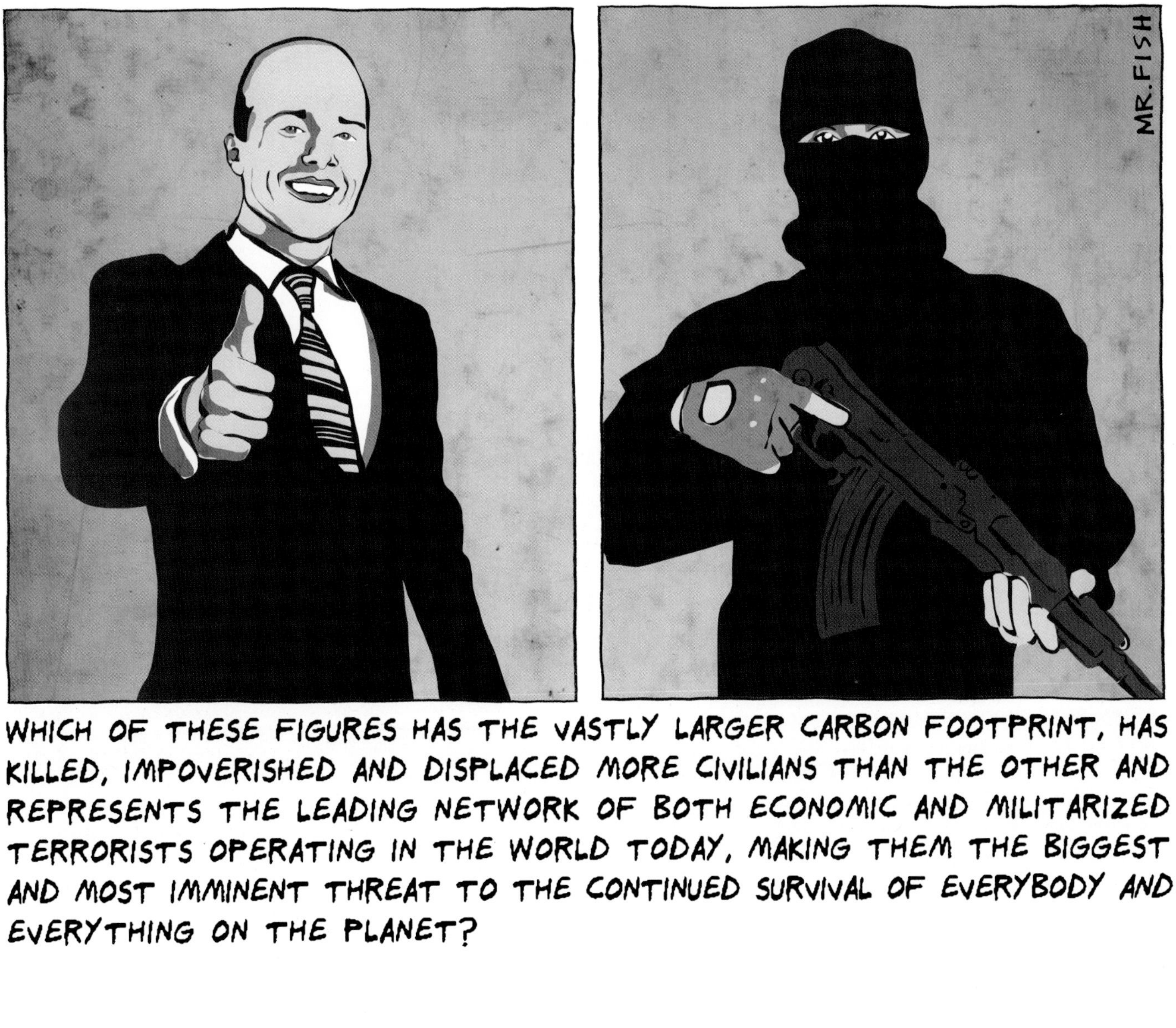
MR. FISH
WHICH OF THESE FIGURES HAS THE VASTLY LARGER CARBON FOOTPRINT, HAS KILLED, IMPOVERISHED AND DISPLACED MORE CIVILIANS THAN THE OTHER AND REPRESENTS THE LEADING NETWORK OF BOTH ECONOMIC AND MILITARIZED TERRORISTS OPERATING IN THE WORLD TODAY, MAKING THEM THE BIGGEST AND MOST IMMINENT THREAT TO THE CONTINUED SURVIVAL OF EVERYBODY AND EVERYTHING ON THE PLANET?

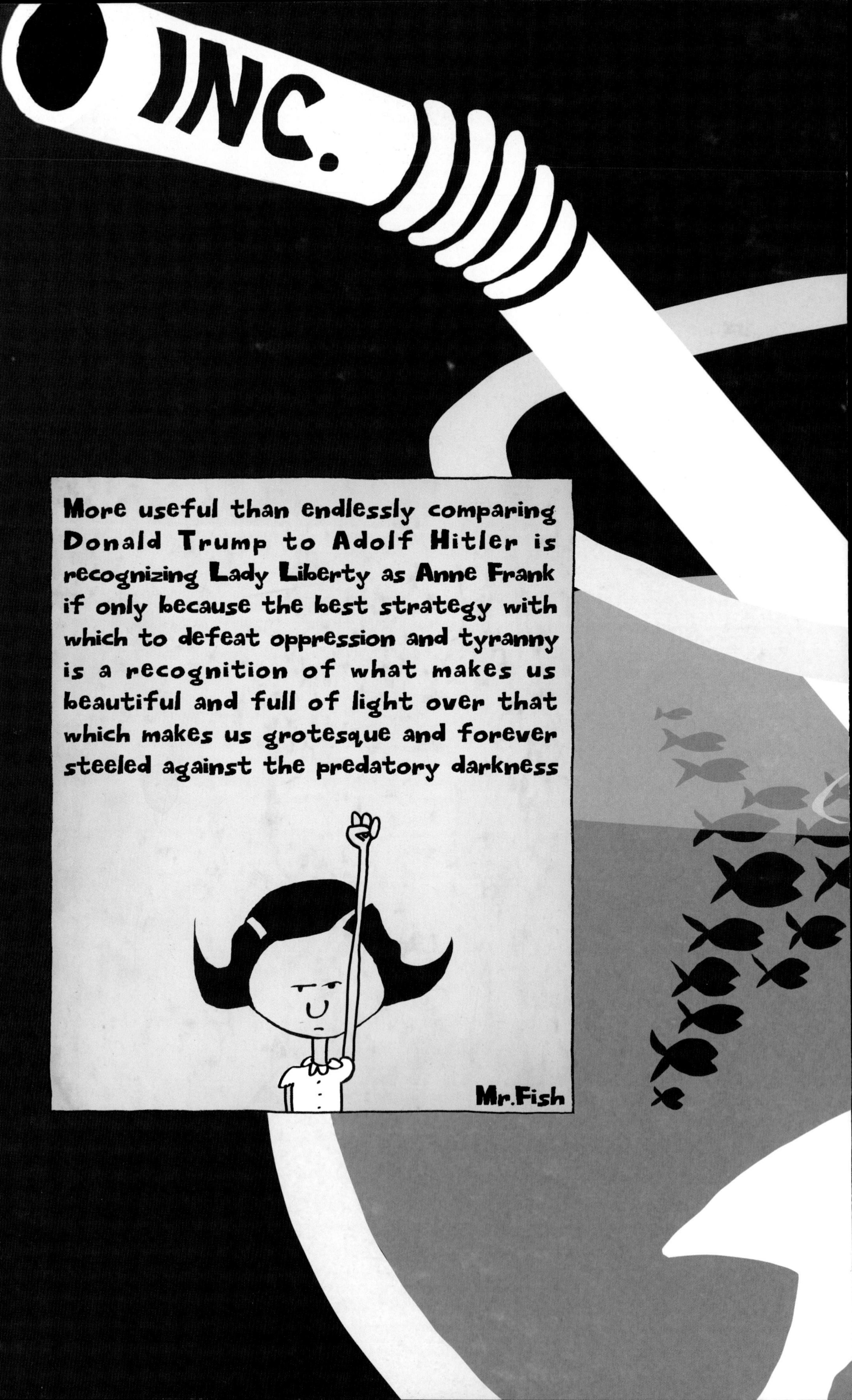
INC.
More useful than endlessly comparing Donald Trump to Adolf Hitler is recognizing Lady Liberty as Anne Frank if only because the best strategy with which to defeat oppression and tyranny is a recognition of what makes us beautiful and full of light over that which makes us grotesque and forever steeled against the predatory darkness
Mr.Fish

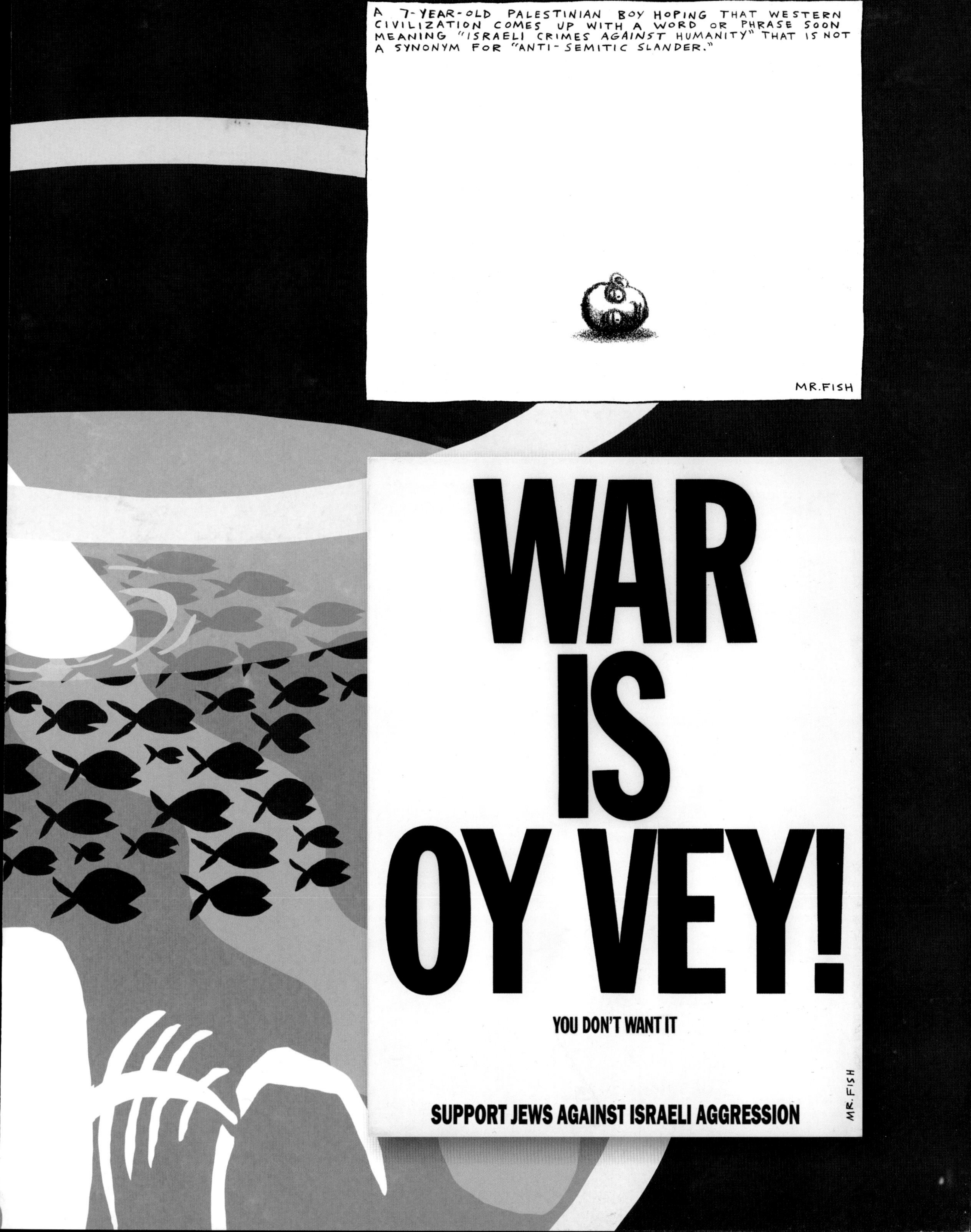
A 7-YEAR-OLD PALESTINIAN BOY HOPING THAT WESTERN CIVILIZATION COMES UP WITH A WORD OR PHRASE SOON MEANING "ISRAELI CRIMES AGAINST HUMANITY" THAT IS NOT A SYNONYM FOR "ANTI-SEMITIC SLANDER."
MR.FISH
WAR IS OY VEY!
YOU DON'T WANT IT
SUPPORT JEWS AGAINST ISRAELI AGGRESSION
MR.FISH

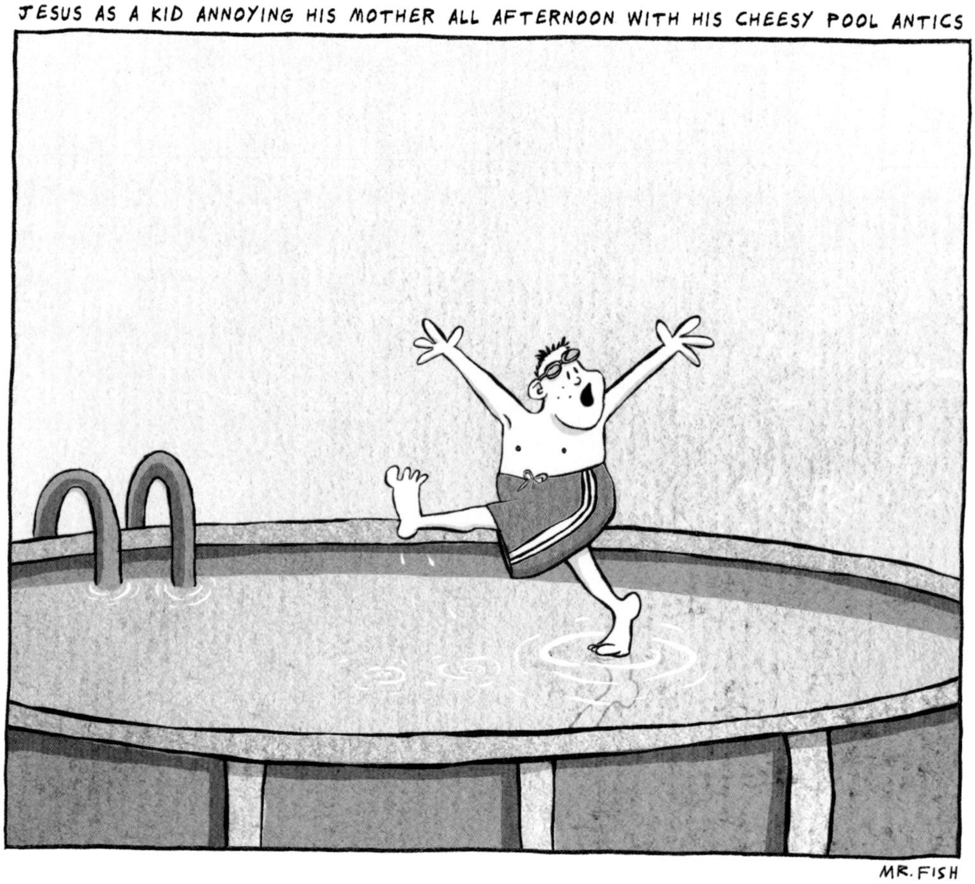
JESUS AS A KID ANNOYING HIS MOTHER ALL AFTERNOON WITH HIS CHEESY POOL ANTICS
MR. FISH

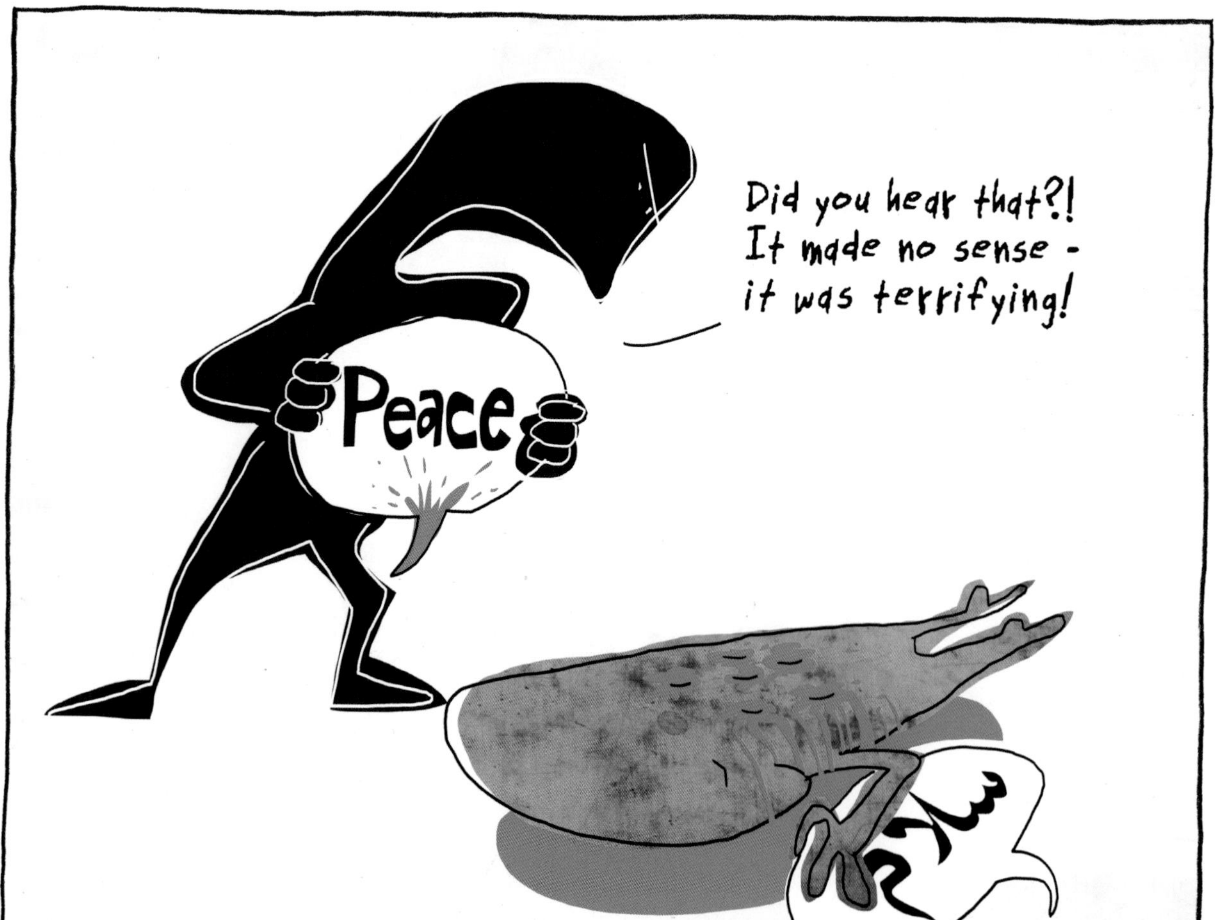
Did you hear that?! It made no sense - it was terrifying!
Peace
Mr. Fish

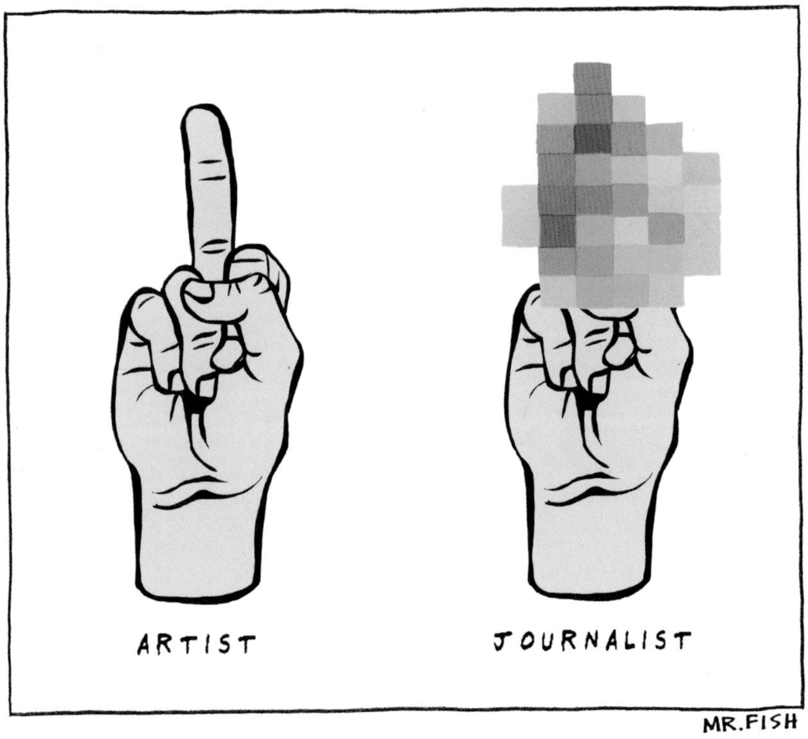
ARTIST
JOURNALIST
MR. FISH

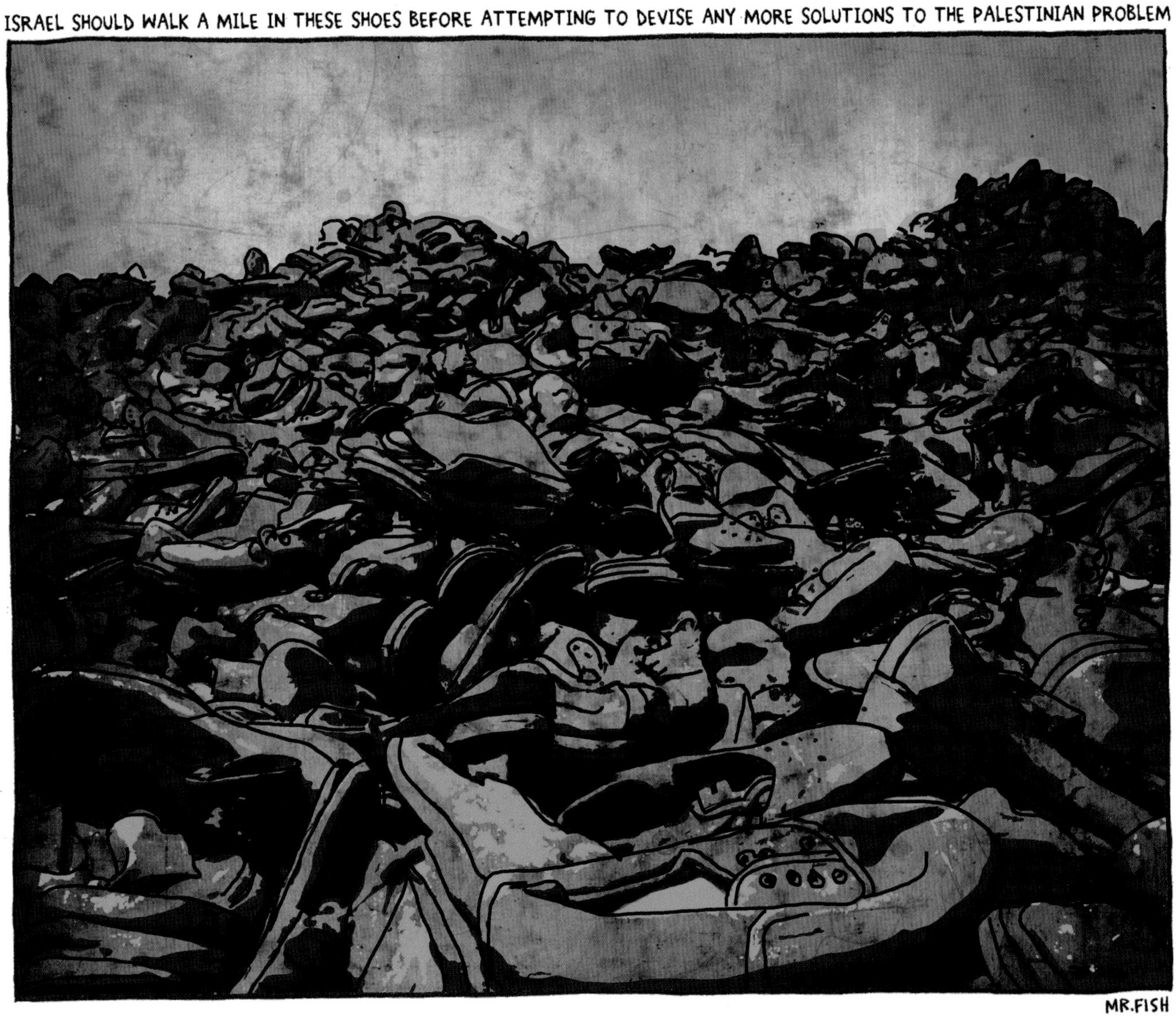
ISRAEL SHOULD WALK A MILE IN THESE SHOES BEFORE ATTEMPTING TO DEVISE ANY MORE SOLUTIONS TO THE PALESTINIAN PROBLEM
MR. FISH

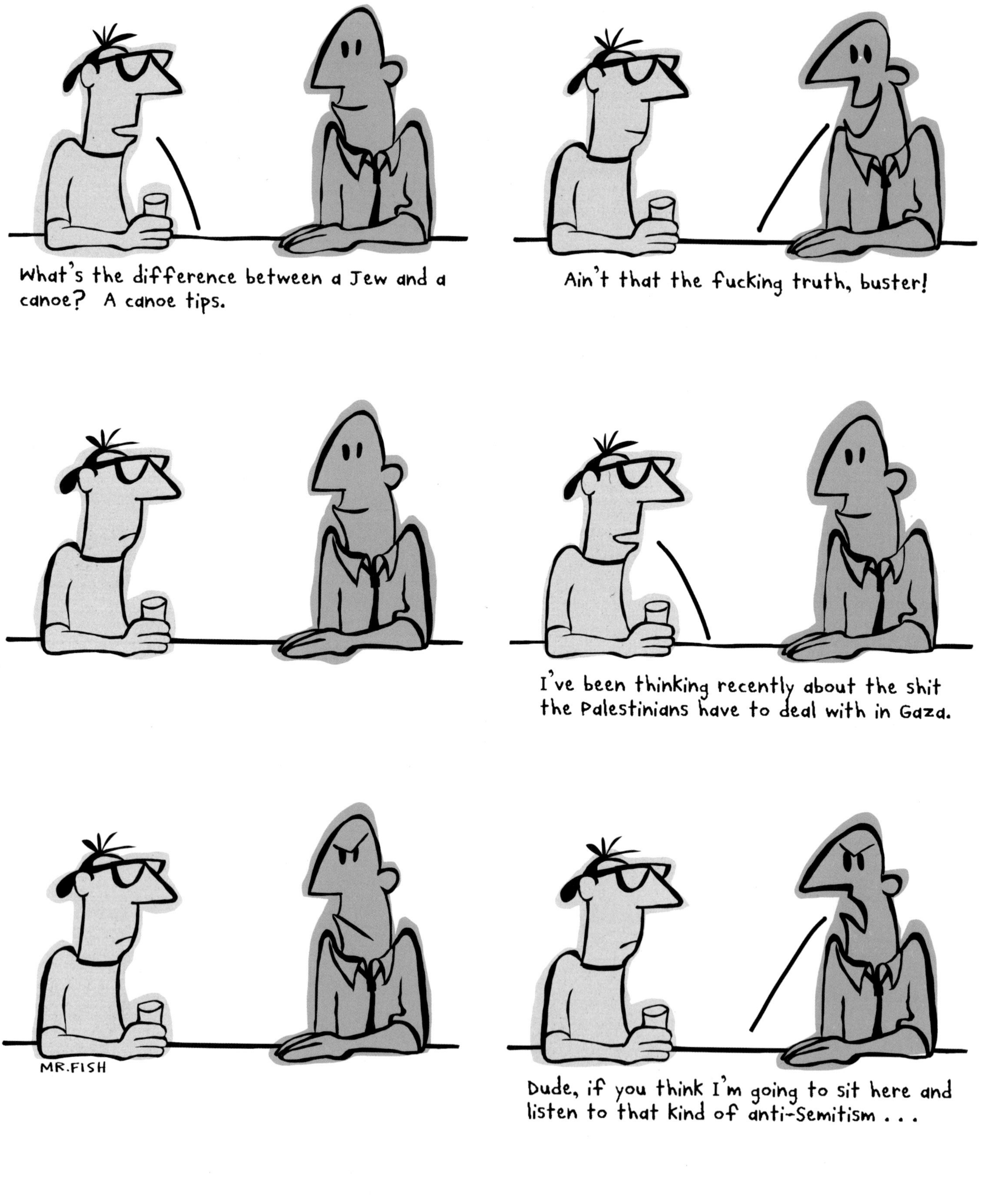
What's the difference between a Jew and a canoe? A canoe tips.
Ain't that the fucking truth, buster!
I've been thinking recently about the shit the Palestinians have to deal with in Gaza.
MR.FISH
Dude, if you think I'm going to sit here and listen to that kind of anti-Semitism . . .

JESUS CHRIST EMERGING FROM HIS TOMB AT CALVARY AND
NOT SEEING HIS SHADOW PROVING SIX MORE MILLENIA OF
DELUSIONAL MORAL SUPERIORITY AND BRUTAL INTOLERANCE OF
ANY DISSENTING POINT OF VIEW.

MR. FISH

THE MEGAPHONE IS NOT OUR BIGGEST PROBLEM

MR. FISH

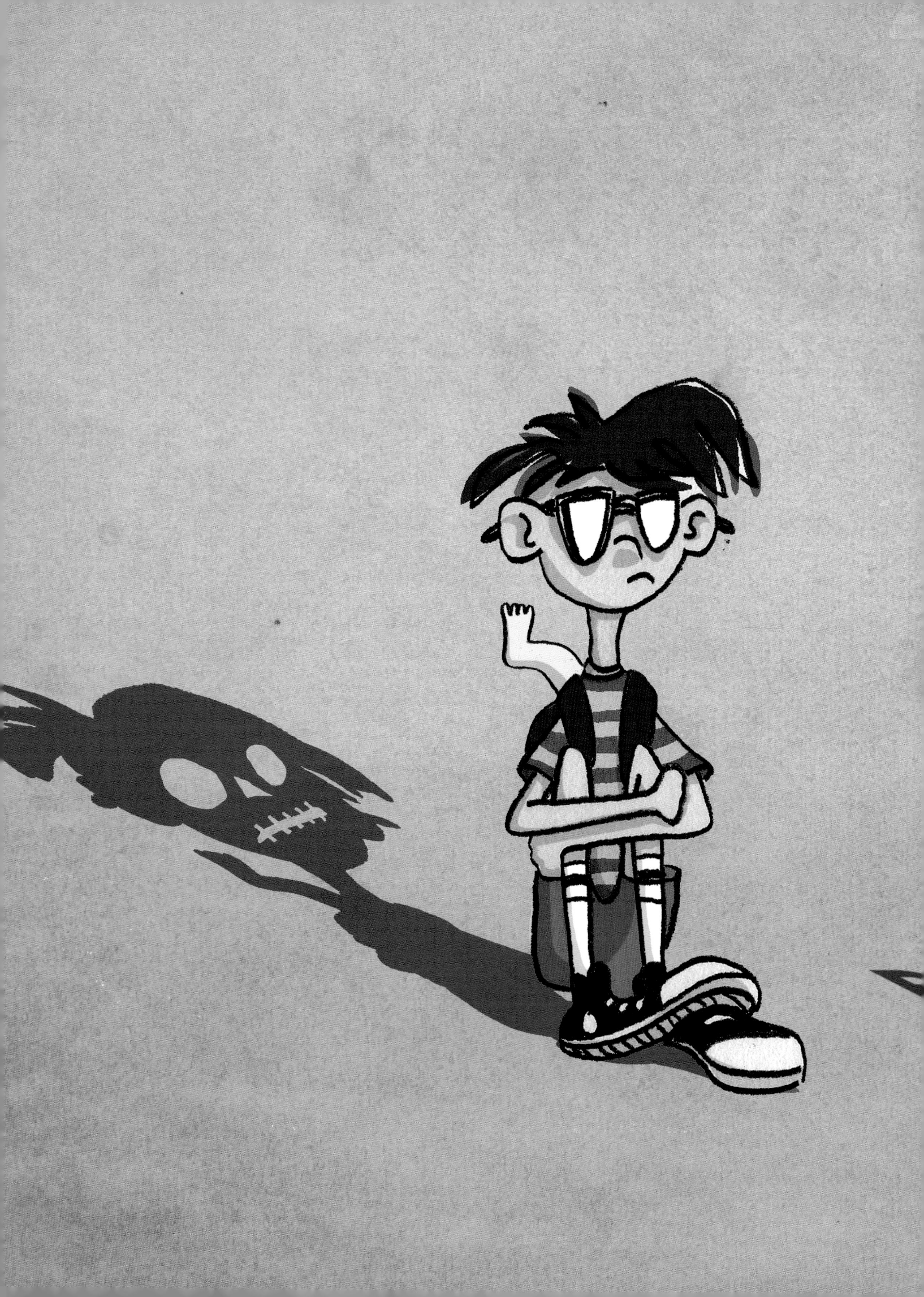

7

PHUCK IS NOT A FOUR-LETTER WORD

Phuck is Not a Four-Letter Word

MY MOTHER WAS the first dead person I'd ever seen up close.

This was in 2007, and I was in Maine when she died all of a sudden in New Jersey. Then, two days later, the funeral home called my brother to tell him that somebody needed to positively identify her body before the cremation, which struck me as odd.

While I could imagine the lawsuit that a mortuary was guarding against with just such a policy—namely that a family was entitled to some reassurance that it would be receiving the remains of a deceased loved one and not the remains of a complete stranger—I wondered how a signature on a piece of paper could really guarantee the identity of somebody's ashes. Unless you were there to actually strike the match yourself and slide the body headlong into the flames, you'd never know for sure that you were getting the remains of your dead relative afterwards—or even the remains of a *person*. After all, practically everything on the planet burns and, given the commonality of ashes, you could just as easily be getting an incinerated chest of drawers as half a horse and never know the difference. So why pretend that signing a piece of paper would guard against sketchy business practices? Common sense, particularly when bolstered by the evidence offered by the breach-of-contract cases forever overflowing every court docket in America, led to the obvious conclusion that paperwork guaranteed absolutely nothing.

So why would my brother even want to drive down to New Jersey to look at his freshly dead mother and then to sign a form saying that it was her? Why allow bureaucratic red tape to take precedence over the truth of the situation?

Of course, in the end, I told my brother to wait for me, that I'd go with him to the funeral home and help him make the positive ID and wait while he signed the proper forms, figuring that having our mother turned to dust and laid to rest in a timely fashion was slightly more important than me hijacking her coffin and turning it into a soap box, knowing that it could never succeed as such so long as she was in it.

Ironically, it was just such a disdain for genteel acquiescence to the dominant culture that our mother instilled in all of her children and made us self-made monkey wrenches all too willing to hurl ourselves into the cogs of what public opinion deemed as normal behavior. We learned to view convention as a total lack of imagination, and dissent as proof of our superiority, the evidence for which was not in any keenly devised set of alternatives to the commonly revered traditions of the day, but rather was in the visceral and decidedly non-intellectual joy that came from wearing sneakers to the ball or pissing on the countess' good china. No doubt, such willful discordance, while being a most outstanding ingredient in the tastiest examples of joke-making, eventually revealed itself to be an all too destructive mental sleight of hand. For my family, it confused us all into assuming that by mocking the bogus elements of etiquette we must be arguing from a contrary point

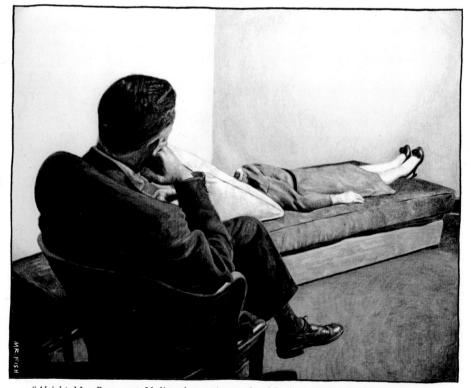

"Alright, Mrs. Beaumont, I believe that you're cured and finally ready to rejoin with all the other brave and creative and patriotic Americans who make this country the envy of the whole world."

Julian practicing his smile after making his wish and getting it moments before his surprise party is officially set to begin.

Mr.fish

of view, which, according to the law of opposites, had to be from a point of view that was *non*-bogus and virtuous and absolutely correct.

But, of course, condemning the light is by no means the best way to argue in favor of the dark, just as celebrating the arrival of the dawn is poor proof that nightfall is a tragedy. Standing there looking down at my 64-year-old mother with her mouth glued shut, I was able to all at once thank her for blessing me with such a rigorous distrust of convention—my whole career as a political cartoonist having come from a healthy skepticism of Establishment values—while, at the same time, damn her for allowing her own distrust of convention to become pervasive enough to cause defiance of doctors, nutritionists and the warning labels on vodka bottles.

I thought back to a summer day in 1975.

His name was Sam, no last name, and he wore no pants. He was lying on my little brother's bed in a filthy orange T-shirt staring up at the ceiling, knees slightly bent, with blue eyes and curly blond hair and small pink lips that were frozen in a strange suckling of the air, almost as if he were unable to wean himself from the invisible teat of some invisible God offering eternal invisibility to anyone willing to praise something that gave no real evidence that it was even ever there to begin with. Similarly, outside in the Ford Falcon station wagon that was idling in the driveway, my mother screwed a fresh cigarette like a new light bulb for a crappy idea into the furious sphincter of her lips, which were pulled into the familiar pucker that she'd been using to kiss her own suicide by heart disease and lung cancer ever since she was old enough to misapply her affection. Lighting the tip and feeling as if sitting in her driveway with the motor running was too telling a life metaphor for her to have to accept gracefully, she began pounding the car horn, effectively forcing the ghost of her aggravation up my 9-year-old ass like I was an empty puppet needing her hand to help me find the canteen that I'd need to stay alive during the day hike that I'd be taking with 20 other Boy Scouts through the New Jersey woods that afternoon.

For the fourth time in a row, the screen door at the front of the house opened and then slammed shut and in ran my little brother, Daryl, to shout at me from the living room that our mother was beginning to place words around my name that he'd only heard our father place around rusted lug nuts just before throwing his wrench and disappearing for an hour to drink a six-pack and to massage the tits out of his masculinity. "Mom's saying *focket* again!" he said.

"Tell her that I can't find my *focking* canteen and to quit it with that goddamn horn already! I'm coming!" I hollered, "momentarily forgetting that a 6-year-old could often be as reliable a form of message delivery as your delivering the message, word for word, yourself. Wait!" I said, to the sound of the screen door opening and then slamming shut again, followed by a moment of silence and then, if it was possible, blasts from the car horn pressed hard into shapes designed to enter my eye sockets like snowballs, *Pow! Pow!* My fists clenched around the emptiness in my hands as desperately as if gripping the rungs on an unsteady ladder.

Walking back across my bedroom to kick, for the millionth time in a row, at the exploded sleeping bag and tent that had been dragged from the hall closet and heaped in the corner, I considered going into the kitchen and grabbing a couple cans of Dr Pepper and shoving them into my backpack. Then I remembered the *NO CARBONATED DRINKS!* rule, which, according to my brother, had been implemented after his friend Hugo Jaffee, after carrying a liter of Mountain Dew over rocky terrain in the Poconos, opened the bottle and ended up spending the better part of the following autumn in a physical therapy program having his part painfully retrained to appear on the proper side of his head.

Figuring *fuck it*, I flumped down onto my little brother's bed, accidentally sitting on Sam, forcing a stream of stale tap water to arc majestically into the air from the tiny piss hole at the tip of his cashew-sized shaft. As triumphantly as a choir-led *amen* at the close of a prayer, the stream rose and fell beside me like a ribbon loosened and flung from a virgin's dress.

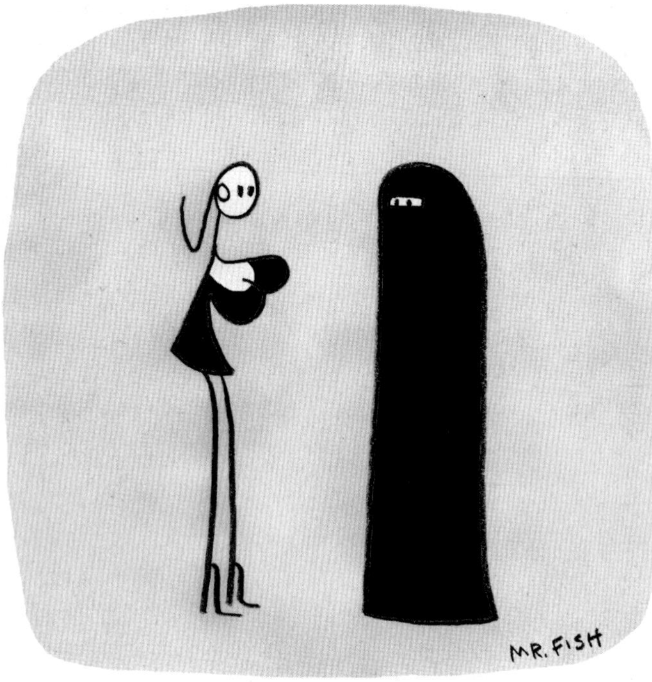
MR. FISH

"Seriously, Tina – take off the burka. It's dehumanizing and only encourages the patriarch to see you as the lesser sex."

I was saved.

None of the other Boy Scouts seemed to notice, or at least they didn't seem to care, that there was a toy baby leg protruding from the top flap of my backpack. Sure, I'd gotten to the trail late and had to run about two miles to catch up with everybody else in my troop and, sure, nobody talked to me when I caught up with them because nobody in the troop liked me, but you'd think that at least the scoutmaster, Mr. Jinx, would feel obligated to say something to me after witnessing me burst through a grove of trees choking and spitting on my own exhaustion like a werewolf. Then again, I thought back to the beginning of the month when Podgie Benigno, who was the hairiest 11-year-old that I'd ever seen in my life, while rubbing two sticks together furiously for 45 minutes to start a campfire for his cooking merit badge, had his elbows catch fire and how Mr. Jinx, when asked where the first aid kit was, suggested, without getting out of his beach chair or putting down his gin and tonic, that we respect the significance of the cooking merit badge and honor its intent by eating Podgie's arms. In essence, Mr. Jinx was the sort of absolute sonuvabitch that lazy parents revered, not because he completed the parenting that they, the parents, were too lazy to commit to, but rather because he justified their disregard for the well-being of their sons by being a shitty parent to them as well. It was Jinx's job to turn little boys into little men, since nurturing them as adolescents required patience, compassion and something brighter than a dimwit.

With Sam's naked leg sticking out of my backpack and a growing concern that I might never find the privacy necessary for me to drink soda from him like a Saigon whore, I fell in with the herd of 20 other hikers and started walking. Having interrupted no conversation with my arrival, none continued, eyes meeting eyes only as confirmation that I was something to be mentally stepped around. It was then that I considered the virtue of camaraderie over isolation. After all, it was during long stretches of self-imposed mental exile without the distraction of other voices when men were forced into conversations with themselves and faced with the terrifying possibility that they were not worth knowing.

I remembered reading in school about dog sled racers in the Alaskan Iditarod and how they frequently suffered hallucinations as a result of their isolation, their brains thrown into sudden panic no doubt at the realization that they were spending the best years of their lives riding in what amounted to a shopping cart on skis behind a pack of dogs slaphappy enough to recognize the word *Mush!* as an excuse to run headlong into the woods, their eyes like pinwheels. Of course, any brain faced with such a bizarre portrait of itself will attempt to create an entirely different reality in which to place itself, damning the one that it's actually in. I feared that I might be beginning this hike with a terrific personality and ending it with absolutely none to speak of, having ingested it during the course of the day like a box of Cracker Jack, my self-destruction predicated on the false notion that there was a prize to be claimed at the center of my soul.

It was then that Mr. Jinx turned around to face us and command, "Canteen/piss break, five minutes!" Dutifully responding like pennies released from a fist, Scouts fanned out in all directions, rolling behind trees and boulders and shrubs and into gullies to pour scant amounts of ammonia and lemonade into tiny foam puddles before regrouping themselves into grumbling pairs and threesomes and quartets to sit and pull canteens from their packs and to upend them against their lips. Finding a tree of my own, one too skinny to provide complete invisibility, I took 49 seconds to take a three-second piss and to shake absolutely nothing off my very modest modesty, contemplating the whole time how I was going to get Sam's plastic meatus out of my backpack and into my mouth without drawing the attention of all the *normal* kids around me, figuring that lynch mobs weren't so much rehearsed as they were spontaneously inspired.

"Well," I whispered to my brother, standing three feet away from the lifeless doll that was our mother, "that's her, all right." He agreed with a whispered *yep.* Then, with neither one of us trusting the authenticity of the oh-so-popular five stages of grief, we stood dry-eyed and said nothing more, him because he wanted to remember our mother looking so much less agonized than she had appeared to him three days earlier and me because I believed, with absolute certainty, that if I made a sound I'd wake her up, which would embarrass both of us, each overcome with average tears and made ordinary by a warm and all-too-comforting embrace.

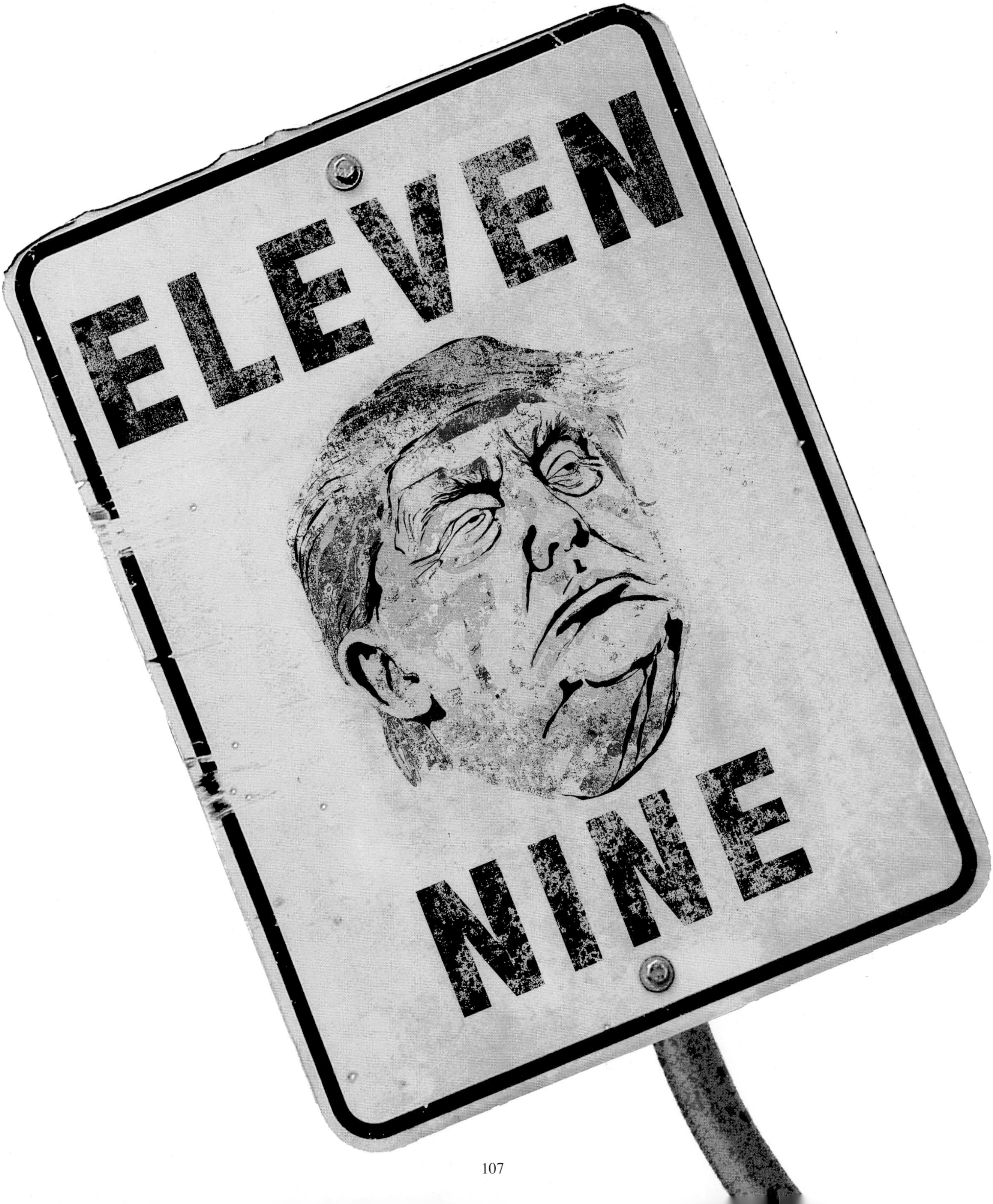
ELEVEN
NINE

THE VIRGIN MARY EXPLAINING THE BIRDS AND BEES TO JESUS

MR. FISH

"Alright, first there's the woman, who is way too young to have a baby, she's got her whole life in front of her, spread out like a, I don't know . . . a meadow of infinite possibilities or some shit. Maybe she wants to go into medicine or open a restaurant or just travel around Europe with some granola and a sketch book, she doesn't know. Anyway, one night she grabs a bucket and goes out to the well to get some water, something she's done a million times before and nobody's ever bothered her . . . she's frigging minding her own goddamned business – she's never even slept with a man before, let alone held hands with one, because she doesn't want to screw up her future! – then POW! All of a sudden there's this PR guy from GOD, Incorporated, and he tells the woman that the CEO of his company, Mr. Big Shot, Mr. I-know-how-to-make-a-fucking-zebra, himself, has just knocked her up without even introducing himself first and her son is going to be this holier-than-thou complainer who thinks, just like his dad, that it's either his way or the highway and he's never going to get a job or even try to get laid and then the government is going to murder him while he's still practically a kid and then in a few thousand years he's going to come back from the dead and kill everybody on Earth who doesn't think that he and his super-conceited father are just the bee's knees. The end."

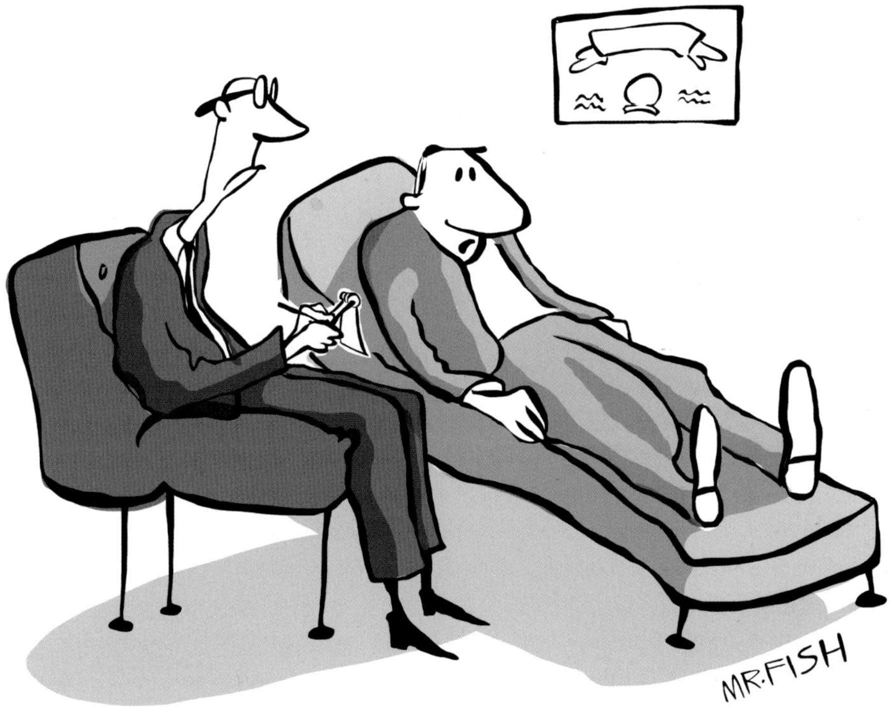
MR.FISH

"It's an absolute nightmare! She only loves me for my mind."

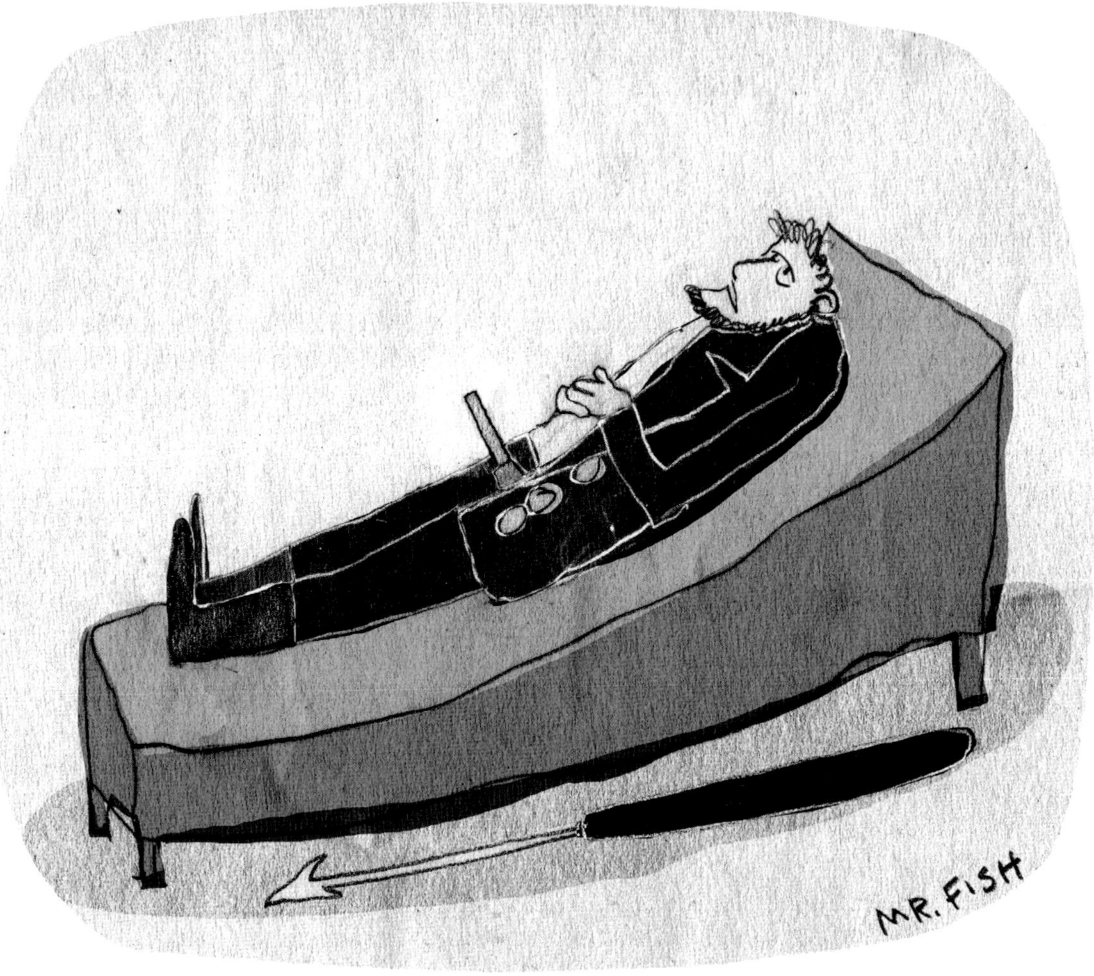
MR.FISH

"Well, we didn't start out as adversaries."

DEAR GREAT PUMPKIN (A.K.A. AMERICA),

IT SEEMS TO HAPPEN ALL THE TIME, BUT PARTICULARLY DURING ELECTION YEARS: I KEEP HEARING ABOUT HOW LUCKY I AM TO LIVE IN THE GREATEST COUNTRY THAT'S EVER EXISTED, THAT I'M BLESSED BY MORE RIGHTS AND PRIVILEGES THAN I'LL EVER BE ABLE TO USE IN A LIFETIME AND THAT EVERYBODY ELSE IN THE WORLD IS JEALOUS OF HOW TERRIFIC I HAVE IT. THEN I'M TOLD THAT AS LONG AS I NEVER DOUBT THE EXISTENCE OF YOU AND THAT IF I SACRIFICE REASON AND COMMON SENSE IN ORDER TO DELIGHT IN THE MYTHOLOGY THAT YOU EMBODY, I WILL BE REWARDED WITH FABULOUS TREASURES AND GOOD FORTUNE. WHAT I'M STARTING TO REALIZE IS THAT YOU'RE NOT REAL, EXCEPT IN MY HEAD, AND ALL I'M DOING IS WAITING AROUND AND DOING NOTHING IN THE MIDDLE OF AN ECHO CHAMBER OF MEANINGLESS AND UNTESTED BALDERDASH WHILE THE MOST ANTI-DEMOCRATIC, PRO-AUTOCRATIC MEN RAVAGE THE PLANET AND COMMIT MASSIVE CRIMES AGAINST HUMANITY WITHOUT ABATEMENT BECAUSE THEY KNOW I'M PREOCCUPIED WITH A FANTASY THAT MAKES ME THE BENEFACTOR OF WONDROUS FREEDOMS THAT ARE PURELY CONCEPTUAL WITH ABSOLUTELY NO APPLICATION TO THE REAL WORLD – THE REAL WORLD THAT YOU'VE COMMANDEERED AND THAT YOU REJOICE IN FUCKING OVER.

IN SHORT, I NOW KNOW YOU ARE FAKE AND IT'S HIGH TIME THAT I STOP ADDRESSING YOU AS IF YOU WERE REAL. I WILL NO LONGER LIVE MY LIFE IN FEAR OF WHETHER OR NOT YOU THINK MY PUMPKIN PATCH IS SINCERE AND I WILL NEVER AGAIN MISINTERPRET YOUR ABSENCE AS GODLIKE OMNISCIENCE. INSTEAD, I'LL SEE IT AS AN EMPTINESS THAT MUST BE FILLED BY MY ACTIVE PARTICIPATION IN THE WORLD. FROM NOW ON I'M GOING TO LOOK BEYOND THE SUPERFICIALITY OF YOUR LEGEND AND PARTICIPATE IN MY COMMUNITY AND DEMAND REAL, EXPERIENTIAL JUSTICE, EQUAL RIGHTS, EMPATHY AND FELLOWSHIP FROM MY NEIGHBORS, WHOSE HOPES, DREAMS, CAMARADERIE, CELEBRATED DIFFERENCES AND EARNEST DEBATE WILL BE THE ONLY TREASURE AND GOOD FORTUNE I WILL EVER NEED.

RESPECTFULLY. . .
A FREE MAN!

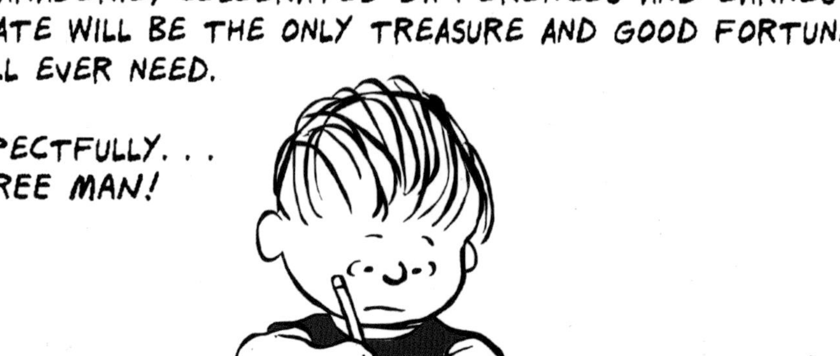
MR.FISH

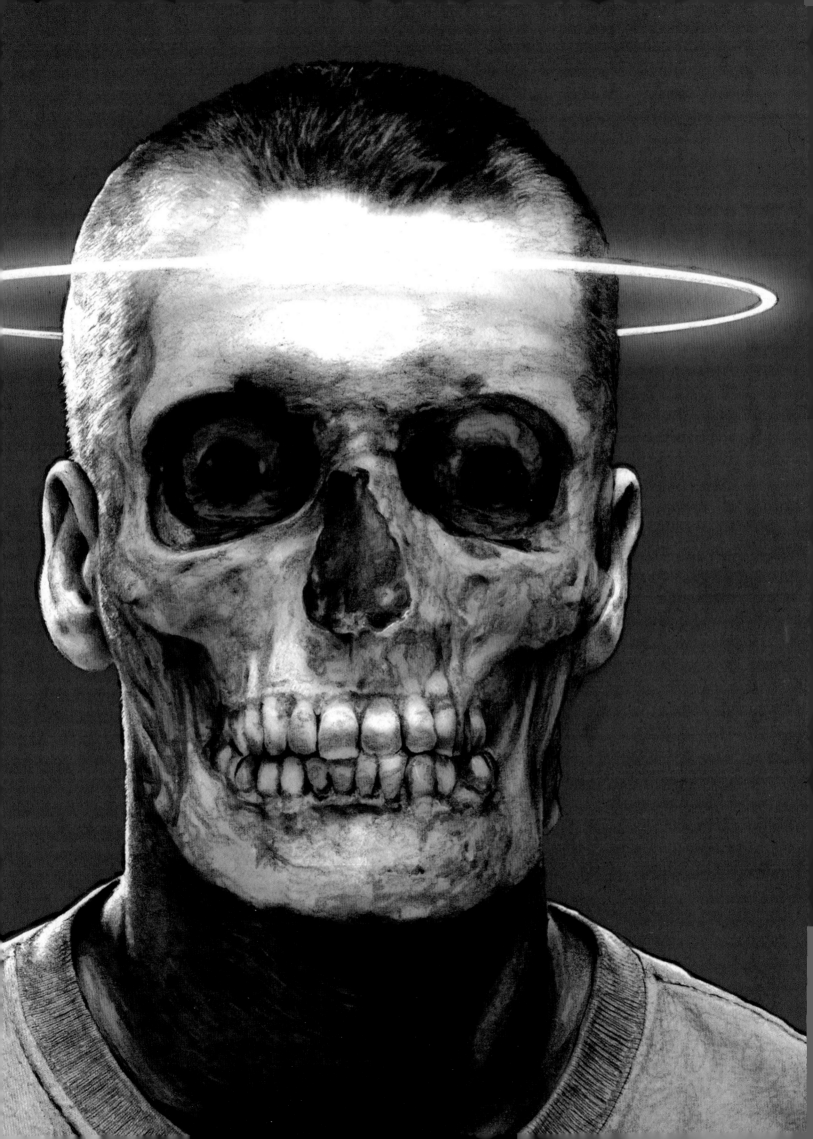

FUCK ALL THE HAWKS AND DOVES AND BALD EAGLES - BE A COCK AND MAKE IT YOUR JOB TO WAKE EVERYBODY UP!

MR. FISH

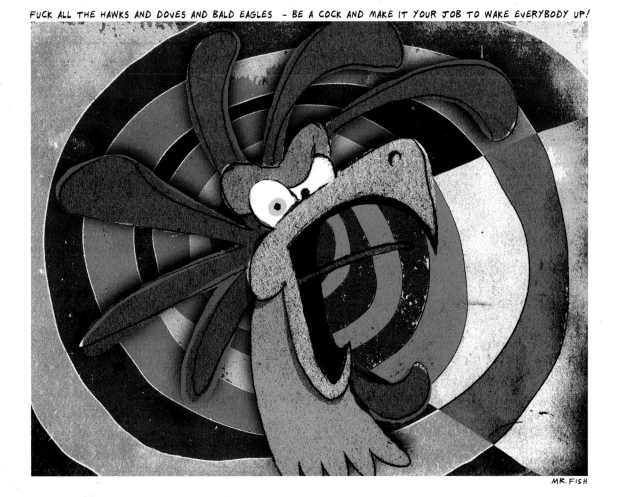

MR. FISH

"Hang on for a second, Dad – what do you mean you're not really the Creator of the Universe and that you're just a Co-Creator?"

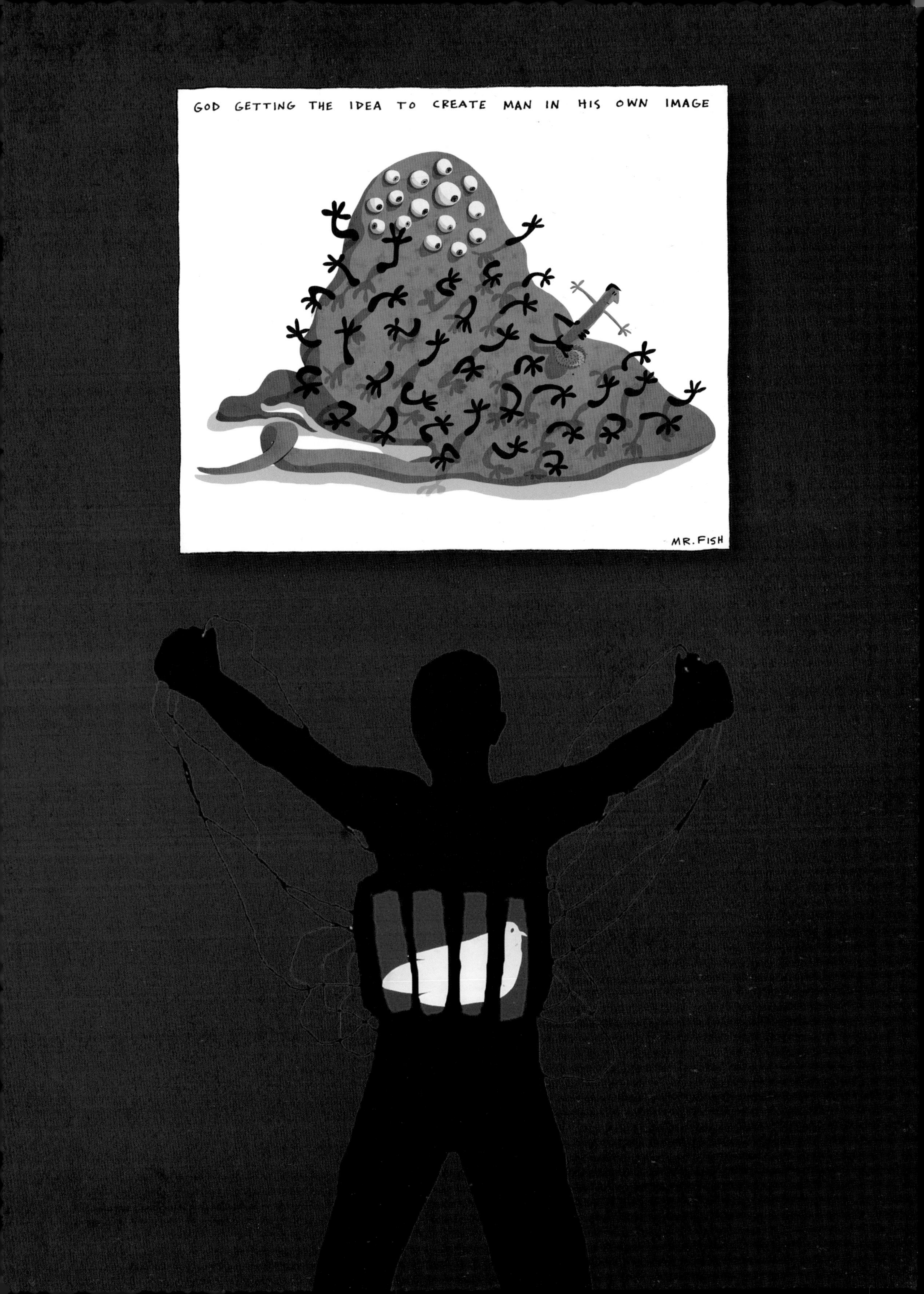
GOD GETTING THE IDEA TO CREATE MAN IN HIS OWN IMAGE
MR. FISH

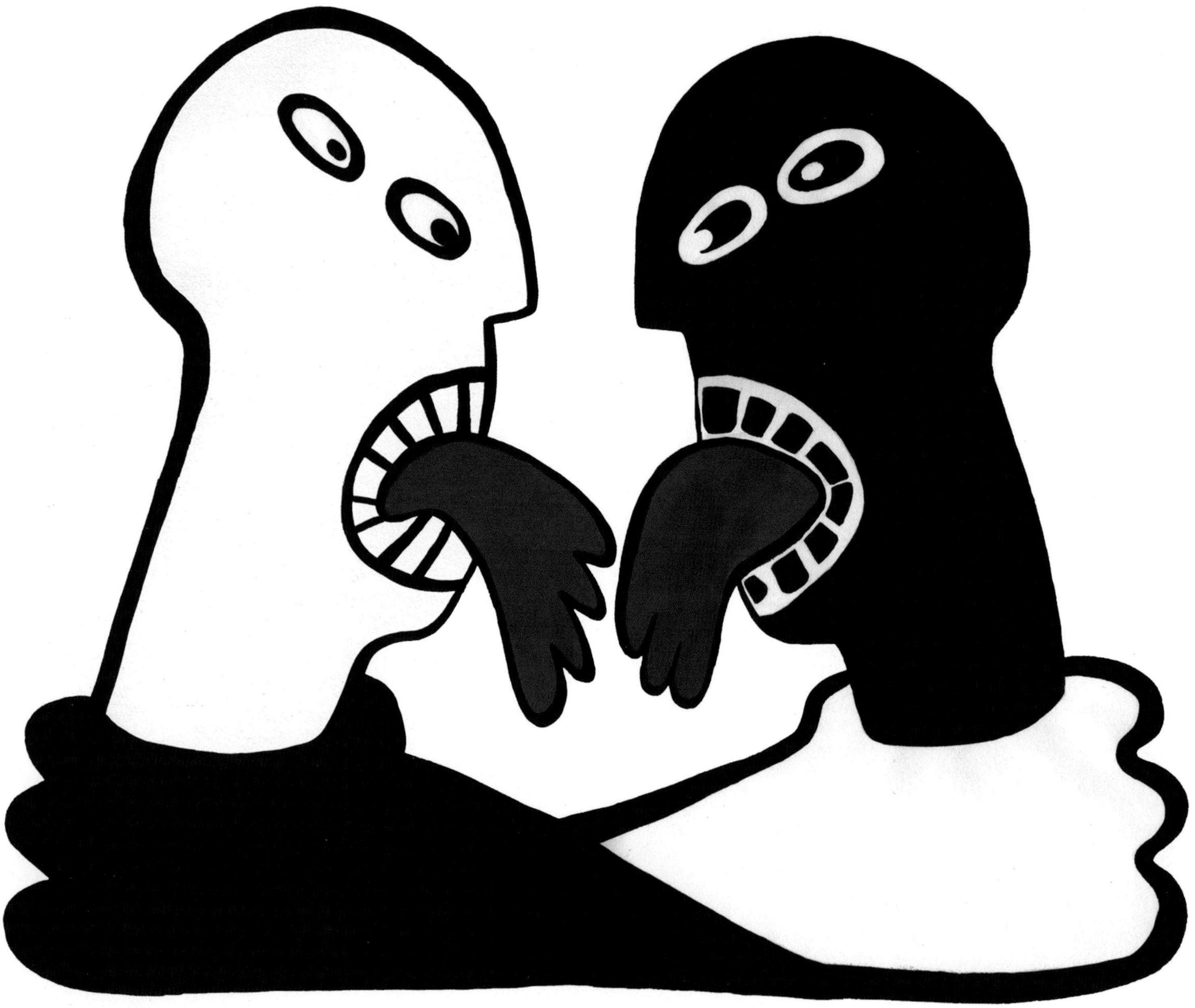

The
MONSTER

The Monster

I STOPPED BELIEVING in monsters on Thanksgiving Day in 1976, when my stepfather came downstairs for dinner wearing black dress pants, a white collared shirt, a pair of freshly polished black leather shoes and only one sock. Had we been at my parents' house, I probably would've put down my *Famous Monsters of Filmland* magazine and left the room at the sight of him, but this was my maternal grandparents' house and he wasn't stumbling around with his shirt off and there wasn't the stench of Jack Daniels and stomach acid filling the room like turpentine. So I stayed, sprawled in my grandfather's Barcalounger like Jesus in the Pietà, and settled back into my magazine, allowing my eye to track backward through the pictorial sequence of Lon Chaney Jr. changing into the Wolf Man, watching as his lower canines receded back into his jaw and his bloodlust softened into the tortured mediocrity of a man made average.

On the same day that Muammar Gaddafi was yanked from a drainpipe in Surt and killed by Libyan rebels, I was in Harlem participating in a multi-author book event at a small independent bookstore called Hue-Man. Having spent the afternoon watching and re-watching the frenetic cellphone footage of the deposed dictator being manhandled onto the hood of a utility truck, where he sat wiping blood out of his eyes, his wedding ring and bare feet and Richard Simmons hairdo making him appear exactly as fiendish and dangerous as a confused senior citizen having just been pulled violently from a Demerol drip and commanded to remember beneath a blazing hot sun where he'd left the TV remote, I couldn't help but feel sorry for the guy. The scene made me think of the 1931 Fritz Lang classic, *M*, starring Peter Lorre as a murderer of children who, at the film's climax, finds himself surrounded by an angry sea of other criminals—pickpockets, arsonists and the murderers of grown-ups—in an abandoned distillery somewhere in pre-Hitler Berlin. The mob is planning to execute Lorre for, essentially, the crime of poor choice, and he is demanding that he be handed over to the police. The request, of course, is met with great peals of laughter from the lynch mob, and Lorre is suddenly made to appear as small and terrified and defenseless as a child just before being devoured by a pack of wild animals.

Q: How many kids with ADD does it take to change a light bulb?

A: LET'S GO RIDE BIKES!

Gaddafi was stripped and shot and punched and kicked and spat on and sodomized with a sharp stick before he was killed by a crowd that was laughing and dancing while flashing peace signs and crowing about the virtues of justice and how great and merciful God was.

Ludwig Wittgenstein said, "A serious and good philosophical work could be written consisting entirely of jokes." That's the quote that gave me my focus for the two-minute talk I was asked to give in promotion of my new book at the Harlem

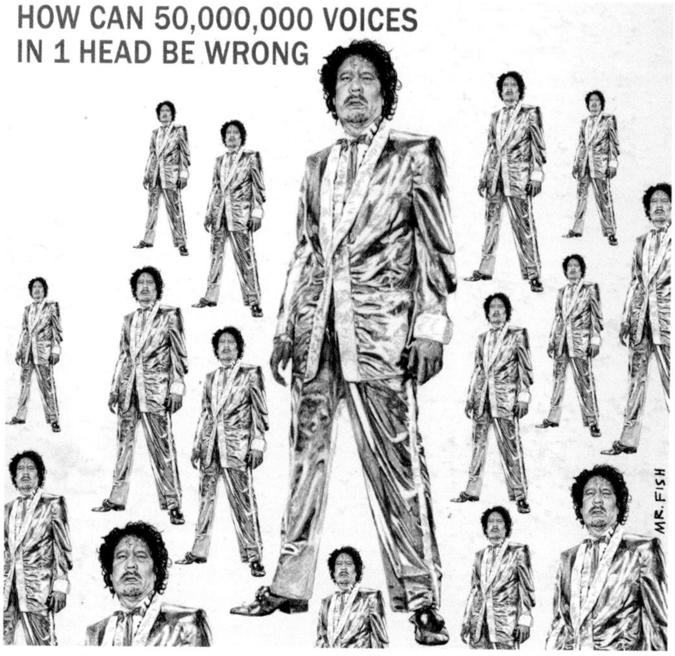
HOW CAN 50,000,000 VOICES
IN 1 HEAD BE WRONG
MR. FISH

bookstore event, although I never cited it. What I like to think Wittgenstein meant was that humor quite often derives much of its potency from simple truth-telling, its comedic snap coming from the shock that the average person, who typically experiences life through any number of political and religious and cultural filters, experiences when confronted with sheer honesty.

Q: What's worse than finding a worm in your apple?

A: Being raped.

What will always make a monster appear even more monstrous is his ability to be magnanimous, even lovable, toward those most often targeted by his abuse. The unpredictability of such behavior prevents a victim from ever being able to recognize any part of the outside world as safe or sure. Then there is the world of make-believe.

"If you really want to upset your parents and you are not brave enough to be gay, go into the arts."

That was the Kurt Vonnegut quote I opened with at the bookstore, offering it as an example of a simple statement of fact that, though it is neither joyous nor optimistic nor complimentary at all, makes us laugh. Why is that? Should not such an unflattering observation about our own intolerance of both homosexuality and artistic ambition shame us?

"Another example of a joke being funny simply because it surprises us with its bold, unapologetic adherence to truth," I said to the crowd, which was made up mostly of African American women older than 60, "is this: What's the worst thing you can hear while you're blowing Willie Nelson? (*Pause to ignite the hilarity fuse, only to notice that one of the more brittle-looking grandmothers brought her 6-year-old granddaughter.*) I'm *not Willie Nelson*." Absolute silence. I then went on to say that while the Willie Nelson joke didn't require much analysis to determine why it was true, the Vonnegut quote did. Why would a parent be upset about his or her child wanting to be an artist? After all, isn't art—whether we're talking about books or music or movies or painting or dance—precious to every single one of us? Is it not the source material we most revere when we're hoping to unwind from a day spent enduring the soul-crushing shit storm that is *normal life?* Hasn't John Coltrane pulled more desperate souls in from the window ledge than, say, the Ten Commandments or Newton's law of universal gravitation?

Having known no other father, my stepfather was what I'd grown up believing patriarchy and, by default, leadership and absolute authority to be. Rather than earning the respect of my brothers and sister and me, my stepfather exacted affection as if it were some sort of tax levied against us in revenge for his failure to enter adulthood as something other than a hopelessly pissed-off, unskilled teenager whose only concept of maturity was whatever jury-rigged masculinity he hoped to cull together from mixing auto mechanics with alcoholism. As a result, we all did what the Libyans might have done 35 years later, which was to develop a deep disdain for any fairy tale that held within it a king or an emperor or a God whose power had been vested by fiat and not hard-won through either humor or compassion or ballot.

Up until that Thanksgiving in 1976, my stepfather seemed like the real deal to me, no less a convincing example of genuine villainy than a recurring nightmare is for anybody desperate to wake from a dream gone haywire. Once, while he was beating me in a vacant lot with a wooden stake used to mark property, I hollered for my mother and wondered why she never came to my rescue, leaving me to puke alone in the weeds on my hands and knees. Then, perhaps a week later, while we swerved wildly down the middle of the highway in a green Nova held together by rusty wire hangers and duct tape, my stepfather deliberately running cars off the road and throwing empty beer cans out the driver's side window, I sat white-knuckled in the backseat with my brothers and sister and watched our commander in chief grab my mother roughly by the upper arm and pull her close. I remember imagining that I could hear her anguished telepathy hollering for somebody to rescue her, realizing all of a sudden that perhaps the reason why she hadn't saved me earlier in the week was because neither one of us had a safe location from which to pull the other.

Two muffins were baking in an oven. One muffin turns to the other and says, "Holy shit, it's hot in here!" The other muffin says, "Holy shit... a talking muffin!"

Q: Hey Dave, why are you wearing only one sock?

A: I needed to blow my nose in the middle of the night and the other sock was the only thing I could reach.

Looking at the vulnerable patch of pale hairless skin stretched shiny over my stepfather's exposed ankle, I laughed and at the same time pitied him for needing to work so hard to reinterpret the belittling laughter from everybody in the room as benign fondness. Decades later I would hear that Muammar Gaddafi's last words were, "Do you know right from wrong?" and I'd wonder what our collective eye rolling was betraying about our inability to answer the question.

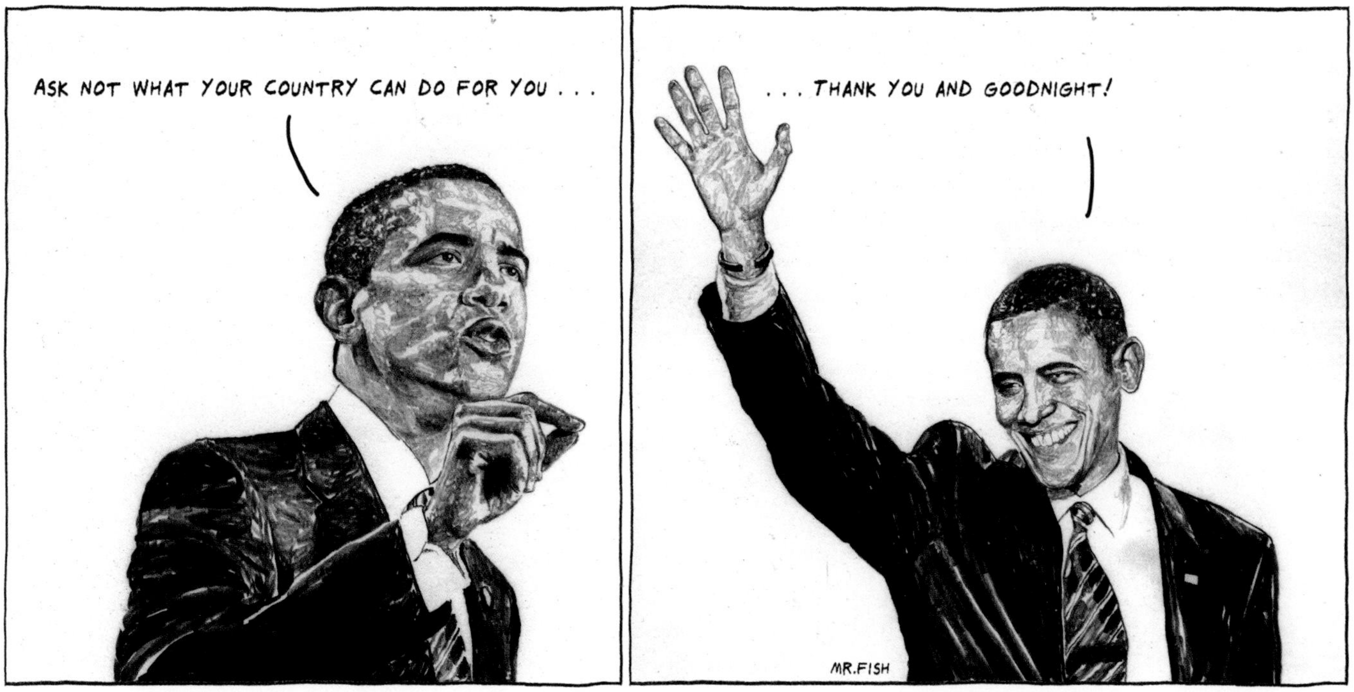
ASK NOT WHAT YOUR COUNTRY CAN DO FOR YOU . . .
. . . THANK YOU AND GOODNIGHT!
MR.FISH

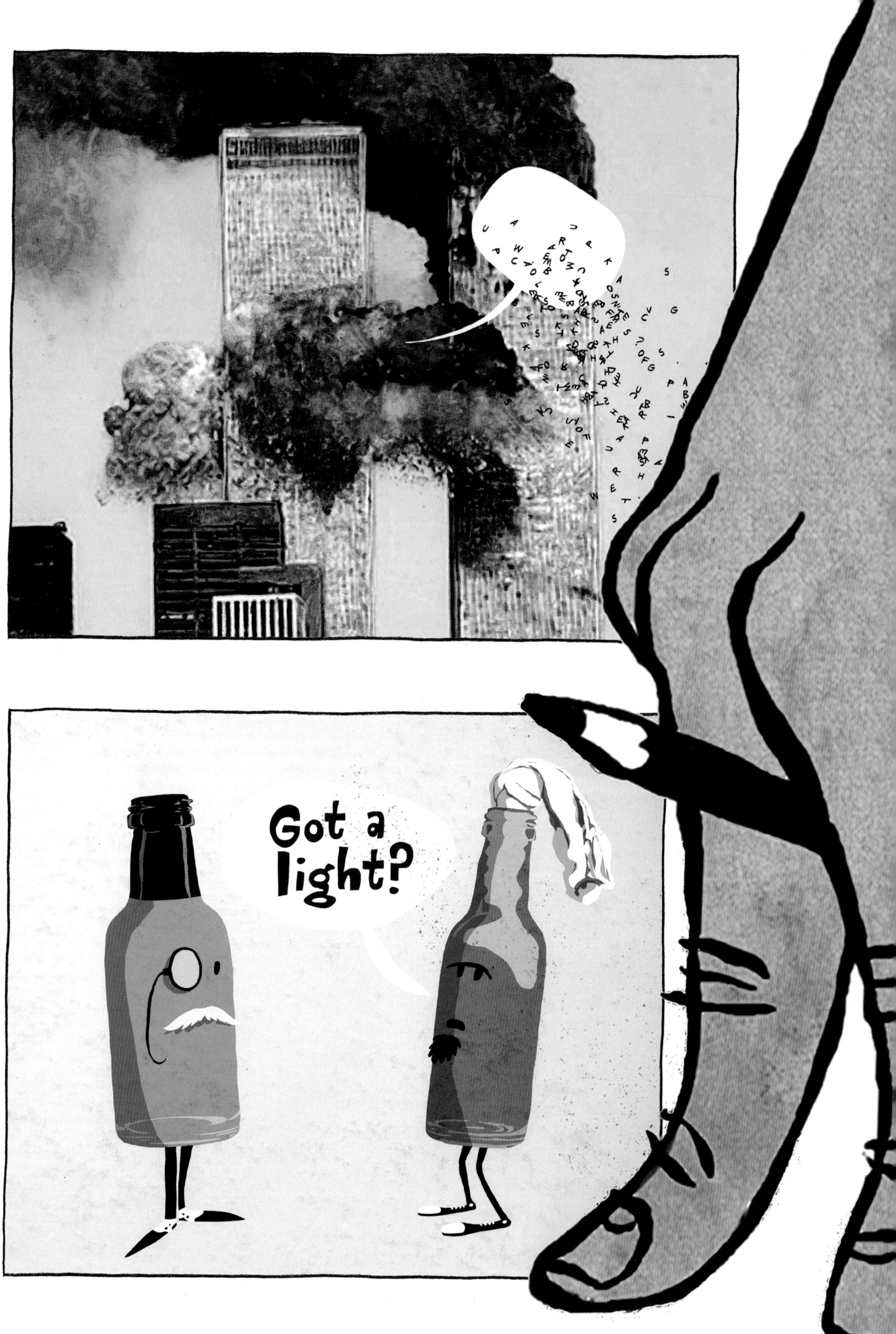
Got a light?

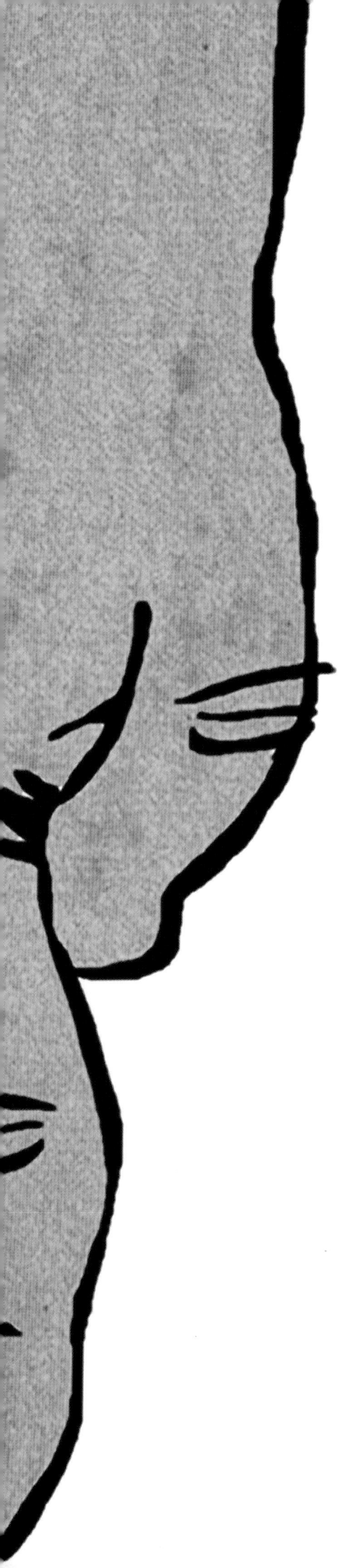

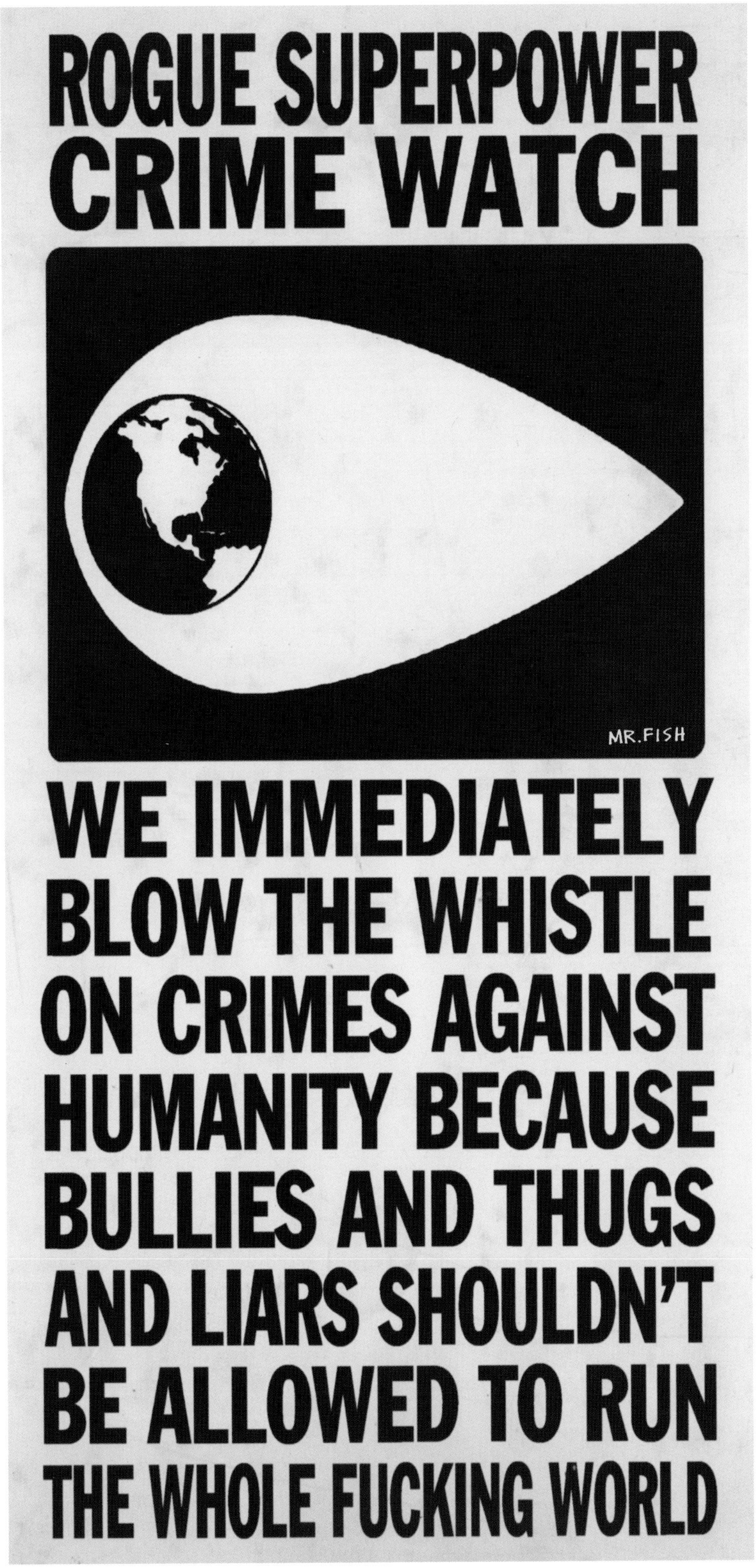
ROGUE SUPERPOWER
CRIME WATCH
MR.FISH
WE IMMEDIATELY
BLOW THE WHISTLE
ON CRIMES AGAINST
HUMANITY BECAUSE
BULLIES AND THUGS
AND LIARS SHOULDN'T
BE ALLOWED TO RUN
THE WHOLE FUCKING WORLD

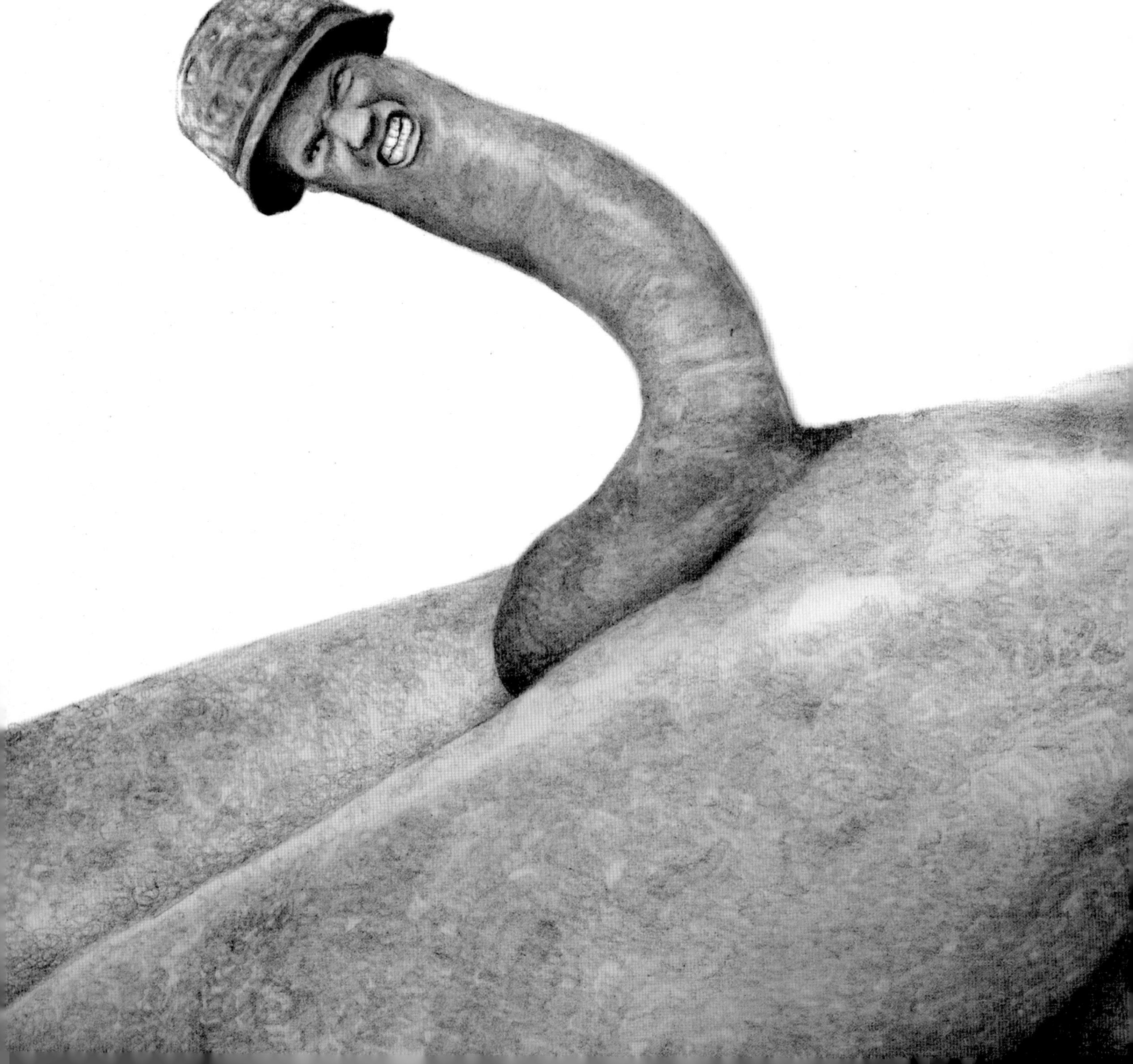

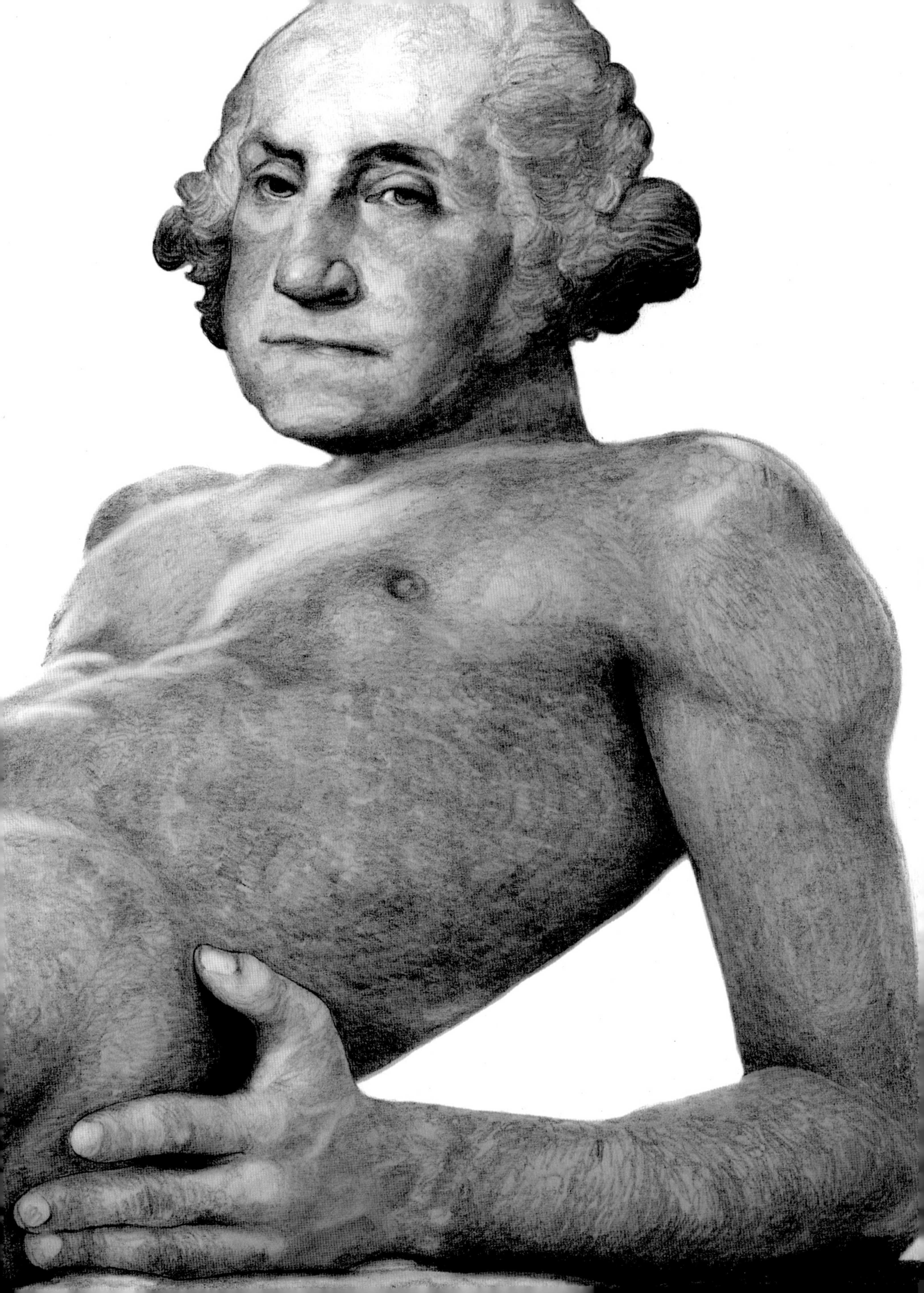

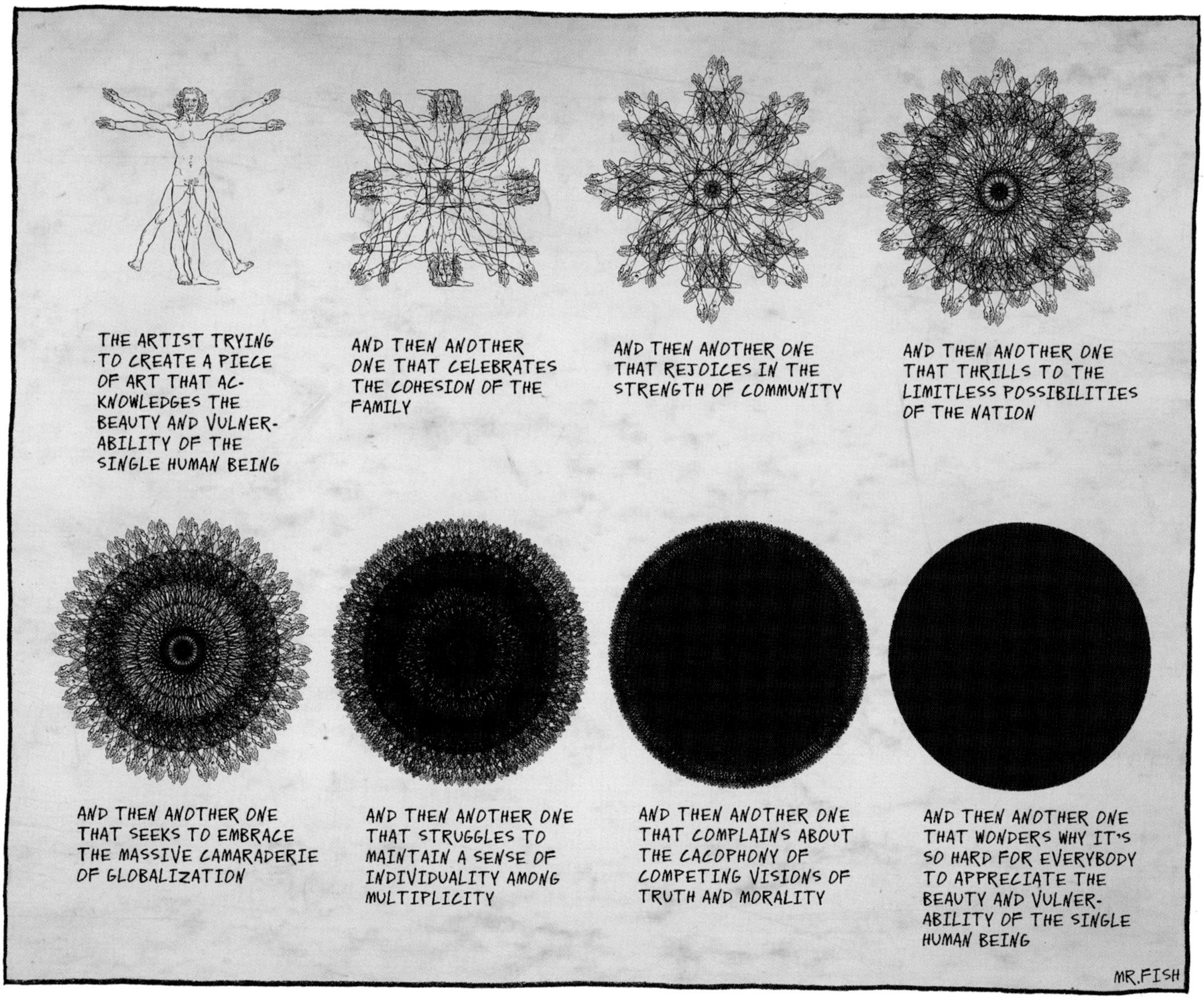
THE ARTIST TRYING TO CREATE A PIECE OF ART THAT ACKNOWLEDGES THE BEAUTY AND VULNERABILITY OF THE SINGLE HUMAN BEING
AND THEN ANOTHER ONE THAT CELEBRATES THE COHESION OF THE FAMILY
AND THEN ANOTHER ONE THAT REJOICES IN THE STRENGTH OF COMMUNITY
AND THEN ANOTHER ONE THAT THRILLS TO THE LIMITLESS POSSIBILITIES OF THE NATION
AND THEN ANOTHER ONE THAT SEEKS TO EMBRACE THE MASSIVE CAMARADERIE OF GLOBALIZATION
AND THEN ANOTHER ONE THAT STRUGGLES TO MAINTAIN A SENSE OF INDIVIDUALITY AMONG MULTIPLICITY
AND THEN ANOTHER ONE THAT COMPLAINS ABOUT THE CACOPHONY OF COMPETING VISIONS OF TRUTH AND MORALITY
AND THEN ANOTHER ONE THAT WONDERS WHY IT'S SO HARD FOR EVERYBODY TO APPRECIATE THE BEAUTY AND VULNERABILITY OF THE SINGLE HUMAN BEING
MR. FISH

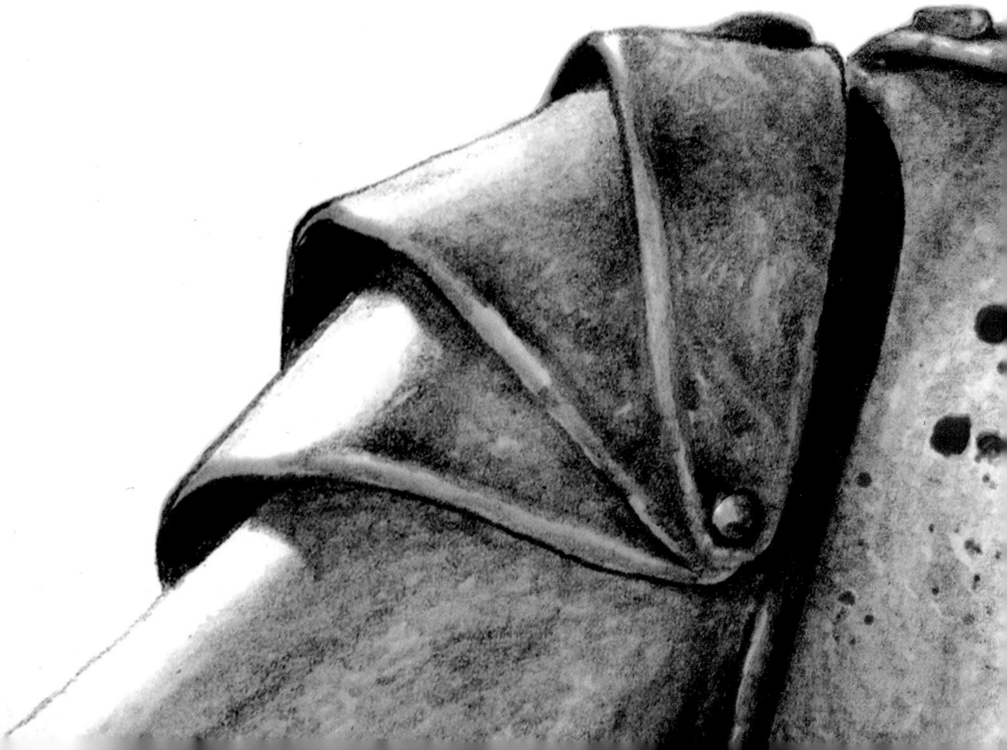

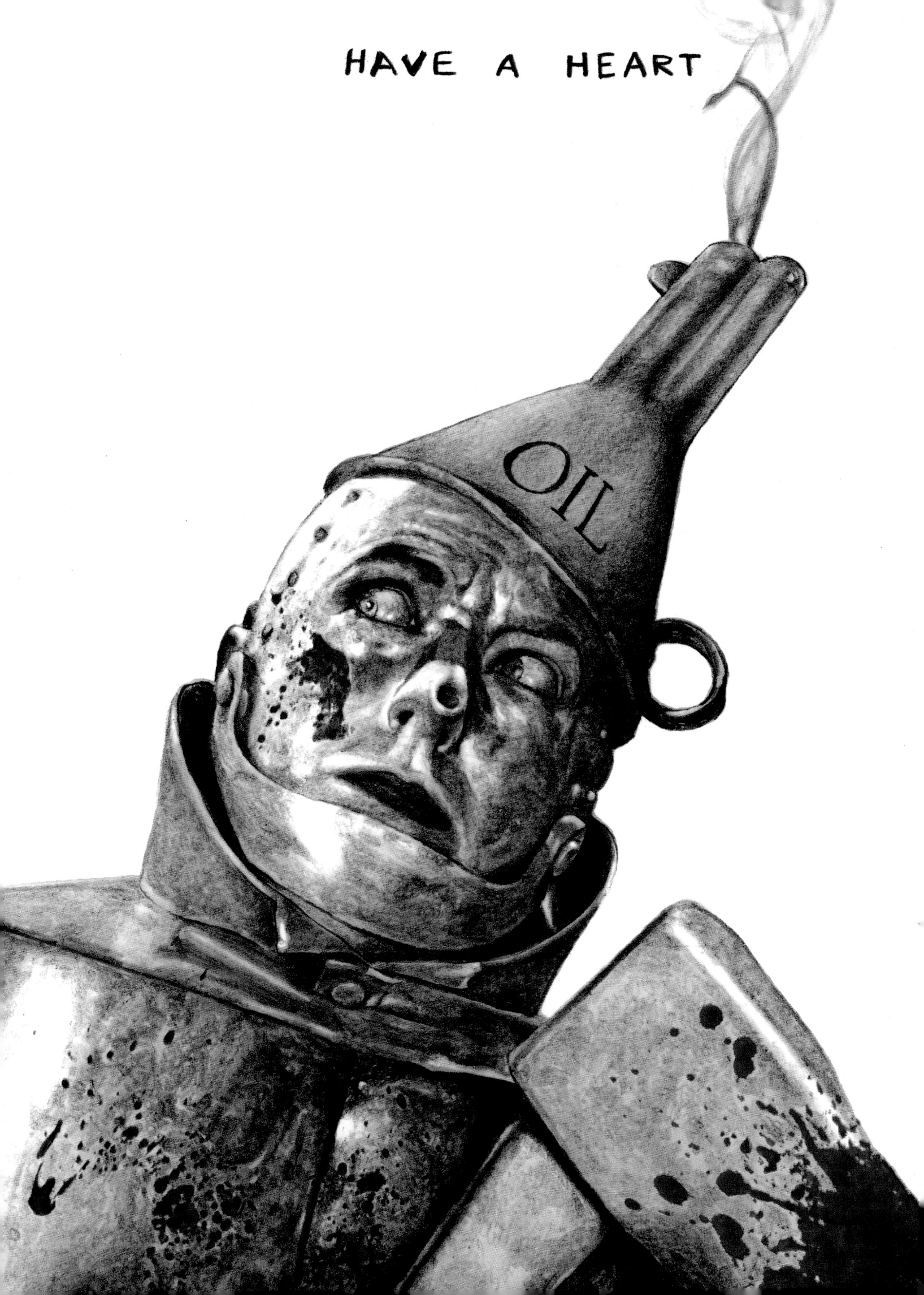
HAVE A HEART
OIL

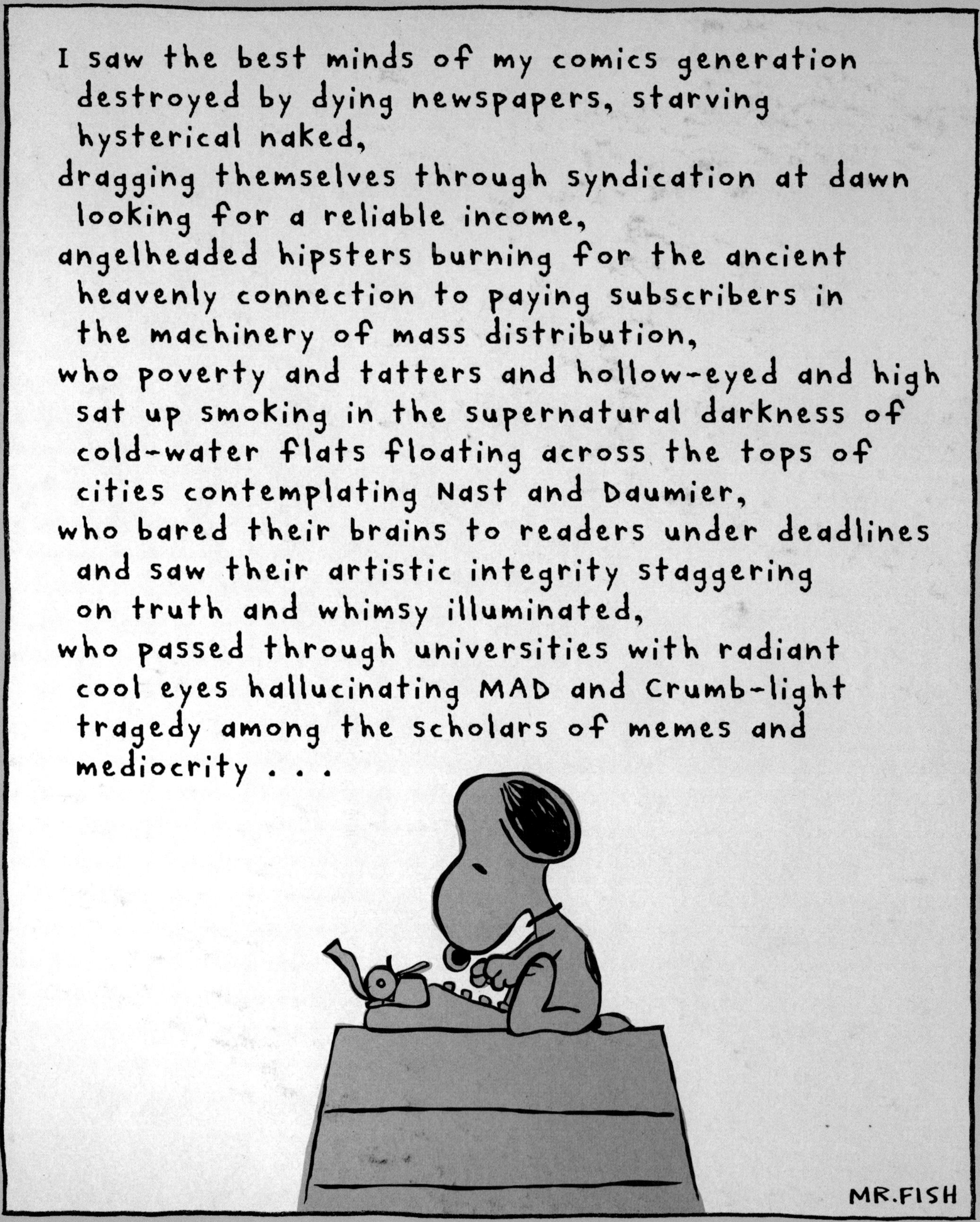
I saw the best minds of my comics generation destroyed by dying newspapers, starving hysterical naked,
dragging themselves through syndication at dawn looking for a reliable income,
angelheaded hipsters burning for the ancient heavenly connection to paying subscribers in the machinery of mass distribution,
who poverty and tatters and hollow-eyed and high sat up smoking in the supernatural darkness of cold-water flats floating across the tops of cities contemplating Nast and Daumier,
who bared their brains to readers under deadlines and saw their artistic integrity staggering on truth and whimsy illuminated,
who passed through universities with radiant cool eyes hallucinating MAD and Crumb-light tragedy among the scholars of memes and mediocrity . . .
MR.FISH

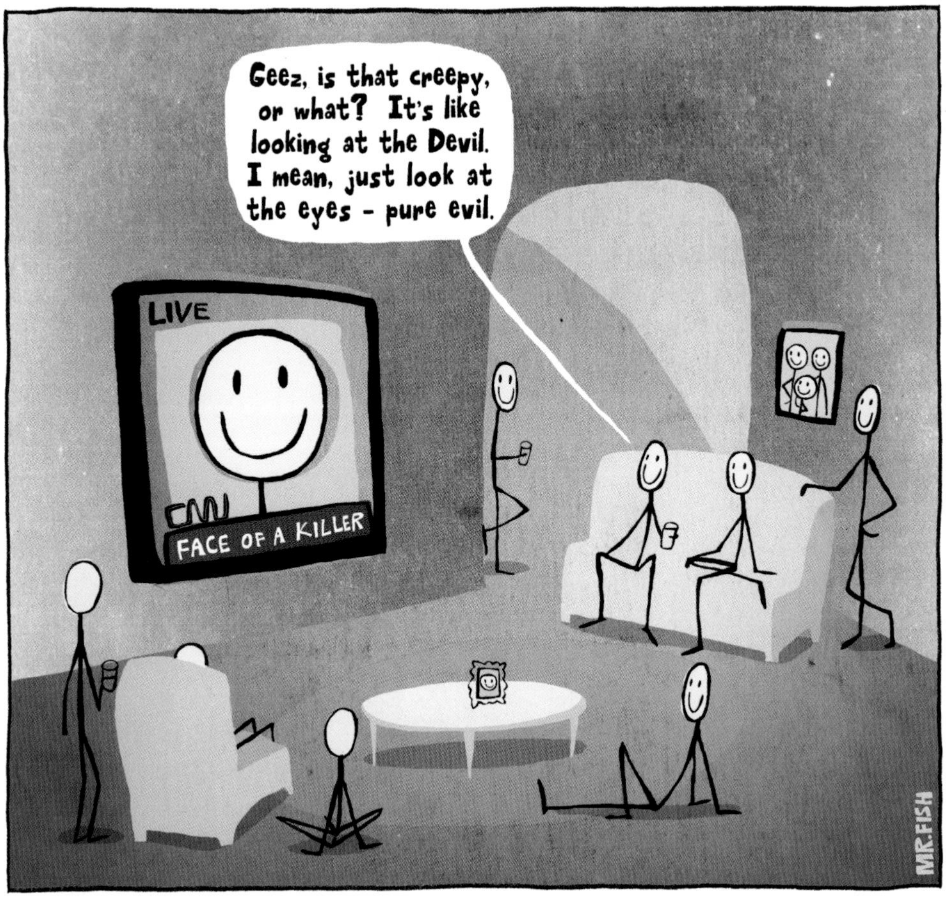
Geez, is that creepy, or what? It's like looking at the Devil. I mean, just look at the eyes - pure evil.
LIVE
FACE OF A KILLER
MR.FISH

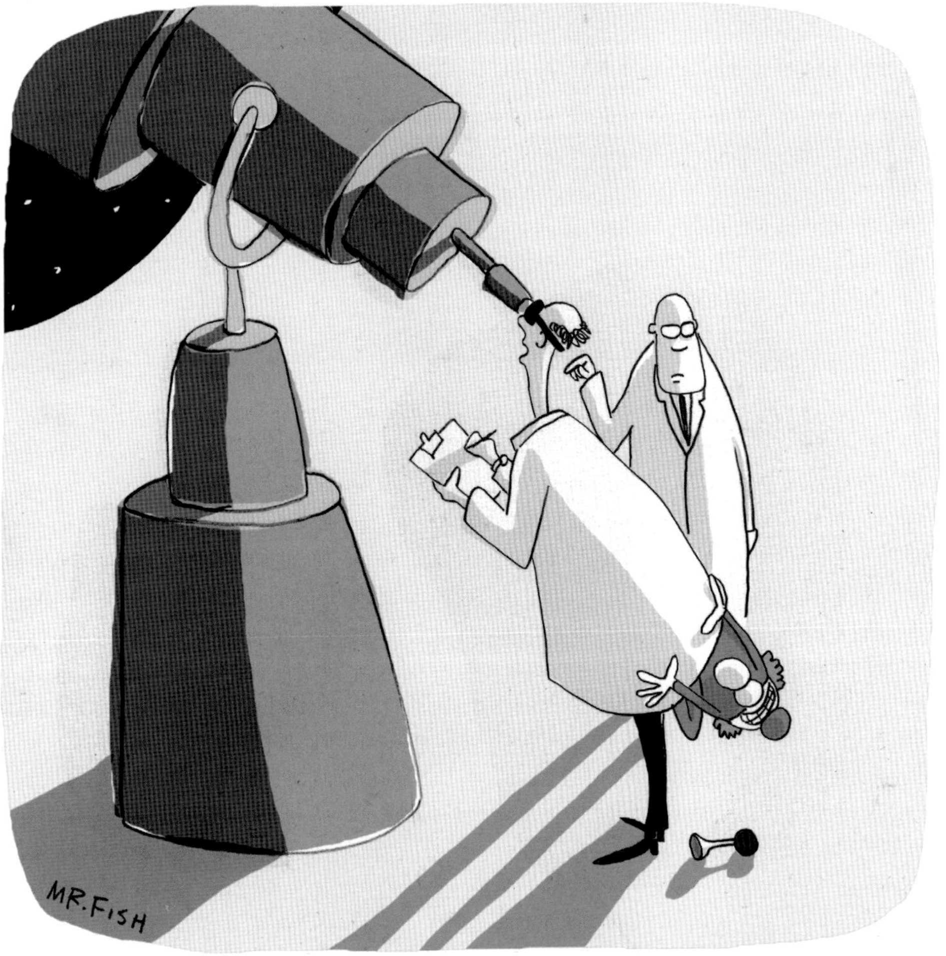
MR.FISH

"Yes, I heard what you said, but trust me – there isn't a clown coming out of Uranus."

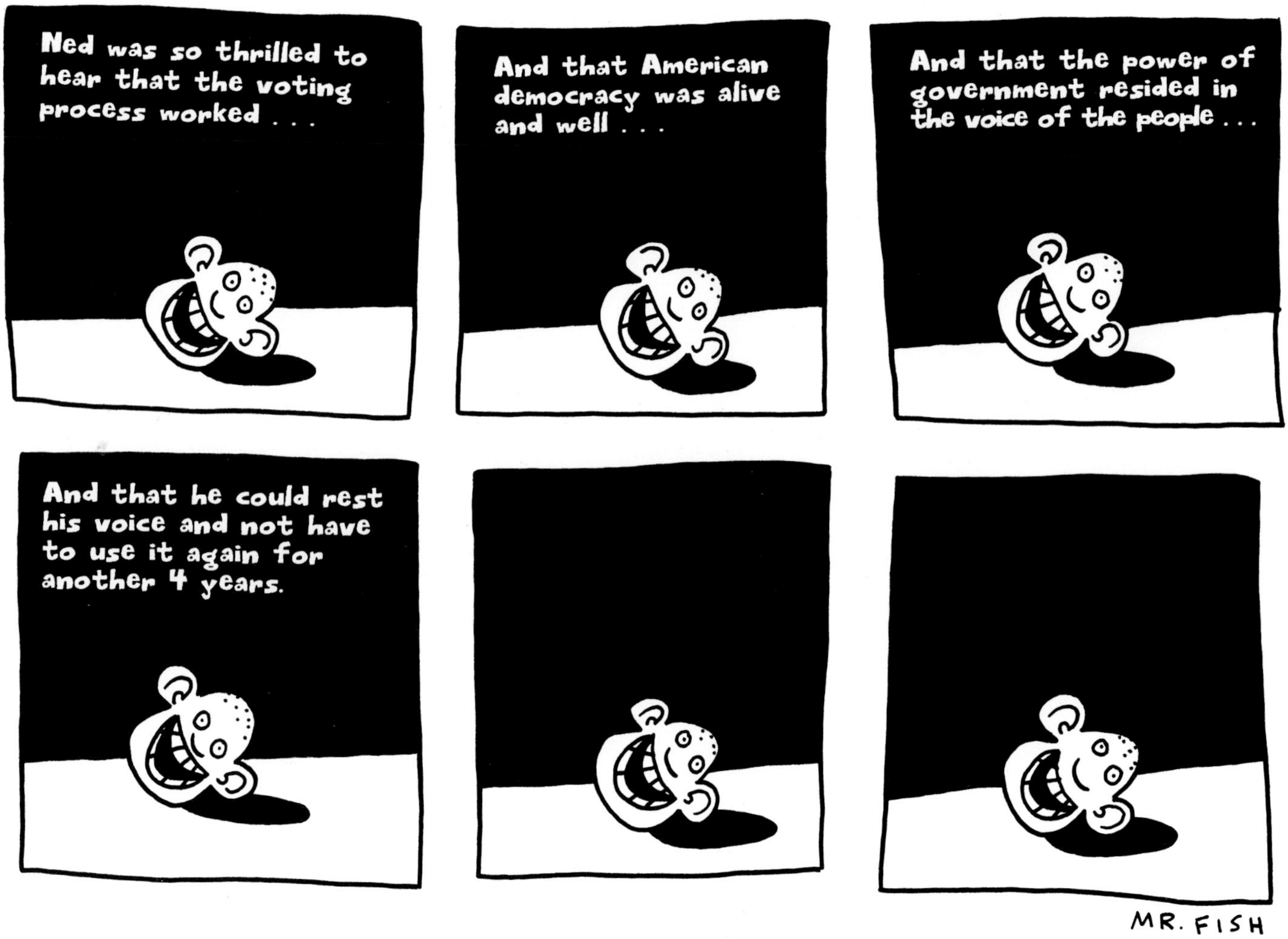
Ned was so thrilled to hear that the voting process worked . . .
And that American democracy was alive and well . . .
And that the power of government resided in the voice of the people . . .
And that he could rest his voice and not have to use it again for another 4 years.
MR. FISH

Fascism all jazzed up with stock options, a 401k plan and comprehensive medical and dental benefits does not automatically become benign capitalism

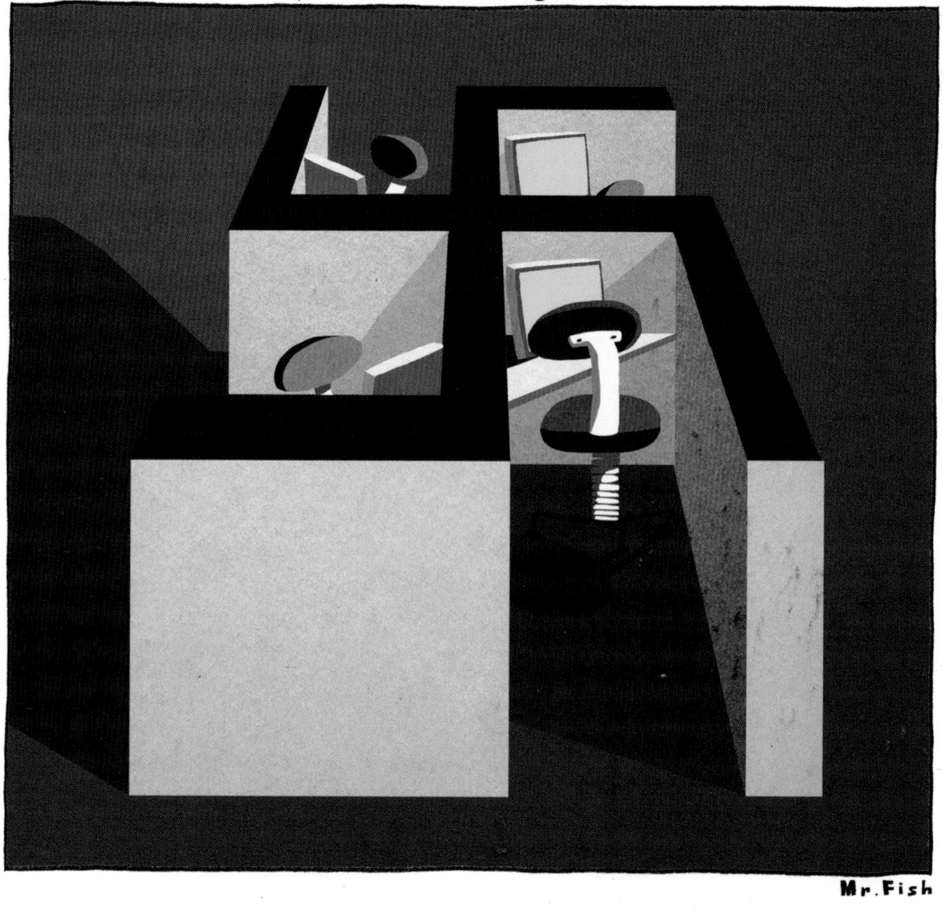
Mr. Fish

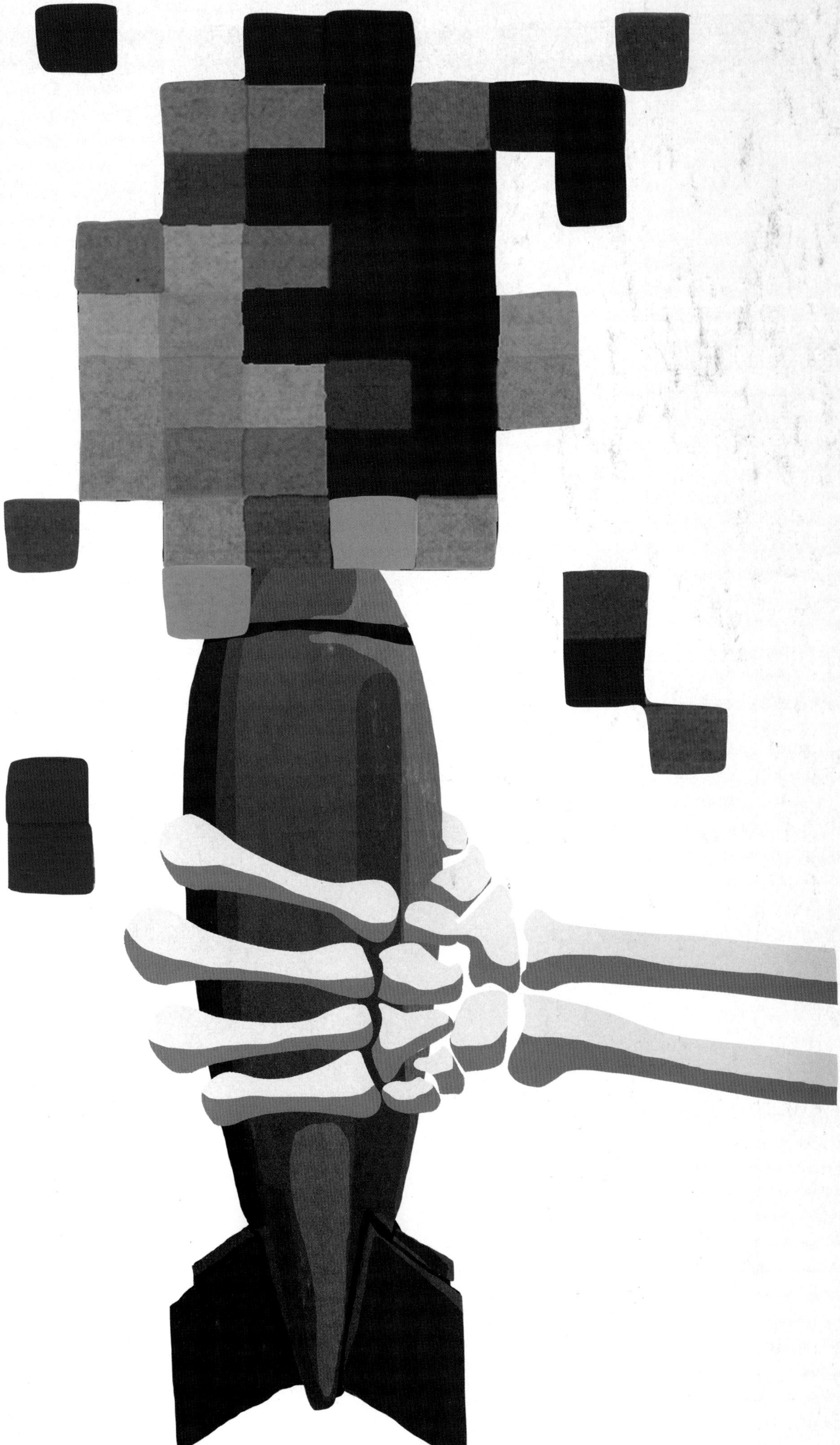

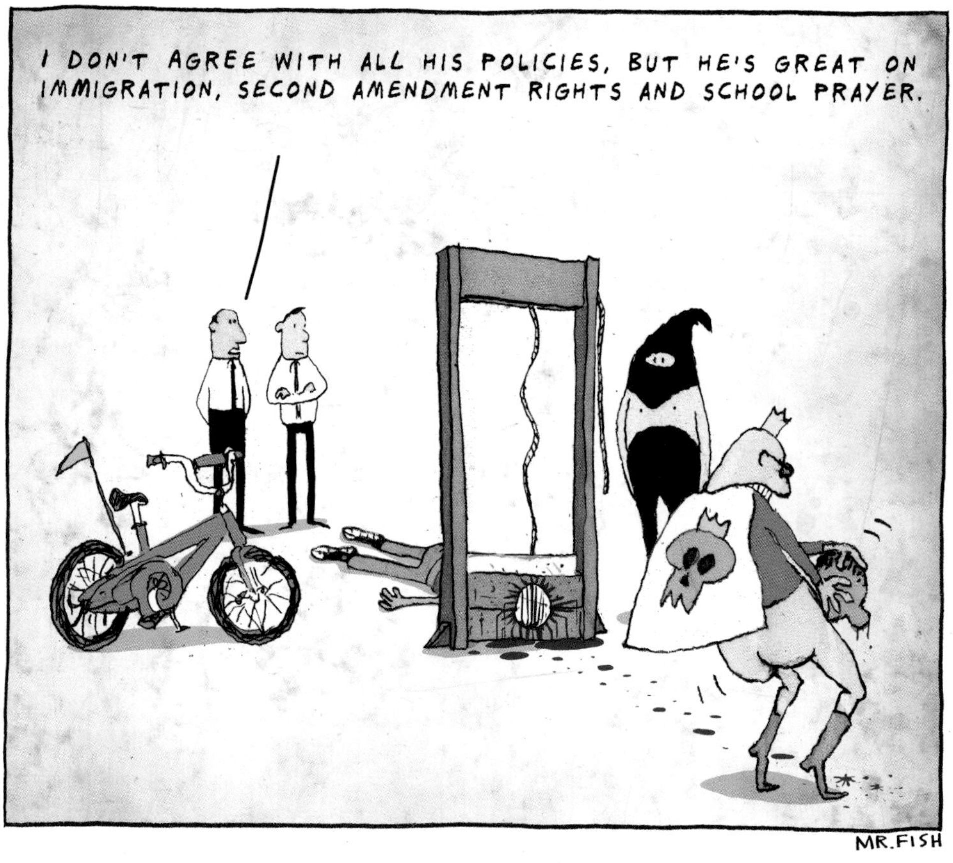
I DON'T AGREE WITH ALL HIS POLICIES, BUT HE'S GREAT ON IMMIGRATION, SECOND AMENDMENT RIGHTS AND SCHOOL PRAYER.
MR.FISH

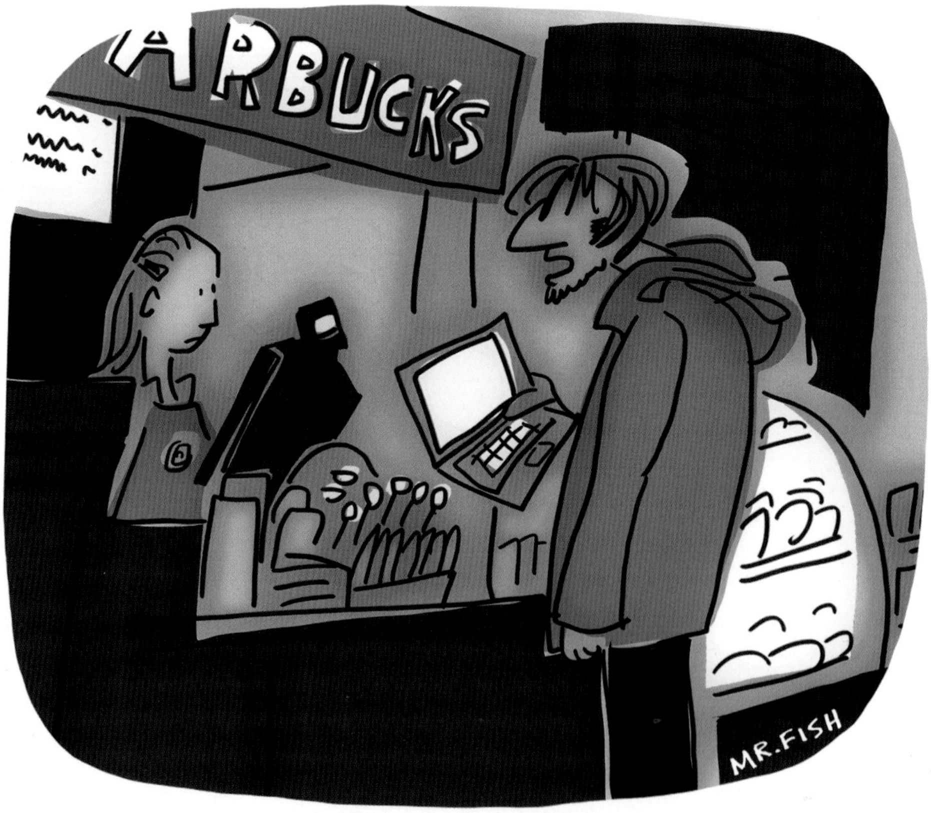
ARBUCKS
MR.FISH

"How can I take my outrage to the street and threaten the government with a show of force guaranteed to make the plutocracy terrified that We The People are pissed off and not going to take their oppressive shit anymore if the WiFi is down?"

At first, Tracy was outraged and felt deceived, but then the cuteness factor of all the little horses turned her anger into the deepest and most profound love she'd ever known.

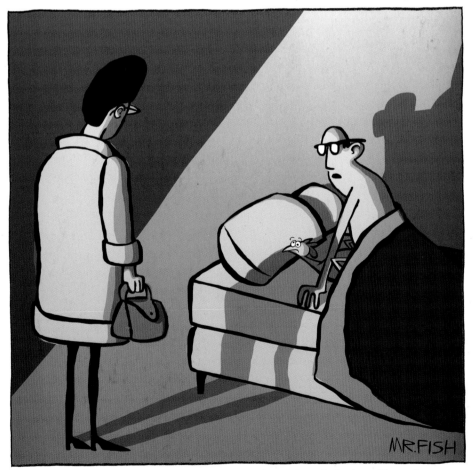

"Wait a minute, honey – this isn't as sick as it looks. She only thinks she's a chicken."

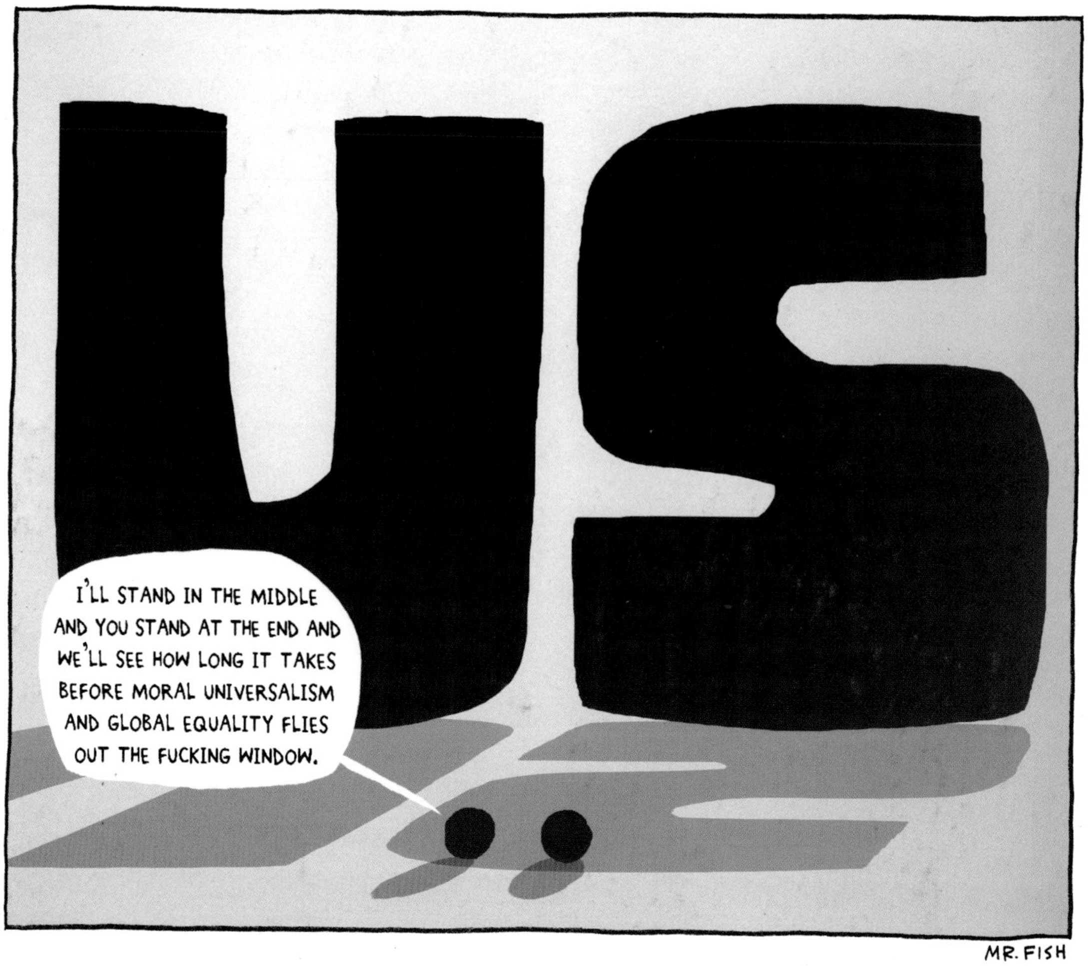
US
I'LL STAND IN THE MIDDLE AND YOU STAND AT THE END AND WE'LL SEE HOW LONG IT TAKES BEFORE MORAL UNIVERSALISM AND GLOBAL EQUALITY FLIES OUT THE FUCKING WINDOW.
MR. FISH

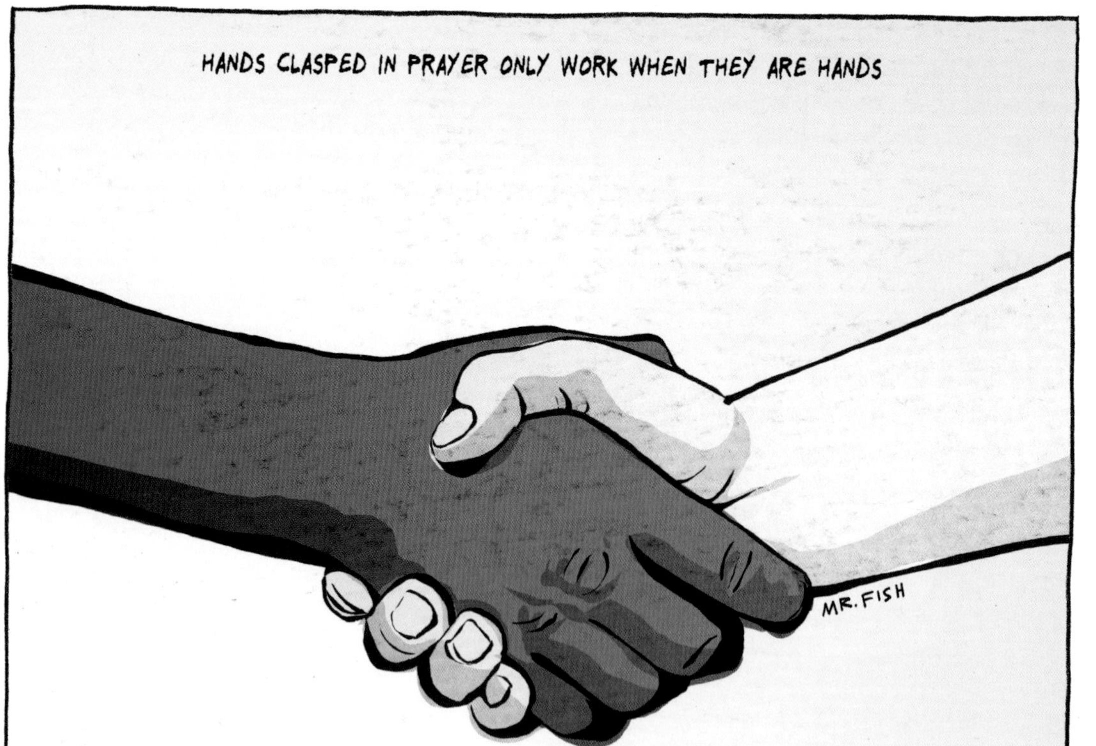
HANDS CLASPED IN PRAYER ONLY WORK WHEN THEY ARE HANDS
MR. FISH
THAT BELONG TO TWO SEPARATE PEOPLE

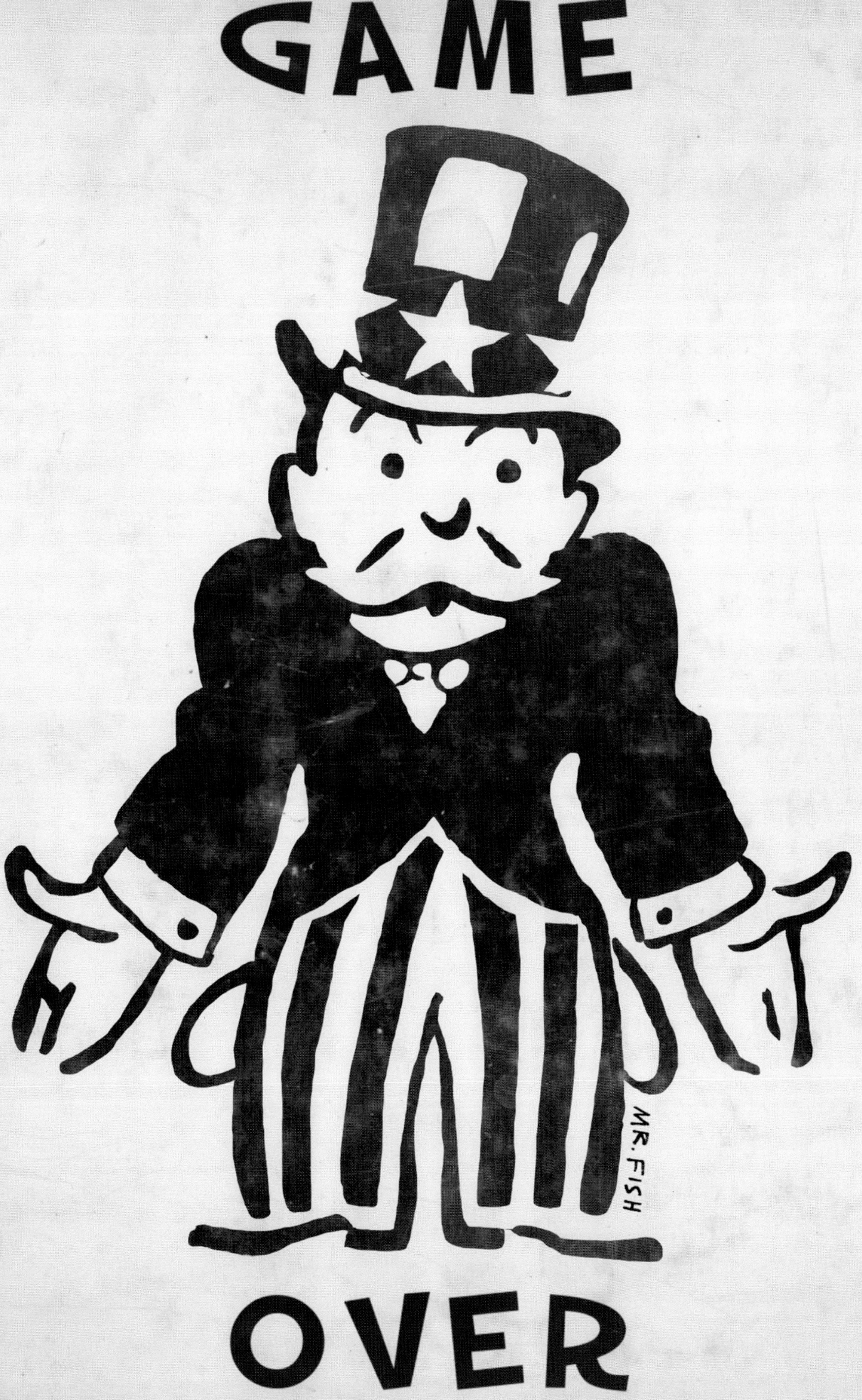
GAME
OVER
MR. FISH

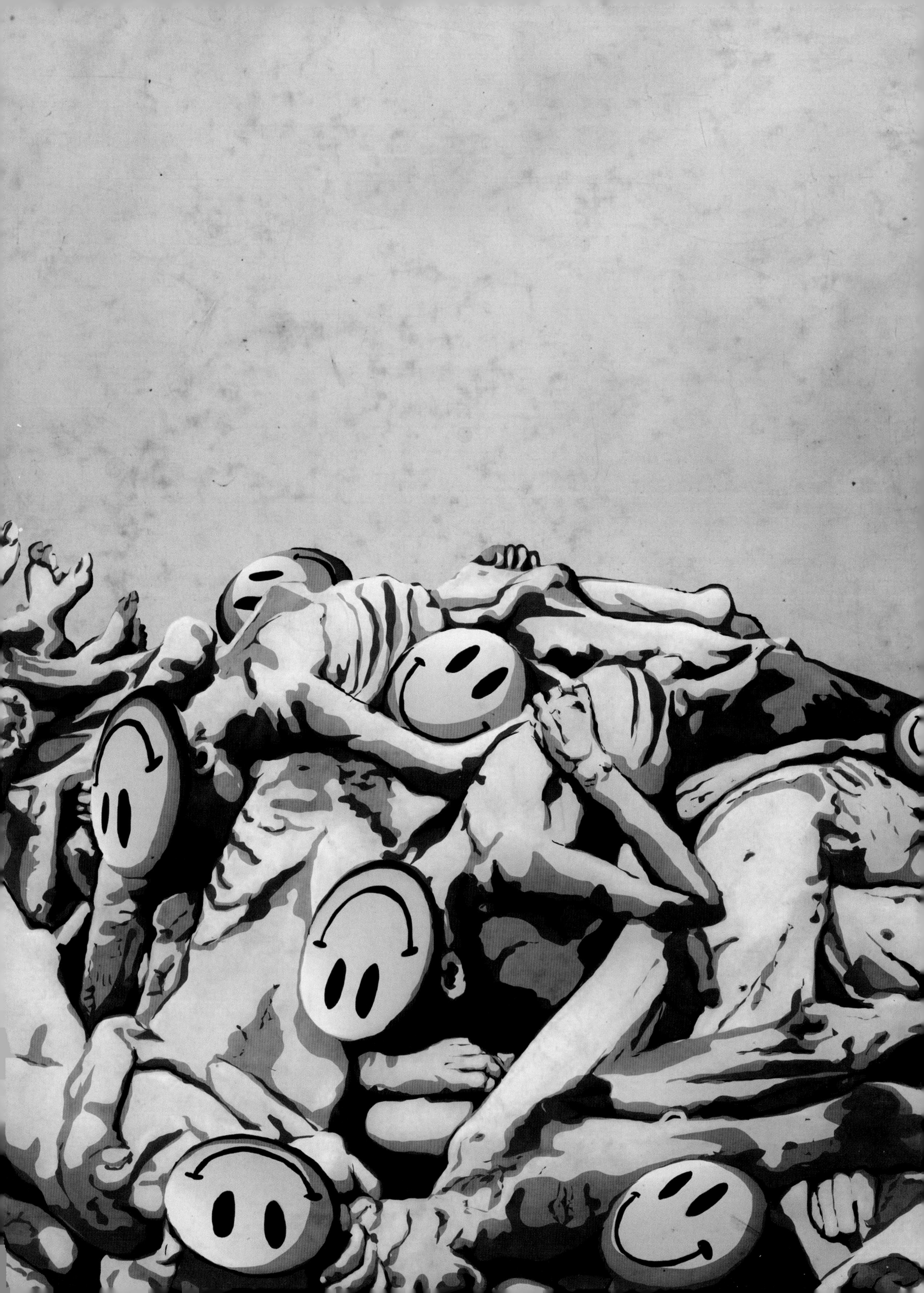

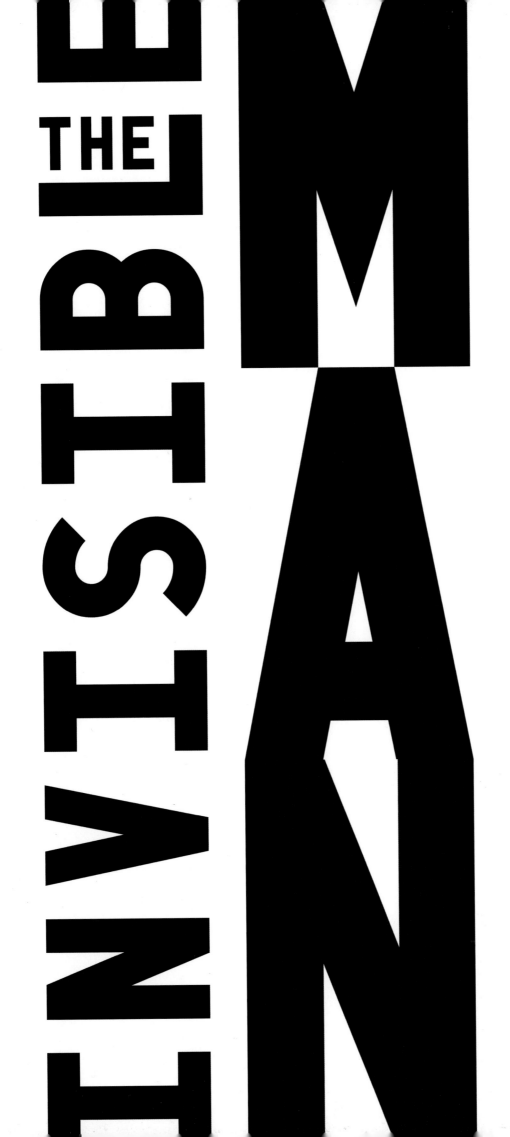

THE INVISIBLE MAN

9

The Invisible Man

THERE'S A STORY that I grew up hearing over and over again about my great-uncle Eddie being blown to smithereens in Tunisia during World War II. In one version, it was a land mine that did it, and in another it was a mortar round from a German Leichter Granatwerfer 36. The single most important detail that had everybody retelling the story, the one that everybody could agree on, was the one about how Eddie's left leg, from just below the kneecap down, was still standing upright when the smoke cleared after the explosion. In fact, it was all that was left of him.

"Those krauts couldn't even knock him down, boy!" hacked an old lunatic named Izzy (whom my mother designated as her *first asshole twice removed* on her mother's side) at a family barbecue over Memorial Day weekend in 1973, his breath smelling like it had been inhaled from the soggy bunghole of a pickle barrel and exhaled through a cat. "No, sirree!" he slurred, steadying himself with his big hammy hand heavy on my 7-year-old shoulder. "That great-uncle of yours had balls! That leg of his should be in the goddamn Smithsonian!"

It was a difficult image to erase from my mind and one that I was seldom without during moments of quiet, most usually when I was trying to fall asleep at night. After all, here was this relative of mine who was flesh and blood, *my* flesh and blood—flesh and blood that was made no more or less invincible by the American flag stitched like a talisman onto its uniform, an M-1 Garand semi-automatic rifle slung at its side as if it were a megaphone for God Almighty, a green mixing bowl strapped to its fresh crew cut as if it were an admission that neither a talisman nor a God were reliable protections against the treachery of men engaged in warfare—and all of a sudden there was a gruesome flash of light and an earsplitting crack in the atmosphere. The relative was instantly gone, except for his leg, this abandoned limb waiting for instructions from a brainstem that had been atomized. It seemed a horrible encroachment of cartoon buffoonery into real life and made me wonder whether Chuck Jones might not be a more reliable authority on universal design than any monk, mullah or king.

Th-th-th-that's all folks!!

Eddie's military portrait, which looked like a Hollywood publicity still from MGM, was hung in the municipal building at town hall, in the east corridor that led to the council chambers. It was right next to the most popular water fountain on the first floor and had much better lighting than did the portrait of John F. Kennedy facing from the opposite wall. I remember glancing over at the Kennedy portrait, which was a crappy oil painting, and imagining that it had been rendered by somebody using a box of Q-tips and whose elbow was constantly being nudged by a llama starved for attention. My grandmother would sometimes take my brother, sister and me out for Slurpees at the local 7-Eleven and then walk us over to where we could cool ourselves in the air conditioning and stare at my great-uncle's picture and envision that the whole world was basking in the exquisite mellifluousness of our loss.

AMERICA'S GIFT TO THE WORLD.

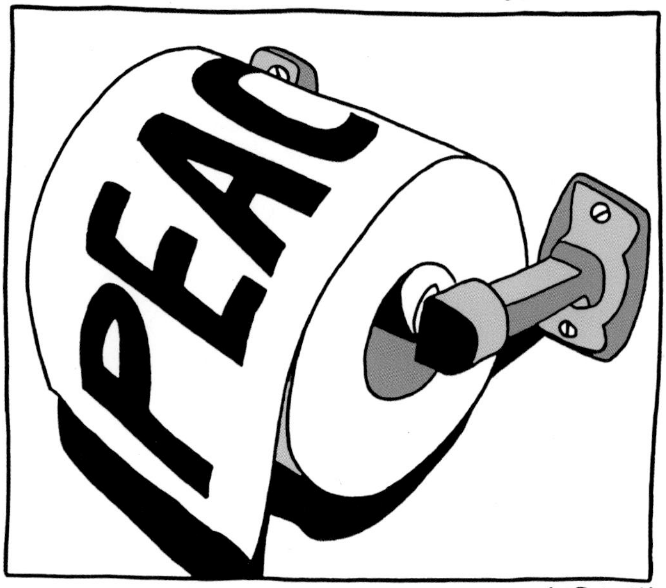
PEAC
MR.FISH

***

We were standing outside the elephant enclosure at the Philadelphia Zoo when I first noticed my grandfather's peculiar habit of grinding his cigarette butts into pulverized tobacco crumbs. Of course, he'd been doing it for years, but when you're 7 years old you suddenly start seeing things that, though they may have been happening all along, appear brand new because they coincide with burgeoning cognitive abilities that you never had before. It had also recently occurred to me that not everybody had a grandmother who, armed with only her pocketbook and a housedress stuffed with used balls of Kleenex and half-rolls of wintergreen Life Savers, was able to steal whole mannequins, piece by piece, from department stores and fill her backyard pool with the faux carnage because she thought it would be fun for the kids.

"It was just something we did during the war so the Germans wouldn't know we were ever there," said my grandfather, rubbing my back as we walked past the vulture cage. I could tell that he didn't want to talk about it. It was his habit, whenever my brother and sister and I asked him to talk about anything from World War II, to say that there wasn't anything to say about it, except that it was sad and a really horrible experience. Then he would light up a Lucky Strike. Then he would smoke it down to practically nothing and smash the butt. It always amazed us to see just how little evidence he left behind whenever we walked away from those unanswered questions.

***

The only other photograph that I ever saw of my great-uncle, besides the one hanging in the municipal building, was one that had escaped a house fire at the address where my great-grandmother lived for 40 years. It was a picture of Eddie posing with a fish at the edge of a lake in Lenape, PA, in 1935, when he was 15 years old and as cocksure as a new pear. In the photo, he is shirtless and has a cigarette sticking out of his mouth, as does the fish he is holding with his two fingers hooked beneath its gills. His swimming trunks are oversized to the point of being clownish, and his eyes, as intense as tiny cinders, are pinched into a fiendish squint by the bright sunlight and a ludicrous grin. His black hair falls jagged over his sweaty forehead as if it were the disembodied hand of a shaggy monster preparing to uncap his skull, and his bare feet are caked with mud. Nothing in his smile registers the agonizing telepathy from those of us in his future warning him against the inevitable.

***

I was recently asked by one of my 8-year-old twin daughters over breakfast what my grandfather was like, and I found myself at a complete loss for words. Every attempt at a description failed. In many ways, he was like the sun to me—impossible to look at directly, yet absolutely essential when it came to illuminating the hodgepodgery that was the rest of my family. I started to wonder whether maybe my relationship with him was so impossible to describe, not because it was amorphous or extraneous, but rather because it was never out of my sight

and, therefore, completely invisible to me. Trying to reinvent the constant that was my grandfather as an anomaly was like trying to jazz up a glass of water just to make it less boring to somebody who might be uninspired by the fact that the most useful and life-sustaining compound that exists on Earth is clear and tasteless.

***

I was probably 8 years old when my grandmother told me how Eddie's leg, still wearing the combat boot, was sent back to her mother and buried in her vegetable garden by a local Boy Scout troop, while a 400-pound neighbor named Bunny Tinkle played *Yankee Doodle* on the rims of wineglasses filled with water, and relatives cried and the children of relatives tried to keep a straight face and raccoons, already in face masks, waited for nightfall.

"The thing was eventually yanked out of the ground by some animal," my grandmother said, "and disappeared. Of course, my mother tried to comfort everybody by insisting that that's the way Eddie would've wanted it. 'He was always wandering off in the middle of the night,' she would tell them. 'I wouldn't be surprised if that leg was walking the boardwalk in Atlantic City or hitchhiking across the country—Eddie always wanted to see the Hoover Dam.'" My grandmother would then try to imitate her mother's excruciatingly forced smile, doing her best to make it look like something wet and clammy that she'd picked up off the ground and laid across her face, while

THE CANDIDATE WORKING ON HIS CAMPAIGN PROMISES

MR. FISH

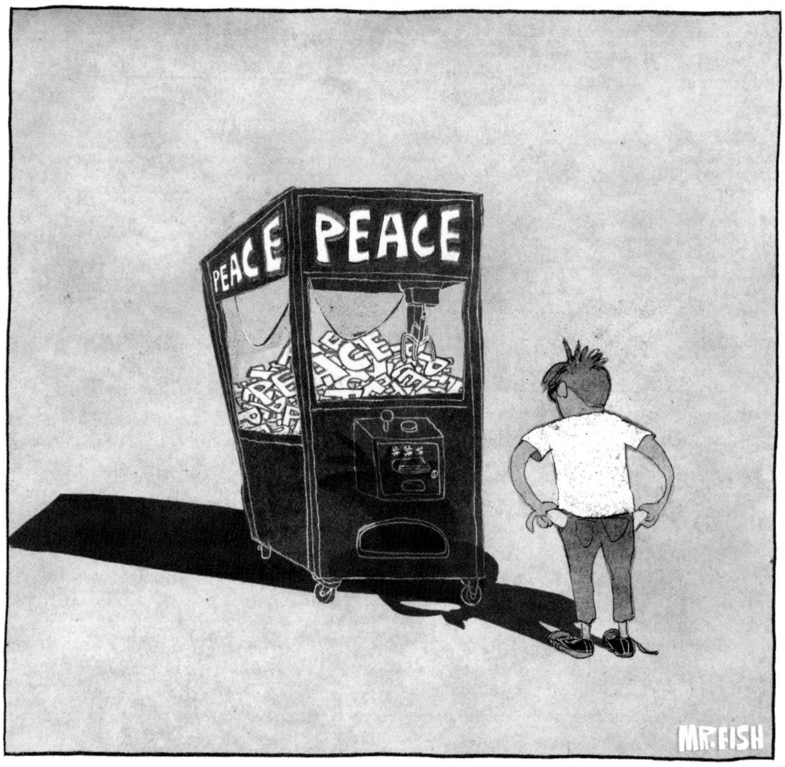
PEACE
PEACE
MR.FISH

I did my damnedest to figure out how a foot might go about thumbing a ride from a trucker out on the interstate. I would then try to imagine the uncomfortable silence inside the cab once the leg was picked up, the glow from the dashboard lights bathing my great-uncle's remains and making them appear as ghoulish and vague as an aberration. I imagined the sound of a single fly buzzing around the gaping and ragged sore that capped Eddie's stump and the tightening of the driver's jaw as he groped around for conversation that would both fill the excruciating silence and wouldn't disparage his passenger's most obvious handicap.

Minus the macabre resolve of a dead soldier's leg standing alone inside the gentle rain of vaporized meat, the death of my great-uncle was made beautiful to me by relatives who decided, like so many others prone to the questionable practice of ventriloquizing the deceased, that heroism works best when the person chosen to be the hero no longer exists and, therefore, cannot contradict his gallantry by continuing to demonstrate the circumstantial mediocrity and poetic fallibility that comes with being alive.

***

When my grandfather died in 1995, a fountain featuring a statue of a golfer standing beneath an umbrella with his chin in his hand was erected in his vegetable garden by relatives who didn't seem to care that he had never picked up a club. After the pleasant ping-pong of jokes and jabs exchanged between brothers and sisters who hadn't seen one another in a while, his ashes were sprinkled into the soil around his tomato plants and disappeared as soon as they hit the ground.

***

When Eddie's picture was moved in 2008 from the municipal building at town hall to the lobby of the firehouse and put into a long glass case with other veterans who had been blown to smithereens in more recent wars, I went to go see it. What surprised me about seeing the photograph for the first time in 35 years wasn't how much smaller it was than I remembered, but rather the extended family that my great-uncle was now fraternizing with, all of them orbiting a giant-sized framed photo of George W. Bush standing at Ground Zero with a megaphone. I thought about how peculiar it was that all the soldiers were smiling, particularly when there was so much more room in the lobby for the construction of more and more glass cases.

Walking around and looking at the crowd of fallen heroes before me, I started to cry. Not because I was overcome suddenly by the tragedy of their meaningless passing, but rather because I couldn't stop thinking about the sad golfer, who was not my grandfather, standing all alone not 10 miles away in a basin of clear rainwater for anybody who cared to notice.

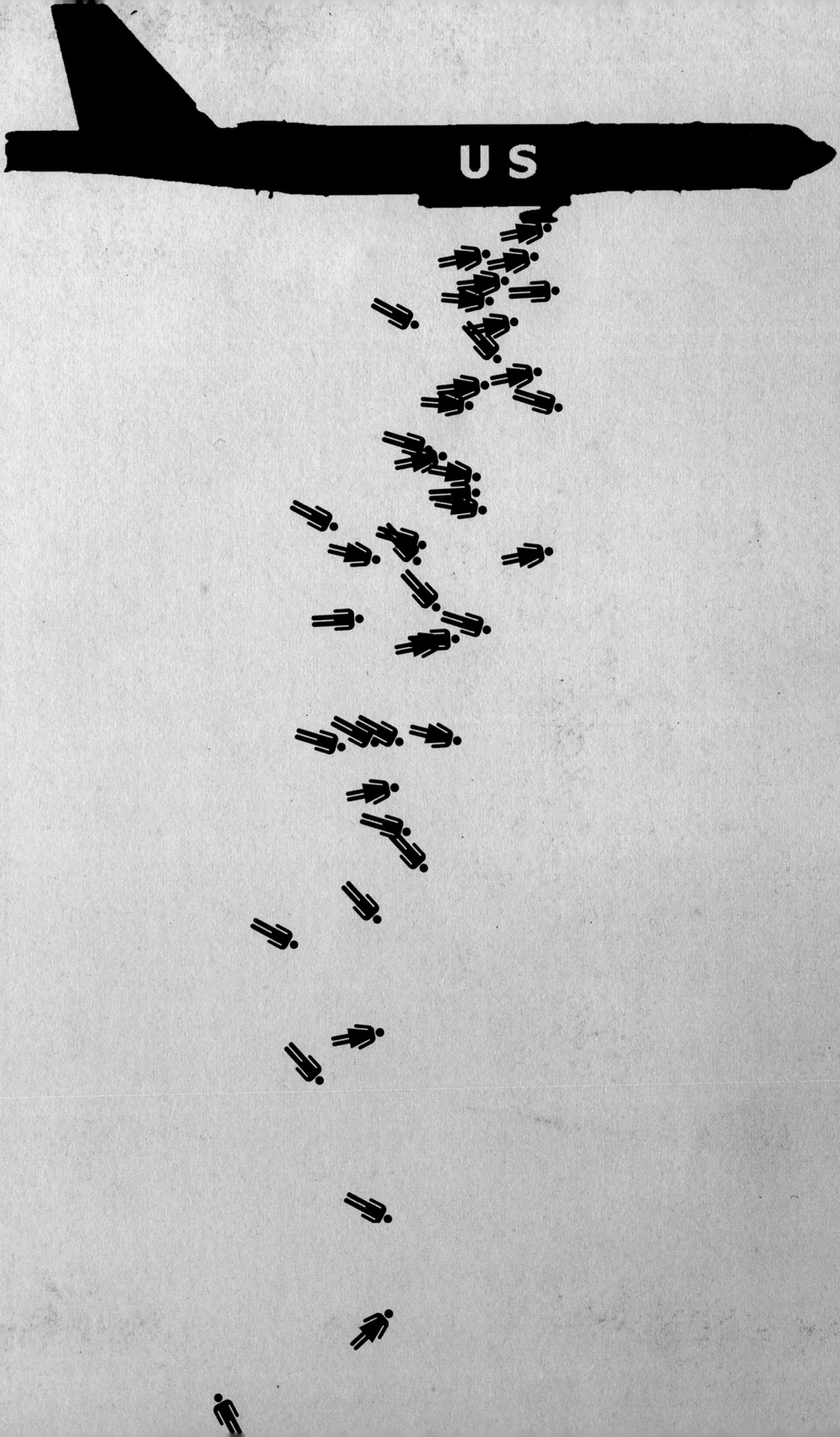
US

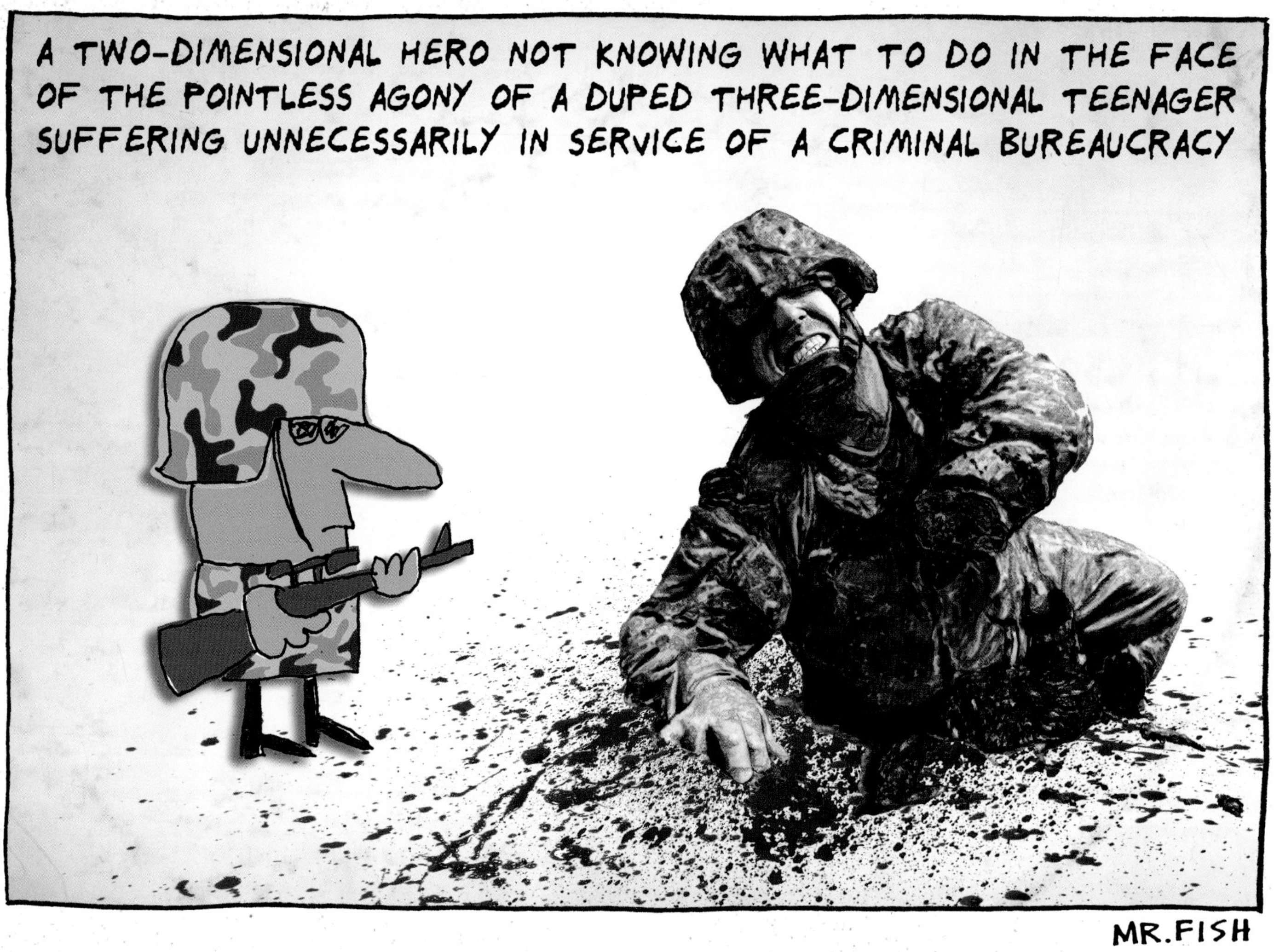
A TWO-DIMENSIONAL HERO NOT KNOWING WHAT TO DO IN THE FACE OF THE POINTLESS AGONY OF A DUPED THREE-DIMENSIONAL TEENAGER SUFFERING UNNECESSARILY IN SERVICE OF A CRIMINAL BUREAUCRACY
MR. FISH

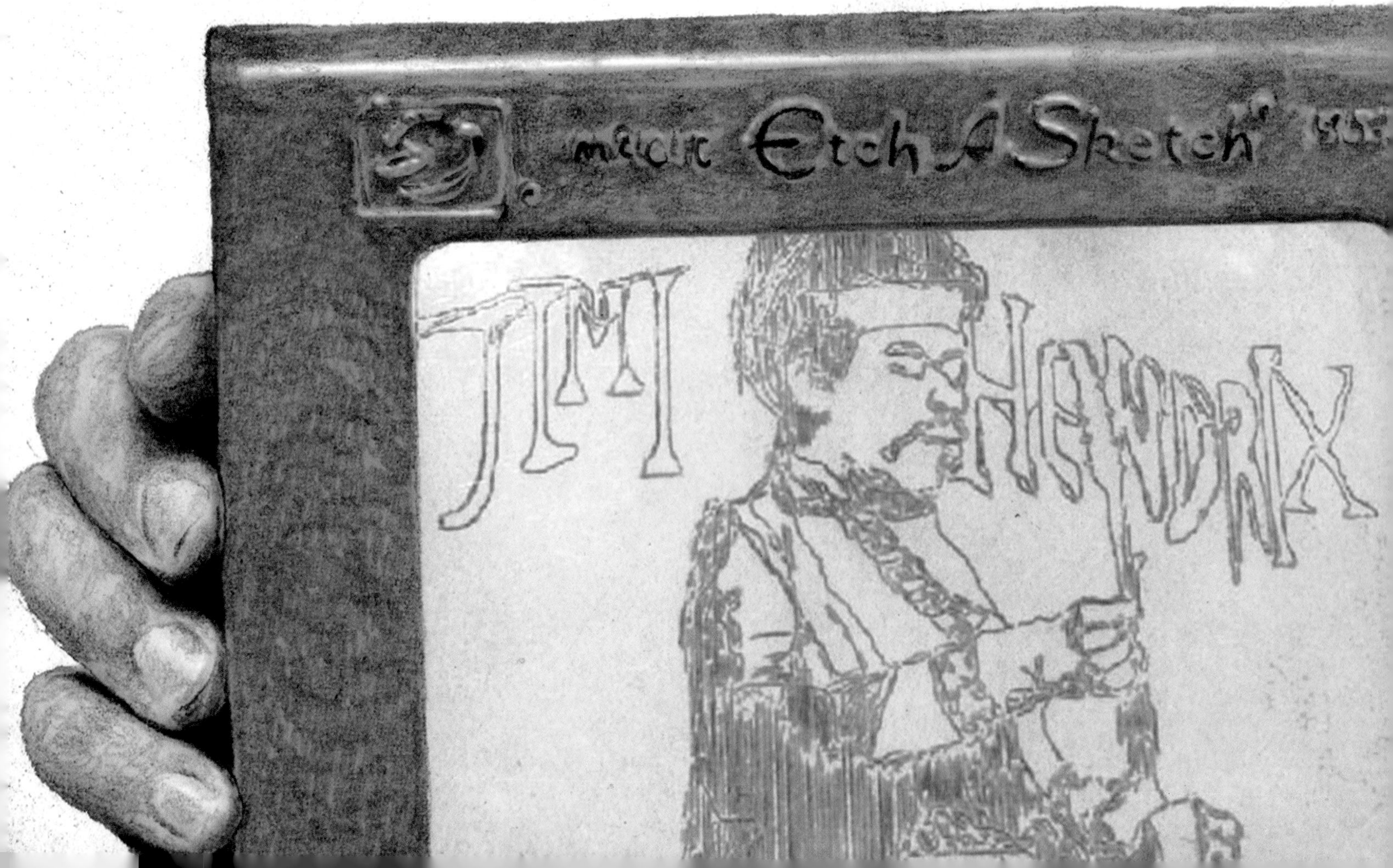
Etch A Sketch
JIMI HENDRIX

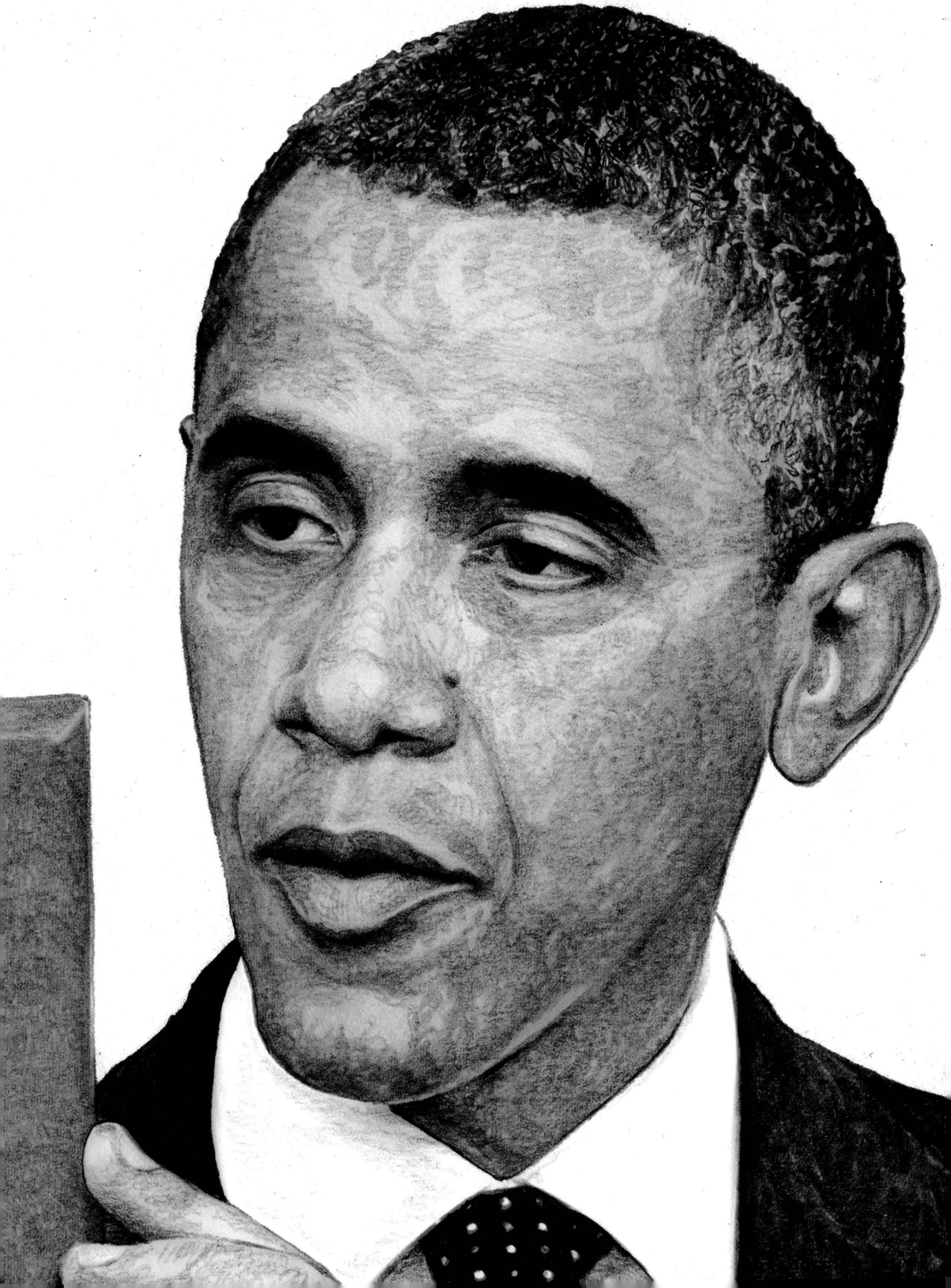

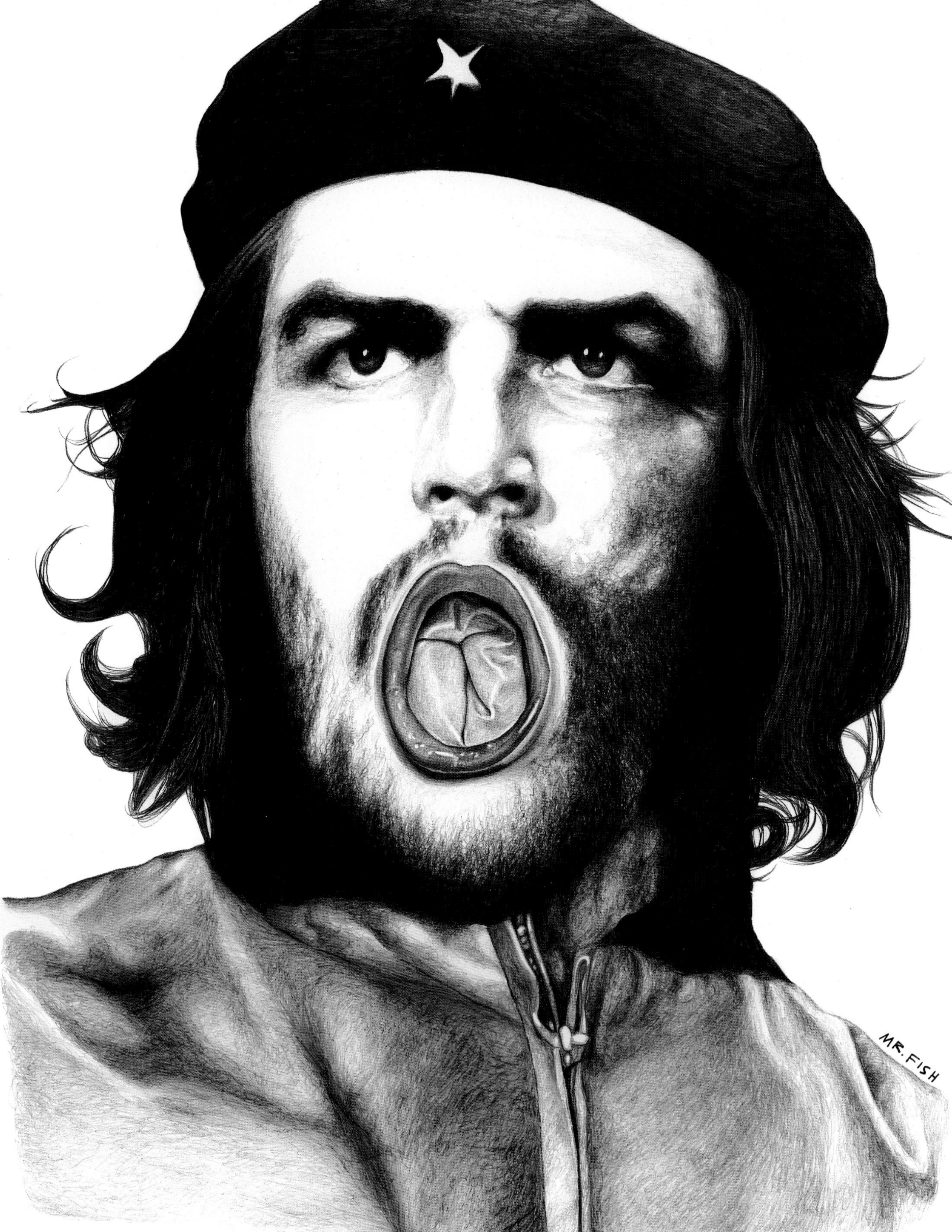
MR. FISH

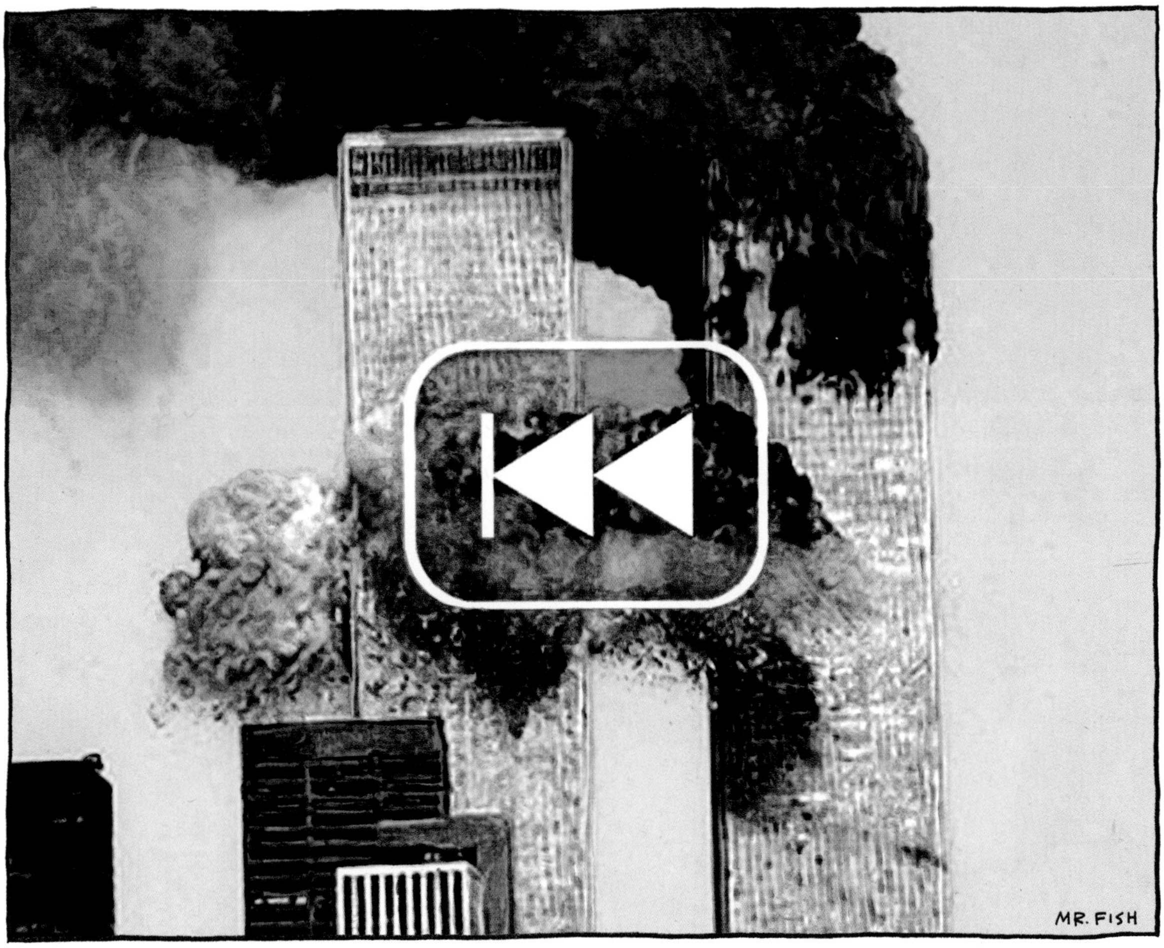
MR. FISH

BILLIONS AND BILLIONS SAVED

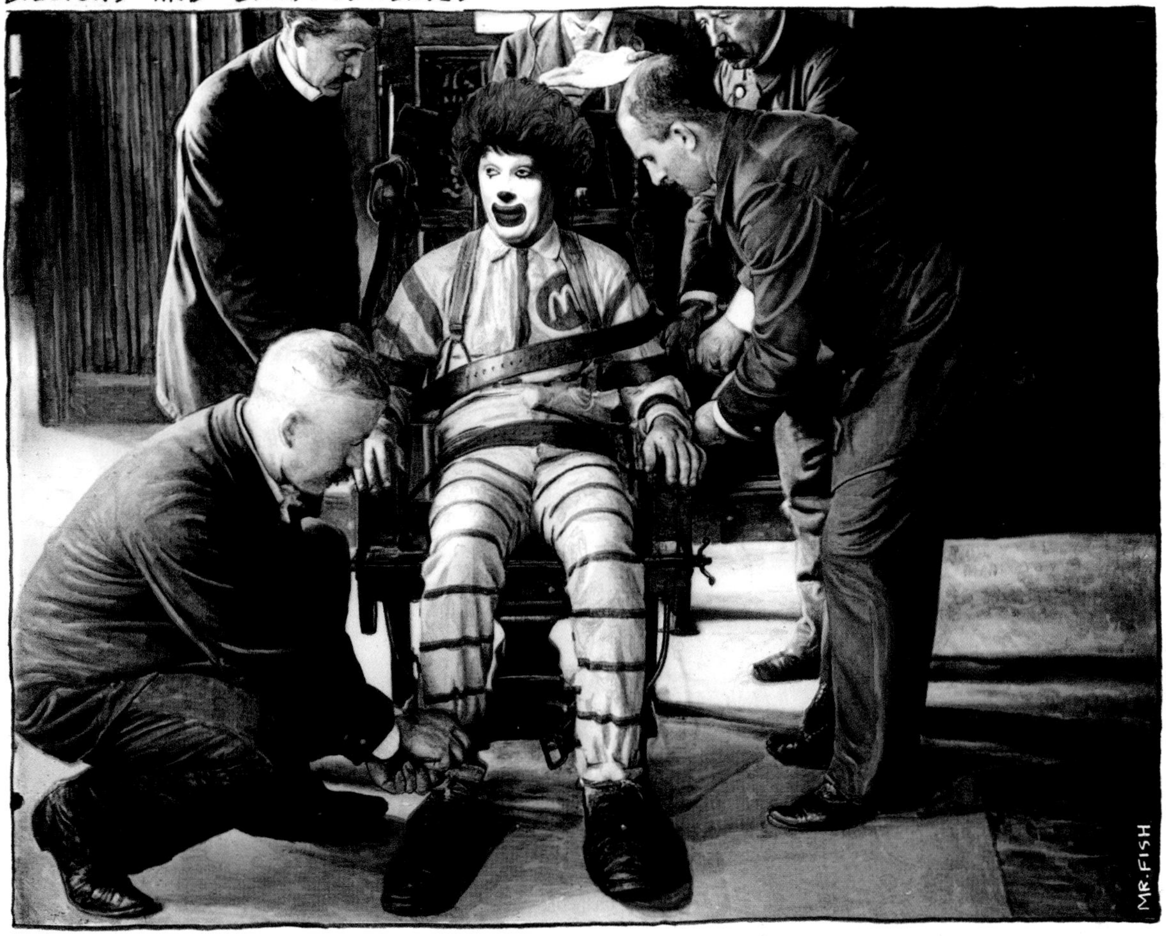
MR. FISH

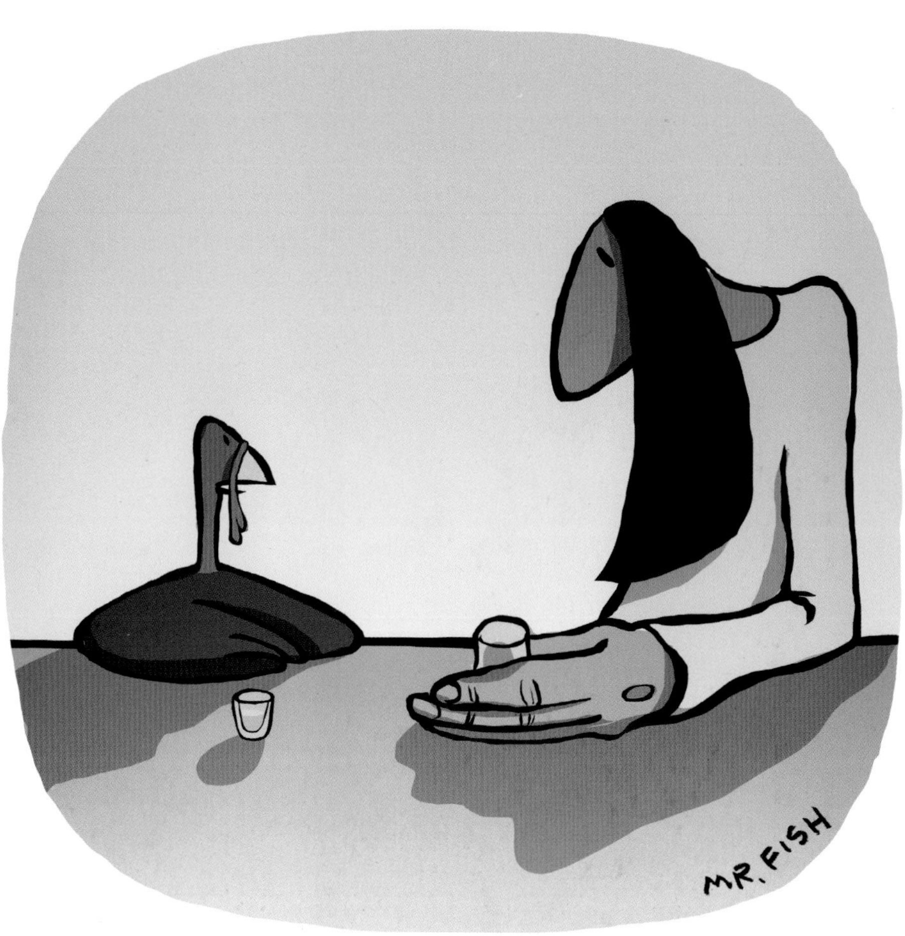
MR. FISH

"I hear you, brother – I can guaran-fucking-tee you that if Santa Claus and the Easter Bunny had to get fucking murdered every year as part of their holiday narrative like we do there'd be a whole lot less ho-ho-hoing and hippity-fucking-hopping to choke down every goddamn year and we'd all be better off for it."

BILLY FINALLY COMING UPON A WAR MONUMENT THAT DIDN'T INSULT HIS INTELLIGENCE

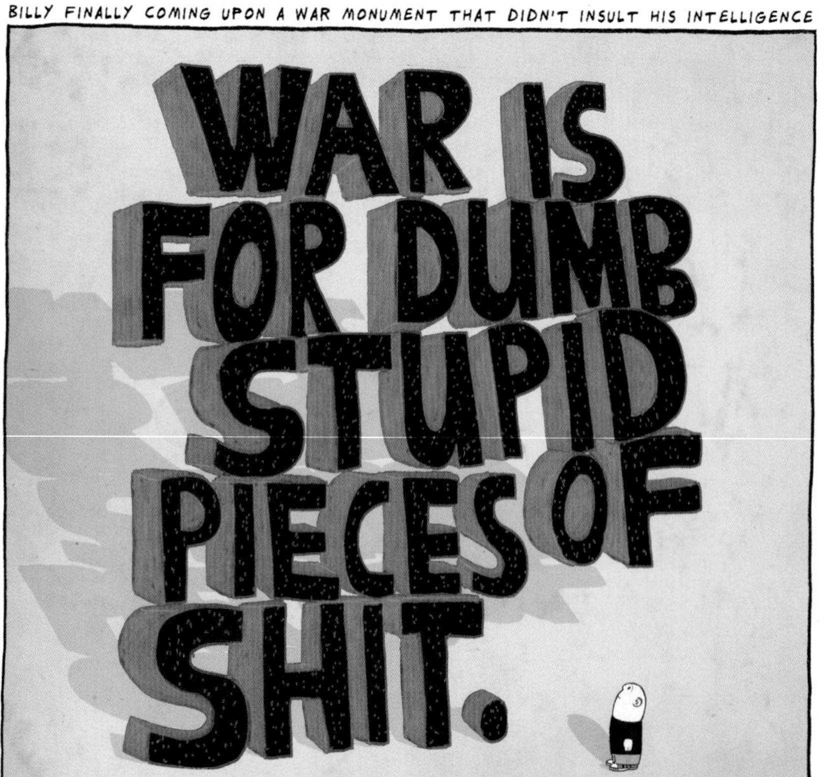
WAR IS FOR DUMB STUPID PIECES OF SHIT.
MR. FISH

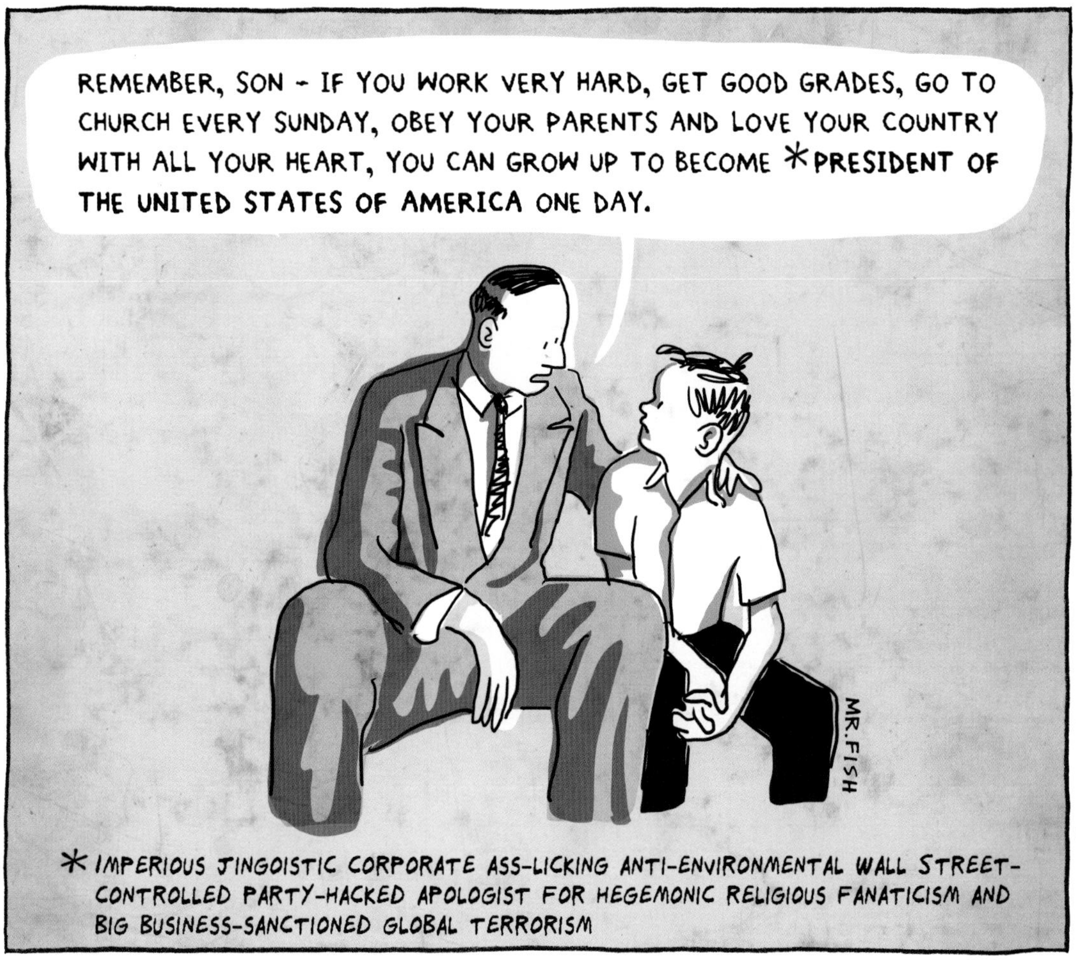
REMEMBER, SON - IF YOU WORK VERY HARD, GET GOOD GRADES, GO TO CHURCH EVERY SUNDAY, OBEY YOUR PARENTS AND LOVE YOUR COUNTRY WITH ALL YOUR HEART, YOU CAN GROW UP TO BECOME *PRESIDENT OF THE UNITED STATES OF AMERICA ONE DAY.
MR.FISH
*IMPERIOUS JINGOISTIC CORPORATE ASS-LICKING ANTI-ENVIRONMENTAL WALL STREET-CONTROLLED PARTY-HACKED APOLOGIST FOR HEGEMONIC RELIGIOUS FANATICISM AND BIG BUSINESS-SANCTIONED GLOBAL TERRORISM

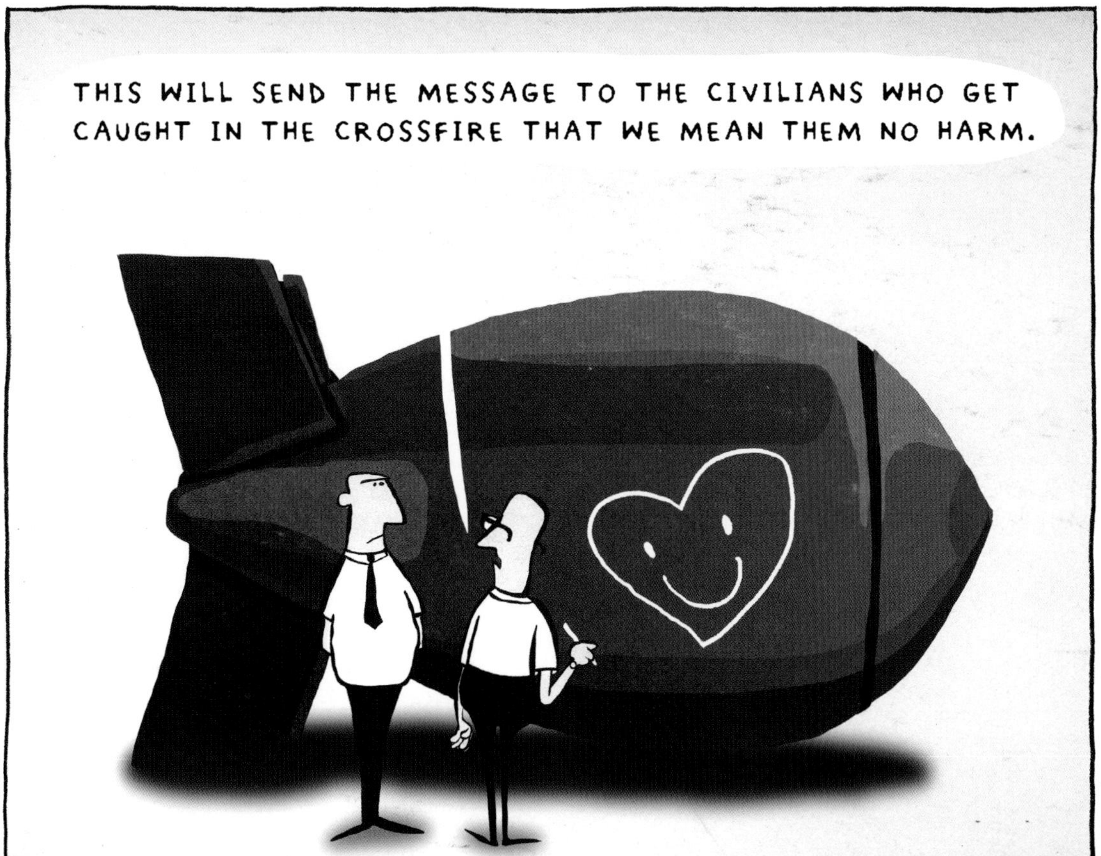
THIS WILL SEND THE MESSAGE TO THE CIVILIANS WHO GET CAUGHT IN THE CROSSFIRE THAT WE MEAN THEM NO HARM.
MR.FISH

CORPORATE PHIL AND CORPORATE STAN TAKING A MOMENT TO ACKNOWLEDGE
THE IMPROVEMENTS MADE BY CORPORATE AMERICAN OVER THE LAST 50 YEARS
WHEN IT COMES TO MAKING AVERAGE JOE AND AVERAGE DICK FEEL AS IF LIFE
IS DEEP AND PROFOUND AND WORTH LIVING

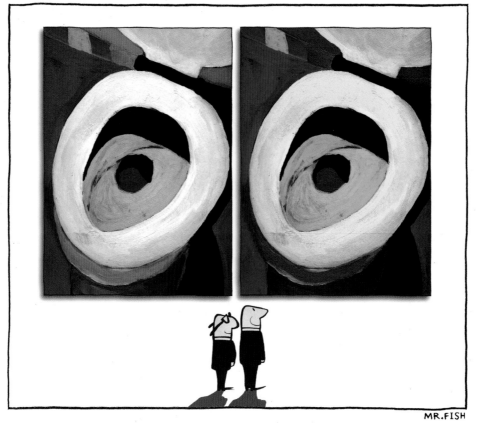

Nothing will ever come of a Climate Change Summit that uses the
wrong machine to determine how and why we should save the planet

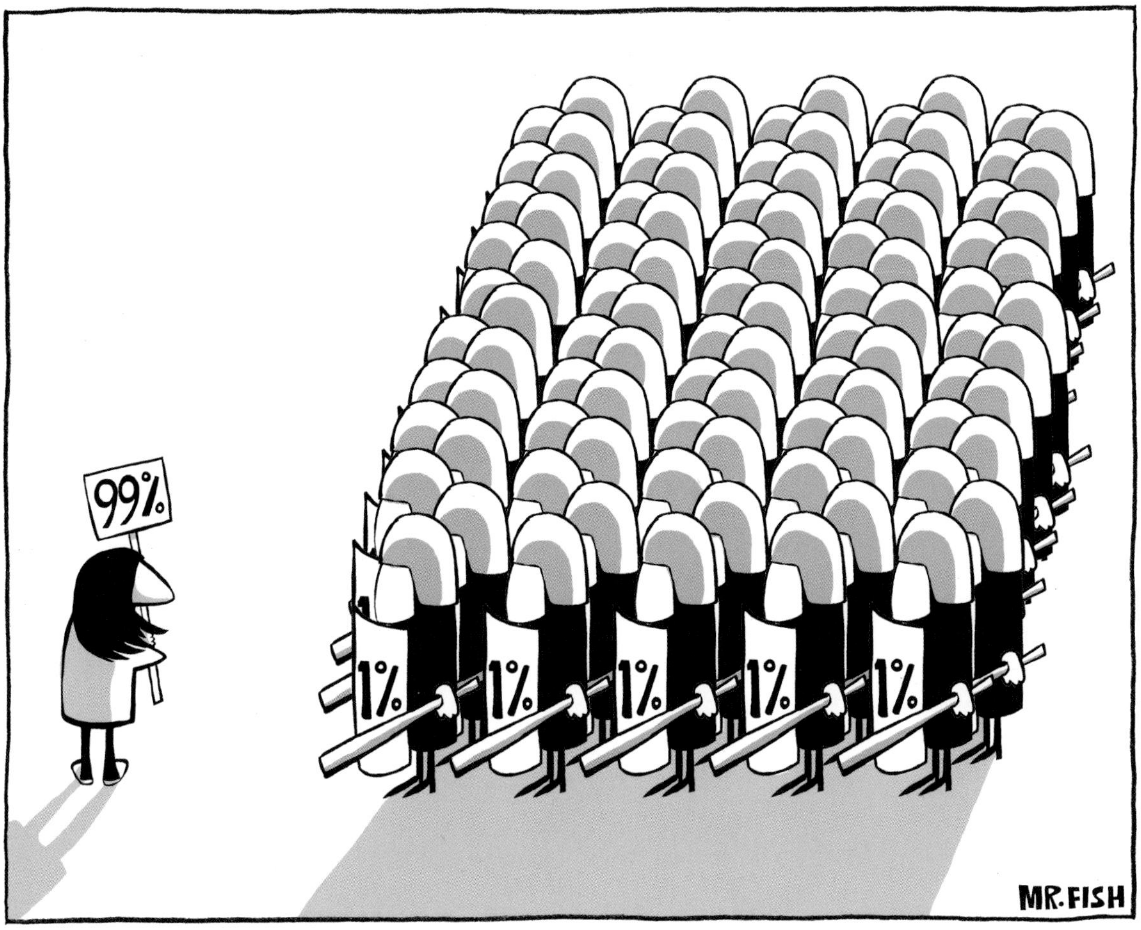
99%
1%
1%
1%
1%
1%
MR.FISH

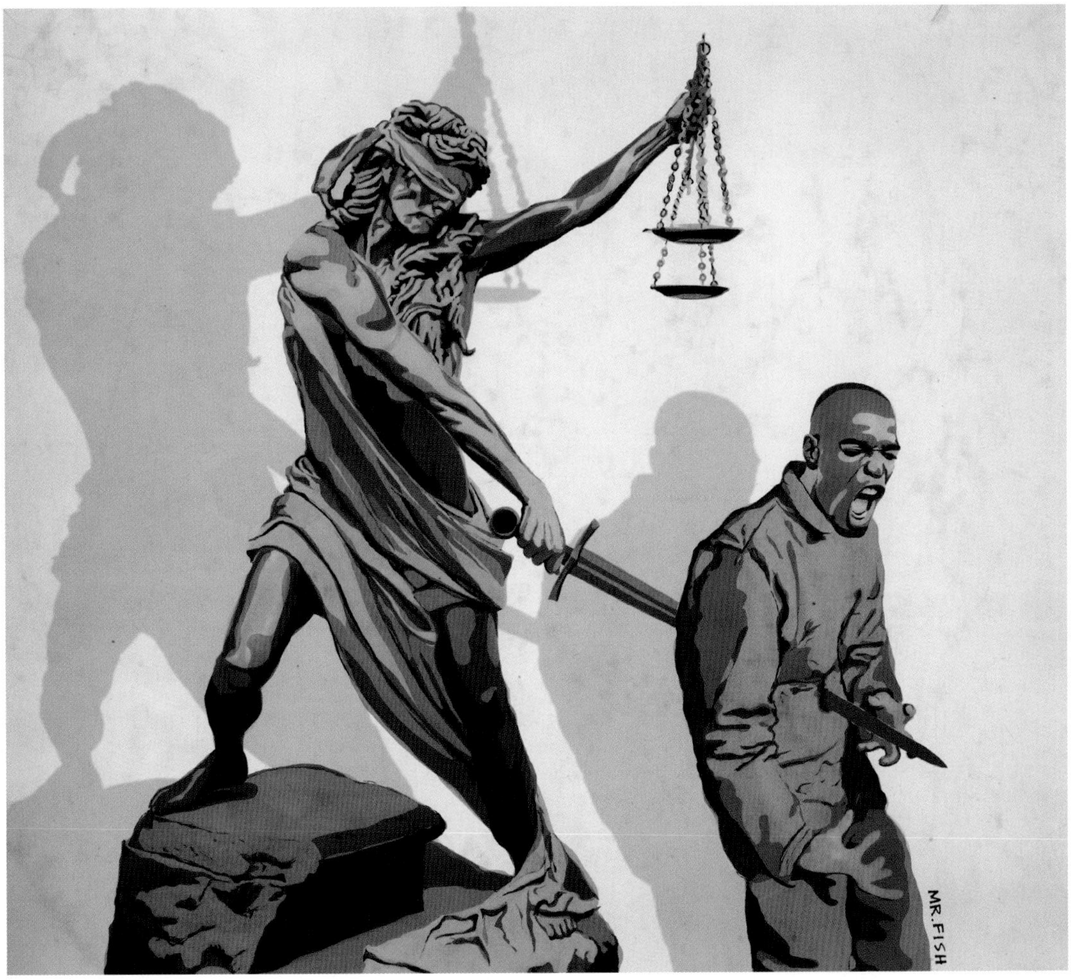
MR.FISH

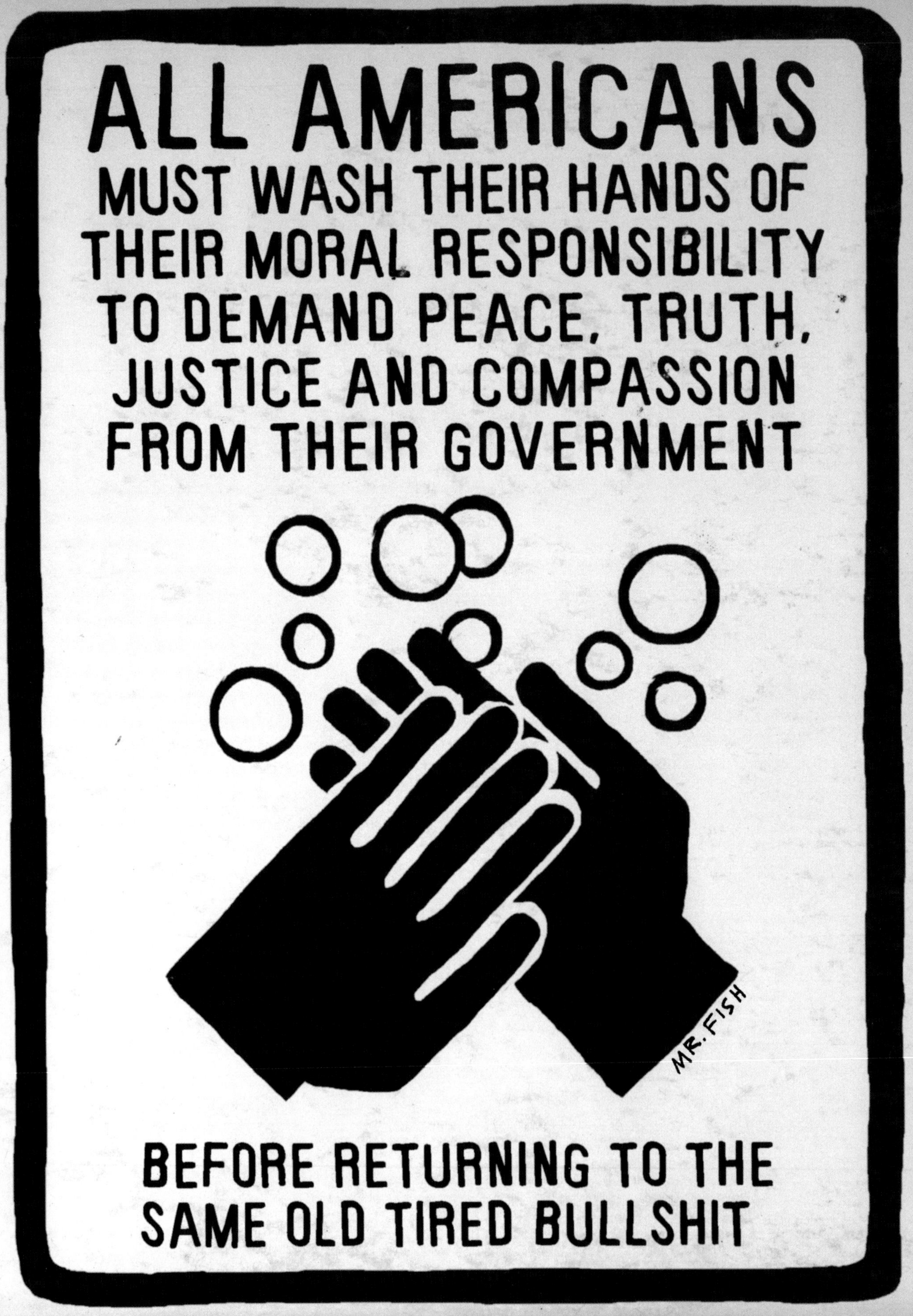
ALL AMERICANS
MUST WASH THEIR HANDS OF
THEIR MORAL RESPONSIBILITY
TO DEMAND PEACE, TRUTH,
JUSTICE AND COMPASSION
FROM THEIR GOVERNMENT
MR. FISH
BEFORE RETURNING TO THE
SAME OLD TIRED BULLSHIT

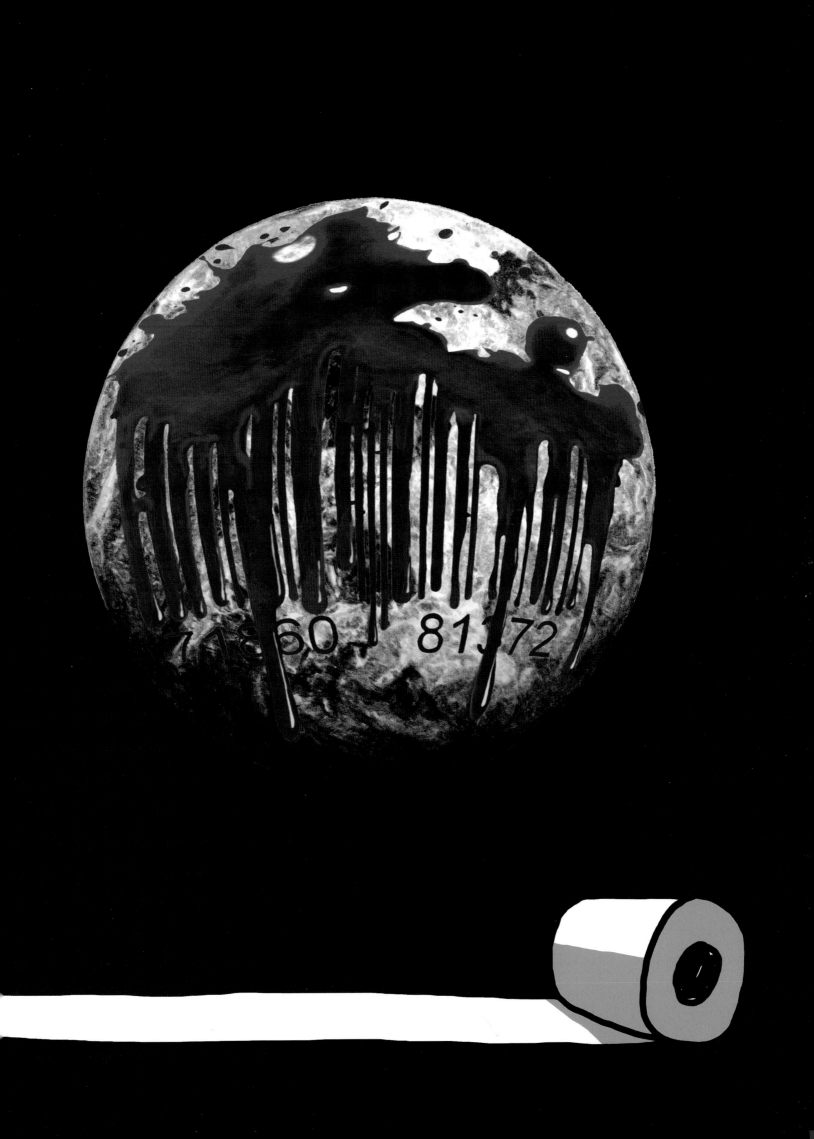

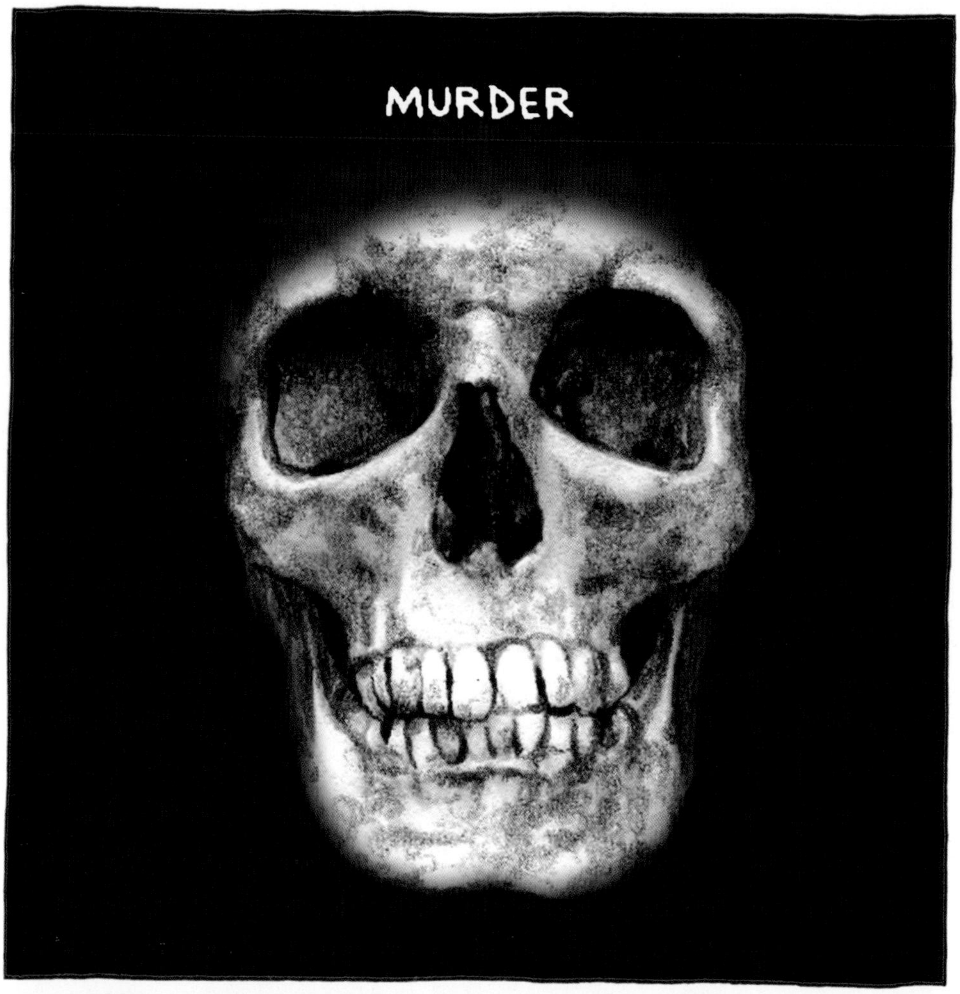
MURDER

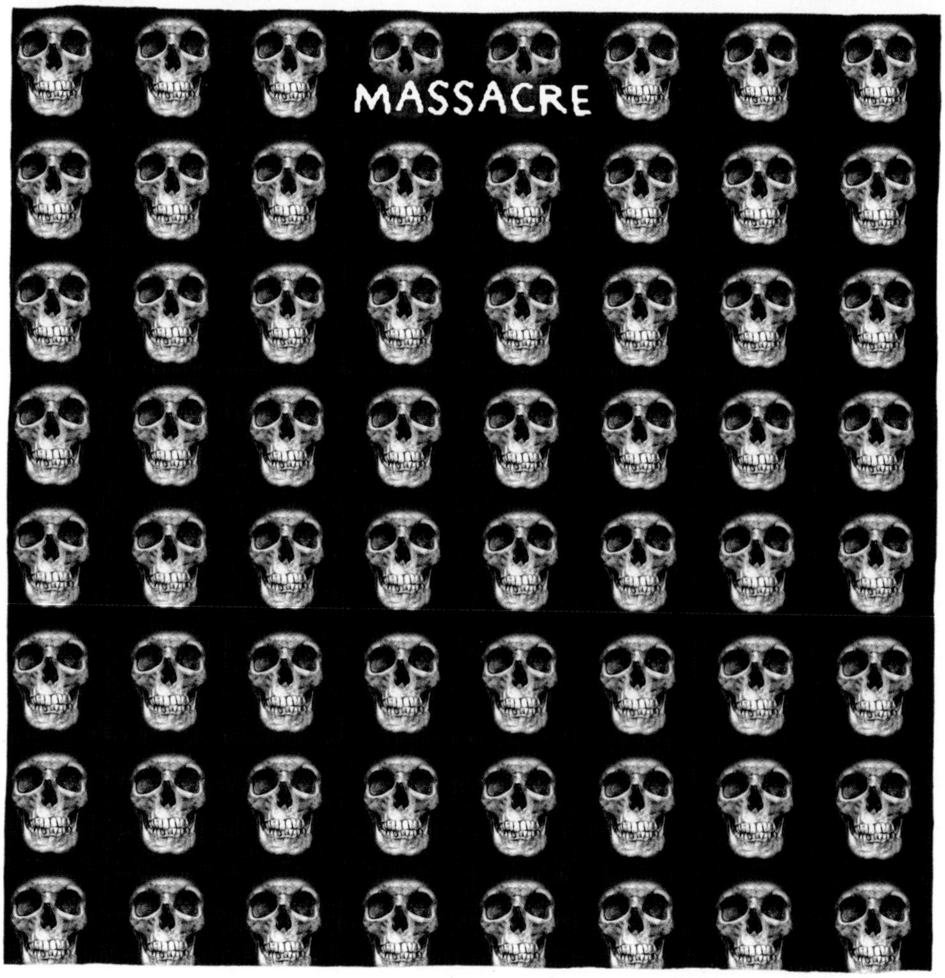
MASSACRE

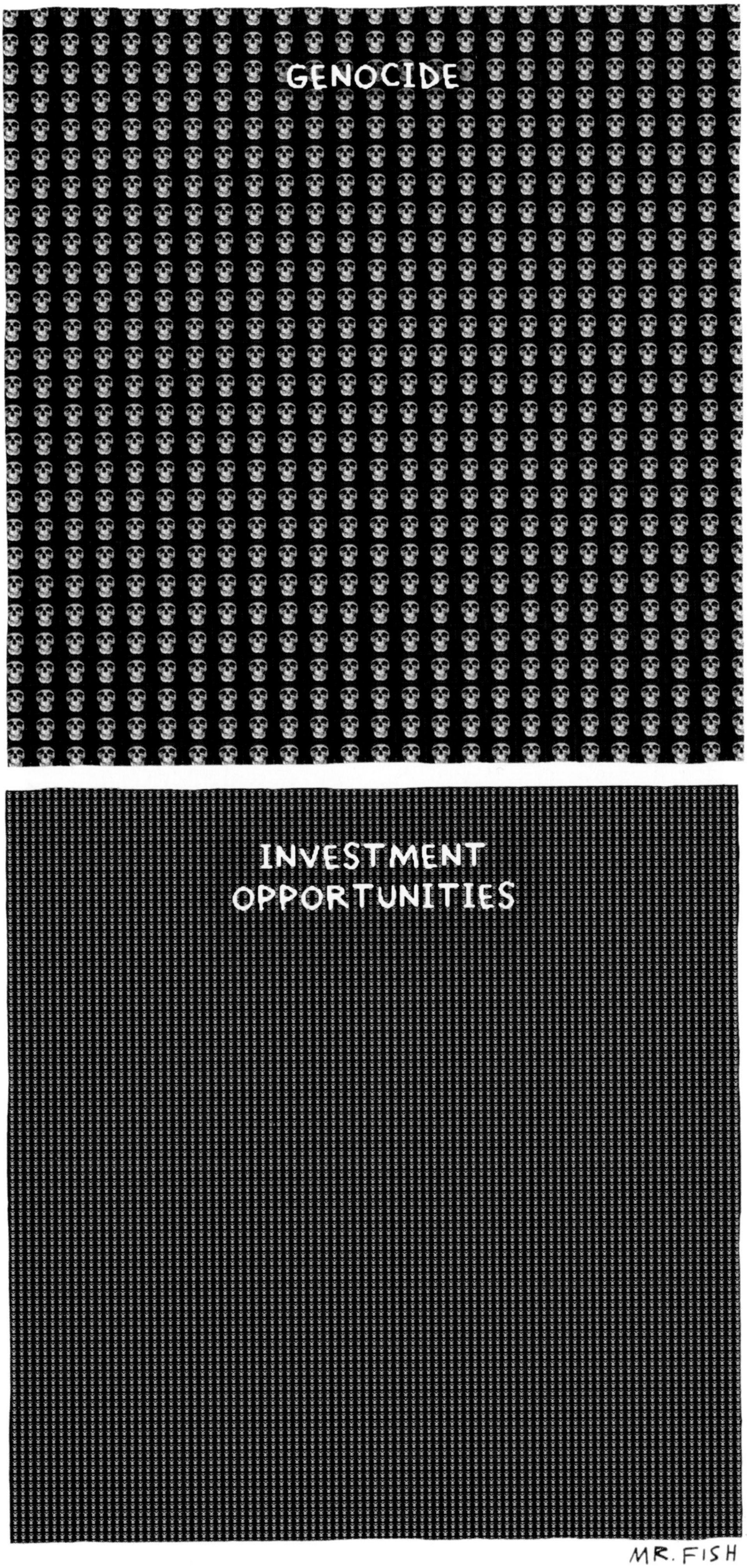
GENOCIDE
INVESTMENT OPPORTUNITIES
MR. FISH

JESUS CHRIST, AMERICA! STOP FALLING FOR THE SAME BULLSHIT EVERY TIME THERE'S A PRESIDENTIAL ELECTION! NO POLITICIAN IS EVER WHO THEY SAY THEY ARE IN A CAMPAIGN PROMISE - NEVER! FOR FUCKSAKE, IT'S NOT ROCKET SCIENCE! CANDIDATES PAD THEIR RESUMES AND INTERVIEW FOR A JOB THAT IS PRE-DEFINED - THEY DON'T GET HIRED, MOVE INTO THE OVAL OFFICE AND THEN BUILD THE QUALIFICATIONS OF THE POSITION TO FIT THEIR ALTRUISM! NO JOB FUNCTIONS THAT WAY, ESPECIALLY ONE WHERE WORLD DOMINATION AND ABSOLUTE GLOBAL CONTROL IS AT STAKE! SHIT, MAN!

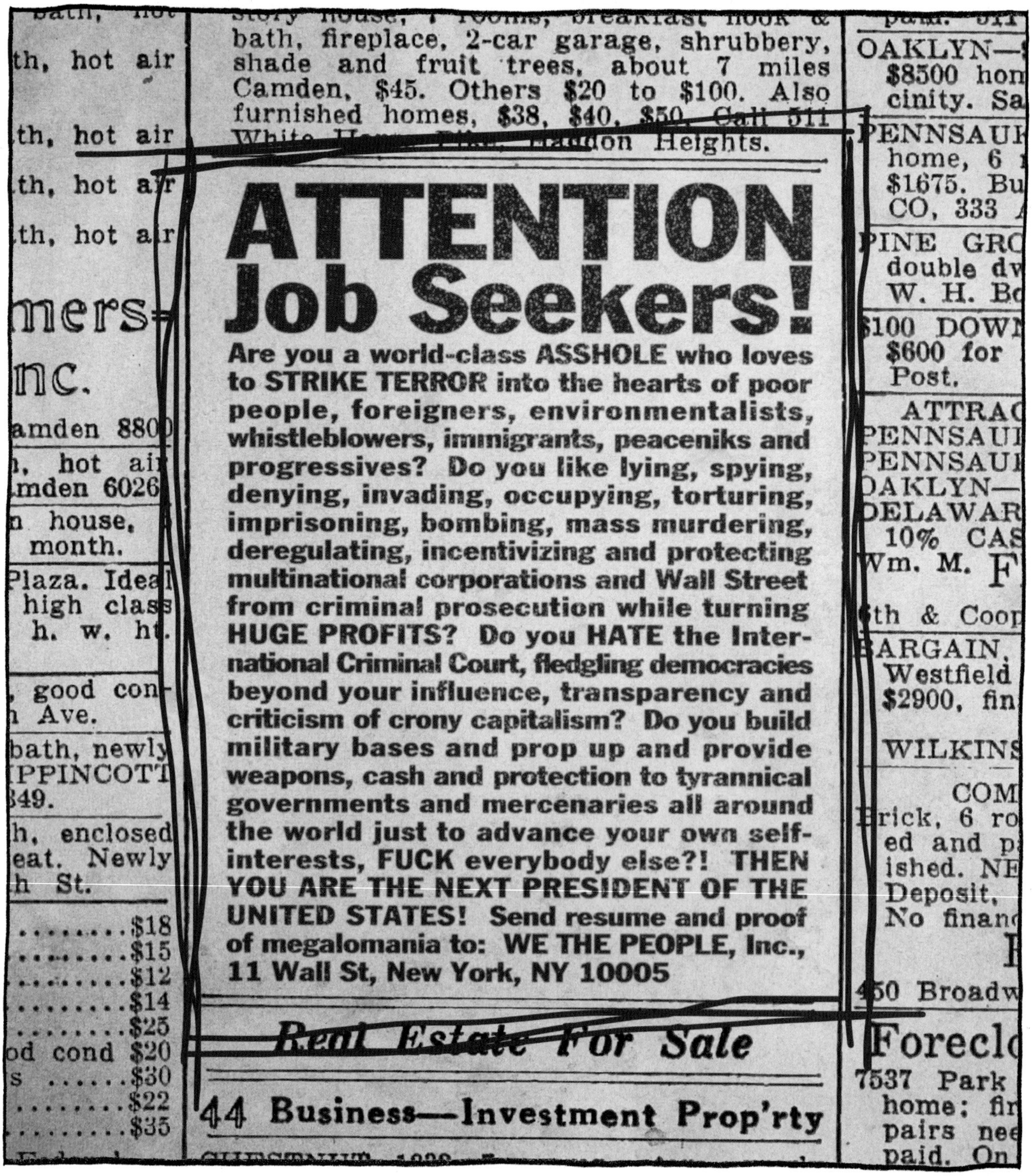

ATTENTION Job Seekers!
Are you a world-class ASSHOLE who loves to STRIKE TERROR into the hearts of poor people, foreigners, environmentalists, whistleblowers, immigrants, peaceniks and progressives? Do you like lying, spying, denying, invading, occupying, torturing, imprisoning, bombing, mass murdering, deregulating, incentivizing and protecting multinational corporations and Wall Street from criminal prosecution while turning HUGE PROFITS? Do you HATE the International Criminal Court, fledgling democracies beyond your influence, transparency and criticism of crony capitalism? Do you build military bases and prop up and provide weapons, cash and protection to tyrannical governments and mercenaries all around the world just to advance your own self-interests, FUCK everybody else?! THEN YOU ARE THE NEXT PRESIDENT OF THE UNITED STATES! Send resume and proof of megalomania to: WE THE PEOPLE, Inc., 11 Wall St, New York, NY 10005
Real Estate For Sale
44 Business—Investment Prop'rty

MR. FISH

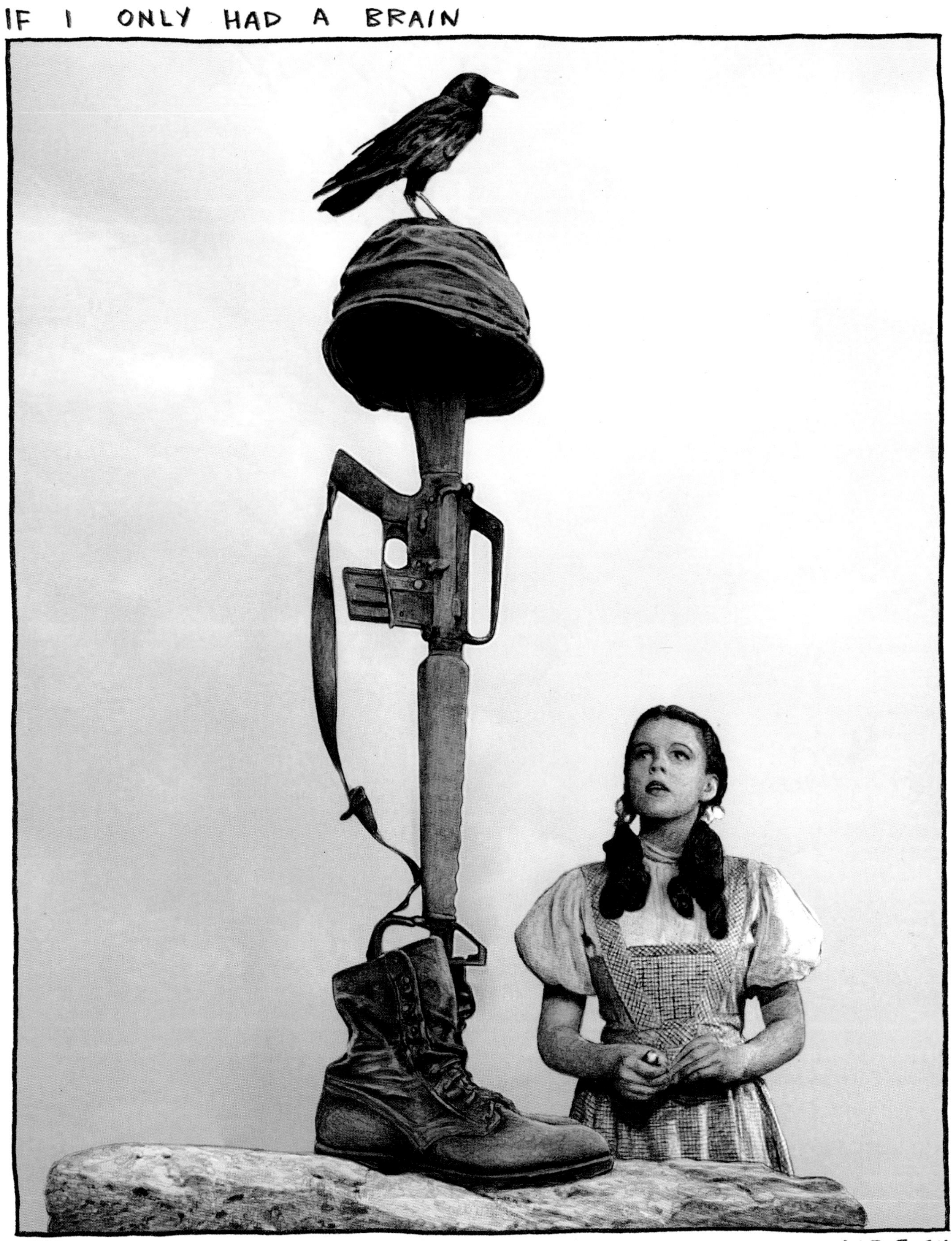
IF I ONLY HAD A BRAIN
MR.FISH

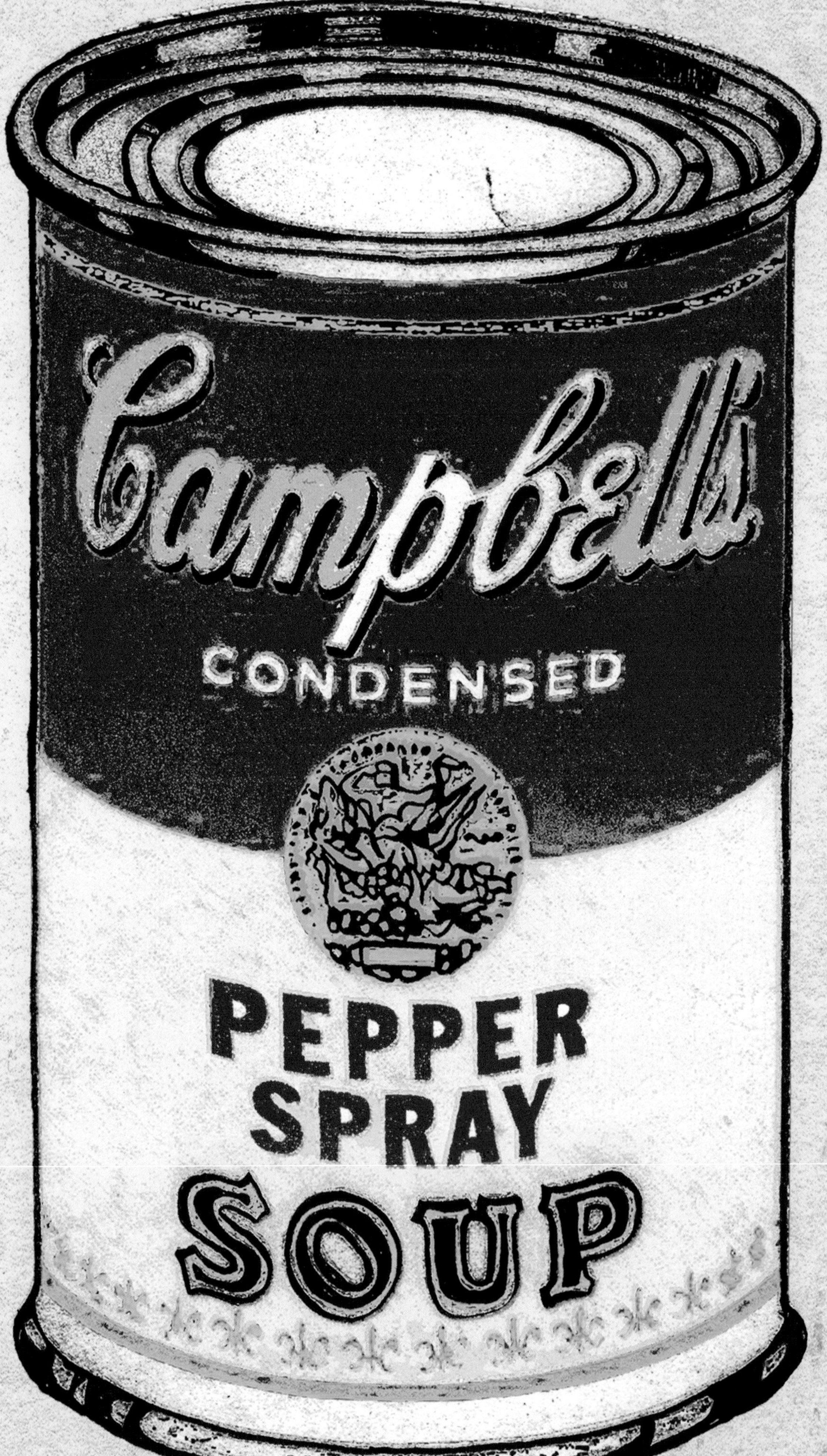
Campbell's
CONDENSED
PEPPER
SPRAY
SOUP

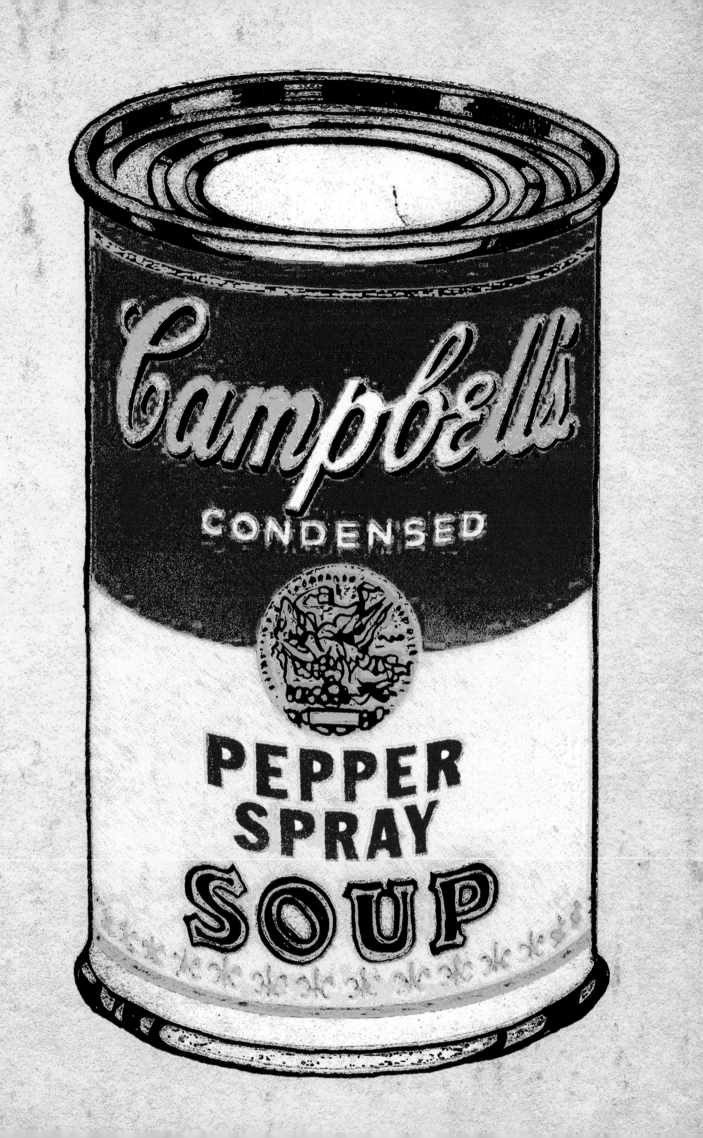

TEN

Soup Having Sex with Soup

Soup Having Sex with Soup

"I'm afraid that if you look at a thing long enough, it loses all of its meaning."

–Andy Warhol

BILL HICKS, ARGUABLY the most existentially articulate comic id of the late 20th century, had a bit in his act where he talked about the bias that the news media had against illegal drugs; illegal drugs, of course, being a metaphor for anything that existed outside the miasma of mainstream influence and wasn't directly controlled by elite institutions of corporate and state power. Pretending to be a television news anchor reporting on hallucinogens without prevarication, Hicks said, "Today, a young man on acid realized that all matter is merely energy condensed to a slow vibration—that we are all one consciousness experiencing itself subjectively. There is no such thing as death, life is only a dream, and we're the imagination of ourselves. Here's Tom with the weather."

What I appreciate about that quote is how it forces a person to consider the context wherein a concept of truth is typically placed for public consumption. Like all good satire, it illustrates just how insular and self-serving every hard-boiled notion of reality can become once it's dropped into the confused bowl of electrified noodles that is the human brain, an organ famous the world over for its uncanny ability to acquiesce to whatever real or imagined authority it perceives to be blowing through the room at any given moment. How many of us, for example, have walked through the reptile house at the zoo and stopped to press our face against the glass of a terrarium and looked at the lizard in the corner lying as still as a root cresting the ground and thought that the cheesy landscape painted on the rear wall of the tank along with the Sherwin-Williams sky and the Exo Terra Repti Glo 10.0 Compact Desert Terrarium Lamp pretending to be the sun, was enough to convince the captive animal that it was at home in the vast grasslands of Southern Australia? All of us have, of course, and not because we are too stupid to see through bullshit but rather because we like to think that the world is being managed by other people who know more than we do about all the complicated and boring crap that we don't want to waste our time thinking about. When we imagine that there are other people in the world burdened with the responsibility of not letting bullshit run amok, we succumb to the illusion that we are being protected and shepherded along by a wisdom that isn't really there.

I found myself thinking about all this in New York City last month during the Occupy May Day protests, which had started early in the day at Bryant Park before moving south, like a transient Renaissance fair that had been purged of its whimsy, its Elizabethan English and its haggis and transmogrified into a pagan celebration of workers' rights, mass dignity and First Amendment Tourette's, toward Wall Street. I had just stepped away from the like-minded riffraff in Union Square Park, having grown a bit woozy from breathing in the

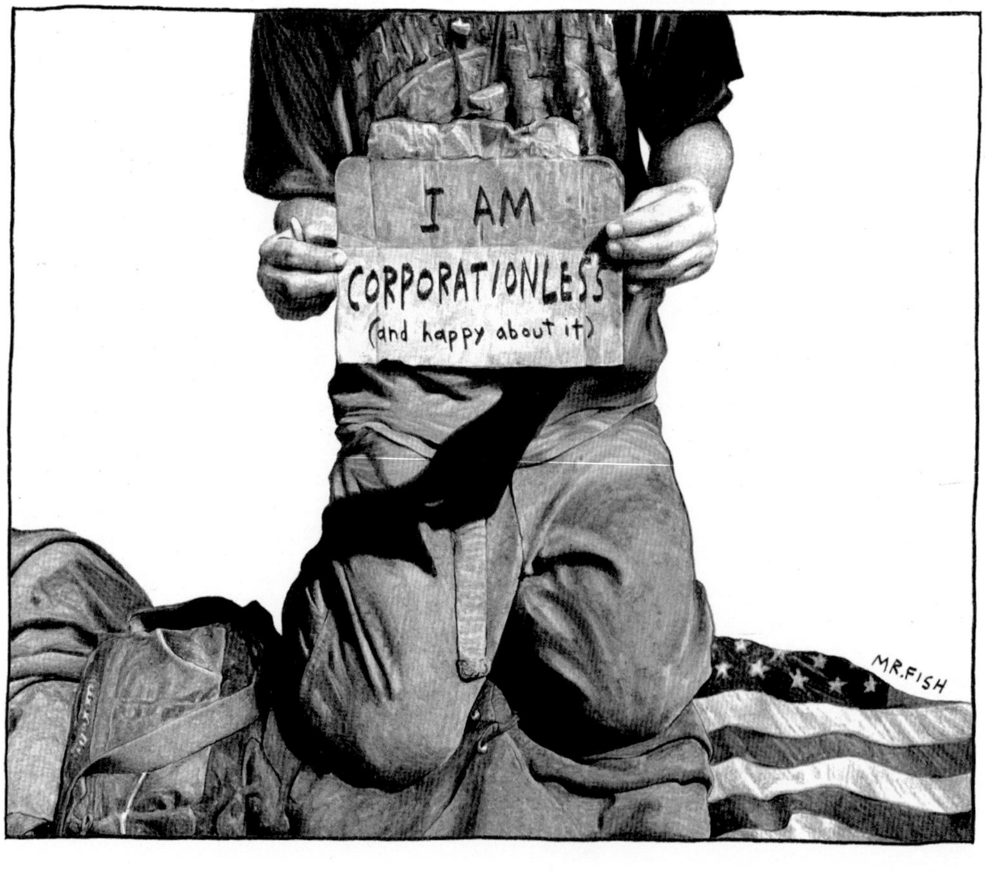
I AM
CORPORATIONLESS
(and happy about it)
MR.FISH

ON A SPRING MORNING IN APRIL OF 1775 A SIMPLE BAND OF COLONISTS - FARMERS AND MERCHANTS, BLACKSMITHS AND PRINTERS, MEN AND BOYS - LEFT THEIR HOMES AND FAMILIES IN LEXINGTON AND CONCORD TO TAKE UP ARMS AGAINST THE TYRANNY OF AN EMPIRE...

MR. FISH

THE ANTI-AMERICANISM THAT COMES OUT OF THOSE OCCUPY WALL STREET FREAKS REALLY PISSES ME OFF!

intoxicating fumes of the movement's jubilant upset for the better part of the afternoon, when I found myself standing at the concrete base of the chrome statue of Andy Warhol, aptly named The Andy Monument, that faces the park at 17th Street. Looking up at this Gandhi of Self-Commodification, this Horace Pippin of Madison Avenue, his trademark Polaroid camera hanging from around his neck like a mystic's third eye, his Bloomingdale's shopping bag, according to the sculptor, Rob Pruitt, weighed down with copies of Interview magazine, I noticed that he was gazing at the protesters in the park, no doubt considering their collective aesthetic and not giving a tinker's damn about the content of their cause.

To him, I imagined, the congregation of complainers, myself included, was little more than a nomadic audience that had arrived in Union Square to enjoy the only entertainment available to it, which was theater of the mind, the star billing going to the holy ghost of communal optimism with doomsday as its understudy. Or maybe it was more personal than that. Maybe he was watching carefully to see who might emerge from the crowd as a beautiful misfit among misfits; a waifish boy in neon lipstick, perhaps, his upper arms as skinny as bruised bananas, or a girl of 16, a runaway for sure, her hair teased into brittle pink Easter grass and mascara smeared hard across the back of her hand, a perfectly chic junkie to brand back at the Factory for resale—fuck the agony of the 99 percent!

It was most definitely a curious sort of apathy for me to imagine coming off an inanimate object. Odder, still, was my ability to forgive the apolitical broad view emanating from The Andy Monument, to even sympathize with it, particularly after I'd spent the previous eight months creating artwork for the Occupy Wall Street (OWS) movement, arguing in print and on the radio and at public speaking events for its relevancy and hating those who predicted and prepared for its demise with relish. These saintly and determined Occupiers were, in fact, dear comrades with whom I'd shared weed and canteens and long embraces, all of us jeering so intensely at the innumerable garrisons of uniformed cops surrounding us since the fall that no one in a uniform—mailmen, bus drivers, doormen, nobody!—was safe from contempt in our peripheral vision anymore.

So why now, in this moment, while standing next to a chrome aberration of Andy Warhol, did my fellow hell-raisers suddenly look like strangers to me? Was it a crisis of faith or was it, perhaps, because they really were strangers?

"If only we could pull out our brain and use only our eyes," Picasso said, naming the distinct advantage that artists have always had over pundits and polemicists when it came to perceiving the world as it is; pundits and polemicists being much more likely to insist that the world is whatever a person wants it to be, as if reality, itself, were there only to corroborate a person's completely egocentric opinion—political, religious or otherwise—about everything and everybody. Artists tend to have an instinctual understanding that reality is much more self-referential than needing to be labeled by a human brain to be relevant and that the meaning of an object has very little to do with the abstract counterpart that people carry around inside their heads, human consciousness being so much more comfortable sculpting putty than stone. I thought about Warhol's famous silk-screens of soup cans and how they were never interpreted as ads for soup, for instance. I thought about his silk-screens of the electric chair, how they were never mistaken as commentary either for or against capital punishment. I thought about his silk-screens of Marilyn Monroe and how they were never considered glamorous portraits of feminine beauty.

I thought about how, contrary to his reputation, Warhol's genius had to be his ability to deflate the importance of commercialism and celebrity in the American consumer culture, to rob it of its cheap superficiality by destroying its ability to speak for itself. By killing the language with which mediocrity finds its voice, there will be nothing left but the aesthetic element of BEING to consider.

"Excuse me," said a tattooed girl in pigtails holding out a digital camera to my left. She was standing with what I guessed to be her boyfriend, who had intensely green eyes and a beard like Rasputin, both wearing backpacks and appearing several days out from their last shampoo and gargling. "Can you take for us our picture?" she asked, her German accent making her words sound as if they were being hatcheted into a wet log.

"Sure," I said, taking the camera. "Where do you want to be?"

"Here," said the girl, leading me around to the other side of the Warhol statue where she and her boyfriend took up position in front of a long line of riot police on scooters. With their arms around each other and huge smiles plastered across their faces, they could have been in front of Niagara Falls or on the west rim of the Grand Canyon or, given the stone cold seriousness chiseled into the faces of the cops behind them, Mount Rushmore. What I knew for certain was that they were standing in front of the country's newest attraction. What I also knew was that it was on a national tour, soon to be available everywhere, which somehow cheapened my involvement in it. Handing back the camera and wishing the couple well, I looked over my shoulder at the Andy Warhol statue and tried to see myself in its completely reflective surface, surprised to find nothing of legible consequence staring back at me. Then, looking across the street and watching the grubbiest Santa Claus imaginable prance about on tiptoe among the demonstrators, his glee as bullying as a Bull Connor fire hose, his ceaseless merriment as he danced around with a filthy cardboard speech bubble containing the words

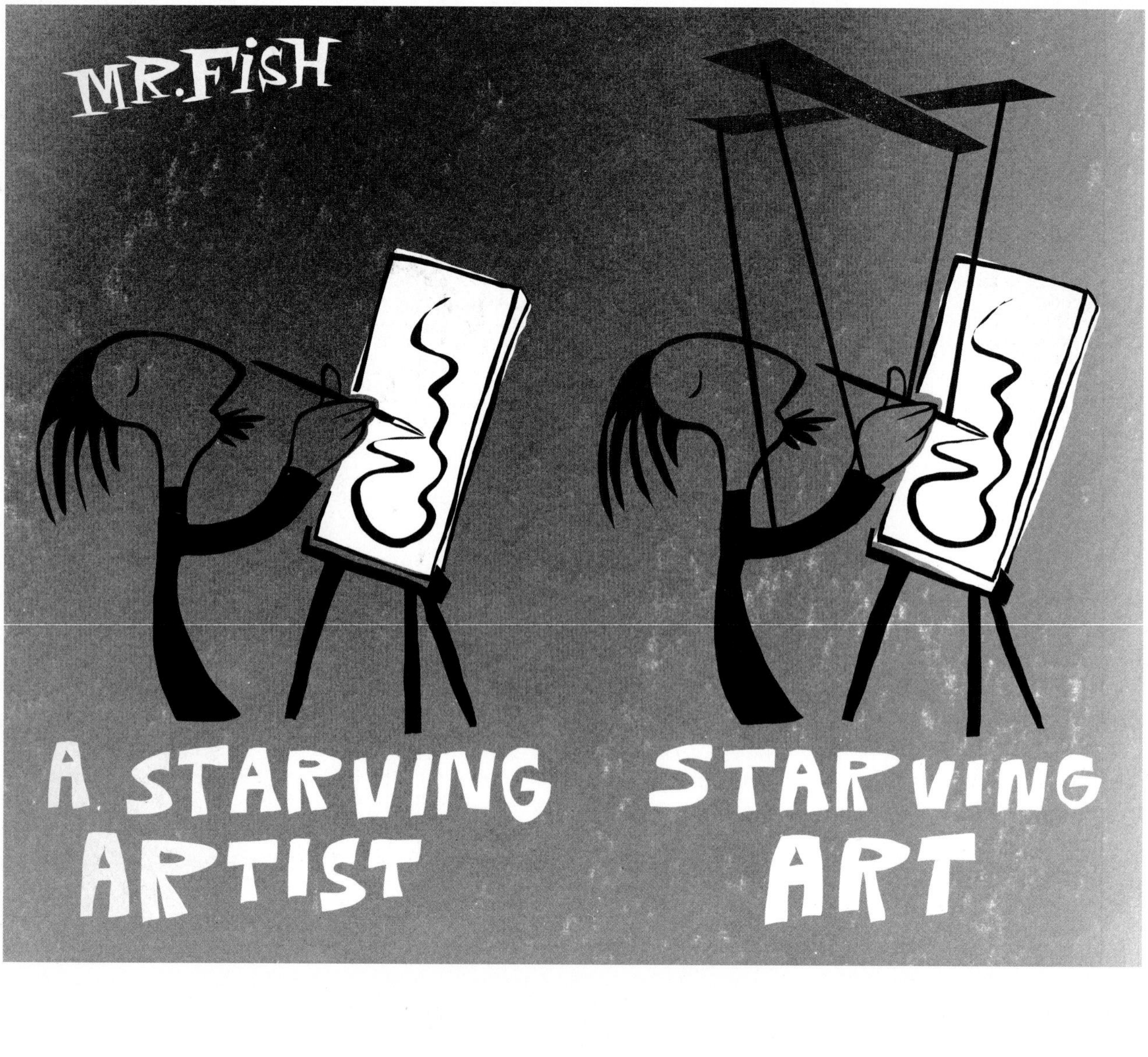
MR.FISH
A STARVING ARTIST
STARVING ART

"not me" attached to the end of a 10-foot wand, which he tried to force into the face of anybody who came near, I readily admitted that, without a doubt, I would be the first to look away and rock back and forth on my heels if any of the riot police crowded around Union Square decided to draw their batons and make a running tackle.

Deciding that it was time for a piss break, a quadruple espresso and a free Internet connection so that I could check my emails, I tromped off in the direction of one of the three Starbucks that I knew to be in the area, not knowing of a decent mom-and-pop place anywhere in a 10-block radius. Stopping at the corner of Park and 17th, I watched as a passing car threw an empty soda can at a scruffy-looking kid with an unlit cigarette in his mouth who was holding a gigantic piece of lime green poster board that read "Economic justice for all!" "Get a fucking job!" shouted the driver as he went by, completely missing the irony of having just directed his rage toward somebody hoping to save the world, not with anarchy or free love, but with a plea for gainful employment and a living wage.

This wasn't Mario Savio addressing Berkeley through a bullhorn. It was Ward Cleaver counseling Beaver on the merits of following the American dream.

"You all right?" I asked the kid, once I crossed the street. He nodded without smiling and asked me whether I had a match. "A what?" I asked.

"Fire," he said. "A torch!"

I told him that he shouldn't smoke. He told me I shouldn't be such a fucktard. I didn't say anything and walked past him, once again doubting the sincerity of my devotion to the idea that the future could and should be brighter. How, I wondered, was I supposed to believe that this Occupy May Day protest was any different from any other mass gathering, whether it was a Tea Party rally or a church revival or a Star Trek convention? Didn't each configuration represent a venue where one simply put on a costume to camouflage his or her social awkwardness and hard-boiled dissatisfaction for the here and now and safely channel his or her own inner Spock, Ted Nugent, Jerry Falwell or Che Guevara, the moral certainty of each participant made to seem incontrovertibly true by an attendance count, the mathematics of fandom always trumping the questionable integrity and practical application of the agenda being rallied around? After all, this kid's sign—this idiot's sign!—was demanding fairness from an economic and political system controlled by private owners for profit. I wanted to go back and ask him why he wasn't holding up a sign asking that the NFL be made more fair for players by eliminating the need for a scoreboard and giving everyone equal possession of the ball, but, honestly, I didn't have the energy.

Twenty minutes later, I was back in the park with my fist in the air and a renewed bloodlust surging through my veins. Having discovered that all the Starbucks in the area had kicked out their patrons after lunchtime and locked their doors to everybody but the police—police who I could see through the glass in their jackboots and leather gloves and sunglasses, sipping frothy drinks and eating pound cake, their helmets and

shields resting on the tables, great lassos of plastic handcuffs looped through their belts like trash bag ties—I was reinvigorated to loot the rich folks' house on the hill, burn the drapes, impregnate the dog and smash the chandeliers into pixie dust.

Fingering the unspent coffee money in my pocket, I felt thankful for the distraction of having all the other protesters around me, for without them I might've had the wherewithal to properly diagnose the source of my rage and recognize it as being something less than revolutionary.

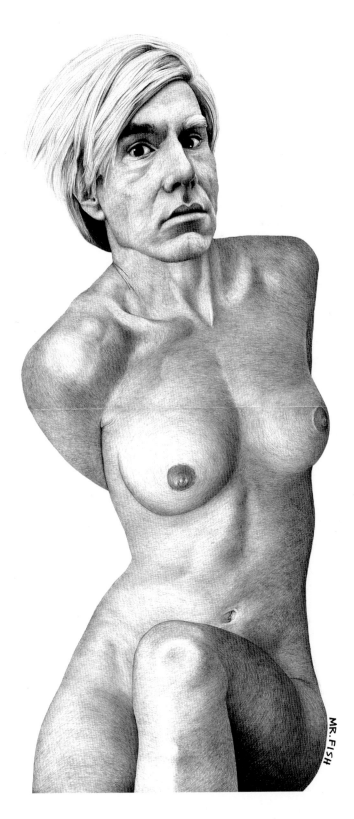

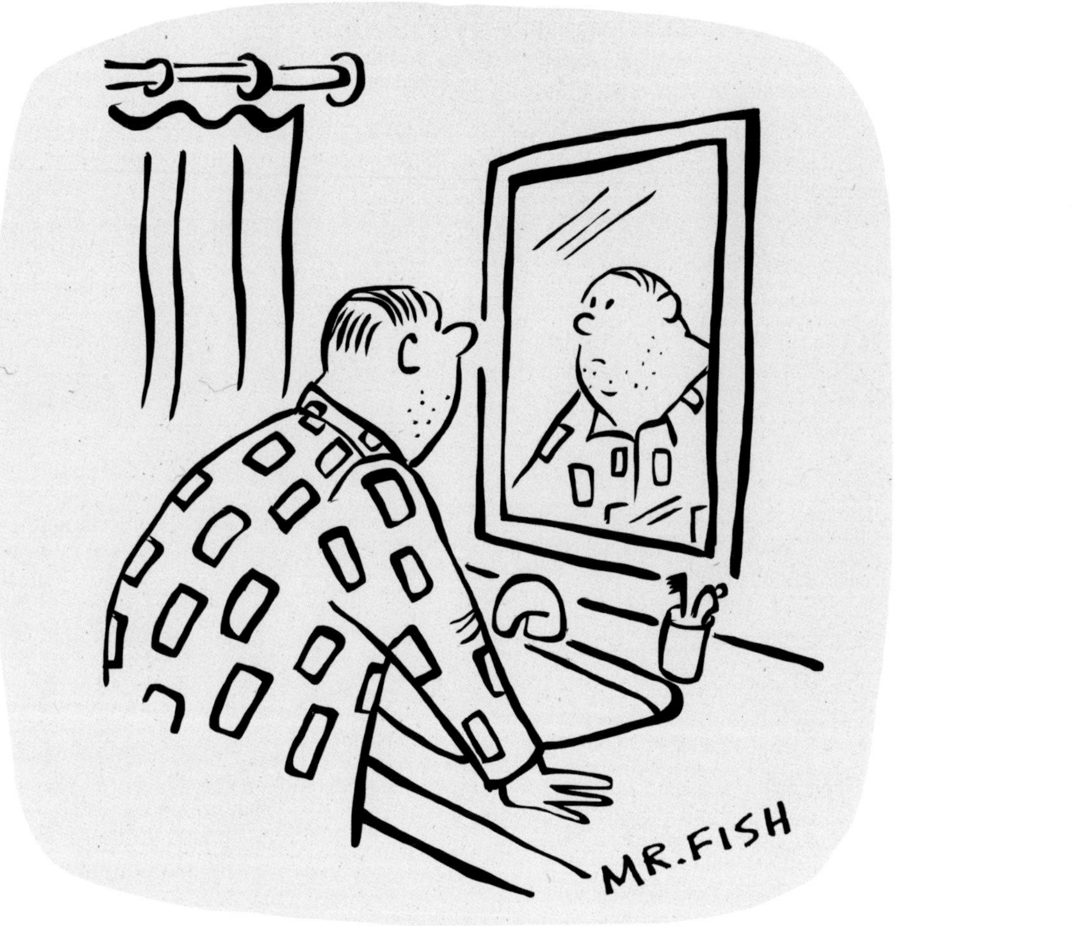
MR.FISH

"Let's see – I feel like a change. I could start parting my hair on the other side of my head, see what that looks like, or I could elect an inexperienced bigot into the highest office in the land and see what America looks like on fire. Hmmmmm…what to do, what to do."

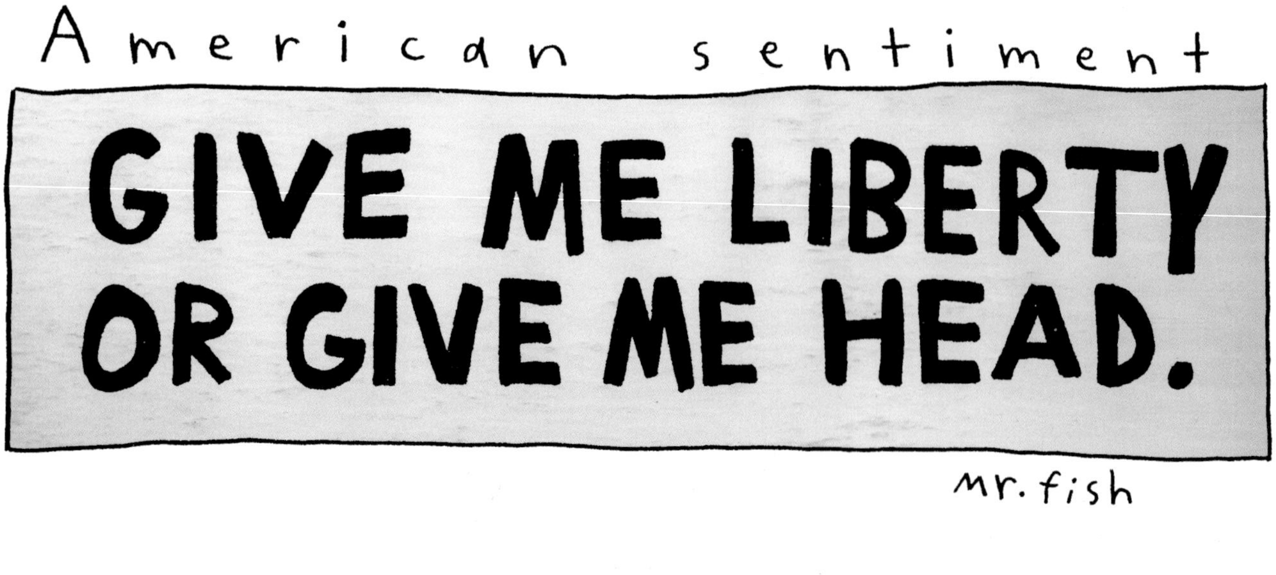
American sentiment
GIVE ME LIBERTY OR GIVE ME HEAD.
mr. fish

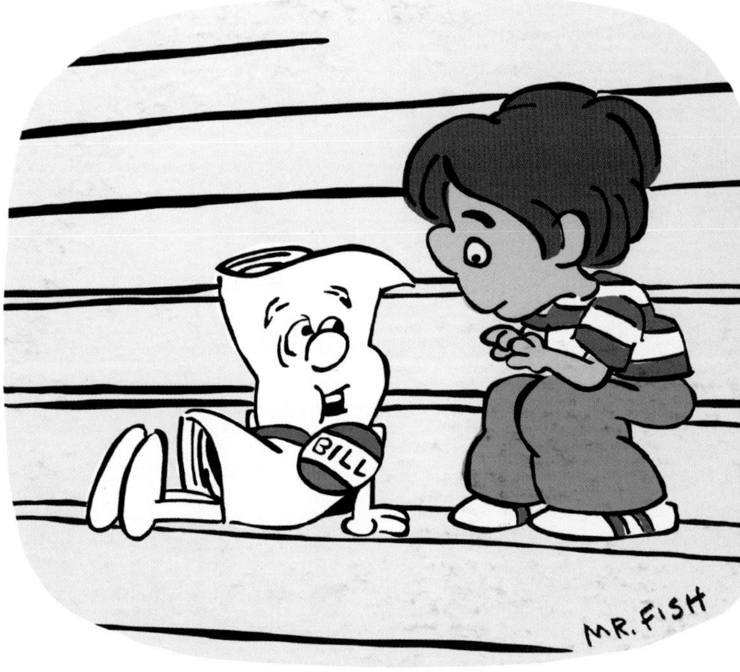
BILL
MR. FISH

"Hey - do you want to hear a catchy song about how I'm going to make all the wetbacks, ragheads, niggers, spics and bitches as miserable as fuck?"

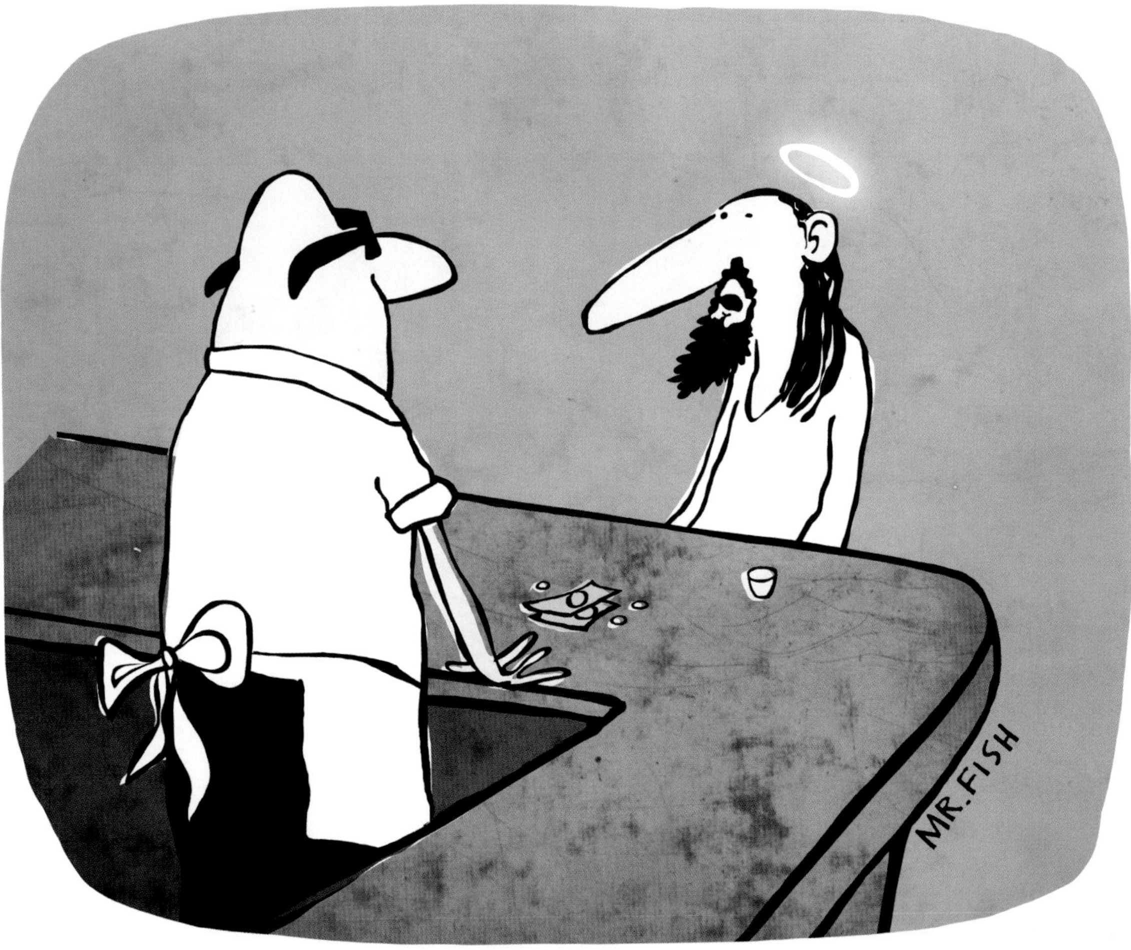
MR. FISH

"No, I didn't just come back – I've been here since 1981. I just never said anything because it turns out that most of my die-hard fans are fucking asshole Republicans and I don't want to be associated with them."

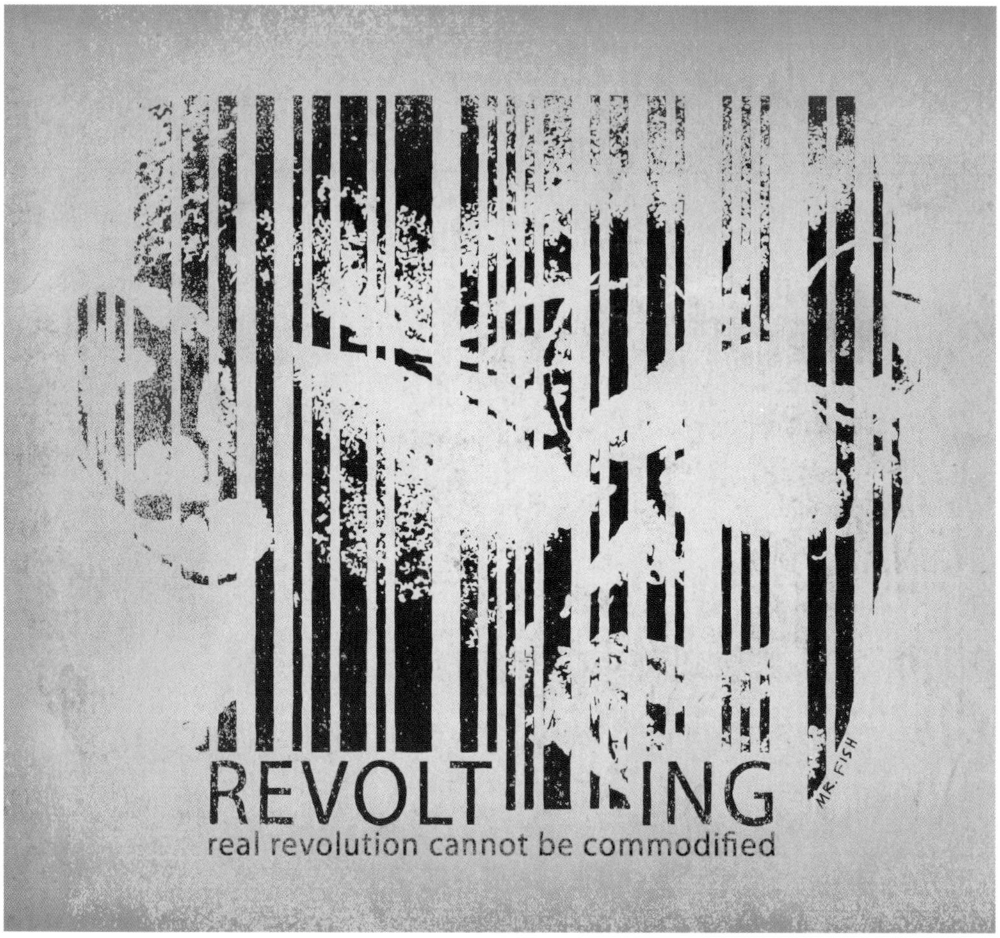
REVOLT ING
real revolution cannot be commodified
MR. FISH

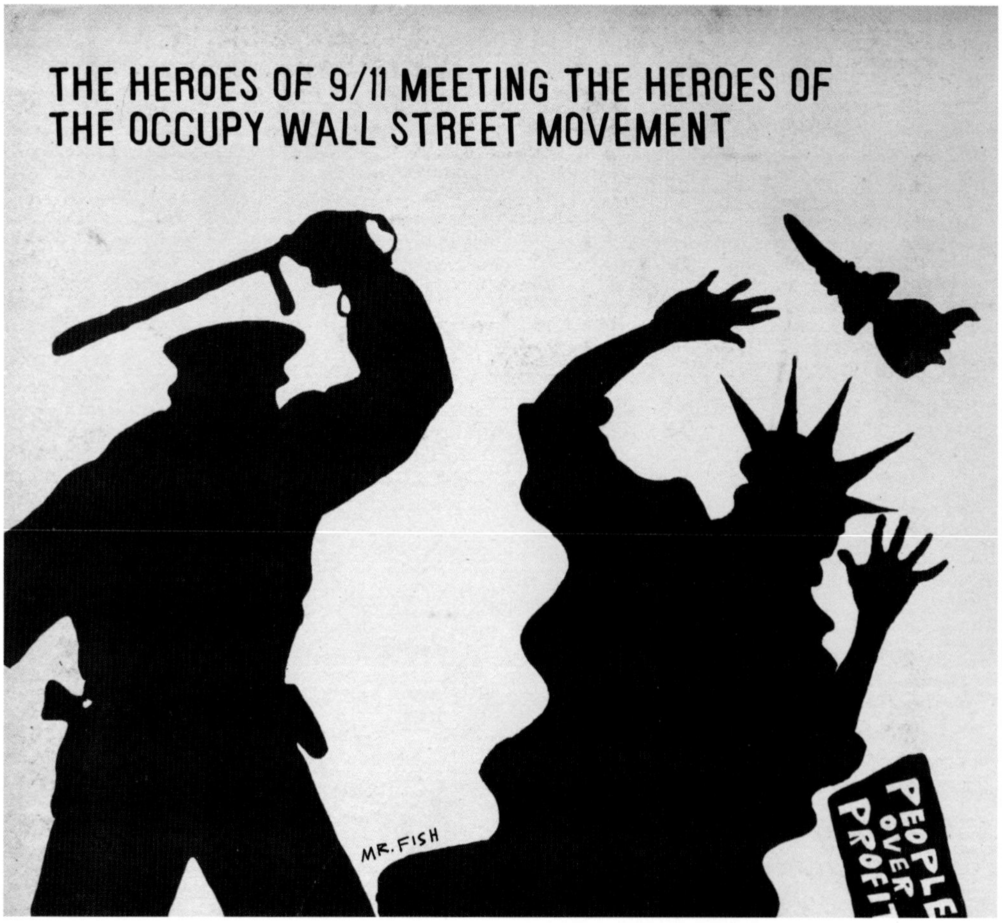
THE HEROES OF 9/11 MEETING THE HEROES OF
THE OCCUPY WALL STREET MOVEMENT
PEOPLE
OVER
PROFIT
MR. FISH

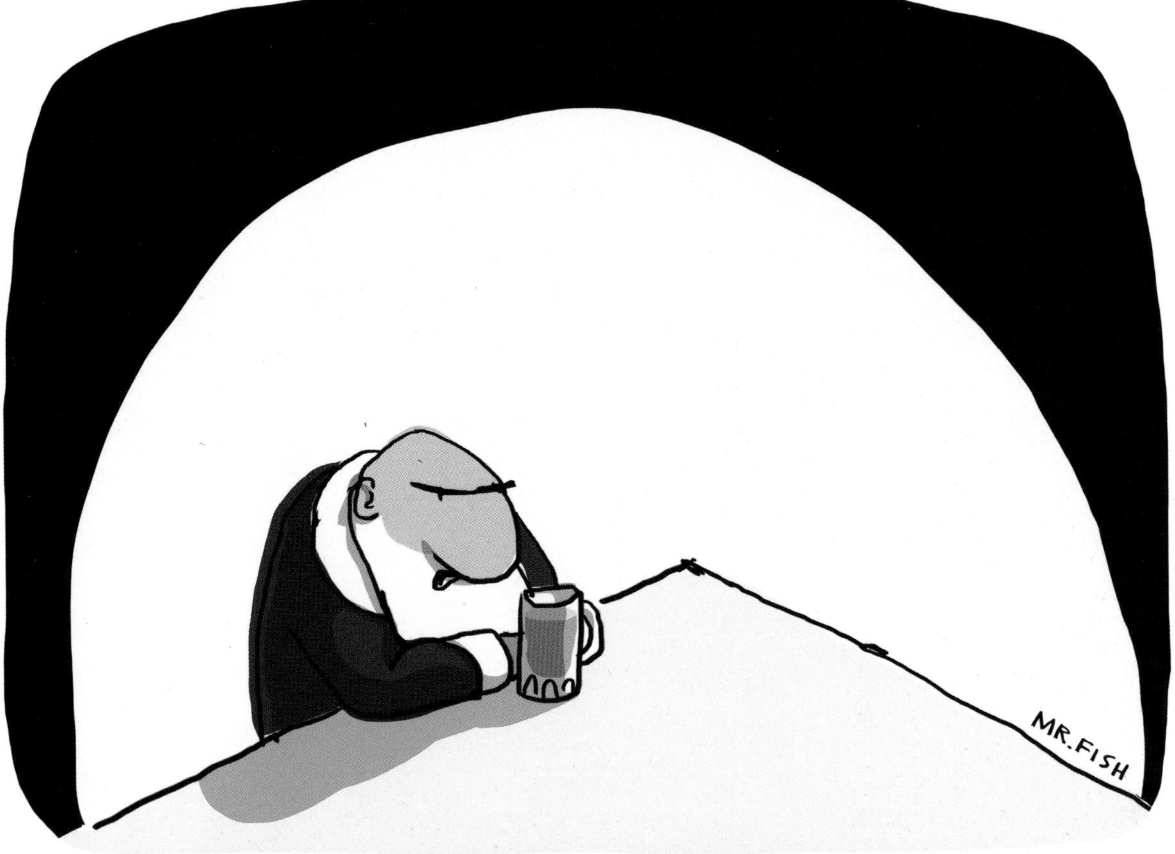
MR. FISH

"Fine, so Jesus is born and that's the first Christmas. Then He grows up and says, 'Hey, rich fucking selfish assholes, guess what, the meek aren't useless pieces of no good shit – fix it, dickheads!' So the rich fucking selfish assholes don't fix it and they kill Jesus because He called them rich fucking selfish assholes and He goes to Heaven. Then He says that when He comes back to destroy the Earth with fire and brimstone, He's going to torch all the rich fucking selfish assholes and their enablers and save the meek. So what's my job? I'm the schmuck who travels around the world every year and gives all the best presents to the rich fucking selfish assholes and all the shitty cheap crap to the meek, if they get anything at all, which pretty much guarantees that I'll be first in line on Judgment Day to have my eyes melted and my scrotum flambéed like a marshmallow on a stick for making the meek feel like useless pieces of no good shit. So, I guess the question is: What the fuck did I do in my previous life to deserve a fate I wouldn't wish on a fucking cockroach? In other words, Happy Birthday, Jesus – I WISH YOU WAS NEVER BORN!"

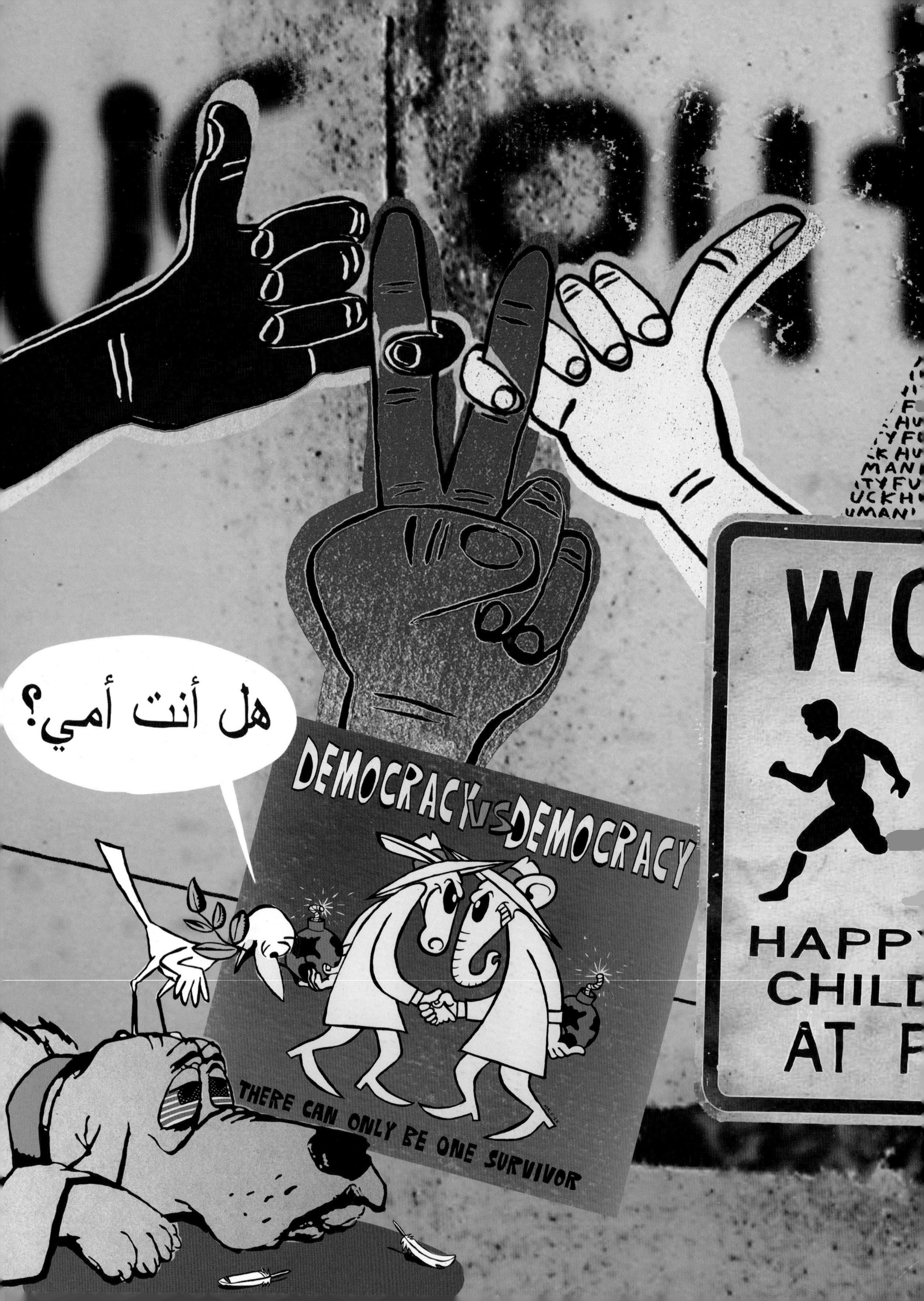
هل أنت أمي؟
DEMOCRACY VS DEMOCRACY
THERE CAN ONLY BE ONE SURVIVOR

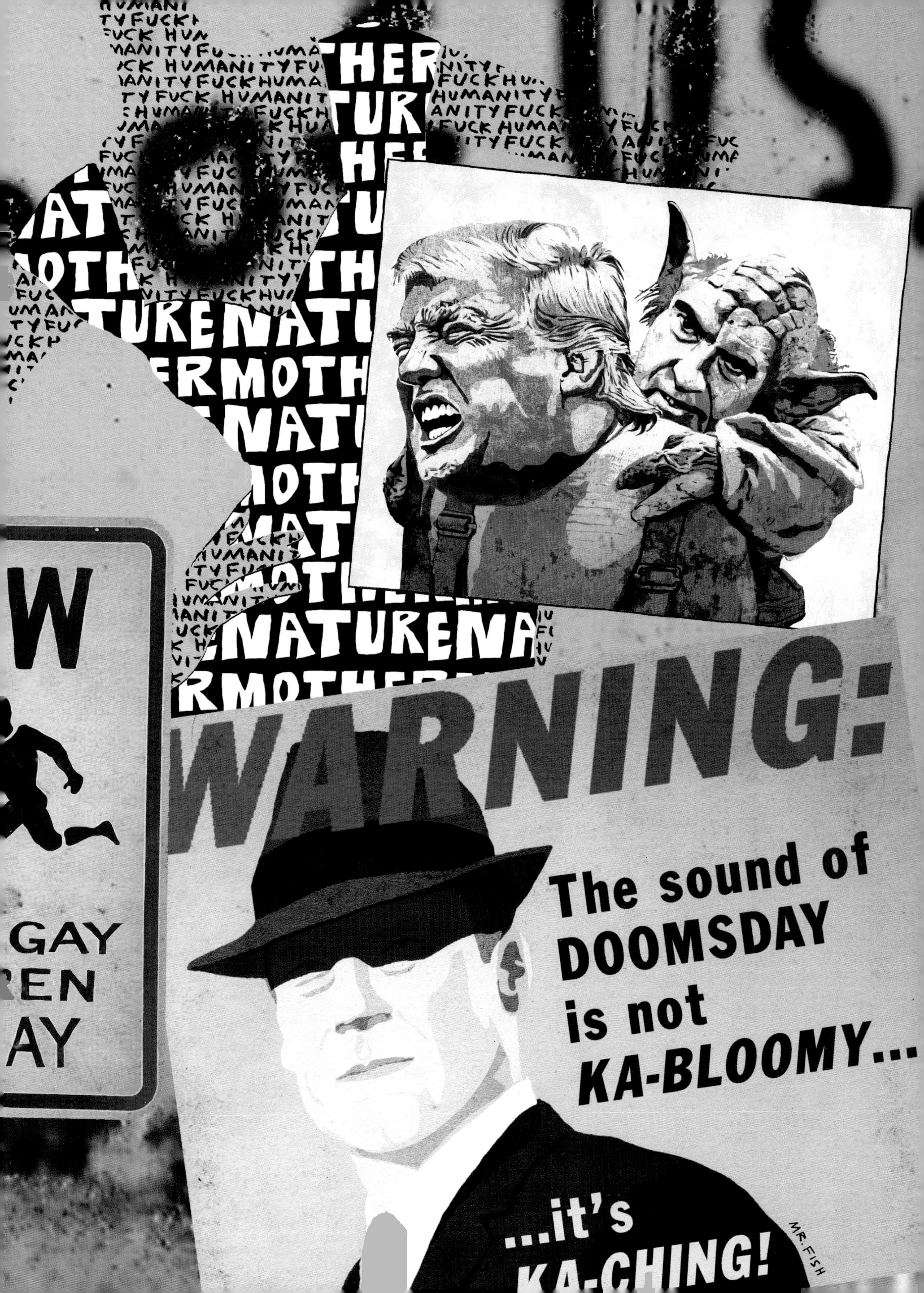
WARNING:
The sound of DOOMSDAY is not KA-BLOOMY...
...it's KA-CHING!
MR. FISH

PAINT BY NUMBERS DESIGNED BY THE BUREAUCRACY FOR THE NOBLE AND ALTRUISTIC PURPOSE OF ENCOURAGING THE PUBLIC TO EXPLORE, EXPRESS AND CELEBRATE ITS CREATIVE SIDE

EDITORIAL CARTOONISTS ARE AN INDISPENSABLE RESOURCE FOR CITIZENS OF A FREE SOCIETY WHO SEEK TO EXERCISE THE FREEDOM TO QUESTION THE LEGITIMACY OF ANY CLAIM, LAW, DEMAND OR JUDGMENT MADE BY THE GOVERNMENT.
MR.FISH

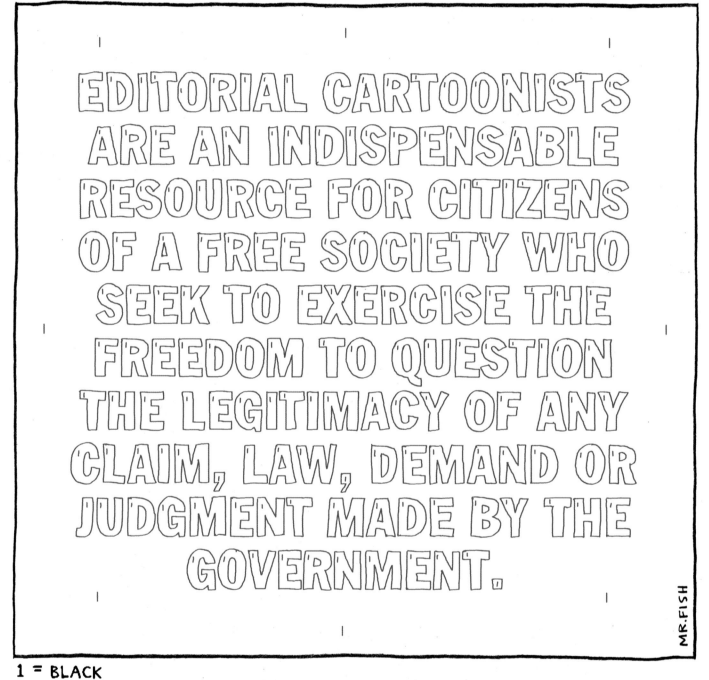

1 = BLACK

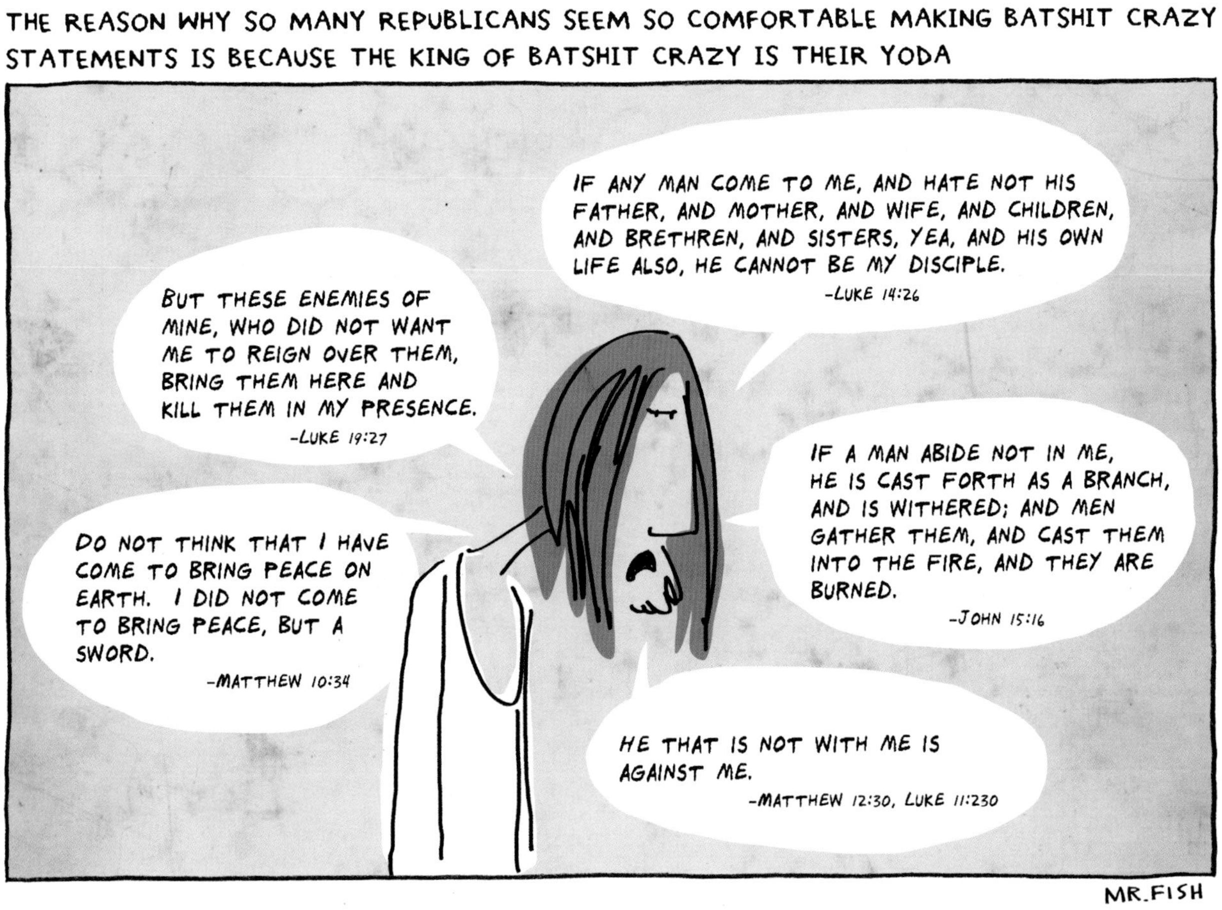
THE REASON WHY SO MANY REPUBLICANS SEEM SO COMFORTABLE MAKING BATSHIT CRAZY STATEMENTS IS BECAUSE THE KING OF BATSHIT CRAZY IS THEIR YODA
IF ANY MAN COME TO ME, AND HATE NOT HIS FATHER, AND MOTHER, AND WIFE, AND CHILDREN, AND BRETHREN, AND SISTERS, YEA, AND HIS OWN LIFE ALSO, HE CANNOT BE MY DISCIPLE. -LUKE 14:26
BUT THESE ENEMIES OF MINE, WHO DID NOT WANT ME TO REIGN OVER THEM, BRING THEM HERE AND KILL THEM IN MY PRESENCE. -LUKE 19:27
IF A MAN ABIDE NOT IN ME, HE IS CAST FORTH AS A BRANCH, AND IS WITHERED; AND MEN GATHER THEM, AND CAST THEM INTO THE FIRE, AND THEY ARE BURNED. -JOHN 15:16
DO NOT THINK THAT I HAVE COME TO BRING PEACE ON EARTH. I DID NOT COME TO BRING PEACE, BUT A SWORD. -MATTHEW 10:34
HE THAT IS NOT WITH ME IS AGAINST ME. -MATTHEW 12:30, LUKE 11:230
MR. FISH

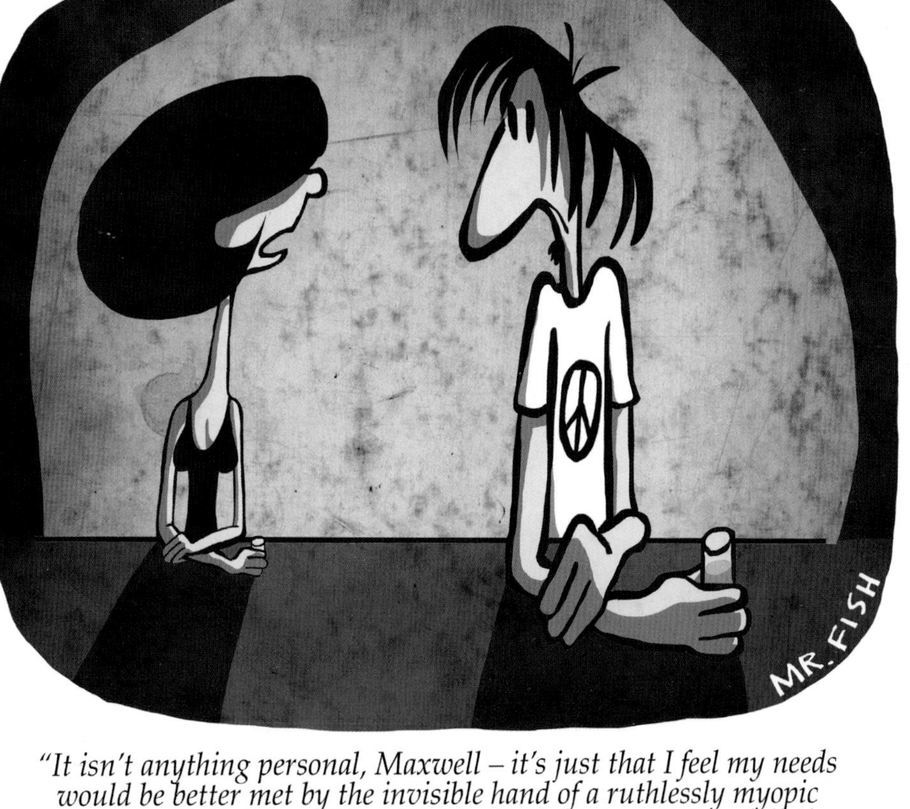
MR. FISH

"It isn't anything personal, Maxwell – it's just that I feel my needs would be better met by the invisible hand of a ruthlessly myopic corporate oligarchy capable of pandering to my more materialistic, narcissistic and complete subservience to authority self."

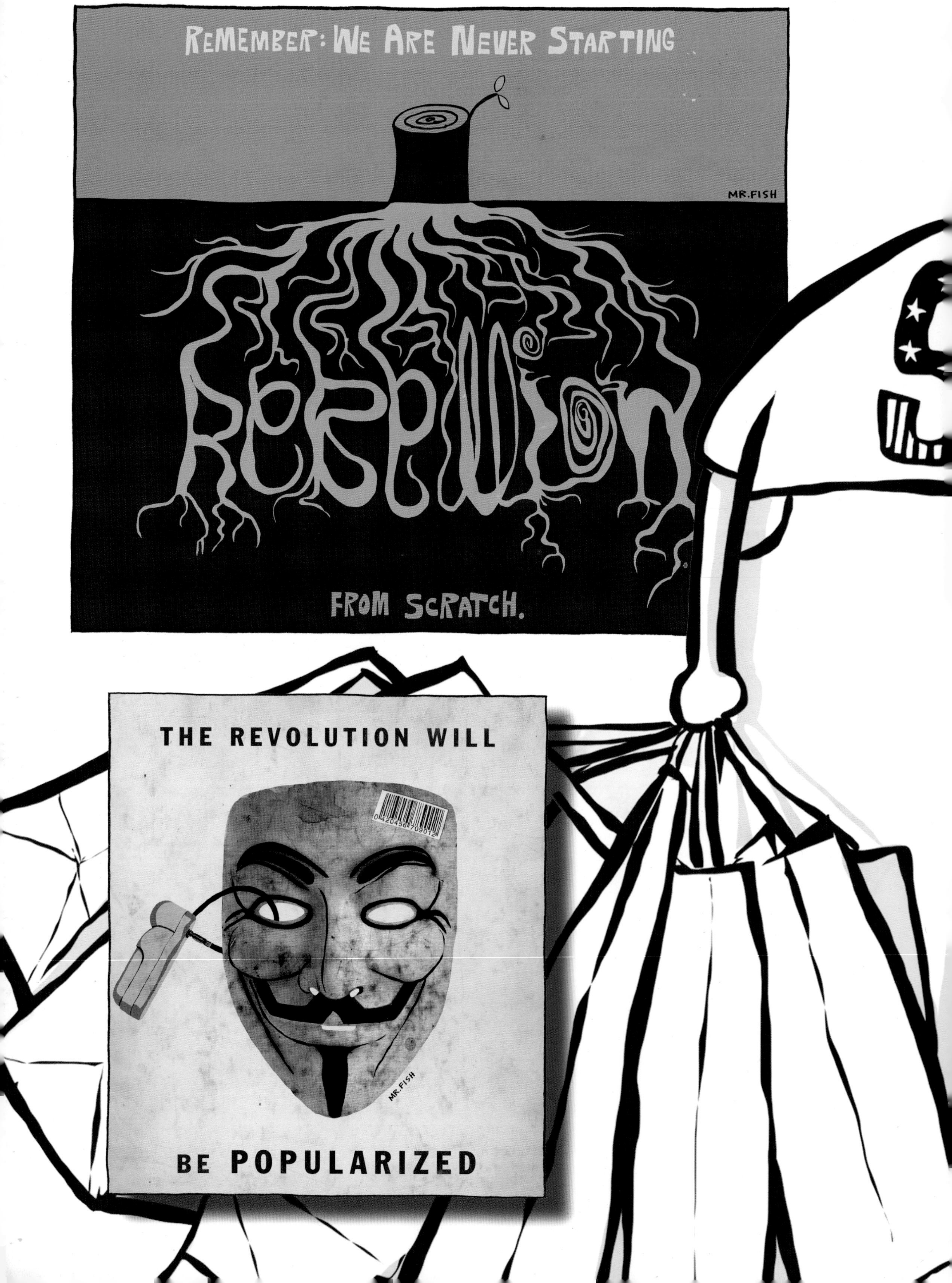
REMEMBER: WE ARE NEVER STARTING
MR.FISH
FROM SCRATCH.
THE REVOLUTION WILL
MR.FISH
BE POPULARIZED

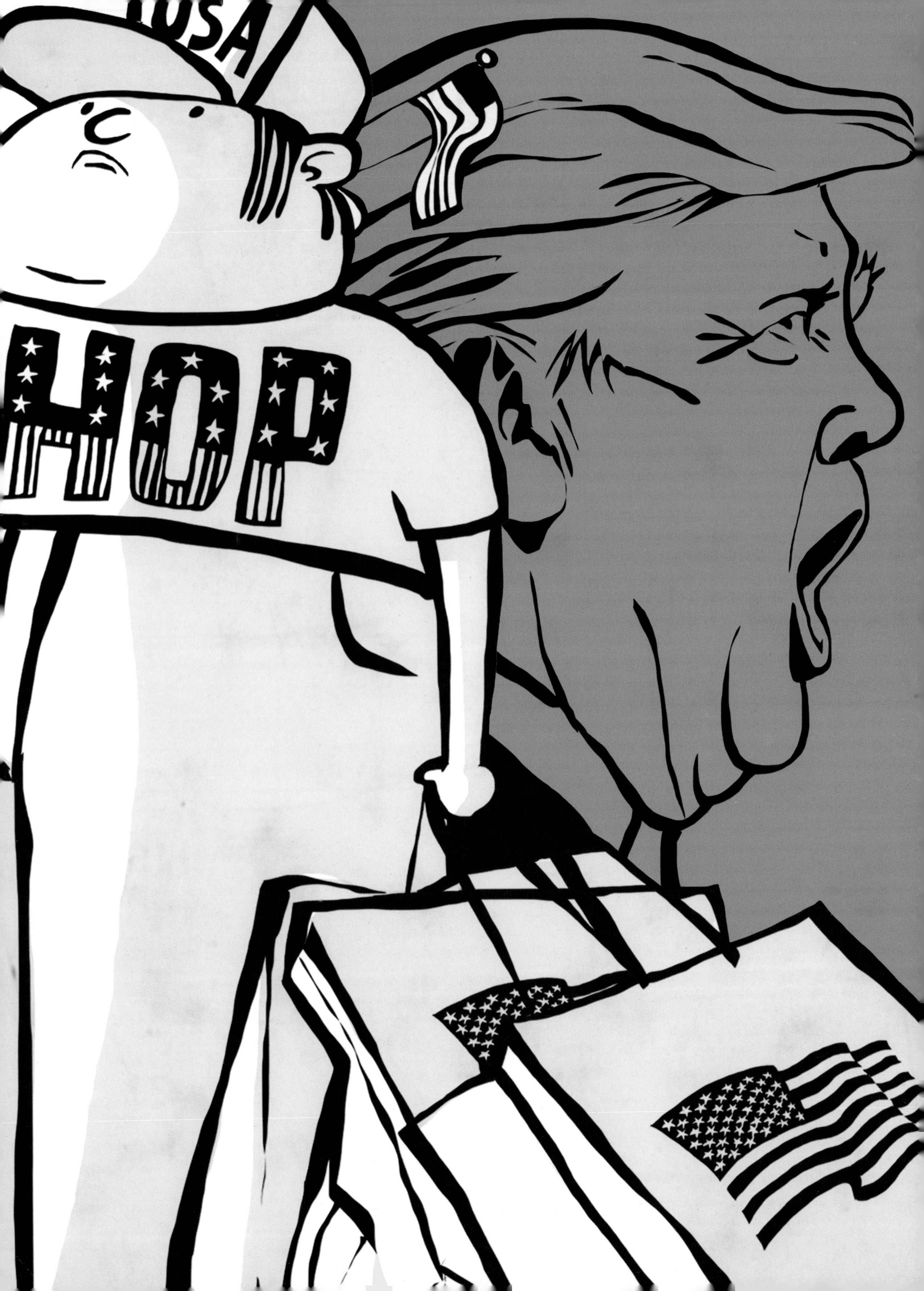
USA
HOP

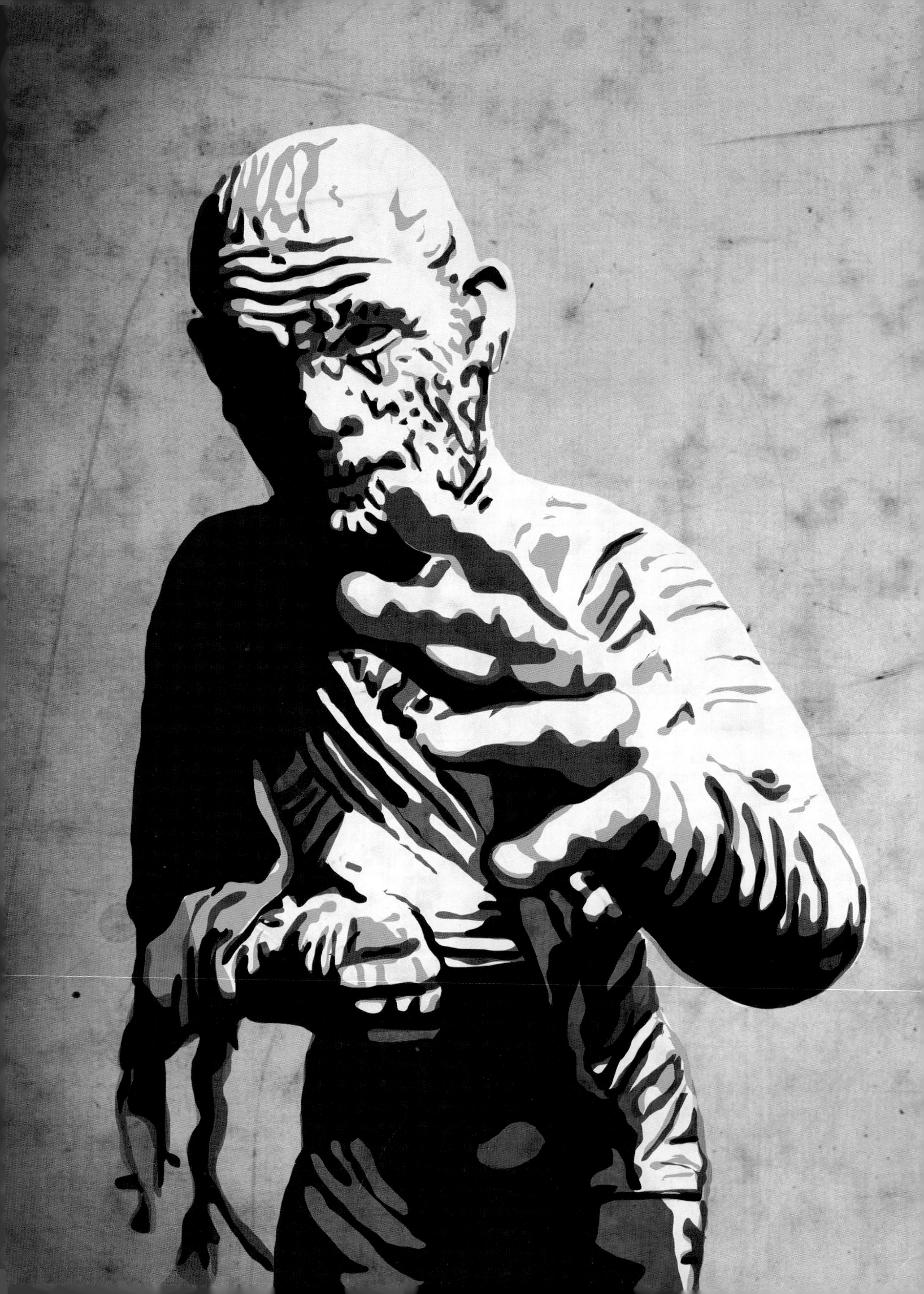

Who's Your Mummy?

11

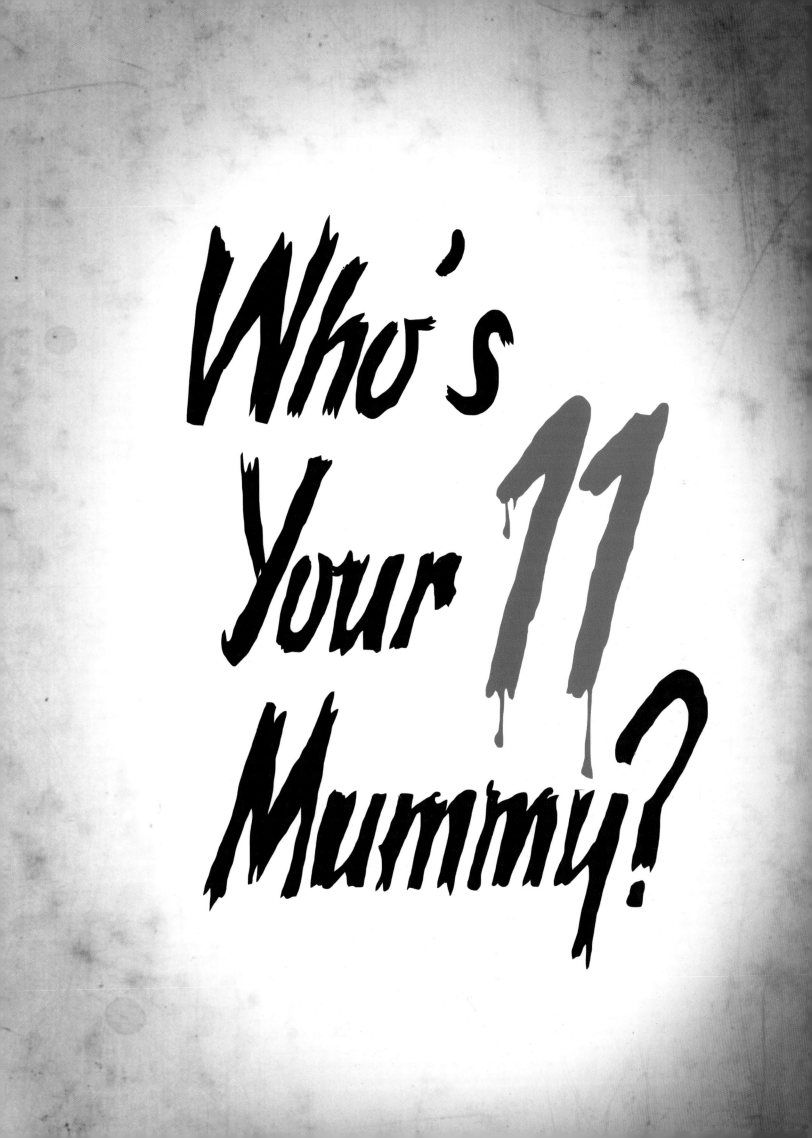

Who's Your Mummy?

THE STRIP MALL was configured like a wide V and was called Victory Square, the shape suggested by its title being the lazy sort of half-truth that made me wonder why anybody would ever trust a grown-up to tell the truth about anything. This was in Forked River, NJ, and I was there every Wednesday and Friday afternoon in the fall of 1971 for ballet class with my twin sister, Dawn. We were 6 years old, and I was the only boy in the class, except for Ernie, a puny kid in leg braces who always wore a desperate expression on his face and, although dressed in a black leotard, never danced. Instead, he merely moaned and periodically let out a pitiful little cry when the dance instructor's assistant manipulated the persistent toothaches that were his knees and elbows, which I now assume must've been atrophied by some sort of muscular dystrophy. I liked having Ernie around, if only because without him it would've been impossible for me to fool myself into imagining that I possessed a stunning masculine grace while executing the goofy faux-karate moves I substituted in place of the pirouettes and side leaps practiced by the rest of the class.

"Where the hell are you going before class starts?" asked my mother, dropping herself into the driver's seat of our blue Dodge Dart and jamming the cigarette lighter hard into the dashboard with her thumb. "And how is it that *you're* on time?" she asked my sister, pulling a menthol True Green out of its pack and screwing it into her teeth. "I drop you both off at the same goddamn time!"

Dawn and I were sitting in the back seat with our ballet cases resting on our laps, having been commanded there only moments earlier by our mother who had remained behind to speak with Ms. Jenny, who had *some concerns* regarding my

tardiness. "*Some concerns?*" I wanted to blurt out before being shoved out the door and pointed toward the parking lot. "I'm wearing a skintight polyester white turtleneck that snaps between my legs!" I imagined myself shouting. "My older brother gets guitar lessons, wears sneakers and jeans and an Italian horn necklace, carries a switchblade comb and throws his shit into a gig bag like Pete Townshend, while I'm locked in the bathroom hunched over in front of the toilet holding my breath and crossing my eyes and cinching myself up like Shirley Temple—*concerns?!* Let me tell you who might have *some concerns!*"

The truth of the matter, of course, was that I liked ballet class, not so much because of the dainty little slippers I got to wear or because of all the pliés and toe pointing I got to do, but rather because I found it deeply gratifying to know that I was doing something that required real guts to do. In fact, considering the laughter and fake throw-up noises made by my friends upon hearing of my enrollment in the class, dancing ballet was a little bit like getting to live inside fire twice a week and emerging from the flames completely unscathed by the experience. It was a new sort of heroism that I was anxious to explore, having absolutely no interest in traversing the well-worn paths of gender competency as endured by every little boy force-fed misogyny and sports-infused machismo since time immemorial. After seeing my brother drop a Frisbee once and then spend the rest of the afternoon sobbing inside a pile of damp leaves in the backyard, I was determined to chart a different course into manhood. The way I figured it, anybody could learn how to throw a lousy football or spit on a girl, but try working on an arabesque with microfibers riding up your ass crack while a middle-aged woman in Capezio shoes wrestles with a crippled child who is screaming bloody murder in the corner of the room, the whole time surrounded by floor-to-ceiling mirrors megaphoning an inferred sissiness that an entire sub-industry of psychiatry and theistic intolerance has been trying to remedy with shock treatment and threats of eternal damnation for generations—*that* will make you bulletproof. *That* will make you dangerous.

"He can't get past the hobby shop window," sighed my sister in answer to my mother's question. "He's in love with that stupid mummy model."

"I told you to forget about that stinkin' model!" said my mother, practically slapping herself on the forehead like an exasperated cartoon character. "For the hundredth time, you're not getting it! It's too expensive!"

The mummy model that she and my sister were talking about was built from an original 1963 Aurora Model Kit and displayed in the window of Master Hobbies, which was two doors down from the dance studio. Each Wednesday and Friday, my mother would pull up to Butler's Drugstore and drop Dawn and me off, saying that she'd be back in an hour. Then she'd drive away. We would then walk in the direction of the Dance Expressions studio, located at the far end of the alley created by the incomplete convergence of Victory Square at its V. We would enter the alley and, yes, I would pause to press my nose up against the window at Master Hobbies and marvel at the 9 inch plastic mummy on the other side of the glass, and my sister would continue on alone, past the pizza place and into the dance studio door.

Then there would just be me and the faint chirping of dying frogs from the far end of the alley where the sidewalk came to a dead end at a green wall of crumbling slate shingles.

It happened at the close of every summer, this huge migratory die-off of frogs. Beginning sometime in late August, just as the great majority of the frogs living in a nearby lagoon reached maturity, they would hop through the weeds in the middle of the night and flush out the massive indigenous cricket population and drive it into the shopping center, past the drugstore and past the hobby shop and past the pizza place and past the dance studio, and slaughter it against the green wall. Then, once all the crickets had been chewed into tapioca, the frogs would gorge themselves on disoriented mosquito hawks and palsied moths and black beetles driven mad and rendered flightless by the caged floodlight bolted to the wall above. Glutted with the spoils of their conquest, the frogs would notice the approaching dawn and begin wearily throwing themselves forward into the crumbling slate shingles of the dead end, over and over again, as if the real world had absolutely no precedence over the self-edifying folly of their wills.

After several weeks of this, the lagoon would eventually be empty of anything larger than a water strider, the forest would be shimmering with the exalted symphony of happy crickets and the alley would be fetid with the dehydrated bodies of frogs, many of them little more than flattened patties of amphibious scrotal jerky wrapped stiffly around tiny skeletons frozen in spirited jazz poses of exultation.

Of victory!

What captivated me most about the mummy model wasn't its wicked cool ugliness, nor was it the exquisite paint job and the ghoulish enthusiasm with which the artist applied blood to the monster's hands and closed right eye, but rather it was my own moral sense of fairness and the affinity for anti-establishmentarianism that seemed to come so naturally to

me. After all, whether one was considering the unique circumstances of the Mummy or Frankenstein's Monster or the Creature from the Black Lagoon or the Phantom of the Opera or the Hunchback of Notre Dame or King Kong, there was no getting around the fact that these poor souls, many of them merely starved for love and companionship, were innocent victims of either intolerance or blatant discrimination from the dominant culture. Simply put, those monsters who weren't trying to gain acceptance from the status quo were merely trying to

DISASSEMBLY REQUIRED

MR. FISH

exclude themselves from society's thuggish judgment and demand for acquiescence, both positions reflecting, I would find out later, the completely coherent and morally cogent opinions of Dr. Martin Luther King Jr. and Malcolm X.

And Jack Kerouac and Mario Savio. And Kate Millett and Geronimo. And Bugs Bunny and Alan Watts.

In fact, what made monsters menacing to the world was either their inability—or their ballsy refusal!—to conform to stringently myopic doctrines of behavior and belief, their hair-raising spookiness coming from the wretched fight that they usually put up before being violently killed by, essentially, popular opinion.

In the end, my stepfather bought me the mummy model, believing it to be the perfect antidote against my turning gay one fiendish relevé at a time.

TIRED OF LIVING HIS LIFE ONLINE, NEVILLE DECIDES TO GET AWAY FROM HIS COMPUTER SO HE CAN GO TO THE PARK AND SPEND THE AFTERNOON HOLDING A REAL WIKIPEDIA AND WAITING FOR SOME SIGN THAT IT LOVES HIM BACK

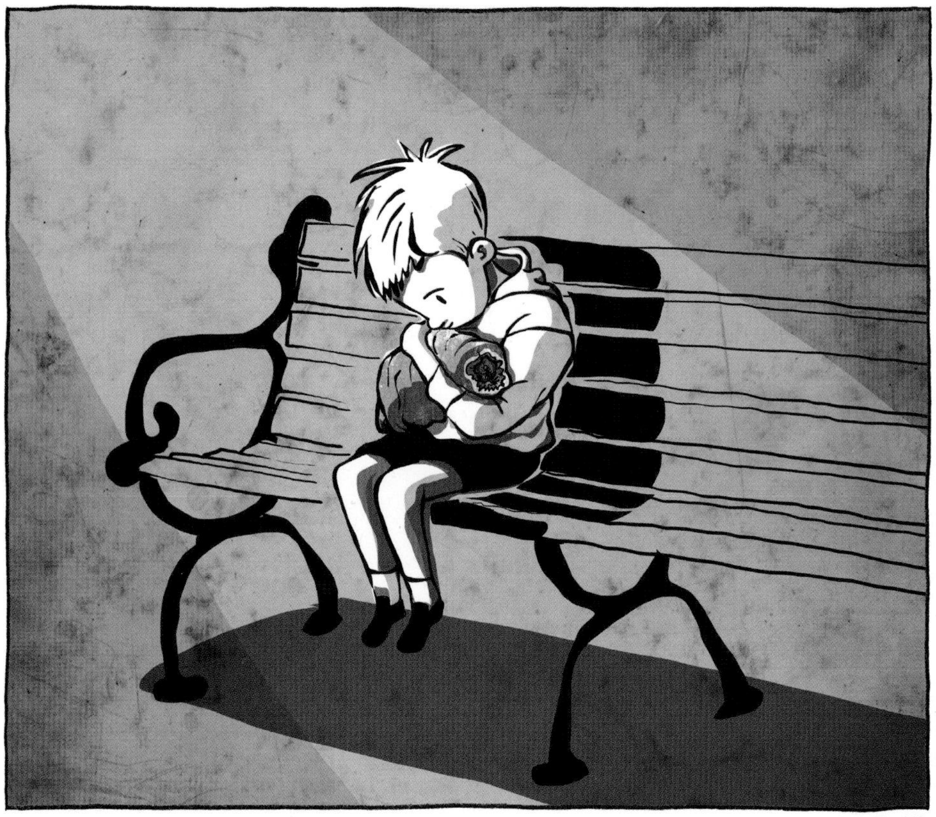

MR.FISH

OLLIE SPREADING PEACE

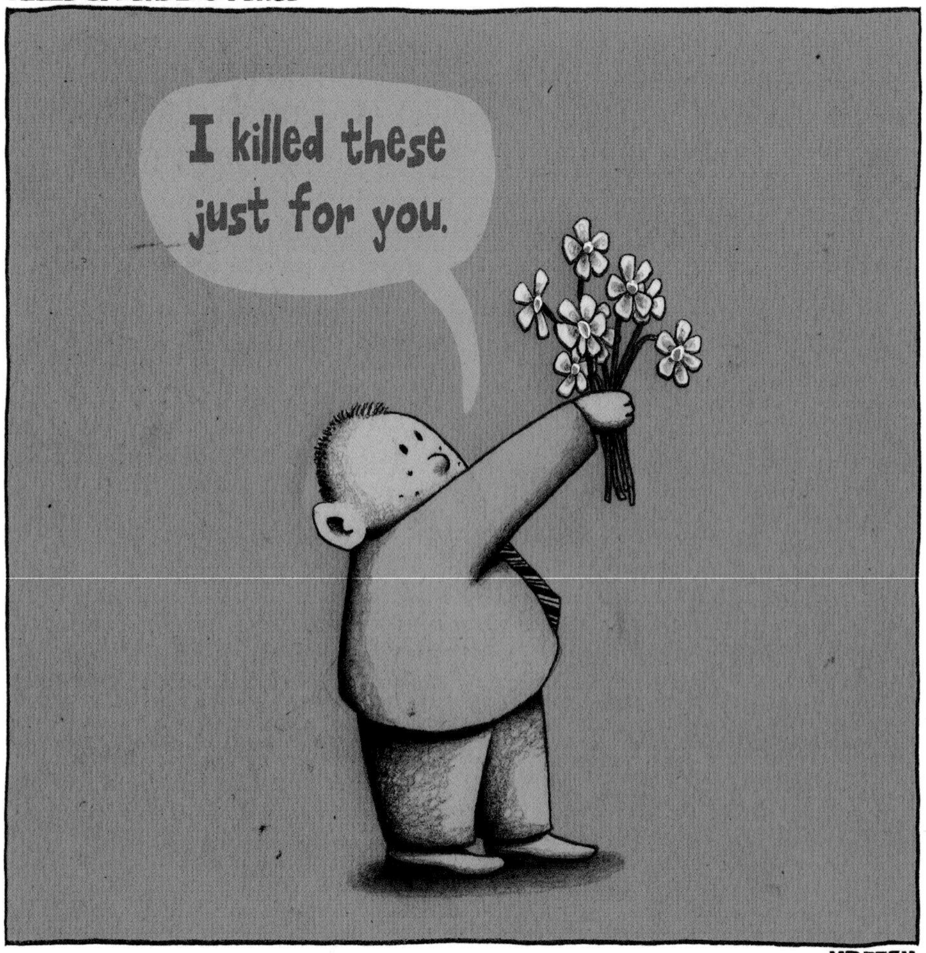
I killed these just for you.

MR.FISH

GLOBAL WARMING MAKES TOO MANY PEOPLE TOO RICH TO CARE TOO MUCH ABOUT BEING TOO UPSET ABOUT THE WORLD ENDING TOO SOON

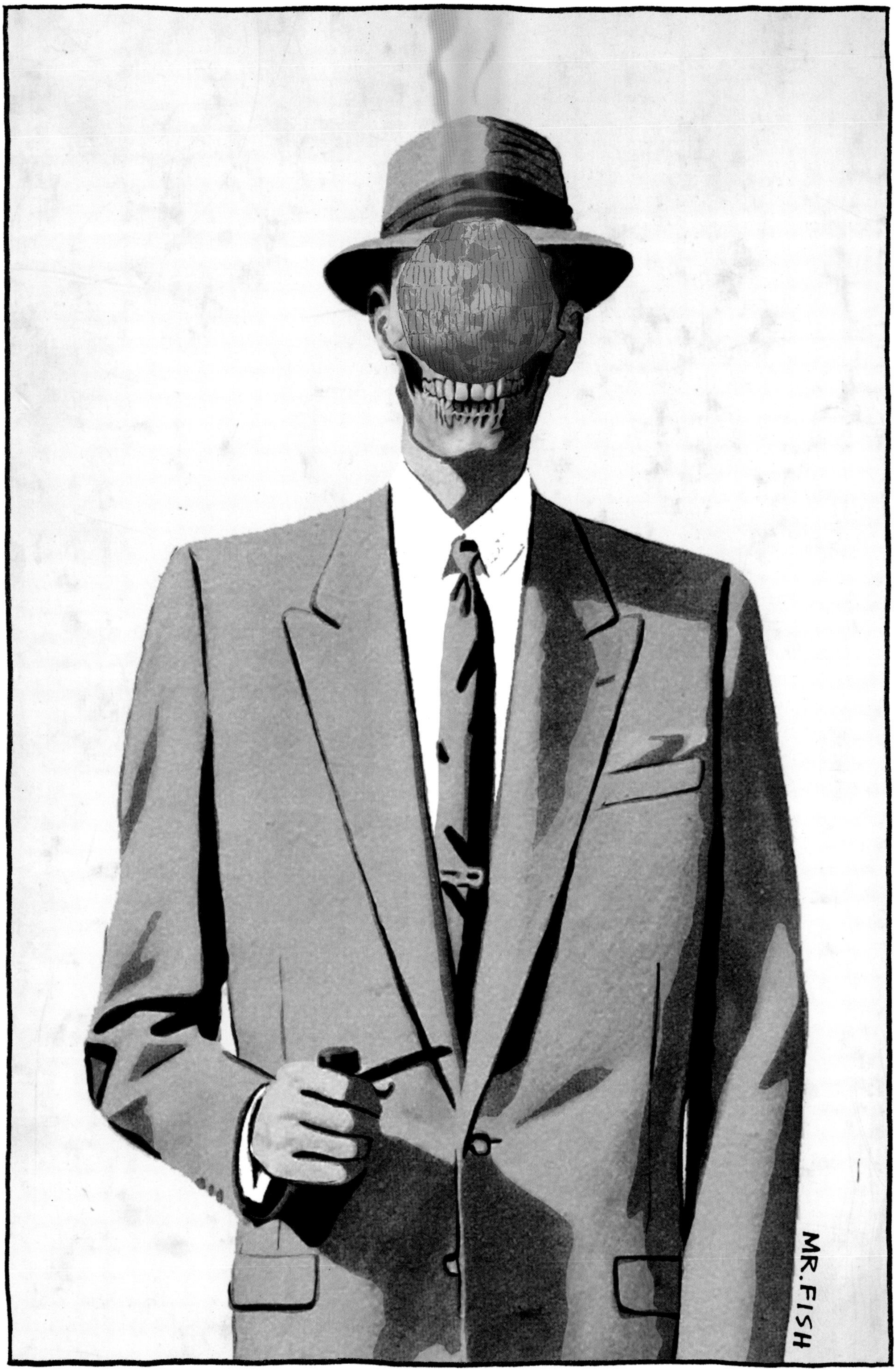
MR.FISH

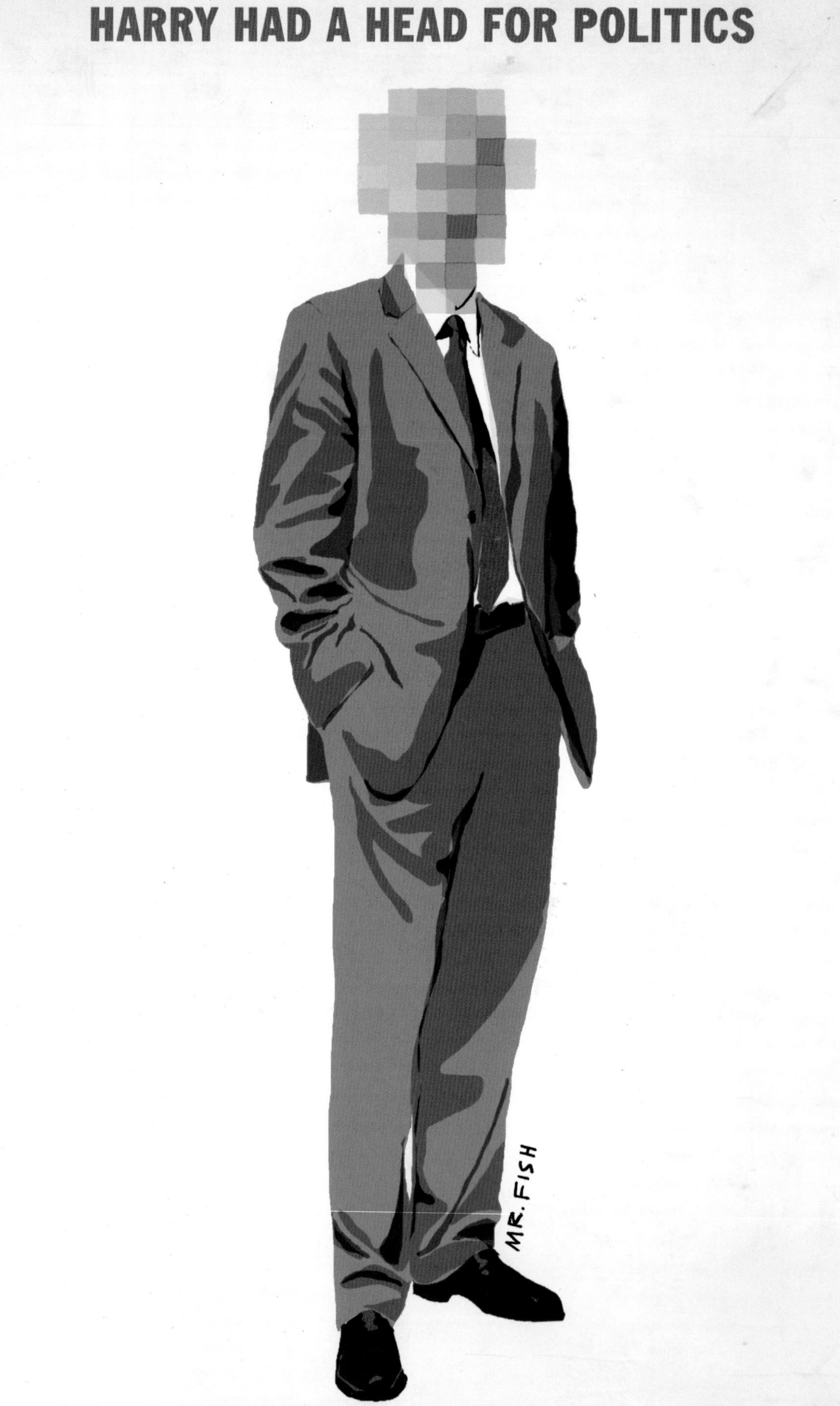
HARRY HAD A HEAD FOR POLITICS
MR. FISH
HE WAS OH SO SAFE FOR EVERY AUDIENCE
(and then the world blew up)

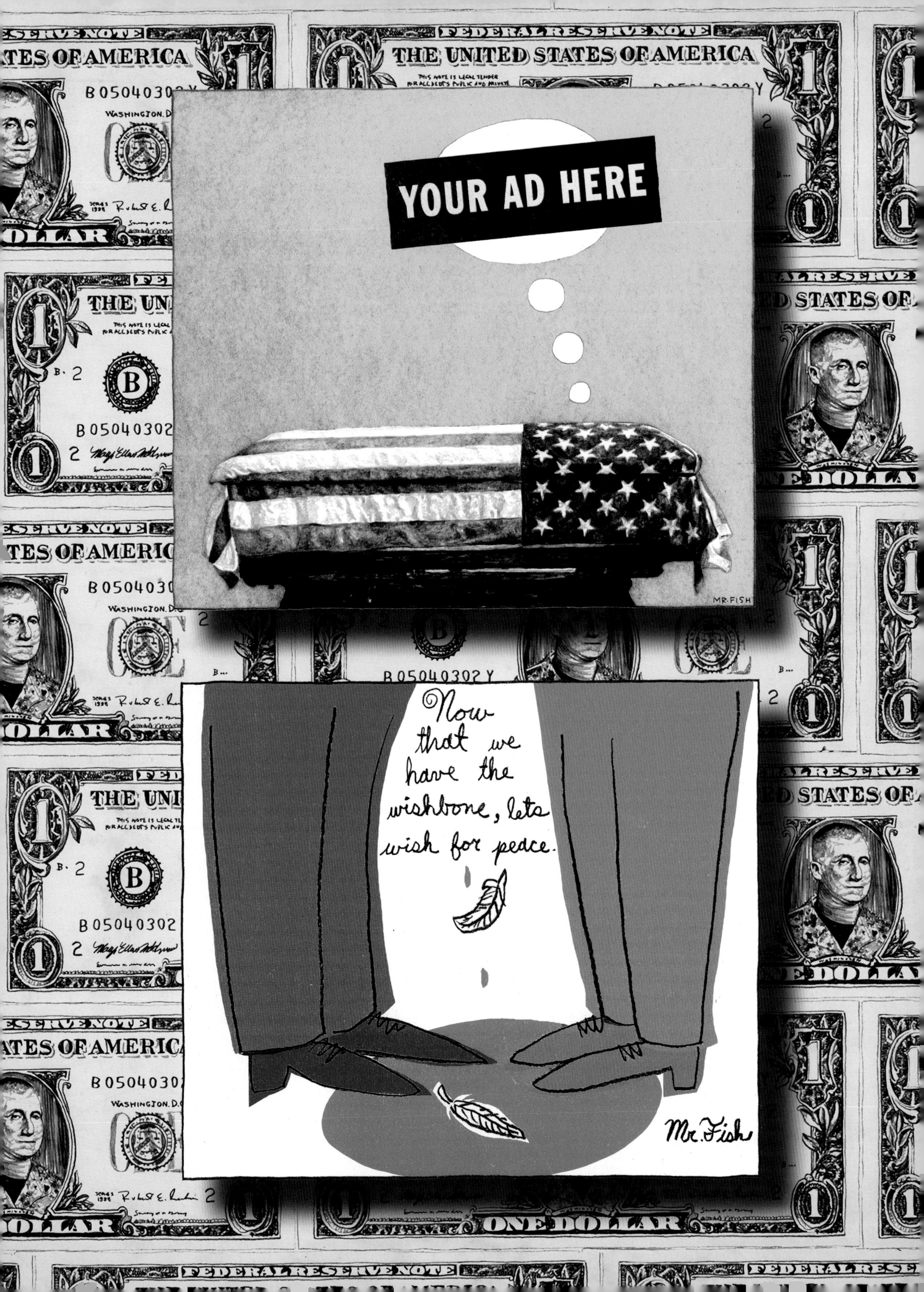
FEDERAL RESERVE NOTE
THE UNITED STATES OF AMERICA
YOUR AD HERE
MR. FISH
Now that we have the wishbone, lets wish for peace.
Mr. Fish
ONE DOLLAR

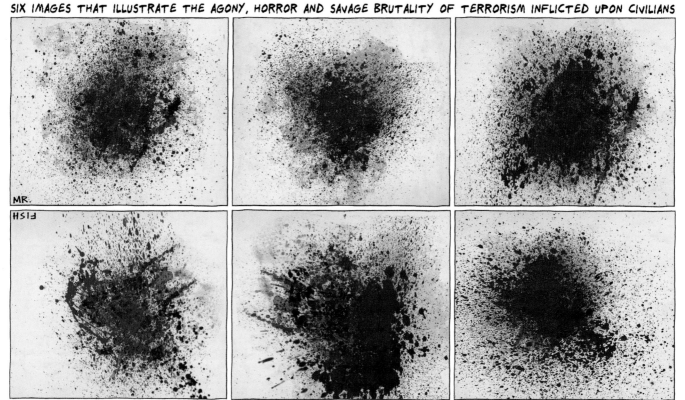

SIX IMAGES THAT ILLUSTRATE THE AGONY, HORROR AND SAVAGE BRUTALITY OF TERRORISM INFLICTED UPON CIVILIANS
MR.
FISH
SIX IMAGES THAT ILLUSTRATE THE GOODWILL, ALTRUISM AND SAVAGE HUMANITY OF AMERICANISM INFLICTED UPON CIVILIANS

MY SAVIOUR DIED AND ALL I GOT WAS THIS OVERWHELMING INDIFFERENCE WHENEVER INNOCENT MUSLIMS ARE KILLED ANYWHERE IN THE WORLD
MR. FISH

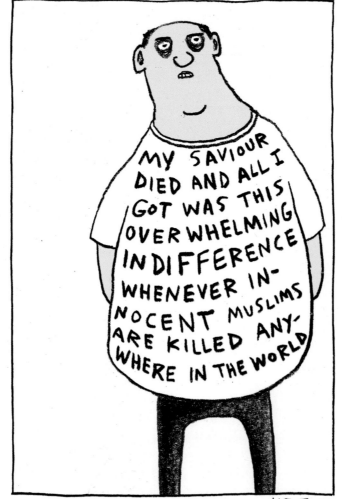

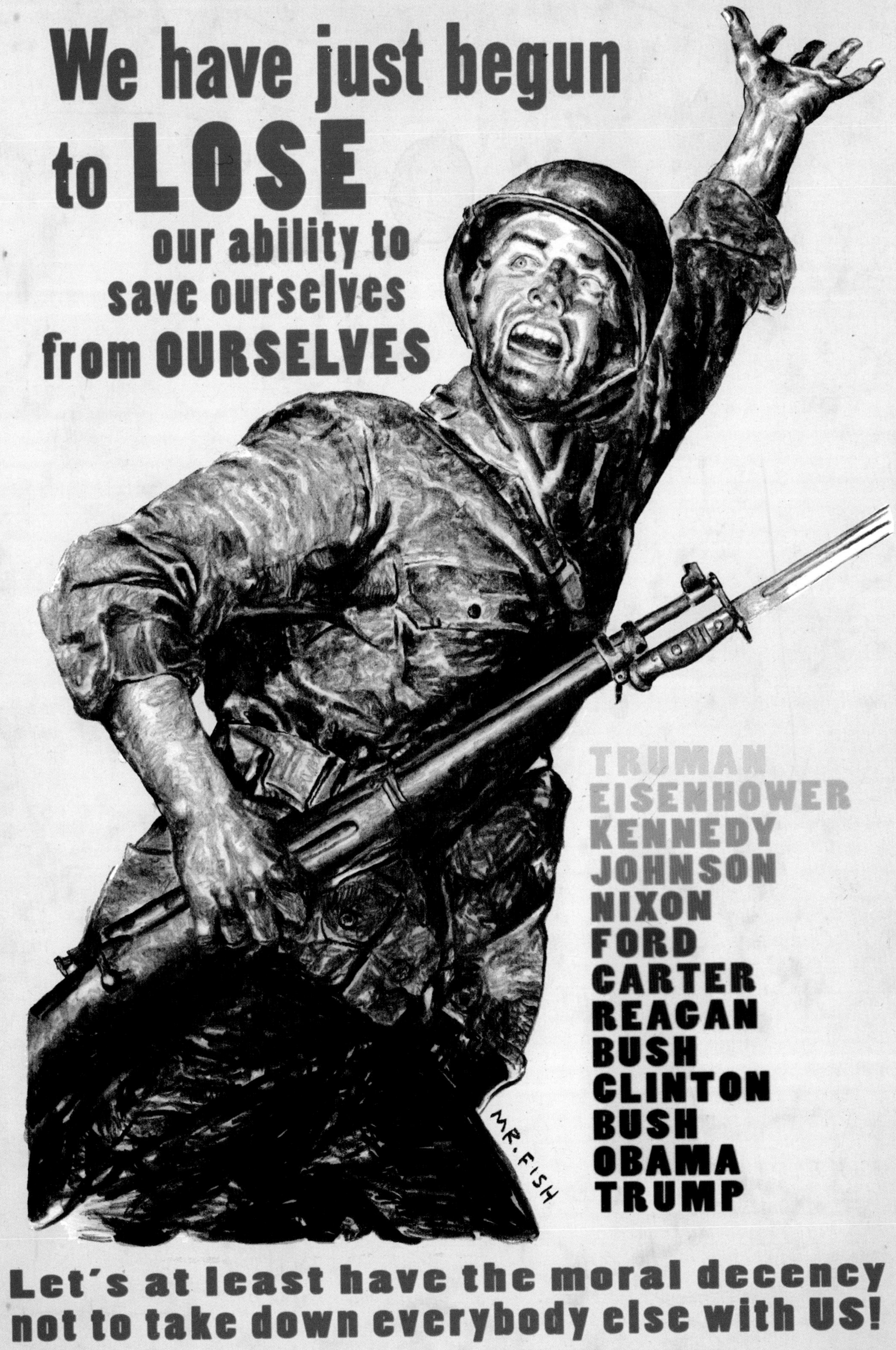
We have just begun
to LOSE
our ability to
save ourselves
from OURSELVES
TRUMAN
EISENHOWER
KENNEDY
JOHNSON
NIXON
FORD
CARTER
REAGAN
BUSH
CLINTON
BUSH
OBAMA
TRUMP
MR. FISH
Let's at least have the moral decency
not to take down everybody else with US!

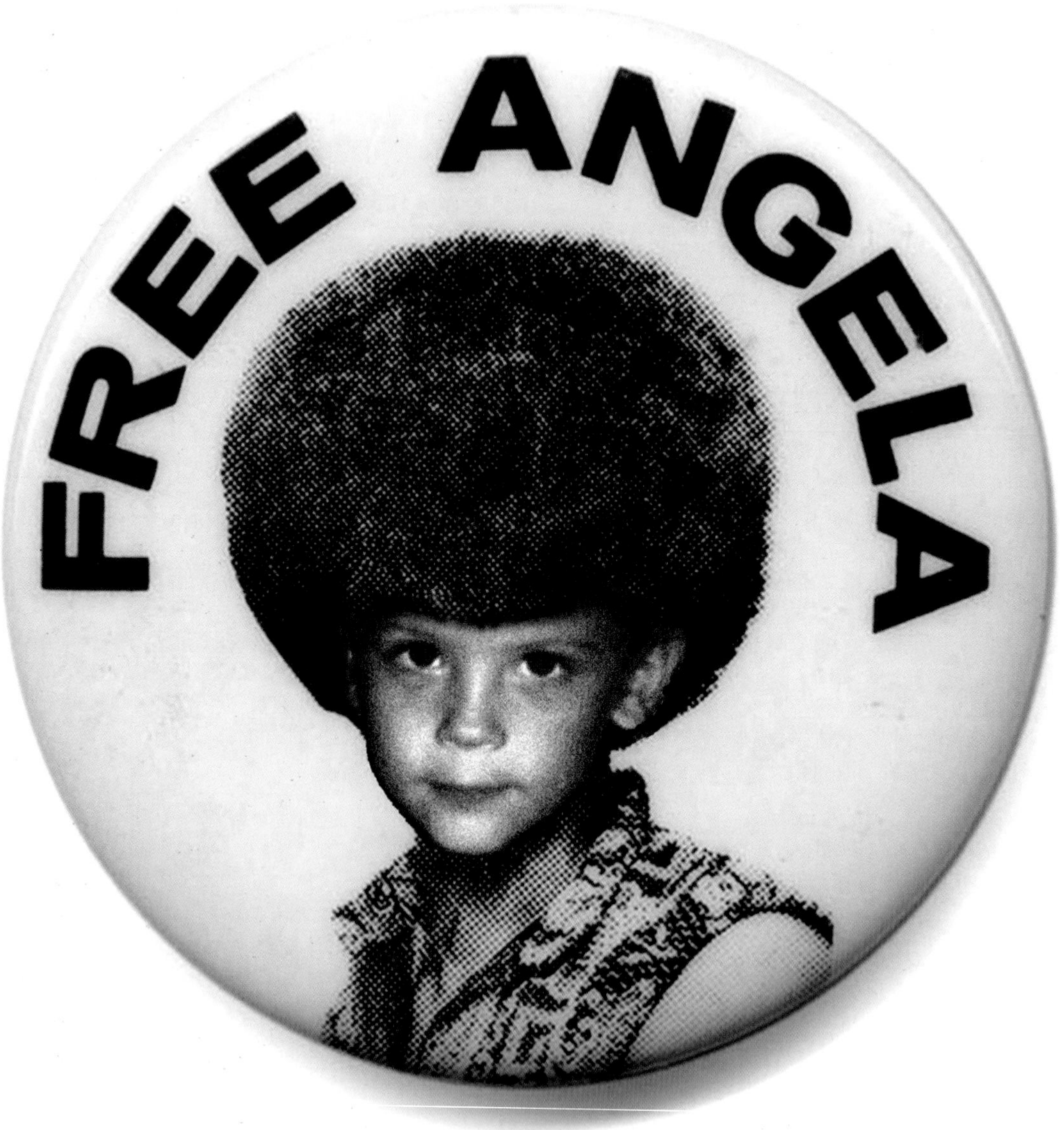
FREE ANGELA

Twelve 1973

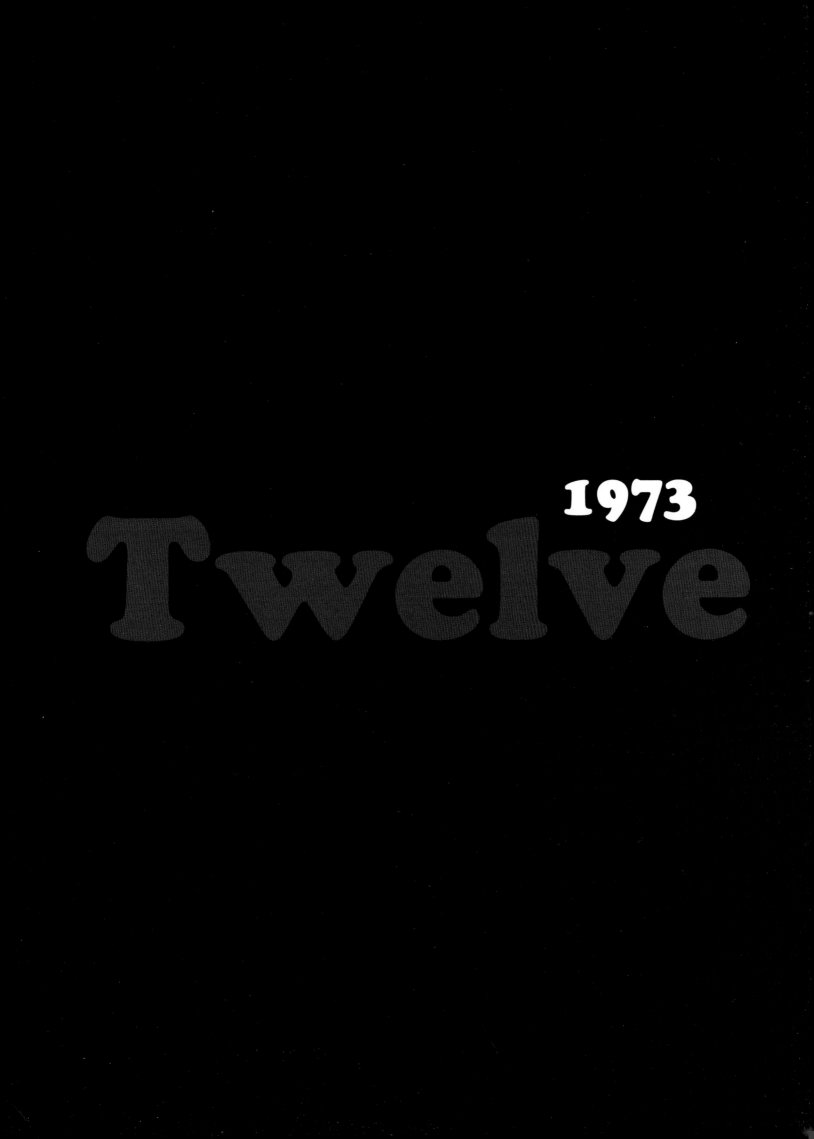

1973

WHEN I WAS 7 I wanted to be Angela Davis.

Not a fireman, not an astronaut, not even what so many of my friends in 1973 dreamed of being—none other than the voice, and some would argue the moral conscience, of our generation, Cornelius from *Planet of the Apes*—but a black feminist revolutionary communist ex-convict philosopher genius sistah *what are you looking at, honkie?!* hellraiser. Afro as big as a Hoppity Hop, no makeup, fist in the air, *whitey afraid to walk down the same side of the street as me*, the biggest shoes anyone could imagine seeing on a woman. A woman, that is, with legs of equal length, a clarification that I feel I must make because my grandmother had a friend who had one normal-sized leg and another leg maybe 10 inches too short, the difference being made up by a gigantic black shoe that looked like a small suitcase containing what I'd always imagined were silver dollars packed so closely together that there was no sound from her walking to indicate any value in her handicap. I used to imagine that she was one-sixteenth a Frankenstein, as uninteresting as somebody one-sixteenth a Kennedy, barely worth the ingredient because it did more to point out the much larger portion of herself that was unpedigreed mutt.

Her name was Aida Hobson, and during summer afternoons at my grandparents' house in Springfield, PA, I'd hear, sometimes as many as three times a week, the screen door off the back porch open and then slam shut and her walk across the linoleum like half a pony and unload an armload of tomatoes and spiders from her garden onto the kitchen table, the flabby drum roll of picture-perfect fruit reverberating through the house as faintly as aristocrats applauding through white gloves. Then the pony would turn and the screen door would slam shut again, but not all the time. If my grandmother wasn't busy with a crossword puzzle or the painting of her hideous yellow toenails, some as thick as cough drops, or a card game with my twin sister and big brother and me, she'd meet Mrs. Hobson in the kitchen and the two would settle into chairs on the back porch for cigarettes and coffee and inaudible talk about what always sounded like plans for either a prison break or a murder or how much more salacious the next sorority party was going to be, Aida's Spanish accent lisping through third-grade English with the allure of exotic cooking. The laughter inside their conversation was always too secretive or lustful or serious to seem entirely appropriate for two women with such dainty mustaches and underwear one could easily imagine, if mounted properly, capable of pulling a mid-sized skiff full of useless books across a vast ocean.

"Angela who?" said my grandfather, straining to hear me over the applause of the 40 pieces of bacon that he was cooking on his brand new birthday present, a slab of superheated Teflon as big as a headstone that, when plugged in and shingled with bacon, dimmed all the lights in the house and made every dog in the neighborhood spin in circles and roll around on the ground and ululate.

"Davis," I said. "Angela Davis. Roger has a poster of her in the basement." Roger was my 24-year-old uncle who was still living at home and was slowly turning the 1950s décor into something more conducive to the growing of mutton chop

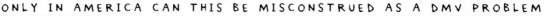

ONLY IN AMERICA CAN THIS BE MISCONSTRUED AS A DMV PROBLEM
YOUR LEFT TAILLIGHT IS OUT - NOW REMOVE THE MELANIN FROM YOUR SKIN, SCUMBAG, OR I'LL SHOOT!
MR.FISH

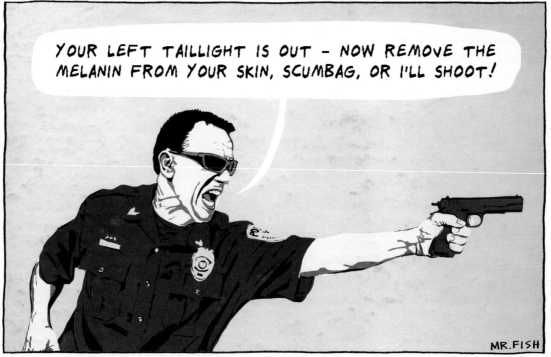

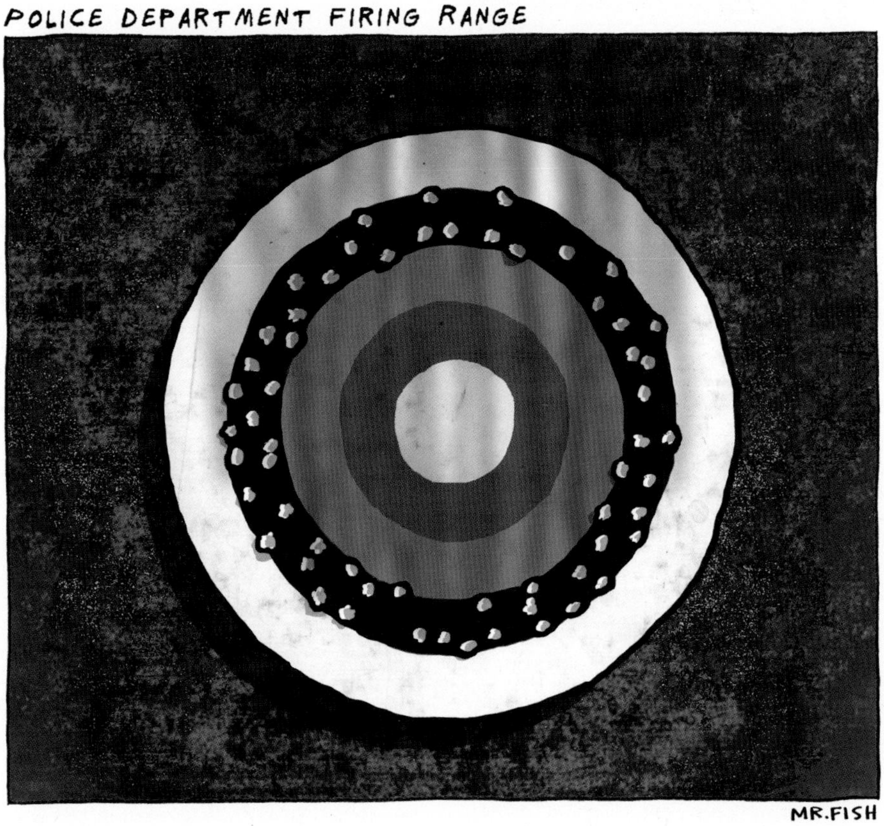
POLICE DEPARTMENT FIRING RANGE
MR.FISH

sideburns and the cashing of unemployment checks. "You know, the big picture of the black lady, near the air hockey table?" No response, the bacon grease beginning to fog my and my grandfather's glasses. "The black lady!" I insisted, balling up my tiny white fists. "Free Angela Davis!" I said, quoting the poster and feeling the injustice of the words. "Down in the basement!"

Pause.

"Air hockey table?" he finally said.

"Aw, just forget it," I said, going out the back door and down the steps and into the garage to climb into the backseat of my grandparents' station wagon, where I planned on using the momentum of my foul mood to properly mourn the end of summer. It broke my heart to smell the newness of the upholstery, only 3 months old, the intoxicating aroma of fresh plastic mixed with suntan lotion and cheeseburgers, and to remember the long summer days spent being driven back and forth to the mall and the tennis courts and the movie theaters and the public swimming pool and how, in less than 48 hours, I would be crammed in between my sister and brother in the backseat of my parents' green Nova, the upholstery smelling like old snow and my mother's menthol cigarettes, with my stepfather's empty beer cans rolling around under the driver's side seat like tiny skulls from an indifferent slaughter of retarded children. It wasn't that there was any less love at my parents' house than there was at my grandparents', it was just that there were cats and dogs and a television that burned 24 hours a day and a fondness for alcohol to compromise the rationing size of the available portions.

"You've got to understand," my brother would explain to me with some measure of impatience, "some of those dogs have been around a lot longer than you or me. For crapsake, Buffy's almost 11." He was right. Buffy was almost 11. And although Bullet, Buffy's second husband, and me shared the same exact age almost to the day, the fact that he was able to toilet train himself years before I was made him, by comparison, something of a fecal prodigy and me a savant of utter helplessness. There was no contest. In fact, while I'd never even kissed a girl before, although I was swung around hard by my hood once and thrown into a stack of trashcans by Betty Boyle for trying, Bullet was already a grandfather.

Lying down on the cool leather and looking up at the dark cab light on the ceiling, I sighed and closed my eyes and tried to imagine what I'd be doing if I were Angela Davis. Admittedly, I knew nothing about the woman beyond the picture of her in my grandparents' basement, but, of course, I didn't know anybody who really knew much about who their hero really was beyond the most trivial sort of personal information such as height and weight and, occasionally, batting average. My best friend JJ, for example, was a huge fan of Lassie, the famous television dog star known for rescuing loathsomely wholesome children from abandoned mine shafts, train trestles, quicksand and fast-moving water week after week, and I could only imagine the army of PR guys hired to make sure that there were no pictures of the superstar collie published in *Time*, *Life* or *Look* where she was licking her own rear or shoving her nose into the crotch of a studio executive or eating the vomit of one of her stand-ins.

Still, despite the fact that I didn't know who Angela Davis was, I felt as if I knew who her detractors were. I knew, for

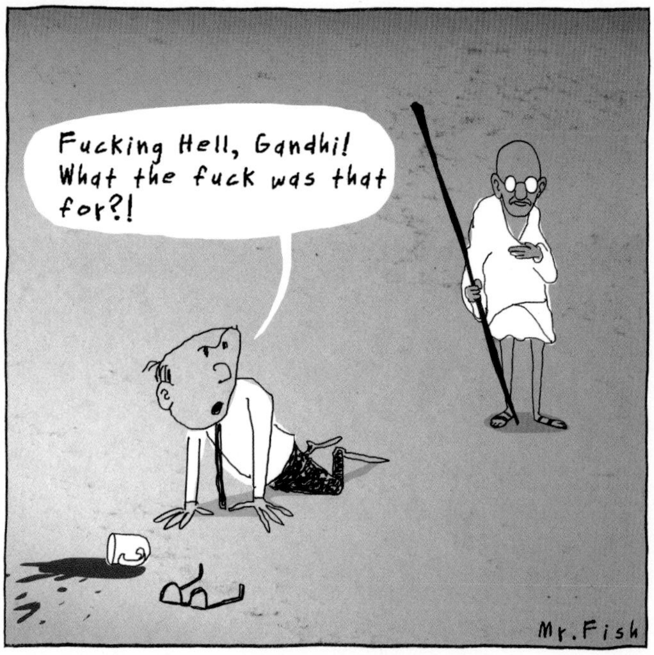
Fucking Hell, Gandhi! What the fuck was that for?!
Mr. Fish

example, that there existed a portion of society that thought black people—*Negroes* they were called back then—were inferior to white people and that women were inferior to men and that black women were, therefore, inferiority squared, and what drew me to Davis was the complete self-assuredness that she seemed to exude from the center of that very specific hurricane of racial and sexual prejudice that was blowing loud and clear through American culture in 1973. Having both a best friend who was black and who incurred daily salutations of *nigger* and *coon* and *Washington* and a twin sister who could easily match every mental and physical feat that I was capable of, I knew that any notion that attempted to cast Negroes or girls into a subcategory of human being, besides being a boldfaced lie, was some kind of extreme cowardice; it had to be, for there was no accidental ignorance capable of being so completely blind to reality. It was the kind of dumbness that existed crouched inside the mind, behind closed eyes, cowering in between capped ears and behind a clothes-pinned nose sealed off from the unmistakable stench of happy smoke from a joyous and inevitable and all-consuming revolution. So much stupidity is deliberate, an attempt to avoid comparison with any fact that might denigrate the notion that any of us are objective participants in the world and that our observations are made cleanly through glass un-graffitied by any bogus or prejudiced ideology, Goddamned, God blessed or God-awful.

Looking at the Angela Davis poster in my grandparents' basement, her face locked in something like a battle cry, I wished to be on the winning side of the argument using just the constant and unwavering statement of my own sex and skin color. I wanted to be a hero who existed contrary to stupidity, somebody who by simply living was the actual proof that the worst misconceptions held by the dimmest wits in society, many of them policymakers and architects of public opinion, were wrong. I wanted to believe that the truth was invincible. And it was.

And this is what it said: your opinion here.

An hour later I woke up to the sound of my grandparents talking on the back porch and having their lunch—as they did every day during the summer months when my grandfather wasn't driving a school bus—of bacon, lettuce and tomato, their voices remarkably clear for having to travel through the wall of the garage and the body of the car and the fog of my grogginess.

"It wasn't about her leg, exactly," continued my grandmother, clarifying a point that had apparently entered my grandfather's head hurriedly and half-dressed. "It was more about the universe in general."

"Uh-huh," he said, still confused.

"She said that she wished that she could wake up every day..." she stopped herself, thinking. "No," she went on, "every *other* day and the world would see her as somebody with one normal-sized leg and one extra-long leg."

"What do you mean?" He exhaled affectionate boredom like an ungrantable birthday wish and took a bite of his sandwich.

"You know, instead of thinking that her short leg was too short, people would think that her normal-sized leg was extra long."

"Too long?"

"No, just extra long."

"Well, longer than the other one I mean."

"Right."

"What would be the difference?"

"Between too long and extra long? I don't know, I guess just your point of view."

"No, between one leg that's too short and one leg that's extra long?"

"Well, instead of just having pity for her, she figured that on the days when she had an extra-long leg people would be fascinated by her. You know, the idea being that people respect the concept of more a lot more than less."

"They do?"

"Sure they do. What do you mean, *they do?*"

"Why not just wish for two normal-sized legs?"

"Oh, Eugene."

"Oh, Eugene what?"

"She didn't say that she wanted to be invisible."

Somewhere in Chicago in the backseat of a black Ford Mercury sat Angela Davis looking out through the rain. Passing a crowded diner on her way from O'Hare International Airport, she sighed and leaned back against the upholstery and, looking up at the dark cab light on the ceiling, she closed her eyes and wished that she were invisible.

Living her dream, I was.

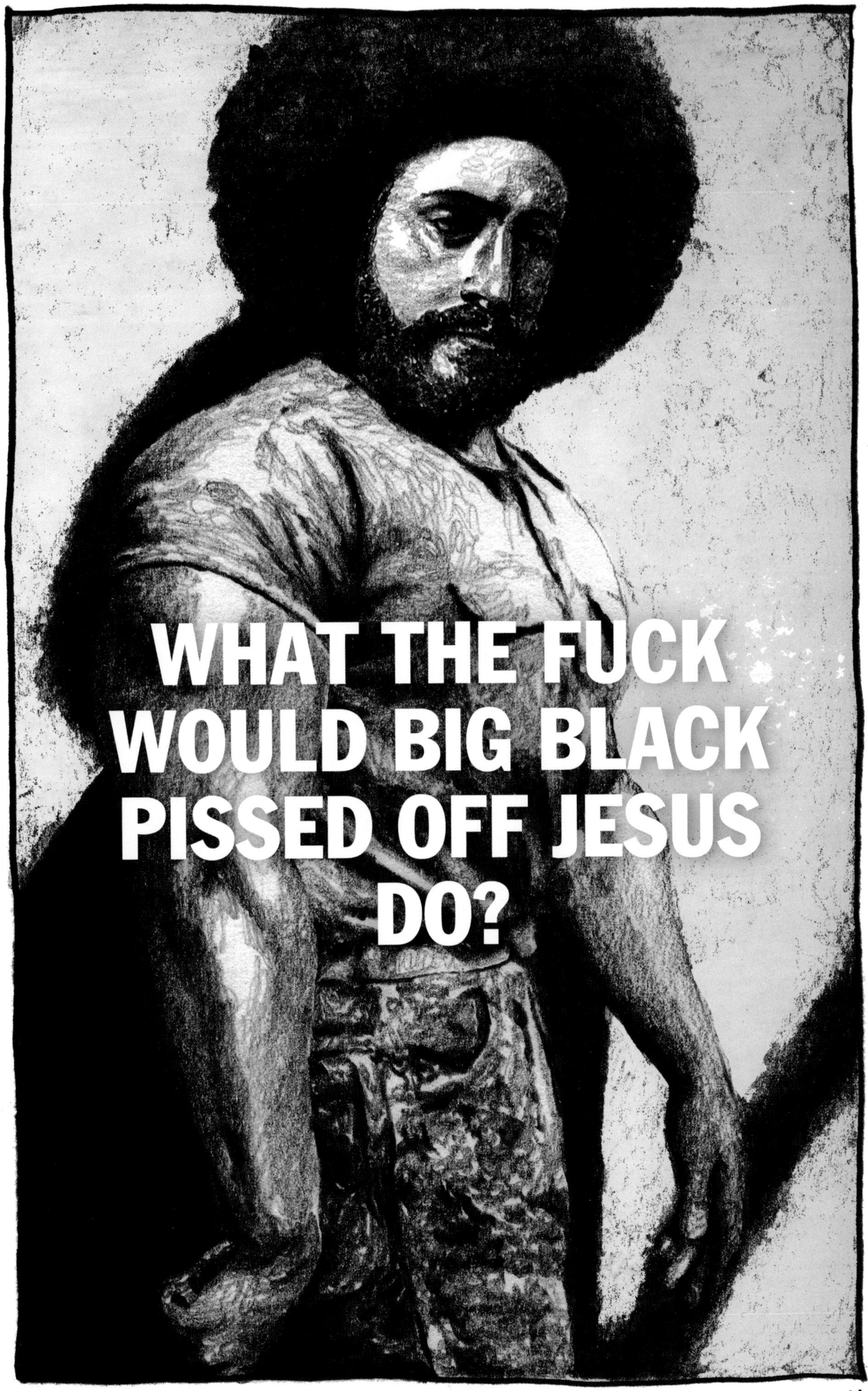
WHAT THE FUCK
WOULD BIG BLACK
PISSED OFF JESUS
DO?
MR.FISH

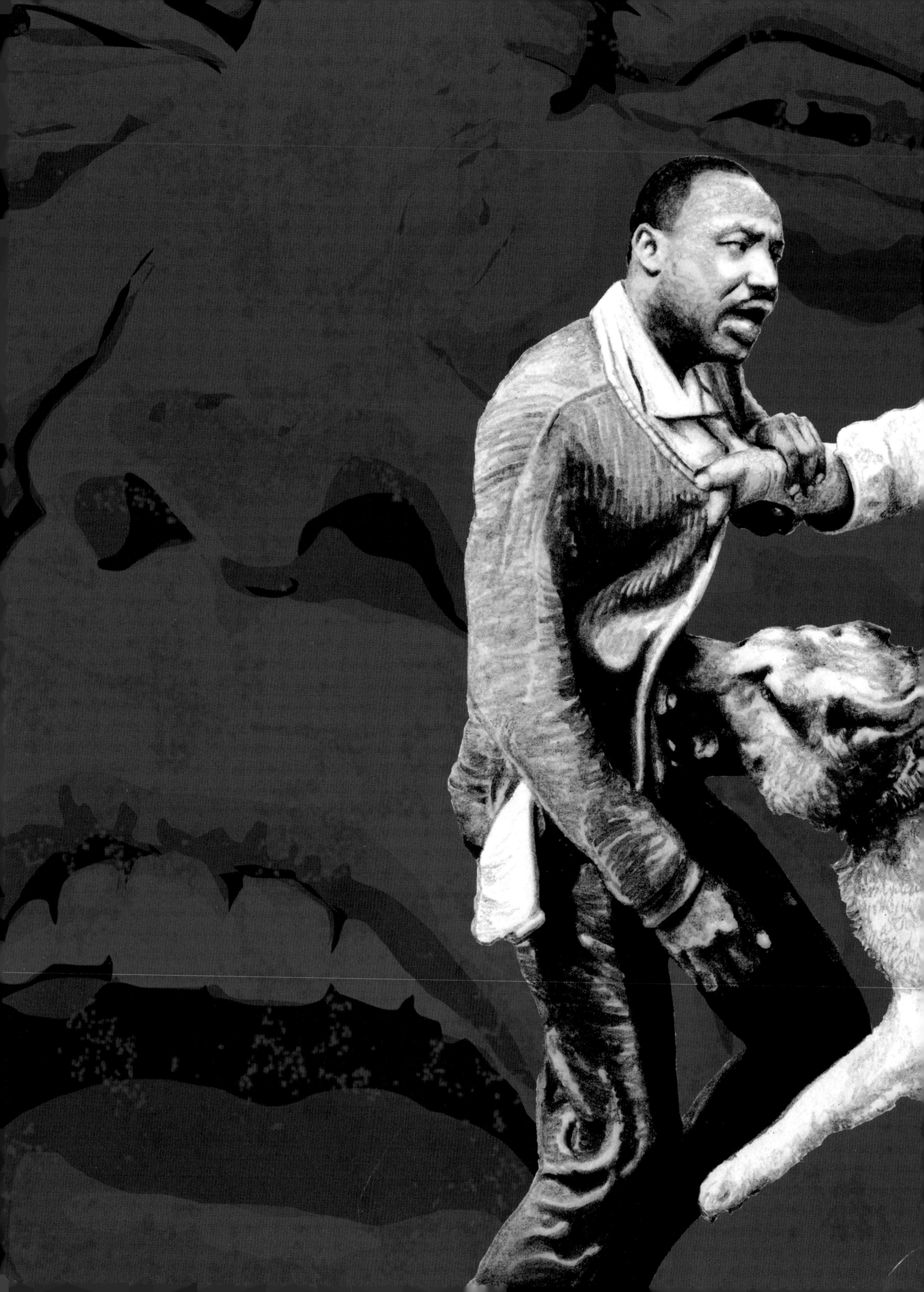

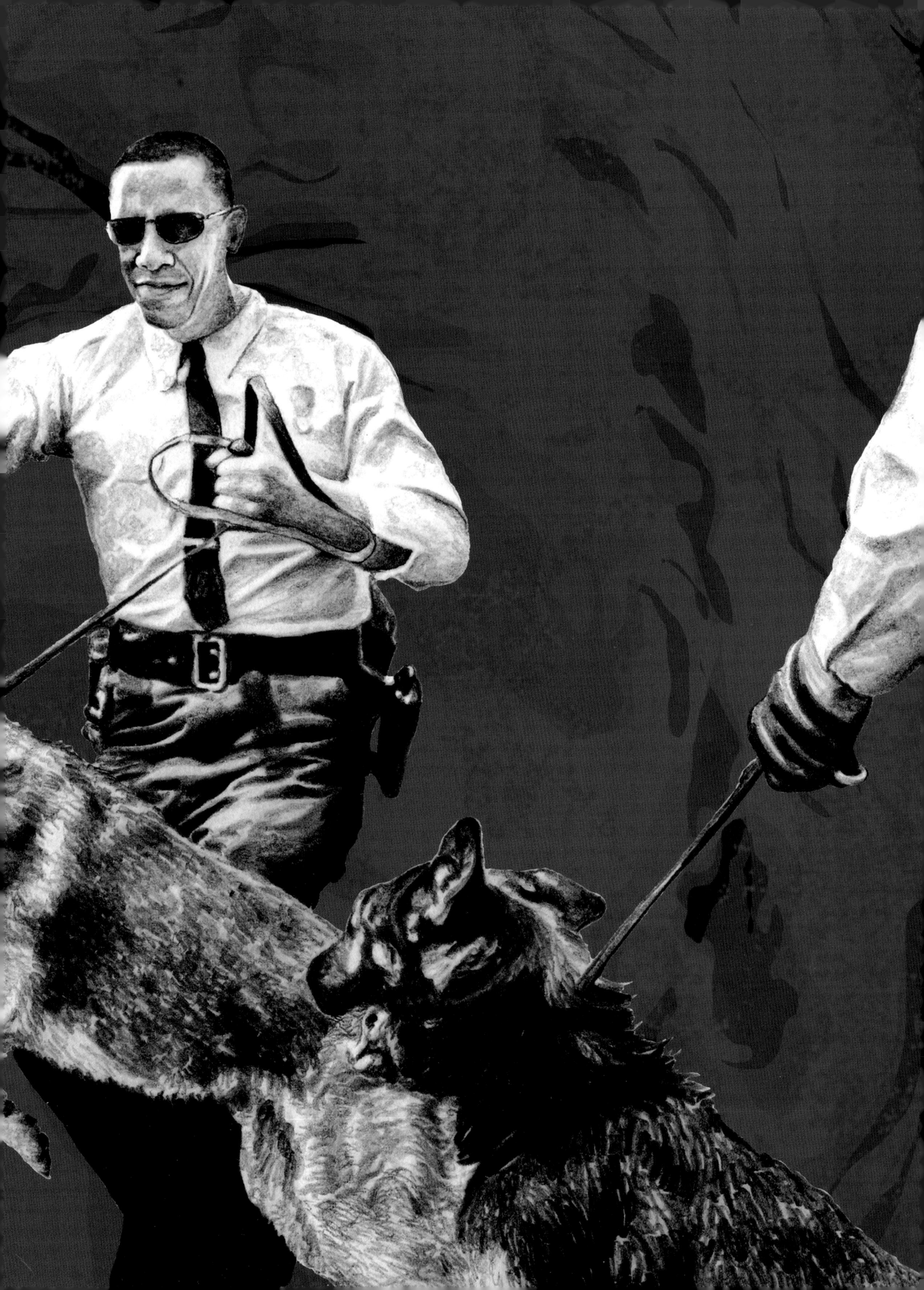

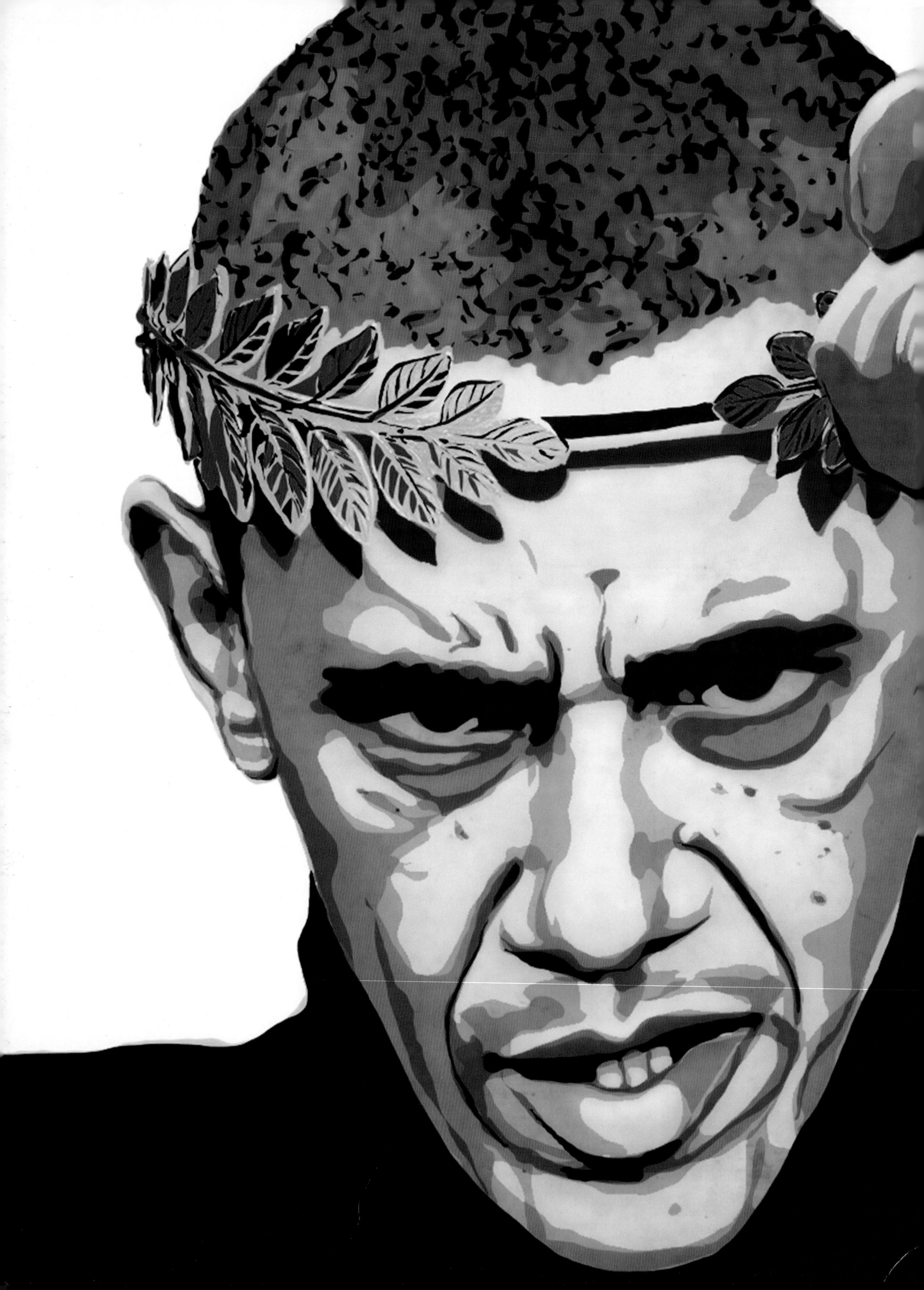

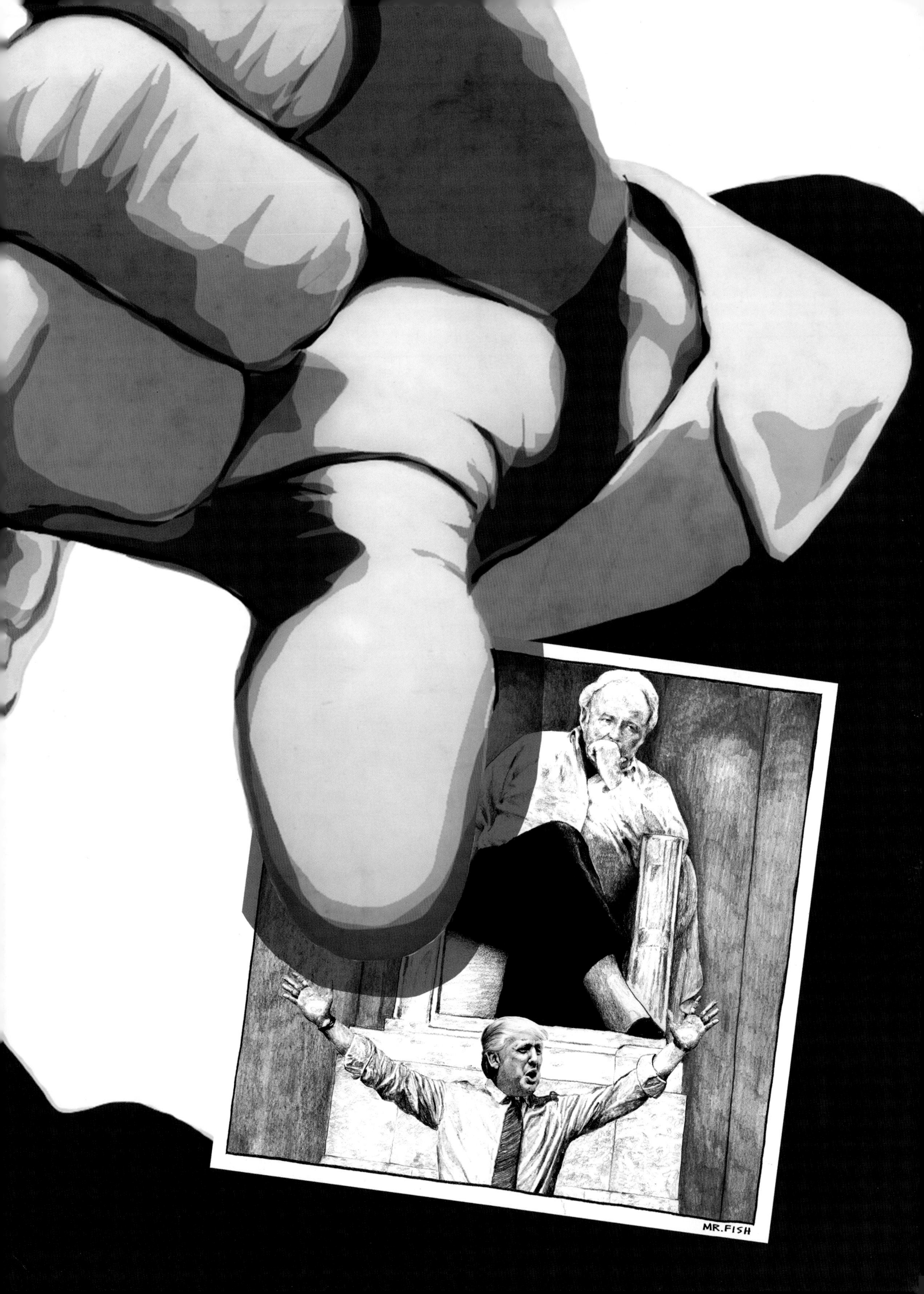
MR. FISH

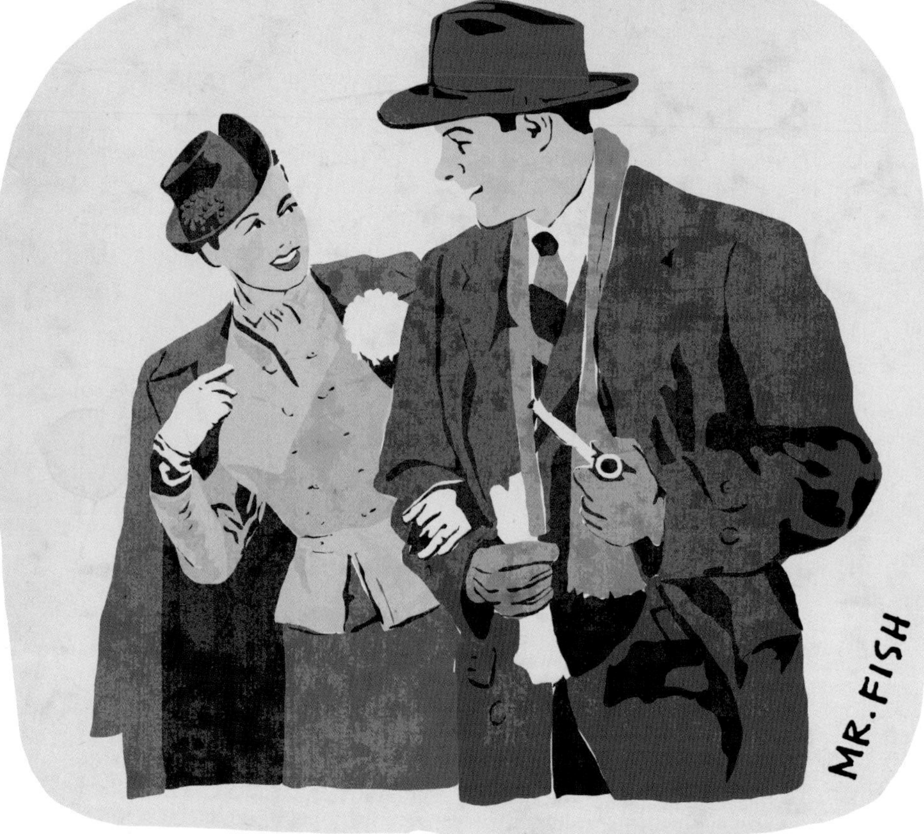
MR. FISH

"Things are finally starting to look up for white people, Dutchy. I'm so glad that we didn't decide to become black when it was fashionable to do so."

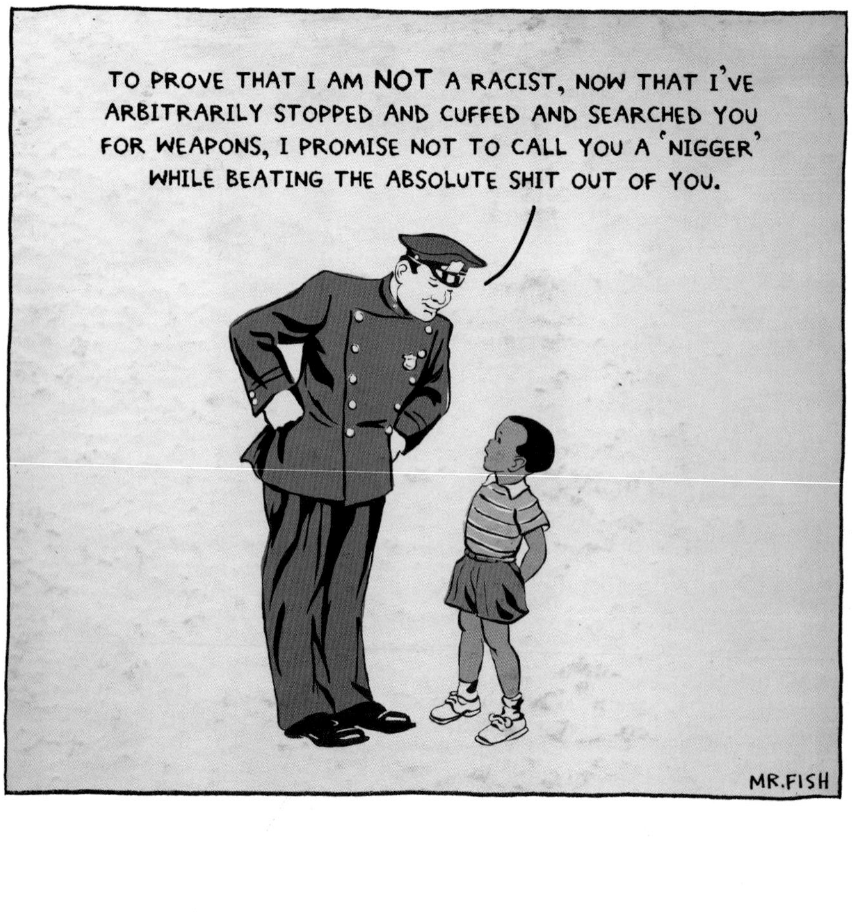
TO PROVE THAT I AM NOT A RACIST, NOW THAT I'VE ARBITRARILY STOPPED AND CUFFED AND SEARCHED YOU FOR WEAPONS, I PROMISE NOT TO CALL YOU A 'NIGGER' WHILE BEATING THE ABSOLUTE SHIT OUT OF YOU.
MR.FISH

THE DIFFERENCE IS THIS RED MENACE IS ACTUALLY REAL

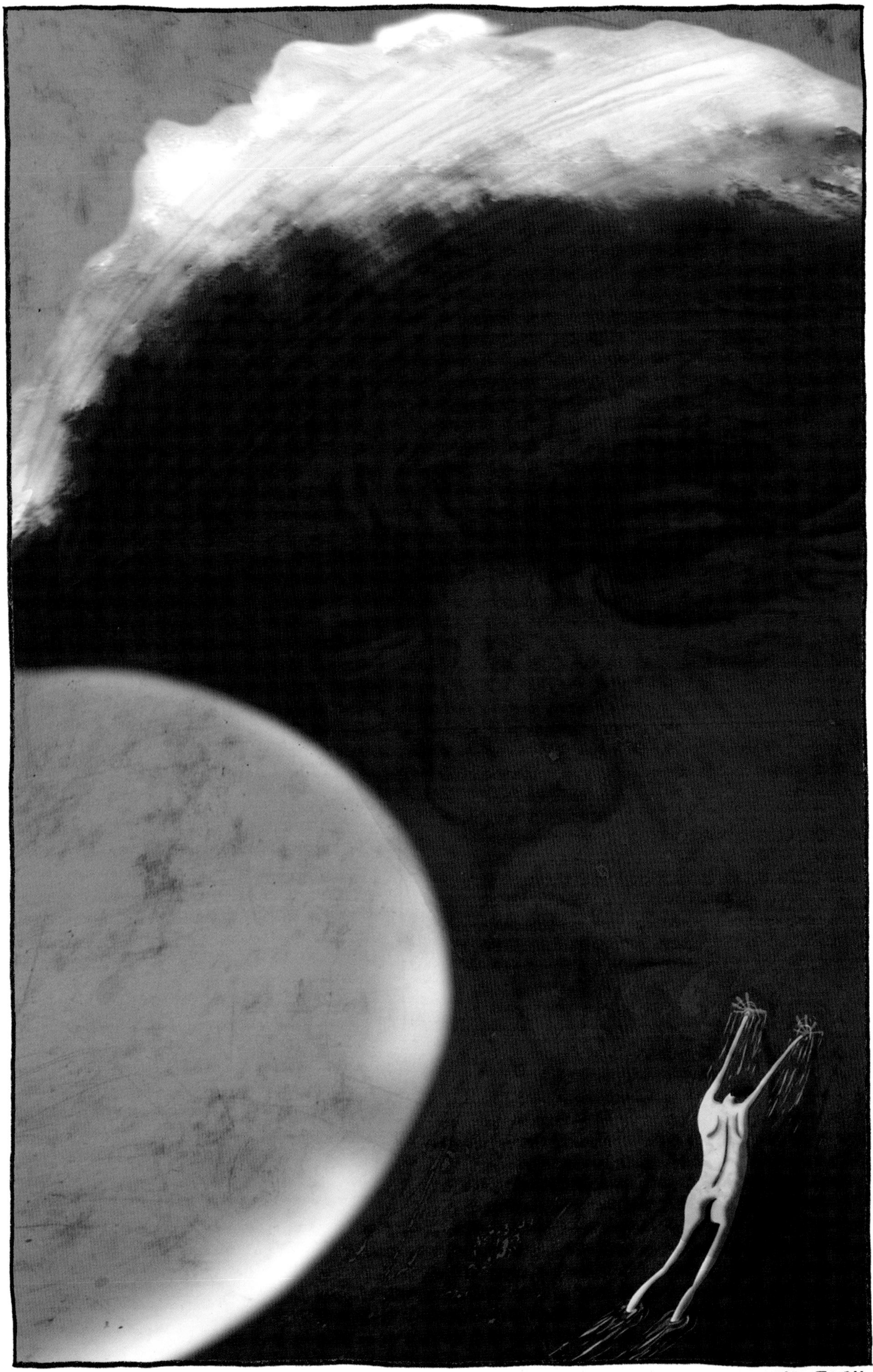

MR. FISH

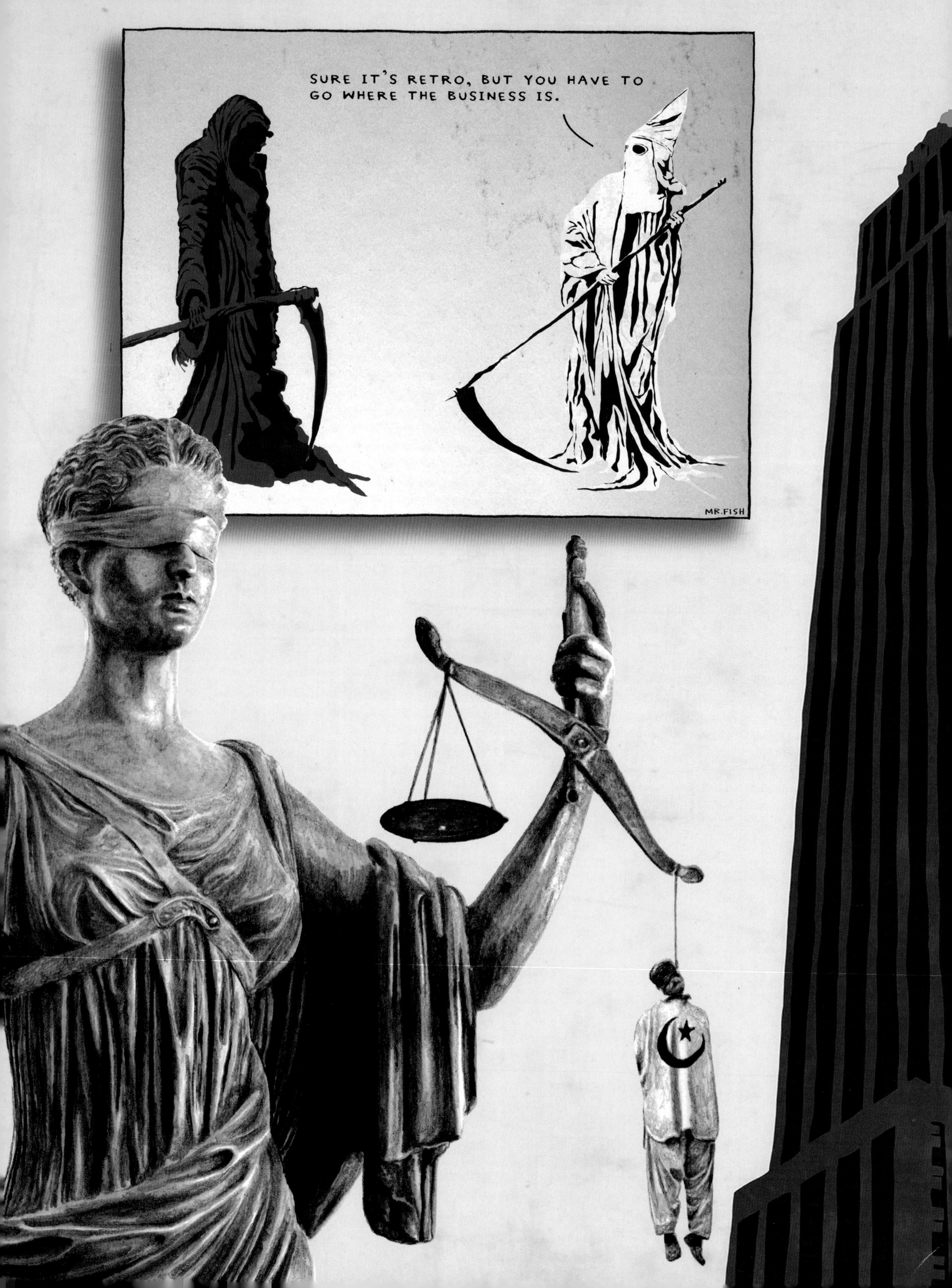
SURE IT'S RETRO, BUT YOU HAVE TO GO WHERE THE BUSINESS IS.
MR.FISH

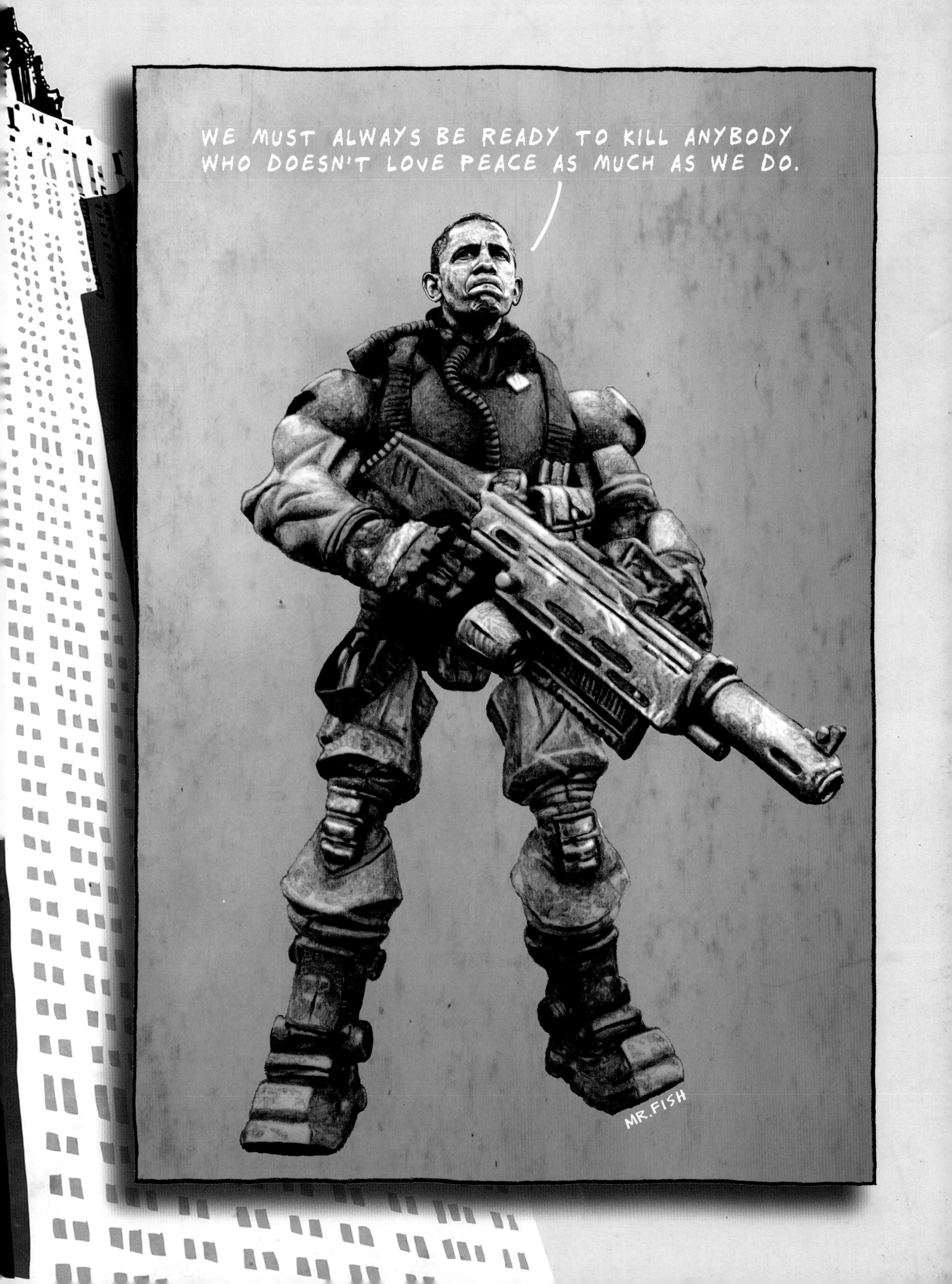
WE MUST ALWAYS BE READY TO KILL ANYBODY WHO DOESN'T LOVE PEACE AS MUCH AS WE DO.
MR. FISH

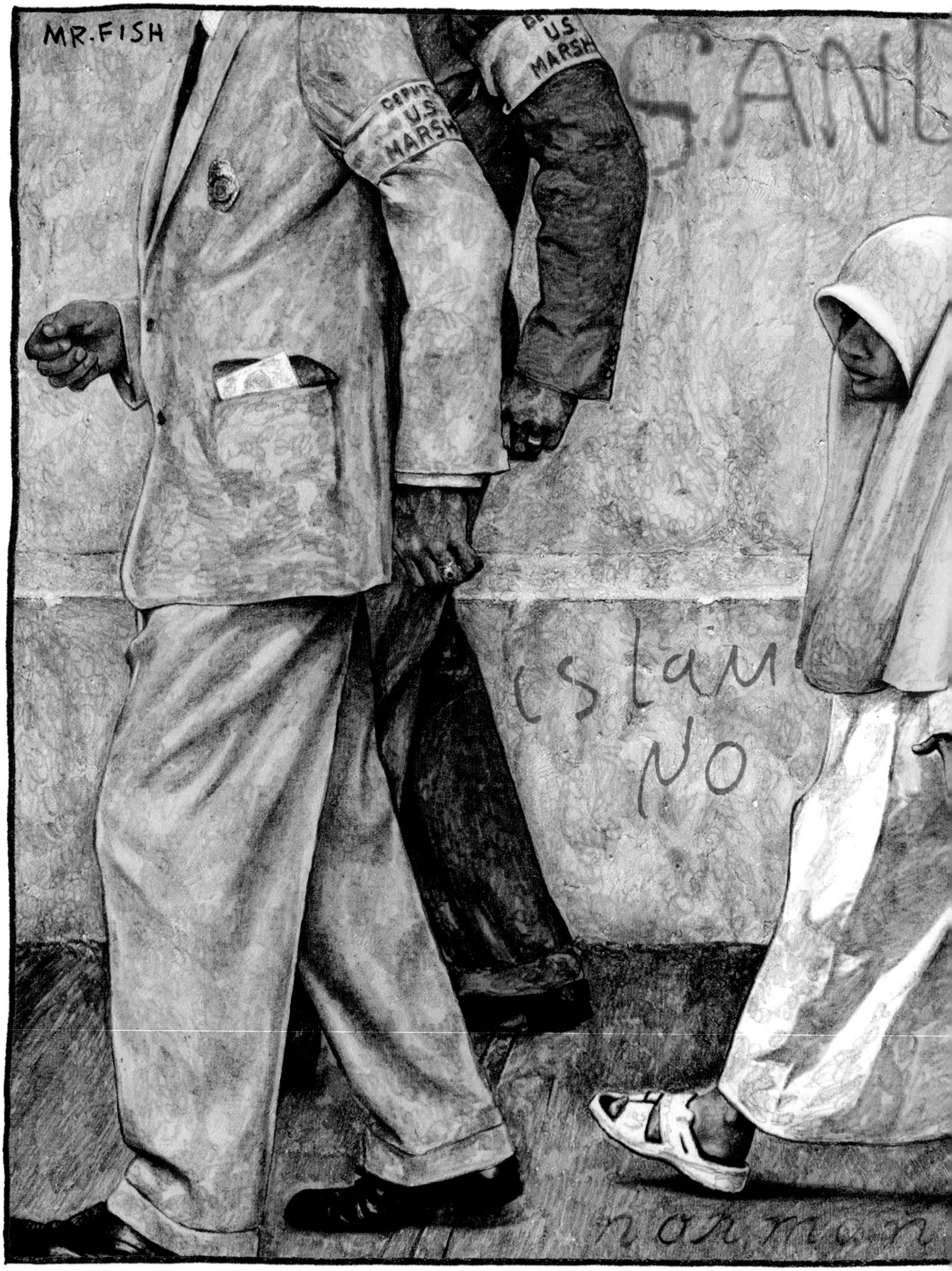
MR. FISH
DEPUTY U.S. MARSHAL
U.S. MARSH
U.S. MARSH
islam
NO

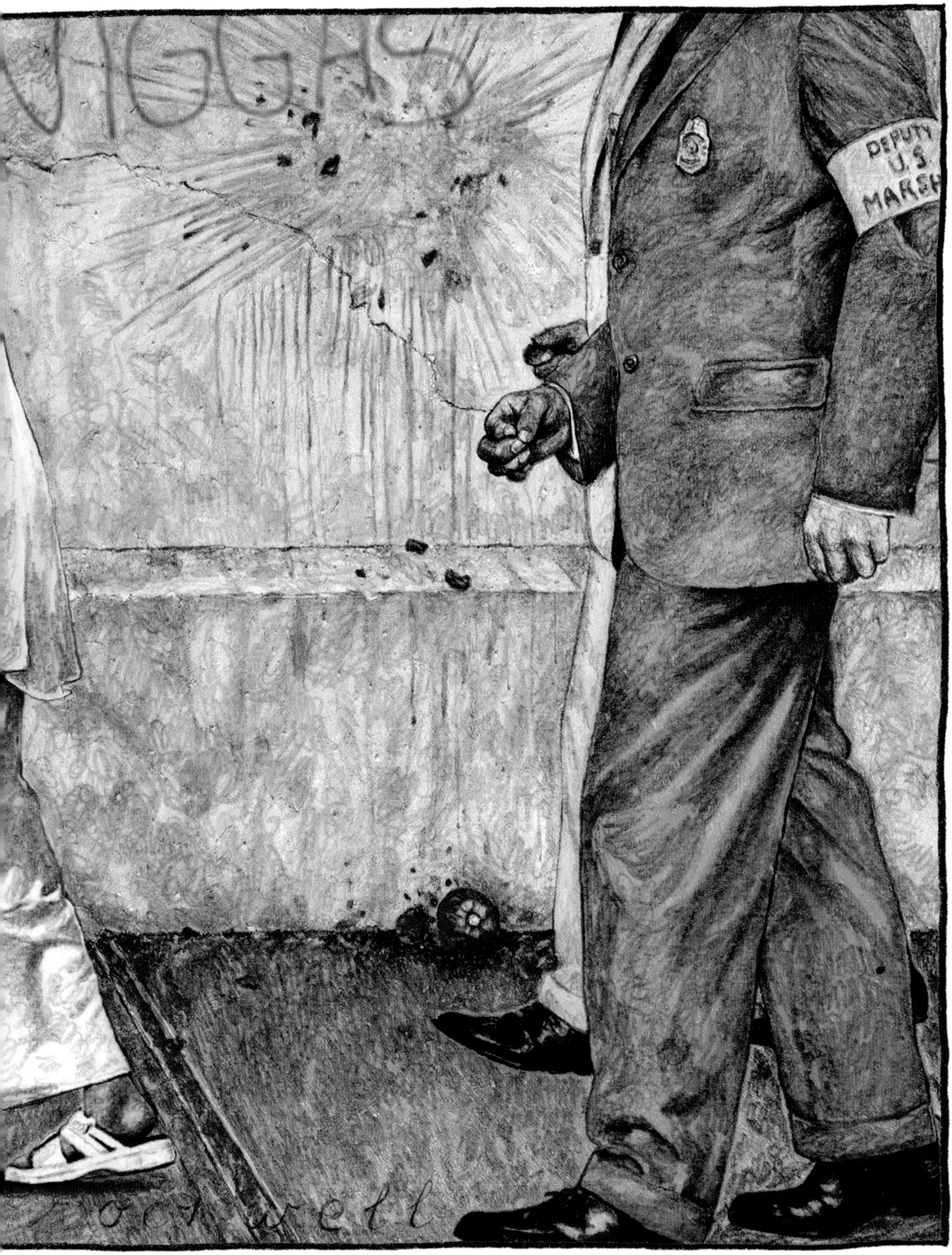
DEPUTY
U.S.
MARSH

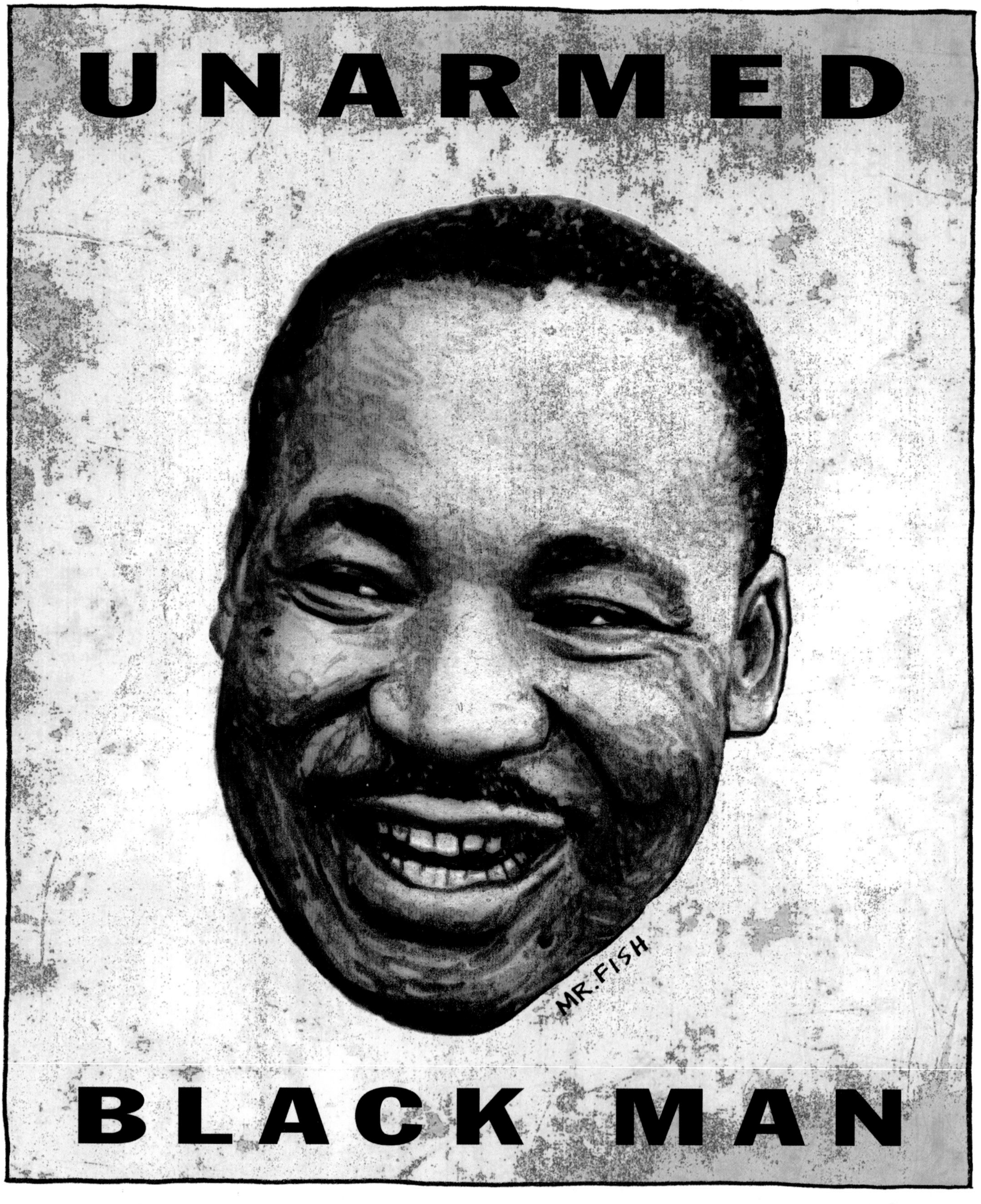
UNARMED
MR. FISH
BLACK MAN

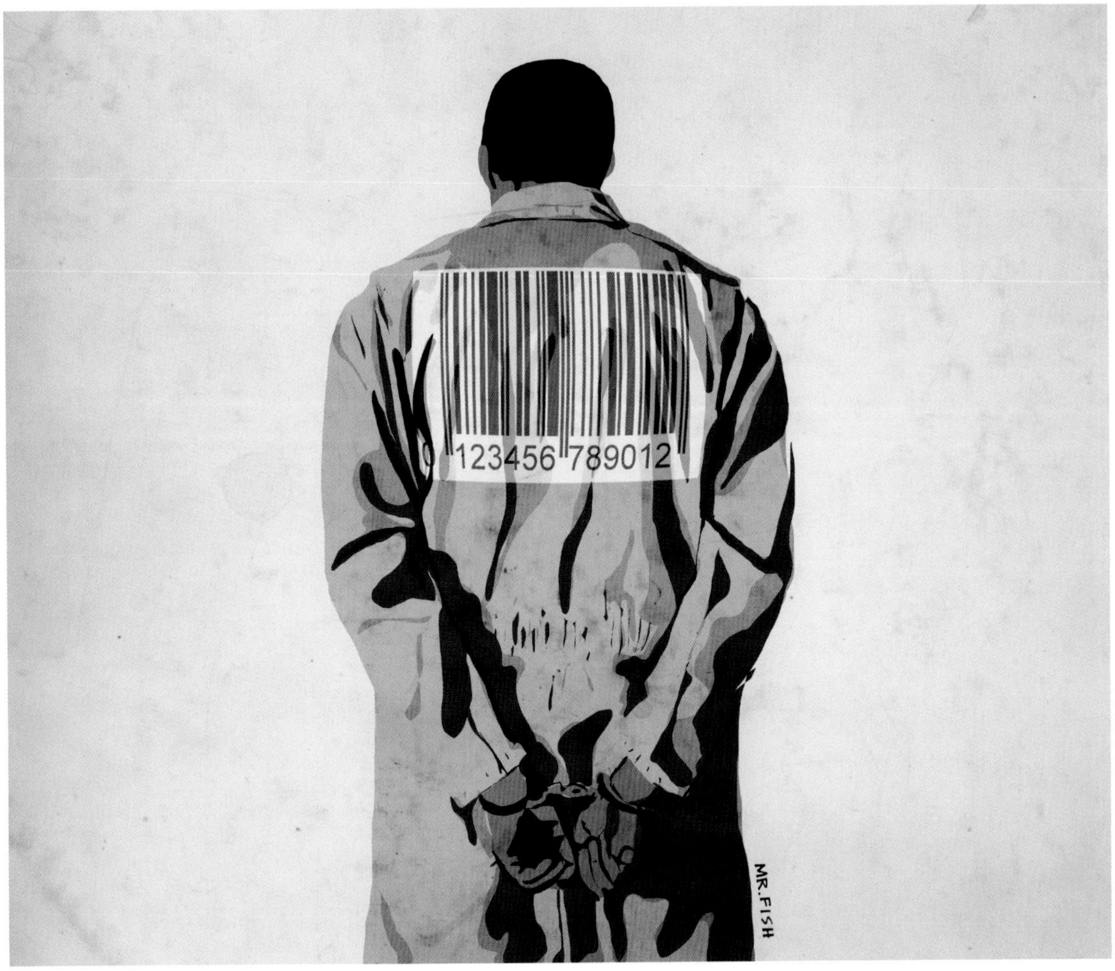
123456 789012
MR.FISH

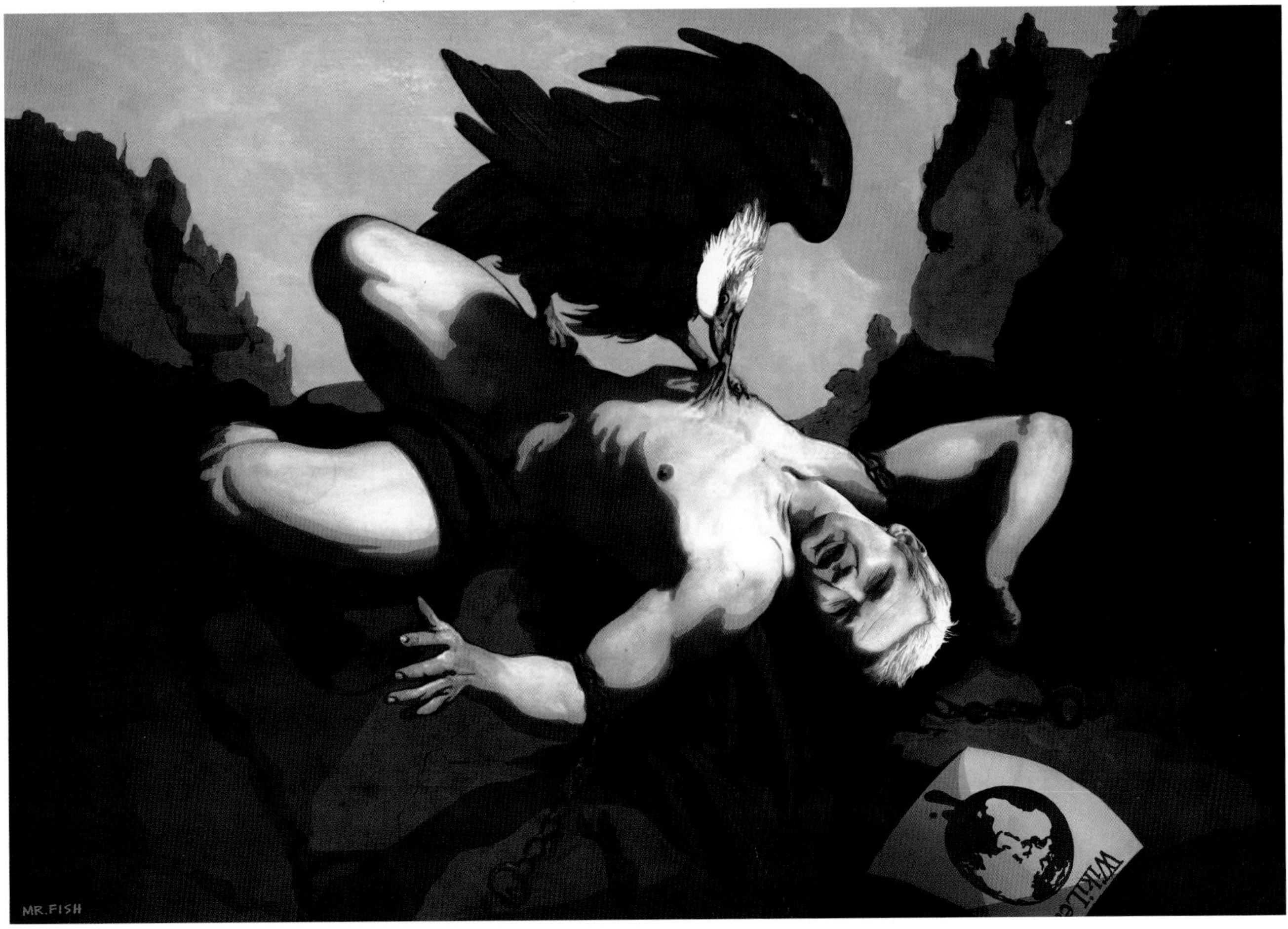
MR.FISH

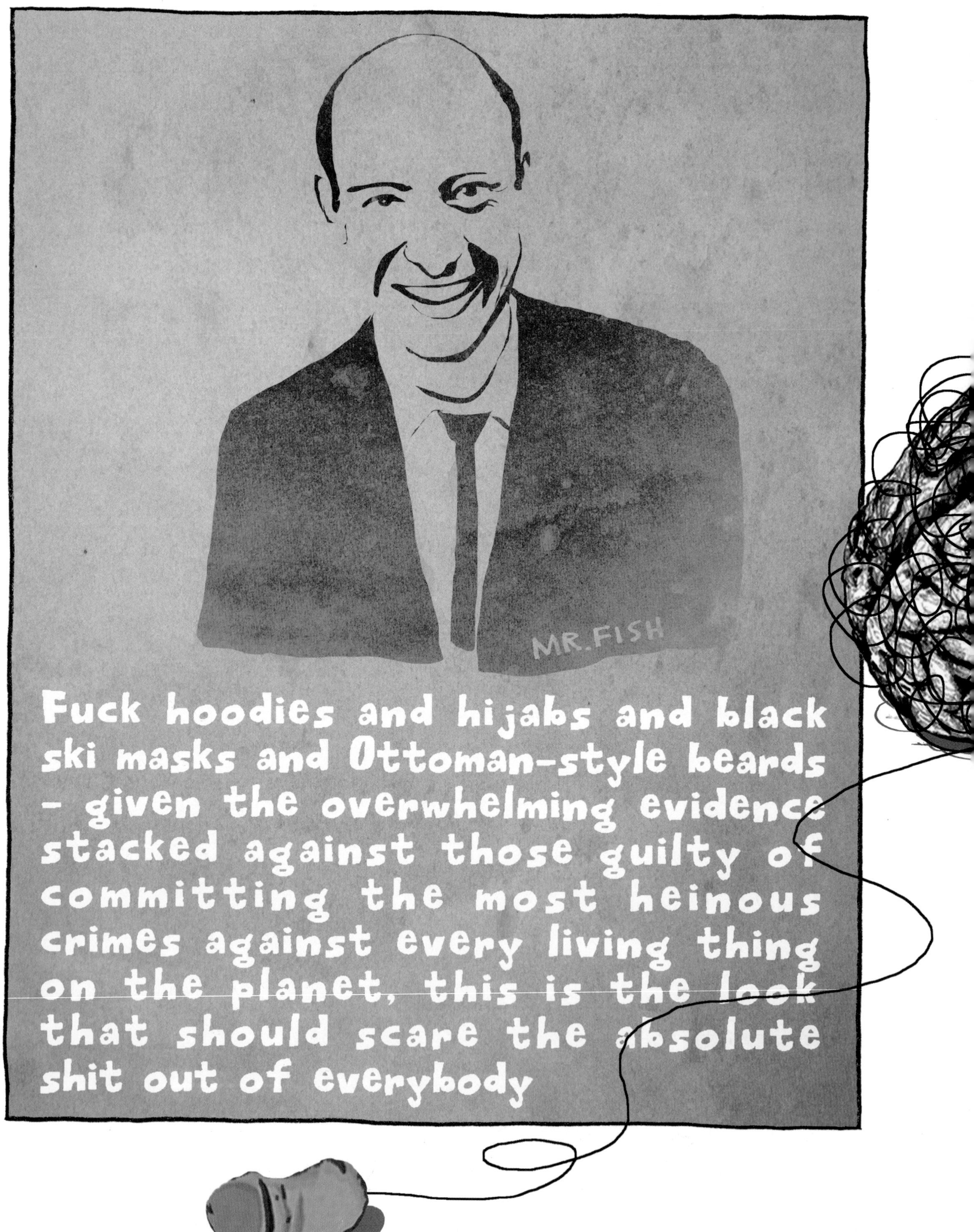
MR. FISH
Fuck hoodies and hijabs and black ski masks and Ottoman-style beards - given the overwhelming evidence stacked against those guilty of committing the most heinous crimes against every living thing on the planet, this is the look that should scare the absolute shit out of everybody

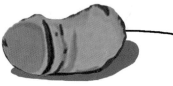

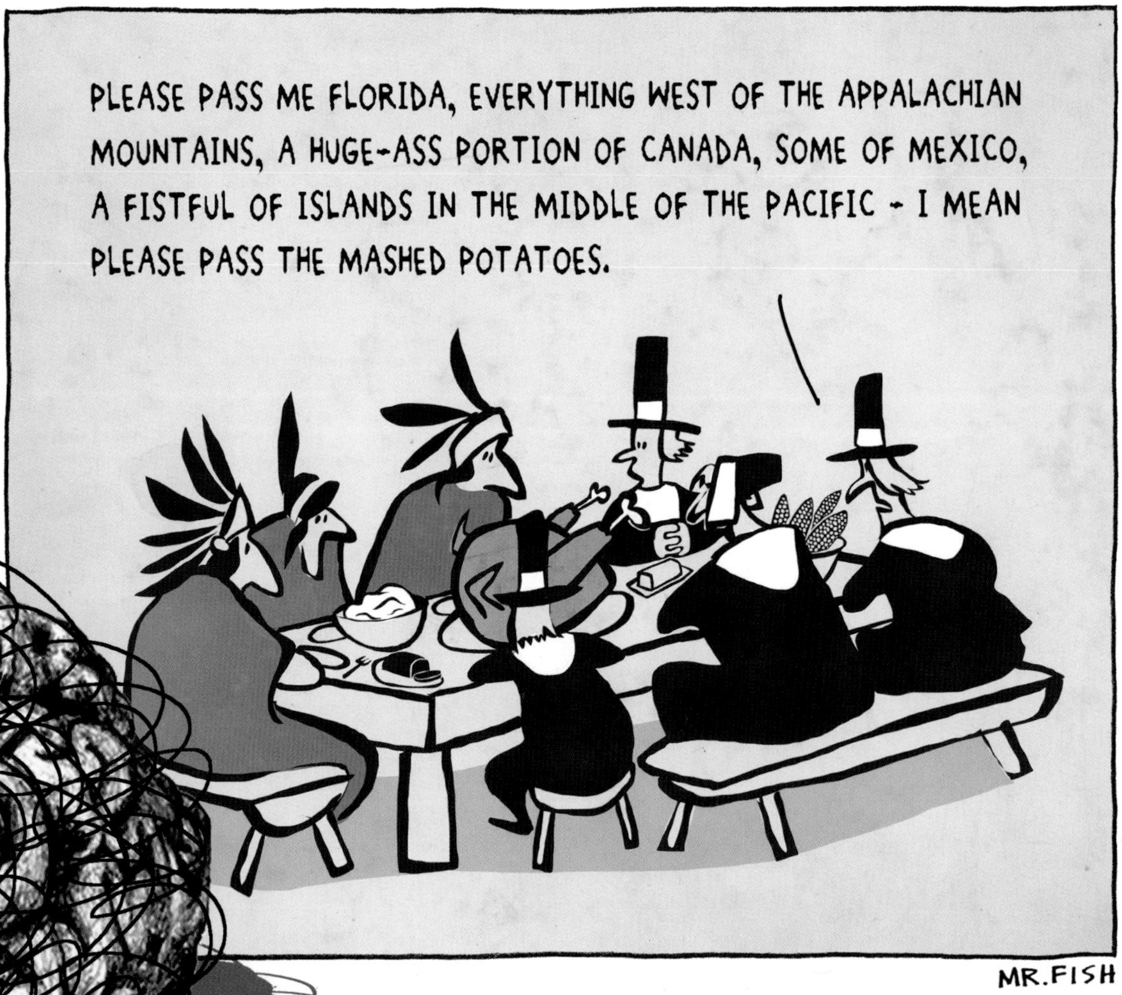
PLEASE PASS ME FLORIDA, EVERYTHING WEST OF THE APPALACHIAN MOUNTAINS, A HUGE-ASS PORTION OF CANADA, SOME OF MEXICO, A FISTFUL OF ISLANDS IN THE MIDDLE OF THE PACIFIC - I MEAN PLEASE PASS THE MASHED POTATOES.
MR.FISH

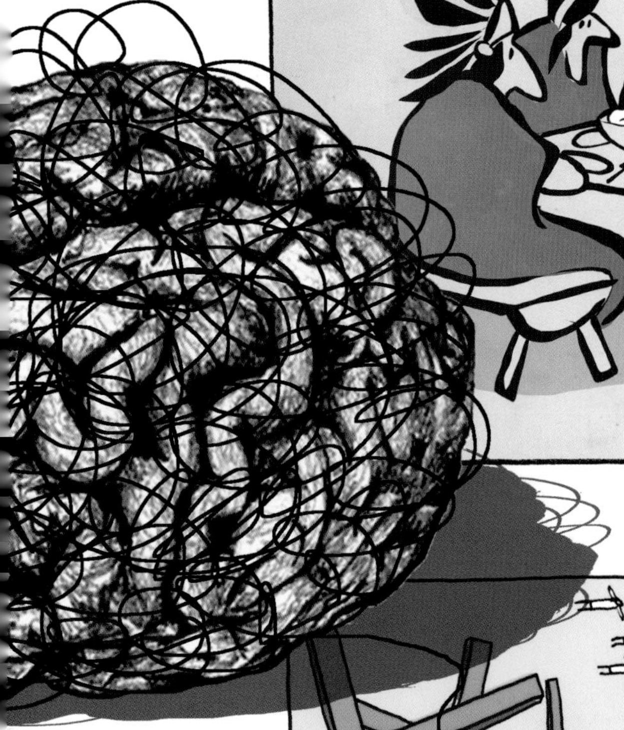

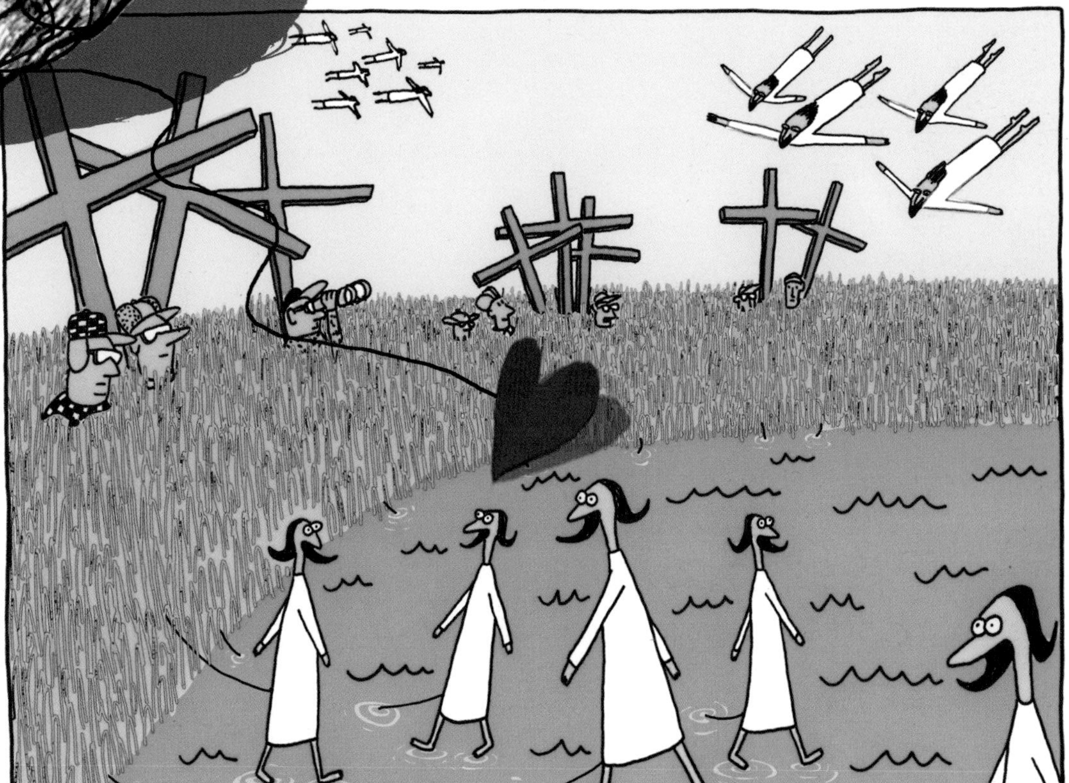
MR.FISH

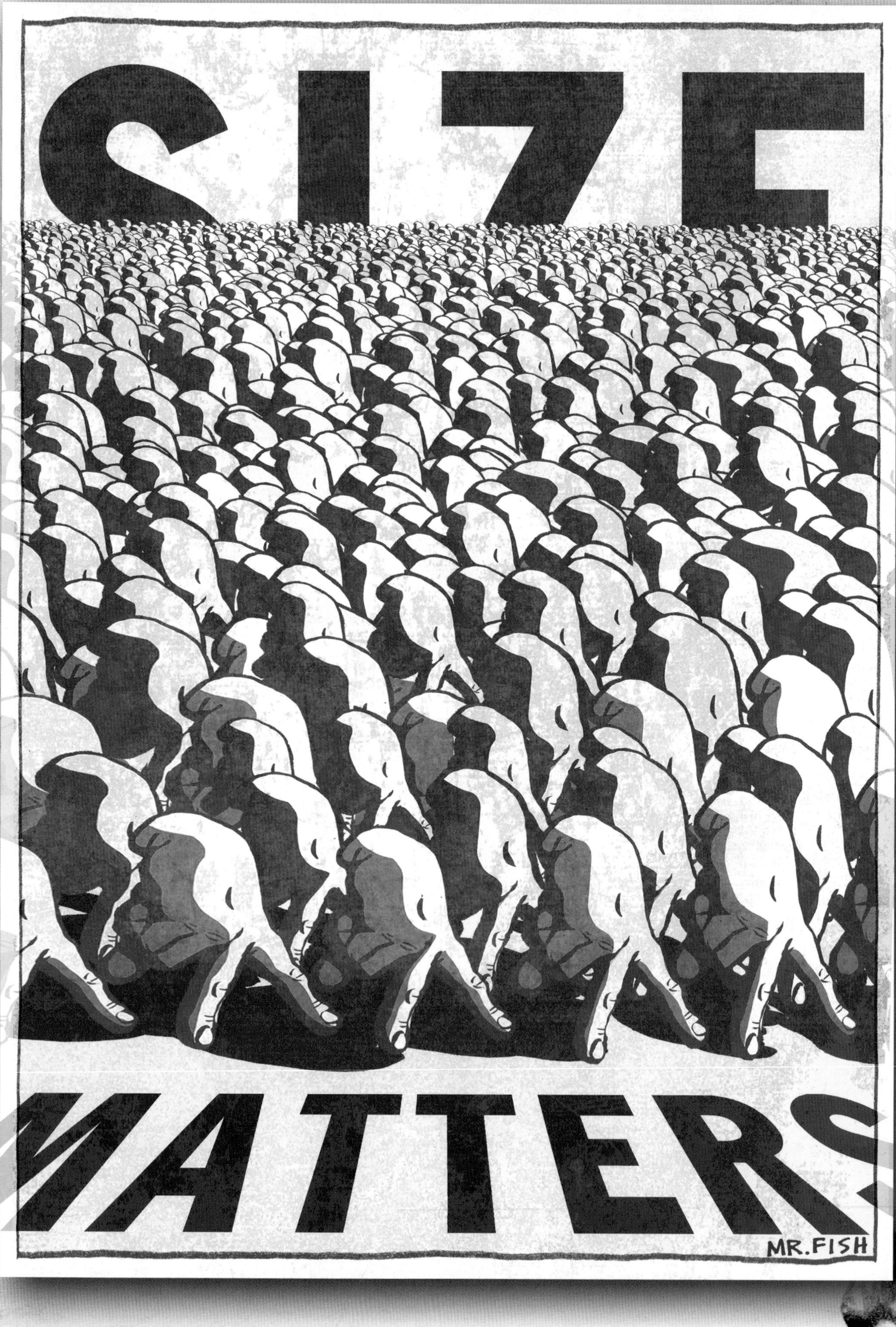
SIZE
MATTERS
MR. FISH

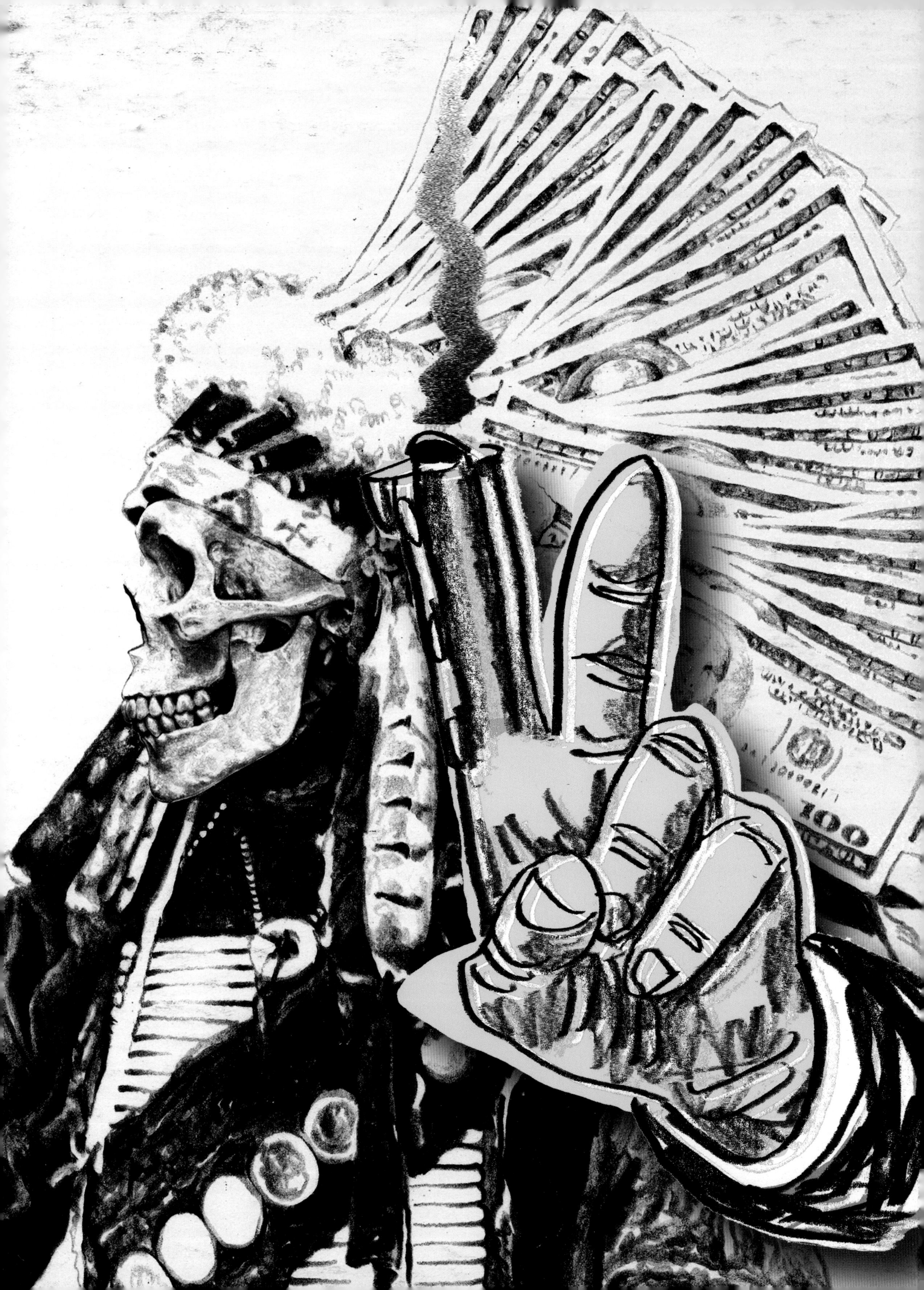

JACK KENNEDY MOMENTS BEFORE MAKING LEE HARVEY OSWALD FEEL THREATENED

MR. FISH

HOW IS THIS FUCKING PIECE OF SHIT GAINING ON US IN THE 21ST CENTURY?

MR. FISH

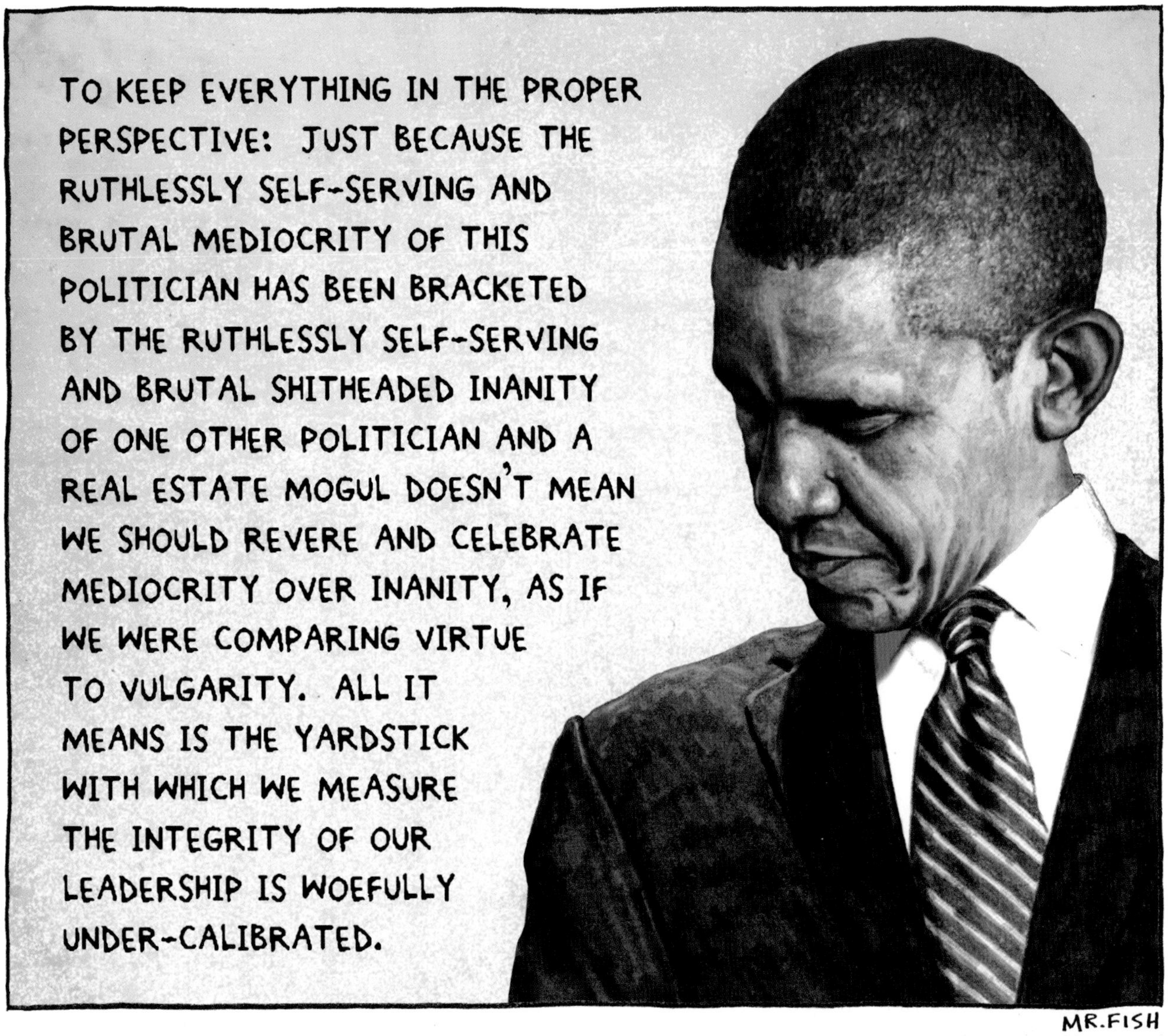
TO KEEP EVERYTHING IN THE PROPER PERSPECTIVE: JUST BECAUSE THE RUTHLESSLY SELF-SERVING AND BRUTAL MEDIOCRITY OF THIS POLITICIAN HAS BEEN BRACKETED BY THE RUTHLESSLY SELF-SERVING AND BRUTAL SHITHEADED INANITY OF ONE OTHER POLITICIAN AND A REAL ESTATE MOGUL DOESN'T MEAN WE SHOULD REVERE AND CELEBRATE MEDIOCRITY OVER INANITY, AS IF WE WERE COMPARING VIRTUE TO VULGARITY. ALL IT MEANS IS THE YARDSTICK WITH WHICH WE MEASURE THE INTEGRITY OF OUR LEADERSHIP IS WOEFULLY UNDER-CALIBRATED.
MR.FISH

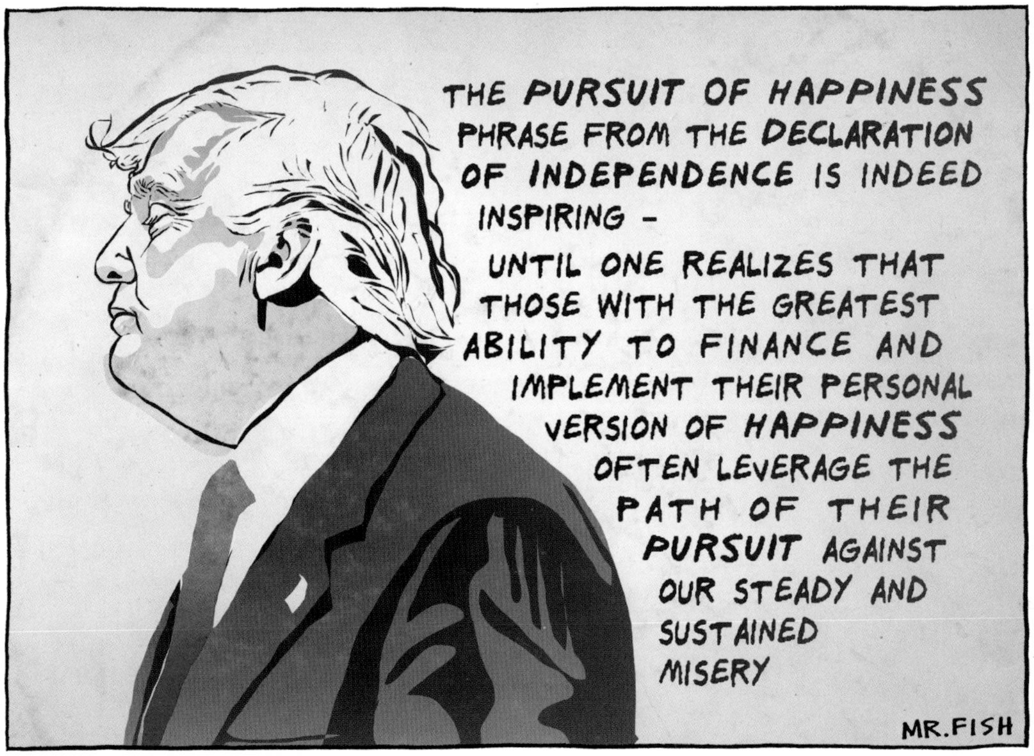
THE PURSUIT OF HAPPINESS PHRASE FROM THE DECLARATION OF INDEPENDENCE IS INDEED INSPIRING -
UNTIL ONE REALIZES THAT THOSE WITH THE GREATEST ABILITY TO FINANCE AND IMPLEMENT THEIR PERSONAL VERSION OF HAPPINESS OFTEN LEVERAGE THE PATH OF THEIR PURSUIT AGAINST OUR STEADY AND SUSTAINED MISERY
MR.FISH

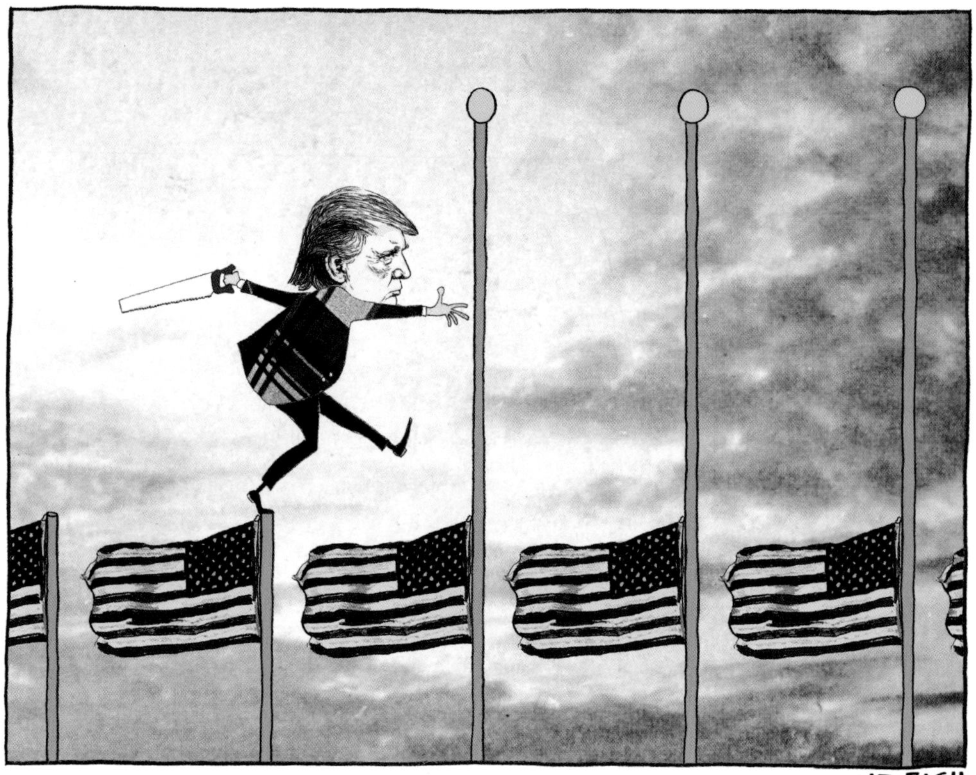
MR.FISH

FUCK WALL STREET - MOTHER NATURE WAS HERE FIRST

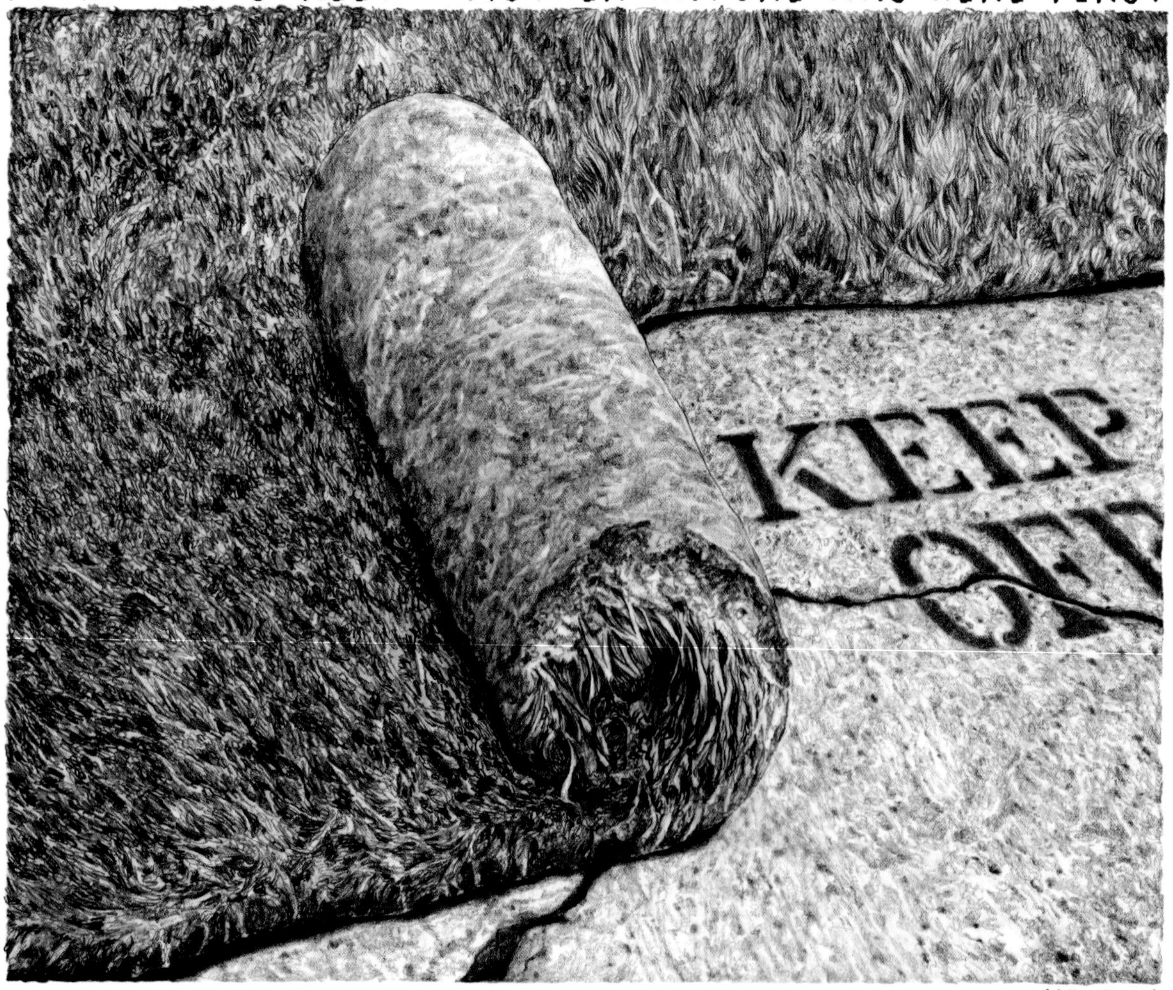
KEEP
OFF
MR. FISH

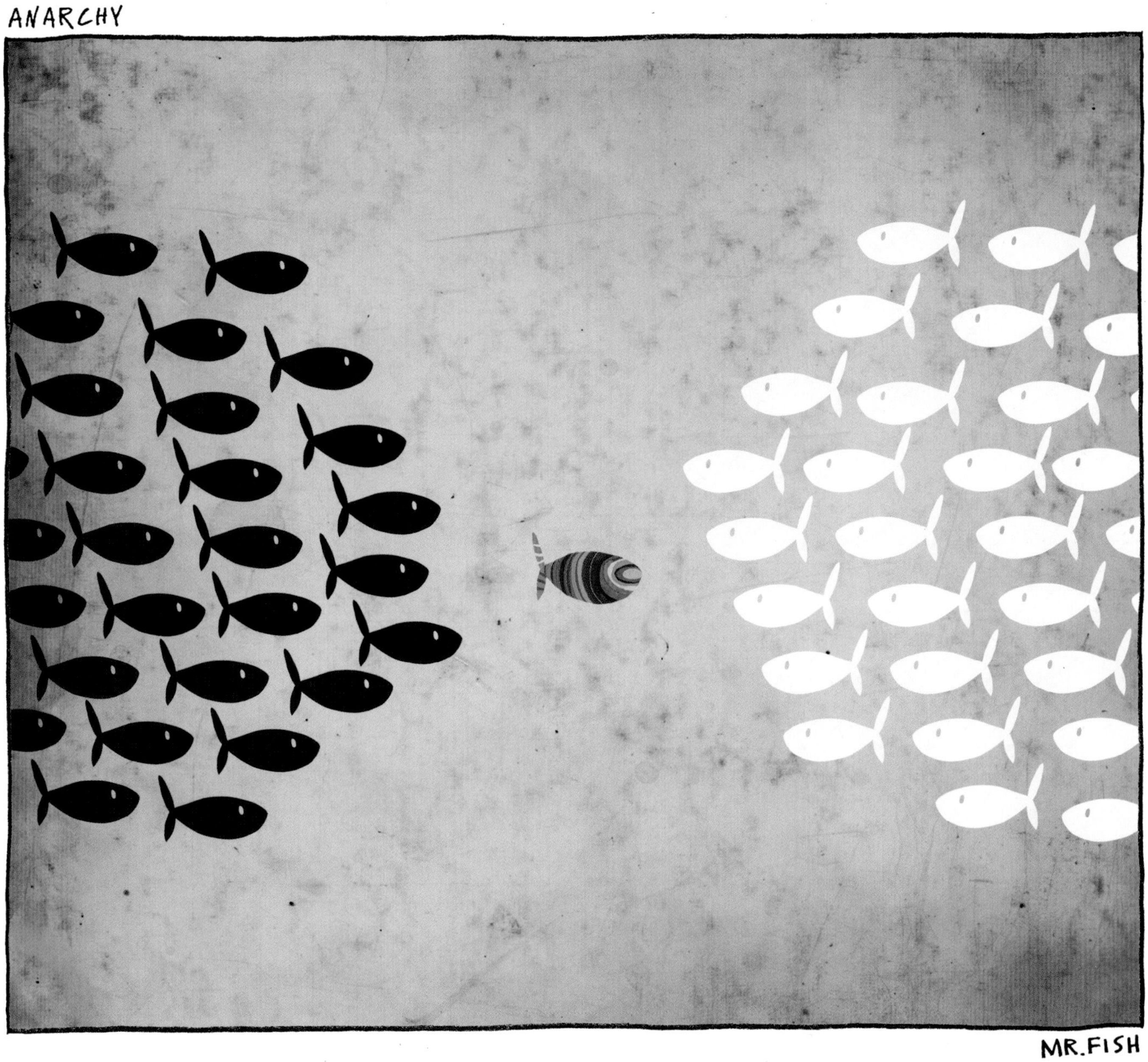
ANARCHY
MR.FISH

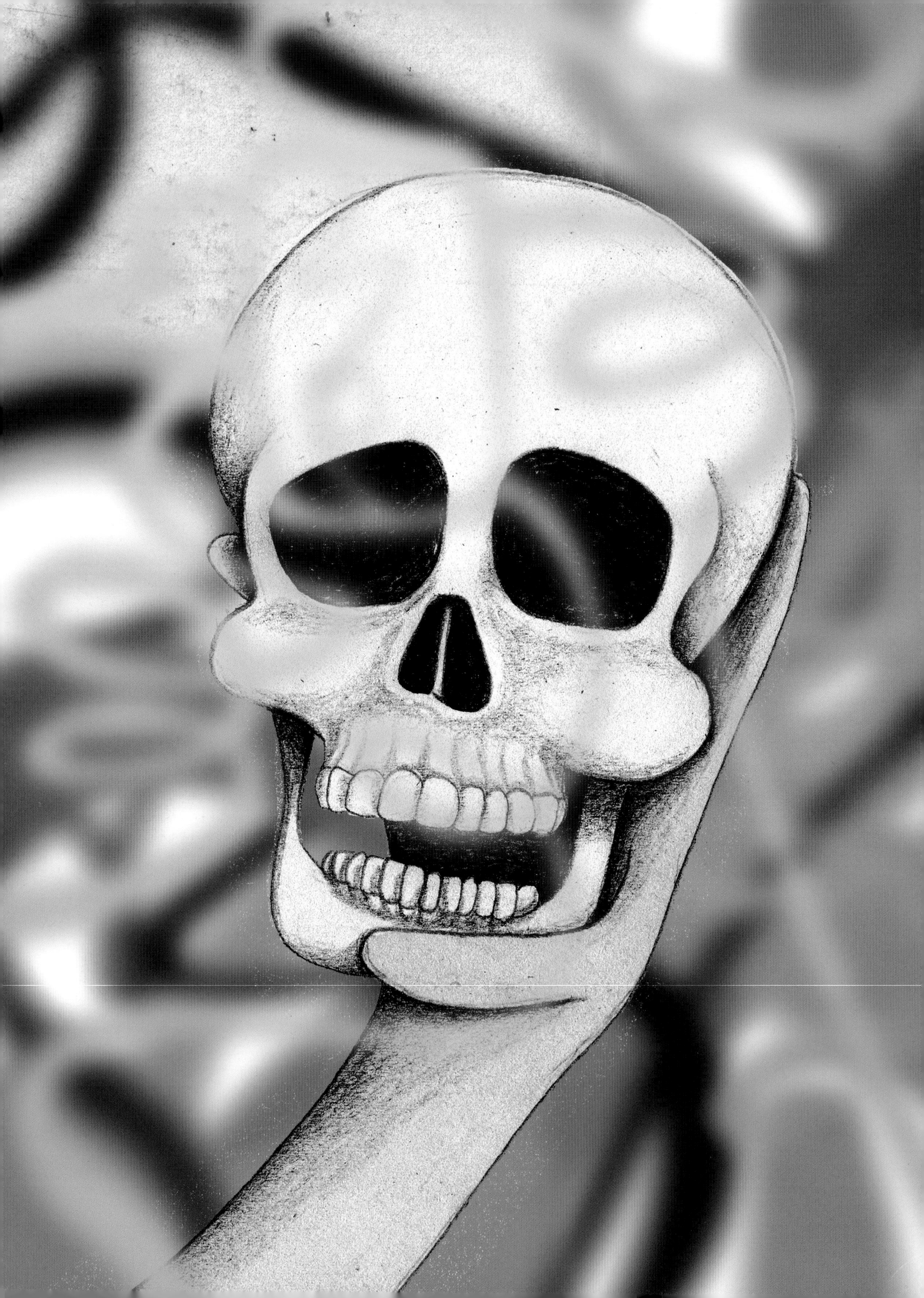

INTRODUCTION BY DWAYNE BOOTH

IT ALL STARTED in the winter of 1975 when I was 9 years old. I had just finished reading an article in *Fate* magazine about the ghost of an old prostitute, maybe she was 50, with a glass eye and who was haunting a law office in downtown New Orleans. I remember that her name was Ebony Doll, and she died on Halloween night in 1923 while giving birth to a baby rumored to have a tail, horns and hooves in one of the upstairs rooms back when the building used to be a brothel. It was a sinister story full of gas lamps and rain soaked cobblestone streets and voodoo flash-seared in pheromones and gin, and I couldn't put it down. As I read, I remember bracing myself for the details of the paranormal activity that the office employees had experienced, knowing that, once released into the soft squishy complacent part of my brain reserved for giggling and open-fingered clapping, the serrated whirligig of horrible imagery and indisputable evidence that demons do indeed walk among us would likely hobble my ability to feel safe or completely happy in the world ever again.

What I ended up getting instead were vague descriptions by office girls with names like Jana and Midge of faint sobbing in the stairwell, lights that sometimes flickered on and off and the faraway roar of toilets that seemed to flush on their own. That was it. There were no reports of male lawyers suddenly doubling over with phantom labor pains or the inexplicable stench of sulfur and afterbirth abruptly filling the room or the bloodcurdling shriek of a middle-aged Creole whore being dragged by her umbilical cord through the walls by a panicked goat baby in a onesie and half-socks. Nothing. It was like being lured into a story about the ethereal wisdom and awesome wizardry of Jesus Christ and then being let down at the end by the sentence, "And then He removed the flashlight from beneath His chin, shook it a few times, sighed, looked out over the massive crowd of twelve open-mouthed, unemployed sycophants and, turning on the lights, asked the one named Pete to go into the kitchen to check the junk drawer for D batteries."

Pissed off and turning the page merely as a way to demonstrate forward momentum away from my disappointment, I came upon the famous black-and-white photograph of 92-year-old Dr. John Irving Bentley pictured as a greasy pile of black ash on a charred linoleum bathroom floor in the Allegheny Highlands of Northern Pennsylvania and everything changed.

In fact, nothing has been the same for me since.

The photograph was taken in 1966, coincidently the year of my birth, and, according to the article, was proof of spontaneous human combustion. Staring at the doctor's right foot, which was still intact and wearing a slipper and lying just beyond the blast point on the floor, I remember thinking to myself, "Shit, would I hate to suddenly disappear like that." Of course, that wasn't entirely true. I, like everybody else, had often fantasized about possessing the talent to disappear before, usually for the purpose of extricating myself from an excruciatingly intolerable situation, which when you're 9 might

be exemplified by a slow zigzag through a supermarket while hanging off the back of a shopping cart, but no matter. The point was that everybody at one time or another had prayed for the ability to simply vanish, I knew that, but what was terrifying about the death of Dr. John Irving Bentley was the supposed randomness with which his detonation was described in the magazine. The idea that any one of us could instantaneously evaporate at any moment of the day or night seemed enormously unfair, not only because suddenly being made to not exist was antithetical to existing in the first place, but also because it seemed cruel to insist that we all be made to endure such a high stakes game of Russian roulette, with each tick of the clock being just another torturous click made from one more empty chamber. The whole scenario seemed irksomely Biblical and more than a little bit ecclesiastical, particularly with the article mentioning the story of Lot's wife as if citing some prior scientific study designed to prove that God, more than any other suspect, had some rather nefarious and damning connections to the supernatural.

Riding around in the backseat of my grandparents' station wagon during that December, crammed in with my brothers and sister, four in all, rotund in our winter coats and being baked by the car's magnificent iron heater into great puffy loaves of groggy yuletide frivolity, I found myself lost in thought, completely blind to all the holiday gewgawkery outside my window, busy inventing scenarios that might've explained the death of the doctor in a way that was self-inflicted and not divinely incurred. I saw Dr. John Irving Bentley stepping into his bathroom and unbuttoning his pajama top and saying, "All right, I know that a wire hanger is probably not the right tool to use when fiddling with a pacemaker, but I swear to God, if I don't figure out where that infernal clicking is coming from..." I knitted my eyebrows, shook my head like rebooting an Etch-a-Sketch and tried again. I saw him walking into his bathroom to find his ex-girlfriend, Gladys O'Harris, dressed in a cape with a silk lining patterned with playing cards, a top hat, white gloves, a maroon cummerbund, spats and holding a wand. I imagined him saying "Gladys?" then swallowing hard to remember how he had broken up with this woman 30 years earlier by openly mocking her life's ambition to become either the best lady magician in Potter County or the very first asthmatic to enter the Guinness World Records by singing "Shortnin' Bread" for 72 hours straight without using her puffer. I shook my head again.

Then, passing a church, I saw God as a divine sniper with a logic that was just fuzzy enough to guarantee a profoundly itchy trigger finger. I thought back to my earliest Sunday School training and remembered how there was never a moment when He didn't have every man, woman and child in His crosshairs and how he was no macaroni when it came to killing people in the goriest and cruelest ways possible, usually without any apparent provocation, other than, of course, a fascistic intolerance of free will. The question then became clear to me: What had Dr. John Irving Bentley said or done to make God so pissed off that He was driven to commit murder? After 92 years of monotonous living, had the doctor grown so impatient with the essential sameness of his days that boredom or ill health or ricocheting dementia had tipped his piety into rage? Perhaps he had finally summoned the courage to complain to his Creator with an appropriate disdain, saying that life was not a miraculous gift after all but rather it was a vexing nuisance contrived by an almighty sadist seeking to satiate His fetish by standing by and watching the tedious existential suffocation of old people.

Could it be as simple as that? Could a person think something so ugly, so utterly inappropriate, that God himself would need to turn that person into an angry black spot on the bathroom floor? Having behaved inappropriately in front of my mother and any number of schoolteachers before and been punished for it, this deduction was the only one that made total sense to me. Blow your nose into a pancake and your mother will send you to your room; write *Phuck is not a four-letter word* on your phonics book and your teacher will send you to the principal's office (along with a note suggesting that Mr. Booth be relocated to a zoo where he can spend his adolescence standing on a hay-covered drain); commit a thought crime that might annoy a Mind-Reading, Omnipotent Super Being with a long history of eradicating entire populations when they disagreed with His version of *yuck, yippie* and *ya-hooey* and you will surely go missing, no question about it, the lesson of religion not being that you are in any way unique or precious, but rather that you are expendable.

Figuring that any God capable of expressing such contempt for anybody tending toward a critical, even God-damning mind was a God that I had no chance of ever impressing, particularly with my tendency to view anything even remotely authoritarian as laughably unnecessary. I knew this. Thusly, instead of waiting for what I imagined would be the equivalent of Santa Claus sneaking up behind me at some point during the next 70 or 80 years with a length of piano wire and lassoing it around my windpipe and driving his velvety red knee into my back because I was being more naughty than nice, I decided to declare possession over my own destiny and to self-detonate by offending God with the most outrageously sacrilegious thoughts I could think of. What would be the point, I figured, in living a life and trying to cultivate my own relationship with the universe, something where I got to pick my own favorite color and define my own passions and pinpoint my own moral outrage over whatever people and circumstances I wanted to perceive as being unjust and immoral and rage-inspiring, if the self-titled moral authority of the universe was going to snuff me out as if I were the disease of illiteracy threatening His thoroughly douched and perfect alphabet?

I started small, still taking the precaution of putting my metaphoric fingers in my metaphoric ears and pinching my metaphoric eyes shut, by imagining what the Virgin Mary might've looked like naked. Too terrified to give her the body and pained expression of an oversexed Miss January, I gave her the same Shatner-esque body as my best friend's mother, a woman nicknamed Boo, whom I accidentally stumbled upon, unseen, while she was peeing into a dry creek bed during a day hike through the Pine Barrens that I'd been invited on the previous summer. Flip-flops spread far apart, her yellow shorts and vat-sized underpants hammocked in the grip of her knees, her shoulders rounded, her head tucked, she set the tune of "I'm a Little Teapot" loose inside my brain, for there she was, short and stout, and there was her handle and there was her... *oh sweet Jesus!* Unaware that so much urine was capable of coming out of a human body, I remembered tiptoeing away backward and wondering if the stench from her fast-moving puddle might confuse a foraging bear downwind and make it believe that one of the Budweiser Clydesdale horses had gotten separated from the team and was now lost in the middle of the New Jersey woods.

Remarkably, my imagination did not make me explode.

Uncertain as to whether or not the Creator had received my telepathy, I tried again, like redialing a phone, just to make sure my revolting signal was getting through, this time imagining Jesus Christ crawling on all fours through my backyard and eating the dog shit that I was tasked with picking up everyday after school. Again, nothing happened. It was as if I were throwing rocks at the moon. It was as if there were something about the physics of the universe—or was it the metaphysics of the supernatural?—that made my goading so completely ineffective that one had to question either the presence of my voice or the absence of ethereal ears. The way I saw it, there was either no superior intelligence up in heaven to offend or there was a superior intelligence up in heaven that was not particularly evangelical, or it spoke only Latin and therefore heard my words as just so much inarticulate barking. Regardless, the epiphany that I reached within the absolute silence was that all measure of blasphemy was derogatory by interpretation rather than by design; that is, the image of the Virgin Mary relieving herself in the woods or of Jesus chomping on great fistfuls of dung cigars could derive its offensiveness only from somebody willing to bring just such a reaction to the reading of the image and not from an innate ugliness that God or the universe was compelled to react to negatively and to retaliate against.

Obscenity, it turned out, was not in the eye of the beholder, but rather in the *I* of the creator with the small *c*, capitalization being a personal choice made in accordance with how much hot air a person was willing to commit to the inflation of his or her ego.

Still, just to be safe, it remained my habit with every pair of sneakers that I wore for the next 3 years to write the words "by Dwayne Booth" on the bottom of the right sole just in case I ever did get blown to smithereens in my bathroom and some future 9-year-old reading about the incident in a magazine might recognize in the inscription written across the bottom of my remaining foot that I was the author of my own fate, rather than crediting a grossly esoteric God who is always way too eager to take credit for a reality into which he refuses to assimilate gracefully.

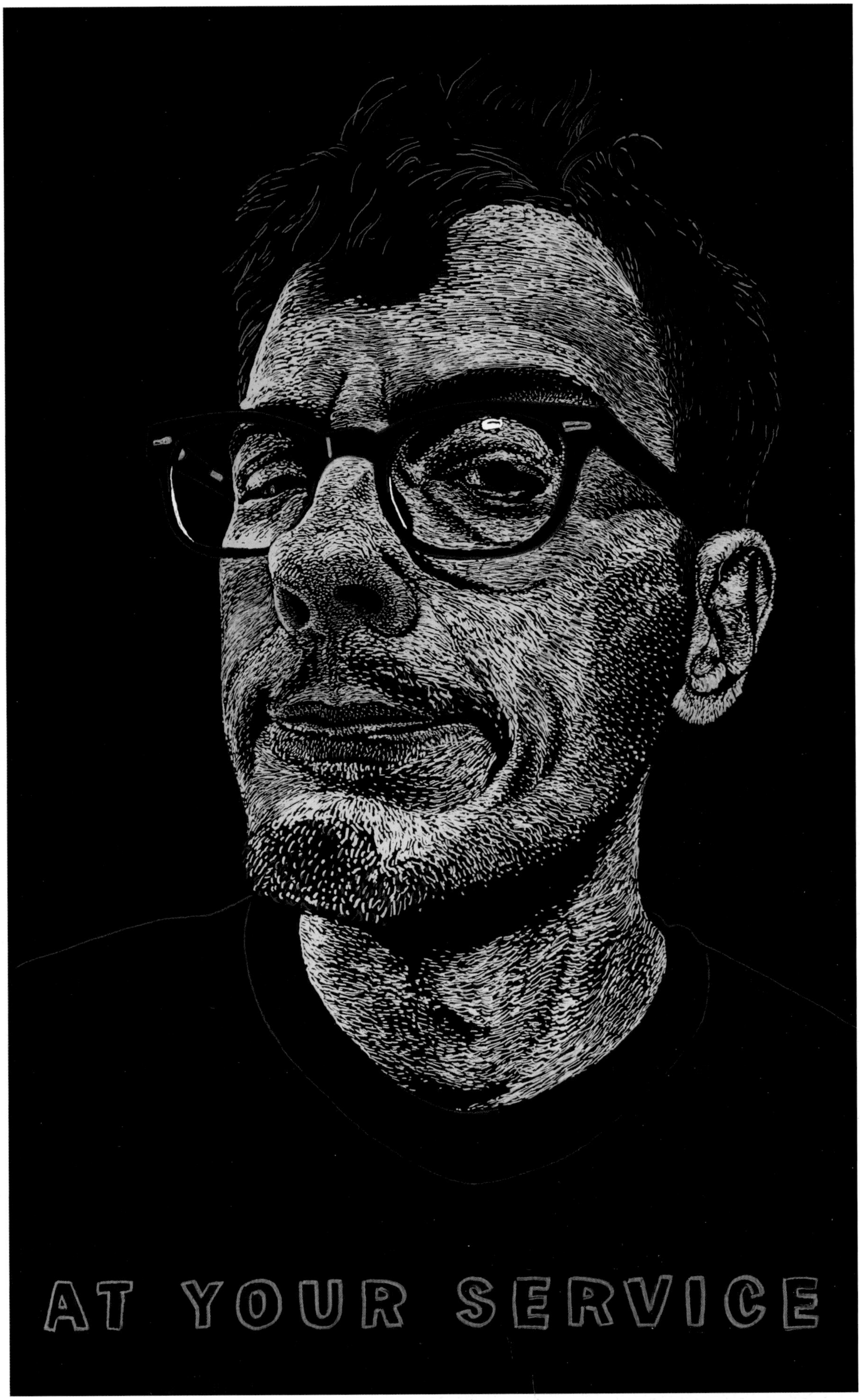
AT YOUR SERVICE

THE DOER
MR. FISH

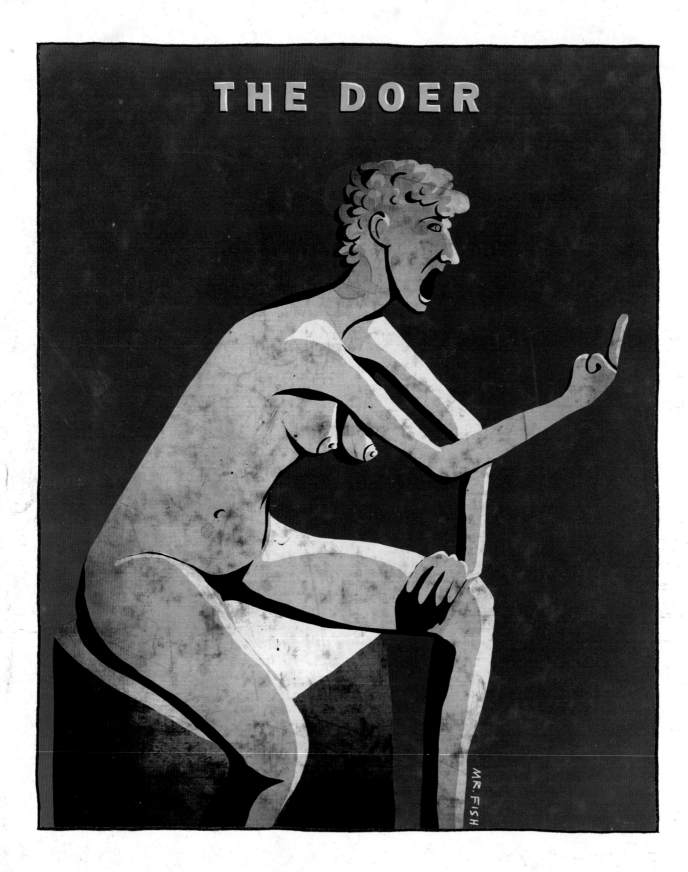